THE JUDAISM BEHIND THE TEXTS

SOUTH FLORIDA STUDIES IN THE HISTORY OF JUDAISM

Edited by
Jacob Neusner
William Scott Green, James Strange
Darrell J. Fasching, Sara Mandell

Number 101
THE JUDAISM BEHIND THE TEXTS
The Generative Premises of Rabbinic Literature
V.
The Talmuds of the Land of Israel
and of Babylonia
by
Jacob Neusner

THE JUDAISM BEHIND THE TEXTS

The Generative Premises of
Rabbinic Literature

V.

The Talmuds of the Land of Israel
and of Babylonia

by

Jacob Neusner

Scholars Press
Atlanta, Georgia

THE JUDAISM BEHIND THE TEXTS
The Generative Premises of Rabbinic Literature
V.
The Talmuds of the Land of Israel and of Babylonia

© 1994
University of South Florida

Publication of this book was made possible by a grant from the Tisch Family Foundation, New York City. The University of South Florida acknowledges with thanks this important support for its scholarly projects.

Library of Congress Cataloging in Publication Data
Neusner, Jacob, 1932-
    The Judaism behind the texts : the generative premises of rabbinic
literature. V, The Talmuds of the land of Israel and of Babylonia /
by Jacob Neusner.
        p. cm. — (South Florida studies in the history of Judaism ;
no. 101)
    Includes index.
    ISBN 1-55540-949-0
    1. Talmud—Sources. 2. Talmud Yerushalmi—Sources. 3. Mishnah—
Criticism, interpretation, etc. 4. Judaism—Essence, genius,
nature. I. Title. II. Series.
BM501.N4834 1994
296.1'2506—dc20   93-48300
                                                   CIP

Printed in the United States of America
on acid-free paper

Table of Contents

Preface ix

Introduction 1

1. The Constitutive Components of the Talmuds and the Issue
   of Premises. Illustrated by Bavli Abodah Zarah 1:1 and
   1:7 9

2. The Premises of the Framers of Composites: A Single Case........ 49

3. The Premises of the Authors of Compositions: Qiddushin 1:1
   in Yerushalmi and Bavli..73

4. The Premises of the Authors of Compositions: Qiddushin 1:2
   in Yerushalmi and Bavli..143

5. The Premises of the Authors of Compositions: Qiddushin 1:3
   in Yerushalmi and Bavli..223

6. Documentary Presuppositions of Composites: Do The Two
   Talmuds' Framers' Premises as to the Character of Talmud
   Compilation Coincide? 257

Index 311

Preface

...one must press behind the contents of the Mishnah and attempt to discover what the contents of the Mishnah presuppose....
E.P. Sanders[1]

The Judaism behind the texts that we seek to document through the texts themselves corresponds to "what the contents of the Mishnah presuppose." It is that corpus of givens – ideas, attitudes, laws, principles, myths – that the writers of documents take for granted and, in one way or another, instantiate in the very concrete writings that they produce. It follows that the only way to find answers to the challenge presented by Professor Sanders is to reread documents, line by line, and see what lies behind what is there. This I do in the multi-volume exercise on selected, critical documents of Rabbinic Judaism that comes to an end here and that will yield *The Judaism the Rabbis Take for Granted*. At this stage of the project, I find myself disappointed that Professor Sanders's question, which has always struck me as apt and provocative, yields no very interesting answer.

This protracted exercise – five volumes, encompassing seven books – concludes with the examination of the two Talmuds, continuing to ask a deceptively simple question of theory, applied systematically now to the principal and final documents of Rabbinic Judaism in its formative age. It is, if I know this, what else do I know? If an author or compiler of a Judaic text tells me something, a moment's thought will show, he thereby tells me also about what he takes for granted. That is the entirely valid point behind Professor Sanders's insistence that we "press behind the contents of a Rabbinic document and discover what the contents presuppose." Here, therefore, I continue to ask about documents' authors' premises: what they know and how they think they know it. In the concluding volume, which will follow very soon, I answer Sanders's

[1]E.P. Sanders, "Puzzling Out Rabbinism," in William Scott Green, ed., *Approaches to Ancient Judaism* (Chicago, 1980: Scholars Press for Brown Judaic Studies), 2:73.

question and tell him precisely what the contents of the several documents presuppose, severally and jointly.

The present project takes a different form from the prior ones, because a special problem defines the work at hand. The two Talmuds are exegetical composites. Two distinct types of materials comprise the documents, and each reveals its own distinctive type of premise or presupposition. Specifically, the two documents are made up of [1] compositions, free-standing and complete statements of one sort or another; and of [2] composites of these compositions. That fact complicates our work. We have to identify the premises or presuppositions of compositions, just as we did for the prior documents, both the Mishnah and the Tosefta, and the Midrash compilations organized around books of Scripture. But we also have to take note of the premises of the framers of composites, since here, too, there are presuppositions of considerable interest. To show what is at stake, and also to spell out the answer to Professor Sanders's question yielded by the Talmuds, I deal with both compositions and composites. And I proceed to ask a still further question, concerning the entire documents and the premises of thought and inquiry characteristic of each. So a single question, concerning two documents, yields three answers for each document: premises of [1] composites, [2] compositions, and [3] documents in their entirety.

In Chapter One I spell out the distinction between the composition and the composite, and in Chapter Two I proceed to the premise of a huge composite and thereby identify a single example of a premise that we can discern in a large-scale composite, one that is not spelled out in so many words but that governs the formation of the composite and yields its principal propositional consequence. Then in Chapters Three through Five, I examine the compositions of the two Talmuds and say what I think is taken for granted in them. In most instances, these premises are limited to the data of the case at hand, deriving from the exegetical problem and process under way. That is not precisely what Professor Sanders appears to have had in mind, and it is not what I expected to find. I thought I would find evidences of a "Judaism," that is, a set of convictions, that transcends the document at hand and animates its framers. But all I seem to have found at the foundations of the compositions before us are premises that sustain the details of those compositions, and these hardly point to those presuppositions that rendered the task at hand consequential for the study of Judaism.

I turn at the end to the entire documents. I ask, do the two Talmuds share premises, at least as to the character of their single task, Mishnah exegesis, that help us to account for the writings we have? If I could find nothing that transcended the specific discussions, that is, the premises of a given composition or even of a large-scale composite, could I at least offer a thesis on what all Talmud writers – authors of compositions, framers of composites alike – shared as the definition of their task?

Chapter Six, finally, draws us back to the issue of the presuppositions of composite compilers, but this time in a different framework altogether. Here I specify what I conceive the governing principles of the framers of the two Talmuds' composites to have been. All of this work, of course, yields answers of diverse kinds to the question that stands at the head of this statement. These results present problems that cannot be addressed within the limits of the kind of research report brought to its conclusion in this book. In due course, the final statement of the work, and the only one that moves beyond the limits of a research report, *The Judaism the Rabbis Take for Granted* will bring to an end the inquiry into premises and presuppositions, so far as that inquiry can be pursued over a variety of documents.

As is often the case, a fresh question turns out to beget more questions, and answers to many of them prove illusory. Once more, as has oftened to me so often in the past, I discover that the way forward requires a full and detailed rereading of the documents. The reason is that, in the logic of making connections and drawing conclusions, we identify the deepest layers of thought that animate the formation of the Judaism of the Dual Torah – of thought, but also, of expression. The results of this volume and the ones that led up to it dictate the next phase in my work, and a protracted one. It will be a complete commentary to the Bavli, under the title, *Making Connections and Drawing Conclusions. An Academic Commentary to the Talmud.* The following indicates where we now stand with this project:

The Judaism behind the Texts. The Generative Premises of Rabbinic Literature. I. *The Mishnah.* A. *The Division of Agriculture* (Atlanta, 1993: Scholars Press for South Florida Studies in the History of Judaism).

The Judaism behind the Texts. The Generative Premises of Rabbinic Literature. I. *The Mishnah.* B. *The Divisions of Appointed Times, Women, and Damages (through Sanhedrin)* (Atlanta, 1993: Scholars Press for South Florida Studies in the History of Judaism).

The Judaism behind the Texts. The Generative Premises of Rabbinic Literature. I. *The Mishnah.* C. *The Divisions of Damages (from Makkot), Holy Things and Purities* (Atlanta, 1993: Scholars Press for South Florida Studies in the History of Judaism).

The Judaism behind the Texts. The Generative Premises of Rabbinic Literature. II. *The Tosefta, Tractate Abot, and the Earlier Midrash Compilations: Sifra,*

Sifré to Numbers, and Sifré to Deuteronomy (Atlanta, 1993: Scholars Press for South Florida Studies in the History of Judaism).

The Judaism behind the Texts. The Generative Premises of Rabbinic Literature. III. *The Later Midrash Compilations: Genesis Rabbah, Leviticus Rabbah and Pesiqta deRab Kahana* (Atlanta, 1994: Scholars Press for South Florida Studies in the History of Judaism).

The Judaism behind the Texts. The Generative Premises of Rabbinic Literature. IV. *The Latest Midrash Compilations: Song of Songs Rabbah, Ruth Rabbah, Esther Rabbah I, and Lamentations Rabbati. And The Fathers According to Rabbi Nathan* (Atlanta, 1994: Scholars Press for South Florida Studies in the History of Judaism).

The place of the final statement then is clear. *The Judaism the Rabbis Take for Granted* will address the claim that we may describe a Judaism behind the texts, taken for granted by them all.

No work of mine can omit reference to the exceptionally favorable circumstances in which I conduct my research as Distinguished Research Professor in the Florida State University System at the University of South Florida. I wrote this book as part of my labor of research scholarship, expressed through both publication and teaching at the University of South Florida, which has afforded me an ideal situation in which to conduct a scholarly life. I express my thanks for not only the advantage of a Distinguished Research Professorship in the Florida State University System, which for a scholar must be the best job in the world, but also of a substantial research expense fund, ample research time, and some stimulating and cordial colleagues. In the prior chapters of my career, I never knew a university that prized professors' scholarship and publication and treated with respect those professors who actively and methodically pursue research.

The University of South Florida, among all ten universities that comprise the Florida State University System as a whole, exemplifies the high standards of professionalism that prevail in publicly sponsored higher education in the United States and provides the model that privately sponsored universities would do well to emulate. Here there are rules, achievement counts, and presidents, provosts, and deans honor and respect the University's principal mission: scholarship, scholarship alone – both in the class room and in publication. Here at last I find integrity, governing in the lives of people true to their vocation and their mission.

I defined the work at hand in conversation with Professor William Scott Green, who gave me substantial help in clearly formulating my problem in its own terms. As ever, I acknowledge my real debt to him for his scholarly acumen and perspicacity. I was originally thinking about the Judaism beyond the texts, and he was the one to explain to me that all any document can tell me is what it knows, not what it does not know. That is a just reward, since, after all, that was what I taught him when he was my student, decades ago.

I wrote this book as Visiting Research Professor of Åbo Akademi Forskningsinstitut, under the sponsorship of Institutum Judaicum Åboense, Åbo Akademi and so express thanks for the research facilities and opportunities provided there. In addition to a generous stipend, my position as Visiting Research Professor at the Åbo Akademi Forskningsinstitut gave my wife and myself five months of residence in a delightful Finnish city, the company of a variety of exceedingly hospitable and interesting colleagues, and a world of new friends.

I express special thanks to Professor Karl-Johan Illman for serving as principal host. Since I worked at a Swedish language university and devoted a fair amount of effort to learning that language, I am indebted, also, to the many Swedish-speaking Finns who accommodated my wish to learn to speak their language, and who, with patience, formed an entire universe of patient teachers.

JACOB NEUSNER

Distinguished Research Professor of Religious Studies
UNIVERSITY OF SOUTH FLORIDA
Tampa, FL 33620-5550 USA

Introduction

Prior to a vast number of rulings, fundamental conceptions or principles, never articulated, await identification. These I call premises, meaning, the givens of argument, or presuppositions, what is implicit in, or taken for granted by, a proposition. The distinction between the two plays no role in this inquiry. For, once identified, these several conceptions or principles demand a labor of composition. Such a substrate of thought forms the datum of that tractate's or compilation's inquiry. Ultimately we shall have to ask how the various premises or presuppositions of various documents fit together with the generative problematic of some others. Once we know what stands behind the law or exegesis of Scripture or theological syllogism, we have to ask, what holds together the several fundamental principles, all of them of enormous weight and vast capacity for specification in numerous detailed cases? Before we know how to define this Judaism, we have to show that a coherent metaphysics underpins the detailed physics, a cogent principle the concrete cases, a proportioned, balanced, harmonious statement the many, derivative and distinct cases of which the law and theology of Judaism are comprised. These questions define what is at stake in the survey that continues in this volume.

What I am trying to do here is to find the correct way to define Judaism in its formative age, which is to say, describe, analyze, and interpret the earliest stage in the formation of the Judaism of the Dual Torah. To that project, which has occupied me for more than thirty years, the question of identifying documents' premises and presuppositions is critical. The explicit statements of a generative text, such as the Mishnah or the Talmud of Babylonia, for example, hardly exhaust all that that text conveys – or means to convey – about God's truth. Even in the earliest generation of the field that used to be called "Talmudic history," the true founder and greatest mind in the field, Y.I. Halevi, in his still unappreciated *Dorot harishonim* (Vienna-Berlin, 1923 et seq.), insisted that a statement rested on a prior history of thought, which

1

can and should be investigated. He implicitly affirmed that the premises of available facts yield a prehistory we can describe. Everybody understands that the definitive documents of a religion expose something, but contain everything.

But it is not enough to posit such premises; we have in detail to identify just what we think that they were. So it is the task of learning to explore the premises, presuppositions, and processes of imagination and of critical thought, that yield in the end the statements that we find on the surface of the writings. But the work has to be done systematically and not episodically. Impressions, episode, anecdote, and example – these standard modes of alleging what "the rabbis" thought – no longer command credence. We have rather to address the entire canon with the question: Precisely what are the premises demonstrably present throughout, the generative presuppositions not in general but in all their rich specificity? Here I continue to investigate this analytical problem, having completed my descriptive work.

This book therefore continues a protracted, systematic and detailed answer to two questions, first, the question set forth in Professor Sanders's quite reasonable proposal, cited at the head of the Preface, to "press behind the contents...to discover what the contents...presuppose." While Sanders speaks of the Mishnah, in fact the generative question – if I know this, what else do I know about the intellect of the writers of a document or a whole canon? – pertains to the entirety of the oral part of the Torah. And the second question, as I have explained, is a still more urgent one: Are there premises and presuppositions that engage thought throughout the documents? Or are the documents discrete episodes in a sustained procession of thought that requires description upon some basis other than a documentary one?

It follows that the project presents an exercise in the further definition of the Judaism of the Dual Torah. Not only what its principal documents make articulate but also what they mean to imply, on the one end, and how what they presuppose coheres (if it does), on the other, define the work. Since many of the answers to those questions are either obvious or trivial or beg the question, we have to refine matters with a further critical consideration. It is this: Among the presuppositions, the critical one is, which ones matter? And how can we account for the emergence of the system as a whole out of the presuppositions demonstrably present at the foundations of systemic documents? Here, then, we shade over from collecting everything to evaluating some things, entering the domain of taste and judgment. The volume that will bring the project to its conclusion, *The Judaism the Rabbis Take for Granted*, will present my best judgment on what else we know, because we have in hand what our sages made explicit.

When I ask the general question about "the Judaism behind the texts," therefore, I refer to a variety of quite specific matters. All of them concern the premises or presuppositions of a document and of important statements within said document. I want to know what someone must take for granted as fact in order to make an allegation of some consequence within a legal or theological writing. Taking as our given what is alleged in a document, we ask, in order to take that position, what do I have to have known as fact? What must I have taken for granted as a principle? What set of issues or large-scale questions – fundamental issues that seem to me to pop up everywhere – has to have preoccupied me, so as to lead me to identify a given problem for solution, a given possibility awaiting testing?

These statements left unsaid but ubiquitously assumed may be of three kinds, from [1] the obvious, conventional, unsurprising, unexceptional, uninteresting, [2] routine and systemically inert to [3] the highly suggestive, provocative and systemically generative.

First, a statement in a text may presuppose a religious norm of belief or behavior (*halakhah* or *aggadah*, in the native categories). For one example, if a rule concerns itself with when the Shema is to be recited, the rule presupposes a prayer, the Shema – and so throughout. Such a presupposition clearly is to be acknowledged, but ordinarily, the fact that is taken for granted will not stand behind an exegetical initiative or intellectual problem to which a document pays substantial attention.

Second, a statement in a text may presuppose knowledge of a prior, authoritative text. For instance, rules in the Mishnah take for granted uncited texts of Scripture, nearly the whole of Tractate Yoma providing a particularly fine instance, since the very order and structure of that tractate prove incomprehensible without a verse-by-verse review of Leviticus Chapter Sixteen. Knowing that the framers of a document had access to a prior holy book by itself does not help us to understand what the framers of that document learned from the earlier one; they would have selected what they found relevant or important, ignoring what they found routine; we cannot simply assign to the later authorship complete acquiescence in all that a prior set of writers handed on, merely because the later authorship took cognizance of what the earlier one had to say. It is one thing to acknowledge, it is another to make use of, to respond to, a received truth.

Third, a concrete statement in a text may rest upon a prior conception of a more abstract character, much as applied mathematics rests upon theoretical mathematics, or technology upon principles of engineering and physics. And this set of premises and presuppositions does lead us deep into the foundations of thought of a given, important and systematic writing. In the main, what I want to know here concerns the active and generative premises of Rabbinic documents: the things the writers had to know in order to define the problems they wished to solve. I seek the key to the exegesis of the law that the framers of the Mishnah put forth, the exegesis of Scripture that they systematically provided. When we can say not only what they said but also what they took for granted, if we can explain their principles of organization and the bases for their identification of the problems they wished to solve, then, but only then, do we enter into that vast Judaic system and structure that their various writings put forth in bits and pieces and only adumbrated in its entirety.

Accordingly, this project, covering the principal documents of Rabbinic Judaism in its formative age, while paying attention to data of the first two classes, focuses upon the third category of presuppositions, stipulating that the first two require no more than routine inquiry. That is to say, we all know that the sages of the Rabbinic writings deemed the Scriptures of ancient Israel, which they knew as the written part of the Torah, to be authoritative; they took for granted the facticity and authority of every line of that writing, to be sure picking and choosing, among available truths, those that required emphasis and even development. That simple fact permits us to take for granted, without laboring to prove the obvious, that the Judaism not articulated in the Rabbinic literature encompassed the way of life and worldview and conception of Israel that, in broad outlines, Scripture set forth. But that fact standing on its own is trivial. It allows for everything but the main thing: what characterized the specific, distinctive character of the Judaic system set forth in Rabbinic writings, and, it goes without saying, how the particular point of view of those writings dictated the ways in which Scripture's teachings and rules gained entry into, and a place for themselves in, the structure and system of the Judaism of the Dual Torah. The present inquiry into the premises and presuppositions of the two Talmuds is so shaped as to take account of the complex literary situation of those writings, dealing with both the compositions of which the Talmuds are made up, and the composites that form the definitive structures of those writings.

The stakes in the project prove weighty. What Rabbinic documents tell us that bears consequence for the definition of their Judaism in particular – not merely what was likely to be common to all Judaism, for example, a sacred calendar, a record of generations' encounter with God and the like – then requires specification, and the third of the three types of presuppositions or premises points toward the definition of what is at stake and under study here. That is, specifically, the deeper, implicit affirmations of documents: what they know that stands behind what they say, the metaphysics behind the physics (to resort to the metaphor just now introduced). For a close reading of both law and lore, *halakhah* and *aggadah*, yields a glimpse at a vast structure of implicit conceptions, those to which Sanders makes reference in his correct prescription of what is to be done: "...one must press behind the contents of the Mishnah and attempt to discover what the contents of the Mishnah presuppose."

When I refer to presuppositions or to "generative premises," I mean to exclude a variety of other givens that strike me as demonstrably present but systemically inert. There are many facts our documents know and acknowledge but leave in the background; there are others, that is, premises and presuppositions, that generate numerous specific problems, indeed that turn out, upon close examination of the details of documents, to stand behind numerous concrete inquiries. The former are systemically inert, the latter, systemically provocative and formative. Such premises as the sanctity of Israel and the Land of Israel, the election of Israel, the authority of the Torah (however defined), and the like in these writings prove systemic givens, assumed but rarely made the focus of exegetical thought.

Not only so: a very long list of platitudes and banalities can readily be constructed and every item on the list shown to be present throughout the documents under study here; but those platitudes and banalities make no contribution to the shaping of our documents and the formulation of their system. Therefore, having proven that the sun rises in the east, from those systemically inert givens, we should know no more about matters than we did beforehand. True, to those in search of "Judaism," as distinct from the diverse Judaic systems to which our evidence attests, that finding – God is one, God gave the Torah, Israel is God's chosen people, and the like – bears enormous consequence. But that God is one in no way accounts for the system's specific qualities and concerns, any more than does the fact that the laws of gravity operate.

What makes a Judaic system important is what marks that system as entire and imparts to that system its integrity: what makes it different from other systems, what holds that system together. Defining that single, encompassing "Judaism" into which genus all species, all Judaisms, fit helps us understand nothing at all about the various Judaisms. But all we really have in hand are the artifacts of Judaisms. As the prologue has already argued in Volume I.A, efforts to find that one Judaism that holds together all Judaisms yields suffocating banalities and useless platitudes: we do not understand anything in particular any better than we did before we had thought up such generalities. So by "generative premises," I mean, the premises that counted: those that provoked the framers of a document's ideas to do their work, that made urgent the questions they address, that imparted self-evidence to the answers they set forth. This brings us to the documents under study in this part of the work. These documents – the two Talmuds – present a set of special problems.

The analysis presented here shifts in character, since the two Talmuds are made up of two different types of components. First, they collect and arrange compositions, for example, completed and free-standing statements; all of these statements provide access to conceptions that are not articulated but that define the framework for those that are set forth. Any account of (some of) the premises and presuppositions of the Talmuds is going to pay close attention to what the authors of the Talmuds' principal components, their compositions, know but do not express, presuppose but do not spell out. Second, the collection and arrangement of said compositions into large-scale composites rests upon important principles of connection, the linking of one thing with something else to produce a conclusion that transcends the items that are linked.

So we have to ask, what do the framers of a composite take for granted or wish to convey without articulation? And, third, the character of the analytical process of the two Talmuds, respectively, demands attention in any study of the givens of thought that define the substrate and structure of a document. These data differ from the earlier Talmud to the later one and require specification. The work here is considerably more complex than what was required for the first four parts of the study, and, as is clear, I offer only a sample.

I begin, in Chapter One, with a clear account of the two distinct elements of any Talmudic composite, the compositions that are utilized, the composite that the framers have made thereof. These have to be carefully distinguished. Recognizing the autonomy of thought represented by each of the two components of the Talmuds, the compositions and the composite, we define for ourselves a much more difficult problem than is presented in the Mishnah, Tosefta, and Midrash compilations. In Chapter Two, I proceed to show, in the setting of two Mishnah units of Bavli Abodah Zarah Chapter One (A.Z. 1:1 and 1:7), how the premises of the framers of a composite come to expression. I give a single example of what is at stake in the differentiation of the composition from the composite. Chapters Three through Five proceed to the examination of the Talmuds' compositions, item by item. Then, in Chapter Six, I return to the much more difficult question of how to identify the premises and presuppositions of documents, this time showing how the two Talmuds themselves, seen whole, flow from quite distinctive premises, respectively, concerning what a Mishnah commentary should accomplish. At that point I have laid out in vast detail the variety and dimensions of the answer to the question presented in the language of Professor Sanders.

That program completed, we shall be ready to address the question I have aimed to answer. The examination of the compositions and composites that comprise the two Talmuds' treatment of the opening three Mishnah paragraphs of Mishnah-tractate Qiddushin Chapter One allows me to make a definitive statement on the question, what else do we know, once we know that our sages of blessed memory have made a given set of statements: the premises and presuppositions of thought? I claim that examining any other sample of the Talmuds will yield equivalent results to those set forth here; I originally contemplated reviewing the entire tractate, but the work proved tedious and one-sided, and I saw no reason to repeat endlessly the few, rather paltry results that emerged in the opening part of the tractate. Answers to that question, drawing together the results spelled out here, will emerge in *The Judaism the Rabbis Take for Granted*, which follows and concludes the project. I suspect some of the answers to the question, what else? are going to produce surprises, but time will tell.

The goal of this project has now clarified itself – one question among a variety of possibilities has taken hold. What I want ultimately to find out is whether I can identify premises that circulate among all or at least most of the Rabbinic compilations of Mishnah and Scripture exegesis through the two Talmuds. In the case of this Judaism, with its sizable canon of authoritative and holy books – Scripture, the Mishnah, Tosefta, two Talmuds, score of Midrash compilations – we want to know how the various writings hold together. That defines the fundamental problem in the analysis of the canonical writings: Can we identify a set of premises that animate all writers, presuppositions that guide every compilation's compositions' authors and compositors' framers?

If we can, then we shall have found what makes that Judaism into a single coherent religious system. If we cannot, then we shall have to ask a fresh set of descriptive questions concerning the theology of that religious system – a different set from those that guide the present work. When at the end of this exercise I reach the conclusion, in *The Judaism the Rabbis Take for Granted*, I shall exploit the facts that will turn up in the present book and its companions: Is there a Judaism behind the texts at all? And if not, what explains the coherence of the Judaism of the Dual Torah – for, by all reckoning, it is a remarkably cogent and stable religious system, with a body of ideas that for centuries have formed a single statement and today, with numerous variations and nuances, continues to say some one thing in many ways. Let me state with heavy emphasis what I want to find out:

At stake is not only the Mishnah and its premises (presumably bringing us back into circles of first-century thinkers) but the presuppositions of numerous representative documents of Rabbinic Judaism throughout its formative period.

The second question vastly outweighs the one that animates interest in premises and presuppositions: Is there a Judaism that infuses all texts and forms of each part of a coherent whole? At issue in the quest for presuppositions is not the Judaism that lies beyond the texts (which the texts by definition cannot tell us and indeed do not pretend to tell us), but the Judaism that holds together all of the texts and forms the substrate of conviction and conscience in each one.

That body of writings is continuous, formed as it is as commentaries on the Written Torah or the Mishnah, and the period in which they took shape for formal and substantive reasons also is continuous and of course not to be truncated at its very starting point, with the Mishnah, as Sanders's formulation proposes. For the Mishnah presents only the first among a long sequence of problems for analysis, and cutting that writing off from its continuators and successors, in both Midrash compilations and Talmuds, represents a gross error, one commonplace, to be sure, among Christian scholars of Judaism, for whom, as in Sanders's case, Judaism ends in the first century or early second and ceases beyond that point to require study at all.

But the Judaism of the Dual Torah, viewed in its formative canon, is single and whole, and the premises and presuppositions of any of its writings, treated in isolation from those of all the others, contain nothing of interest for the analysis of that massive and complex Judaic system, only for the Judaism of a given piece of writing. The future of research into the formation of Judaism now is clear. The analytical work having been concluded, the constructive and synthetic venture begins: how we can identify the bases for the conclusion, universally self-evident to the faithful of holy Israel of the Dual Torah, that both parts of the Torah, the oral and the written, are one, and, it goes without saying, all parts of the Oral Torah, that is, each of the documents we now have, make a single statement on the foundations of a single, coherent set of premises. If the Torah of Sinai really is one, wherein do we locate its unity? That question must find its answer in detailed, documentary description. The analytical work has now set the rules for synthesis and reconstruction.

1

The Constitutive Components of the Talmuds and the Issue of Premises. Illustrated by Bavli Abodah Zarah 1:1 and 1:7

Before we can ask about the premises and presuppositions of the two Talmuds, we must specify what we mean by the two Talmuds. The reason is that we have to take account of the types of units of thought that make up those Talmuds, which form composites of several types of materials. Only when we have differentiated among them shall we have defined the arena of inquiry, specifying the kinds of completed compositions or composites that are subject to inquiry as to premises or presuppositions. These different types of writings yield wildly diverse types of premises, and to speak of the premises and presuppositions of the Talmuds requires a clear definition of the frame of reference.

The two Talmuds are made up of four components, of which only two will demand our attention. The first two, the Mishnah and passages of the Written Torah, Scripture, obviously need not detain us. We have already examined the former and systematically reviewed the premises of those who commented upon the latter. Nor shall we dwell on the premises that accord a privileged status to those writings, for obvious reasons. The Mishnah forms the structure around which both Talmuds are built. Scripture defines the court of last appeal for each. We cannot assign to the framers of the Talmuds responsibility for the character of those documents. An account of what the authors of compositions and framers of composites took for granted need not attend to the givens of the Torah, oral and written. In any event we have already paid ample attention to the premises of the Mishnah, as well as to the presuppositions that generated readings of Scripture in the Midrash compilations.

But there are two other components that play a central role, the completed compositions that are gathered and organized, and the formulation of the composites of those compositions. The former convey one set of propositions, the latter, a different set altogether, and the premises or presuppositions of each require attention. These now require close attention.

COMPOSITIONS AND COMPOSITES: Rabbinic documents draw upon a fund of completed compositions of thought, compositions that have taken shape without attention to the needs of the compilers of those documents. At the same time these same documents also draw upon materials that have been composed with the requirements of the respective documents in mind. We understand the character of the Talmuds's principal unit of completed discourse as a composite only when we fully grasp the types of writing that a given passage holds together. Specifically, within the distinction between writing that serves a redactional purpose, the composite, and writing that does not, the composition, four types of completed conglomerates of thought find a place in rabbinic documents.[1] Each type may be distinguished from the others by appeal to a single criterion of differentiation, that is to say, to traits of precisely the same sort.

The indicative traits in particular concern relationship to the redactional purpose of a piece of writing, viewed overall. Some writings serve the purpose of the compilers or redactors of a document, others were formulated independent of the needs of a larger compilation. The latter I call compositions, complete in themselves, the former, composites, made up to be included in a larger construction. These distinctions are objective and factual; anyone should be able to replicate my classification of a completed unit of thought as a composition or a composite.

> [1]   Some writings in a given compilation clearly serve the redactional program of the framers of the document in which those writings occur. The Mishnah is one striking example of a piece of writing that has been formulated in the process of redaction, or, to put it differently, that has been written by those responsible for the final compilation, with only limited evidence of the utilization of writings prepared

---

[1]I review the argument of my *Making the Classics in Judaism: The Three Stages of Literary Formation* (Atlanta, 1990: Scholars Press for Brown Judaic Studies).

earlier and for a different kind of document from the one in which they now take their place.

[2] Some writings in a given compilation serve not the redactional program of the document in which they occur, but some other document, now in our hands. There is no material difference, as to the taxonomy of the writing of the classics in Judaism, between the first and second types; it is a problem of transmission of documents, not their formation. Where authors or compilers of a given document made use of some other document, for example, Scripture or the Mishnah, they ordinarily gave a signal that that other document was cited, for example, "as it is written" or "...said," for Scripture, and, "as we have learned as a Tannaite statement" (TNN), for the Mishnah. It is exceedingly rare that a document will fail to insert an explicit mark that another piece of writing is cited.

[3] Some writings in a given compilation serve not the purposes of the document in which they occur but rather a redactional program of a document, or even of a type of document, that we do not now have *but* can readily envision. In this category we find the possibility of imagining compilations that we do not have, but that can have existed but did not survive; or that can have existed and were then recast into the kinds of writings that people clearly preferred (later on) to produce. Numerous examples of writings clearly have been redacted in accord with a program and plan other than those of any document now in our hands.[2] Stories about sages were told and recorded, but not compiled into complete books, for example, hagiographies about given authorities. The criterion here is not subjective. We can easily demonstrate that materials of a given type, capable of sustaining a large-scale compilation, were available; but no such compilation was made, so far as extant sources suggest or attest.

[4] Some writings now found in a given compilation stand autonomous of any redactional program we have in an existing compilation or of any we can even imagine on the foundations of said writings.

---

[2]See the many examples in my *Making the Classics in Judaism: The Three Stages of Literary Formation*. In *Why No Gospels in Talmudic Judaism?* I was able to point out one kind of book that we can have received but were not given.

The first of those four kinds of completed units of thought (pericopes) as matter of hypothesis fall into the final stage of literary formation. That is to say, at the stage at which an authorship has reached the conclusion that it wishes to compile a document of a given character, that authorship will have made up pieces of writing that serve the purposes of the document it wishes to compile. The premises or presuppositions of such composites tell us about the purposes of the redactors of compositions into composites. The second through fourth kinds of completed units of thought come earlier than this writing in the process of the formation of the classics of Judaism represented by the compilation in which this writing now finds its place. The premises or presuppositions of these compositions tell us about the generative conceptions of those who wrote them, not (necessarily) about that of those who selected them for the larger composite in which they are now located.

The distinction between the goal of the author of the composition and the purpose of the author of the composite in which said composition is utilized is readily grasped. We may ask ourselves a simple question: Can this composition have been drawn together, with its beginning, middle, and end, without reference to the composite in which it occurs? If it can, then the goal of the author of the composition is exhaustively realized by what he has written, without reference to the further uses to which (later on) his writing has been put. If a composition is best explained only within the framework of its broader context, so that the part can be properly read and interpreted only in that larger context, then, of course, the compositor has had a hand in the whole. So the issue concerns the problem of relevance, the judgment that the Bavli's authors or editors too often forget their starting point and wander off in odd directions.

How did the compositor of a document know what sort(s) of materials he wished to introduce into a talmud, that is, a document that served as an amplification of the Mishnah, then as an extension of that amplification itself? That question can be answered, because it is the fact that, while the thirty-seven tractates of the Talmud of Babylonia cover a substantial topical program, respectively, each of them different from the others, all of them utilize a single and uniform set of markers. That is why we always know the character of the discussion at hand, its place in the larger sequence of analysis, and its contribution to the order and structure of the whole. And that explains how the document, within the chaos of its excess of information, everywhere proves purposive – once we know the purpose of each bit of information. The building block of thought and therefore writing is not the composition but the composite. Then the composite must constitute a complete and fully articulated discourse. But when it comes to the examination of givens of thought, both the composition and the composite demand attention, the one speaking in behalf of the authors of the completed writings upon which the framers drew, the other making the statement of the compilers of the document's principal parts. These represent very different types of premises, as the contrast between Chapters Two and Six, on the one hand, and Three through Five, on the other, will show us.

FOOTNOTES AND APPENDICES: If we wish to present valuable facts that our argument requires, facts that are necessary for the argument but not sufficient to warrant a position in the exposition and argument at hand, we resort to footnotes. There we fill in the factual gaps and so inform our readers of things they need to know – but not within the rush of exposition and flow of argument. But the framers of the two Talmuds did not have the possibility of burying footnotes at the bottom of a page. Nor could they add appendices at the end of a document; these gifts of printing were not imagined. It follows that compilers of compositions introduced not only those compositions but also footnotes, themselves (ordinarily) brief compositions on their own. These form compositions within compositions.

A CONCRETE CASE: COMPOSITION, COMPOSITE, THE SHANK OF DISCOURSE, FOOTNOTES AND APPENDICES: These theoretical remarks require instantiation. What I now want to show is how the entirety of a vast, run-on and continuous passage in fact forms a single entity, a composite made up of available compositions in part. These compositions may well bear in their midst insertions as well, compositions within compositions, as I said, which function as do footnotes or appendices for us. But the composite is the thing, for, as we shall observe, the whole makes a single enormous point, and all of the details of the composite – each of the compositions that have been used – contribute to making that one point. So what appears to digress in fact wanders back, time and again, to a single position. Because each composition in the enormous composite that follows will be seen to be linked to the others, fore and aft, we must classify the whole composite that follows as a single, sustained composite, to be classified whole and all together.

In what follows, I refer to I.1 with its footnote at I.2, and then with that footnote's extended notes, glosses, appendices and the like, through to I.32. Even attention to the subject matter – the theme and recurrent propositions – justifies treating all thirty-two compositions as a single cogent composite. For the whole of the composite when seen all together addresses only the single issue introduced by the Mishnah and addressed in the exercise of text criticism of I.1: gentile idolatry, Israelite service of God but also Israelite sin, and the punishment to be exacted on some one day – the day of judgment – on the gentiles for their idolatry and on Israel for its perfidy. Then we recognize how a single, sustained program or problem, which we can readily identify, has guided the compositor in writing up his complete statement – footnotes, appendices, and all.

But most of what is before us comprises footnotes and appendices, secondary developments, expansions and clarifications, information fully spelled out to which, in a prior statement, allusion is made – a pedantic exercise of high consequence, in which everything we require is provided, and perhaps rather more than by our tastes we might have inserted. Each composition is inserted whole and complete, but given a (to the framers, natural and logical) position well integrated into a single running discussion. Each one then exists in two dimensions, the one defined by its writers, the other by those who utilized the composition for the present purpose. An account of the premises at hand would encompass both unstated but governing conceptions, and, in the nature of things, these conceptions in fact scarcely intersect.

How to proceed to identify the arena for analysis of premises and presuppositions? The graphic way in which I show what I conceive to be a footnote is to indent a discussion that seems to me secondary, for example, filling out what is stated in a prior matter. As I proceed I shall explain why I represent matters as I do, and then at the end is a summary of the whole. In this way I show that a composite in fact forms a single, continuous, and, properly read, coherent and cogent, even economical statement. What is in italics is in Aramaic in the original and ordinarily stands for the compilers of the composite, not the authors of the composition that is discussed.

1:1

A. [2A] **Before the festivals of gentiles for three days it is forbidden to do business with them.**

B. **(1) To lend anything to them or to borrow anything from them.**

C. **(2) To lend money to them or to borrow money from them.**

D. **(3) To repay them or to be repaid by them.**

E. **R. Judah says, "They accept repayment from them, because it is distressing to him."**

F. **They said to him, "Even though it is distressing to him now, he will be happy about it later."**

I.1 A. [2A] Rab and Samuel [in dealing with the reading of the key word of the Mishnah, translated "festival," the letters of which are 'aleph daled, rather than 'ayin daled, which means, "calamity"]:

B. *one repeated the formulation of the Mishnah as, "their festivals."*

C. *And the other repeated the formulation of the Mishnah as "their calamities."*

D.   *The one who repeated the formulation of the Mishnah as "their festivals" made no mistake, and the one who repeated the formulation of the Mishnah as "their calamities" made no mistake.*

E.   *For it is written, "For the day of their calamity is at hand" (Deut. 32:15).*

F.   *The one who repeated the formulation of the Mishnah as "their festivals" made no mistake, for it is written, "Let them bring their testimonies that they may be justified" (Isa. 43:9).*

G.   *And as to the position of him who repeats the formulation of the Mishnah as "their festivals," on what account does he not repeat the formulation of the Mishnah to yield, "their calamities"?*

H.   *He will say to you, "'Calamity' is preferable [as the word choice when speaking of idolatry]."*

I.   *And as to the position of him who repeats the formulation of the Mishnah as "their calamities," on what account does he not repeat the formulation of the Mishnah to yield "their festivals"?*

J.   *He will say to you, "What causes the calamity that befalls them if not their testimony, so testimony is preferable!"*

K.   *And as to the verse, "Let them bring their testimonies that they may be justified" (Isa. 43:9), is this written with reference to gentiles? Lo, it is written in regard to Israel.*

L.   *For said R. Joshua b. Levi, "All of the religious duties that Israelites carry out in this world come and give testimony in their behalf in the world to come: 'Let them bring their witnesses that they may be justified' (Isa. 43:9), that is, Israel; 'and let them hear and say, It is truth' (Isa. 43:9) – this refers to gentiles."*

M.   *Rather, said R. Huna b. R. Joshua, "He who formulates the Mishnah to refer to their calamities derives the reading from this verse: 'They that fashion a graven image are all of them vanity, and their delectable things shall not profit, and their own witnesses see not nor know' (Isa. 44:9)."*

That much of the discussion under study here serves as a systematic commentary to the Mishnah. The operative presuppositions concern Mishnah exegesis. There are other premises, those of substance, which the reader will readily identify.

Now we proceed to ask about how someone would have strung together a long series of compositions into a single, I maintain coherent, composite. In what follows, every item fits together with its predecessor and leads us without interruption to its successor, from the starting lines of I.1 to the concluding ones of I.32. When I have made that claim stick, I shall have justified my insistence on seeing the whole as a coherent composition, to be classified in its entirety in a single entry, within a single rubric. And that is what is at stake in this long and detailed examination of four folios, eight pages, of the Talmud. Indentations mark footnotes, insertions into the text, secondary amplifications of minor details; double indentations mark appendices, for example, to footnotes themselves.

I.2 A. R. Hanina bar Pappa, and some say, R. Simlai, gave the following
          exposition [of the verse,"They that fashion a graven image are all of
          them vanity, and their delectable things shall not profit, and their
          own witnesses see not nor know" (Isa. 44:9)]: "In the age to come
          the Holy One, blessed be He, will bring a scroll of the Torah and
          hold it in his bosom and say, 'Let him who has kept himself busy
          with it come and take his reward.' Then all the gentiles will crowd
          together: 'All of the nations are gathered together' (Isa. 43:9). The
          Holy One, blessed be He, will say to them, 'Do not crowd together
          before me in a mob. But let each nation enter together with [2B] its
          scribes, and let the peoples be gathered together' (Isa. 43:9), and the
          word 'people' means 'kingdom': 'and one kingdom shall be
          stronger than the other' (Gen. 25:23)."

     B. *But can there be a mob scene before the Holy One, blessed be He?*
         Rather, it is so that from their perspective they not form a mob, so
         that they will be able to hear what he says to them.

     C. [Resuming the narrative of A:] "The kingdom of Rome comes in
          first."

     D. *How come? Because they are the most important. How do we know*
         on the basis of Scripture they are the most important? Because it is
         written, "And he shall devour the whole earth and shall tread it
         down and break it into pieces" (Gen. 25:23), and said R.
         Yohanan, "This Rome is answerable, for its definition [of
         matters] has gone forth to the entire world [Mishcon: 'this
         refers to Rome, whose power is known to the whole world']."

     E. *And how do we know that the one who is most important comes in*
         first? It is in accord with that which R. Hisda said.

     F. For said R. Hisda, "When the king and the community [await
          judgment], the king enters in first for judgment: 'That he
          maintain the cause of his servant [Solomon] and [then] the
          cause of his people Israel' (1 Kgs. 8:59)."

     G. *And how come? If you wish, I shall say it is not appropriate to keep*
         the king sitting outside. And if you wish, I shall say that [the king is
         allowed to plead his case] before the anger of the Holy One is
         aroused."

     H. [Resuming the narrative of C:] "The Holy One, blessed be He, will
          say to them, 'How have you defined your chief occupation?'

     I. "They will say before him, 'Lord of the world, a vast number of
          marketplaces have we set up, a vast number of bathhouses we have
          made, a vast amount of silver and gold have we accumulated. And
          all of these things we have done only in behalf of Israel, so that they
          may define as their chief occupation the study of the Torah.'

     J. "The Holy One, blessed be He, will say to them, 'You complete
          idiots! Whatever you have done has been for your own
          convenience. You have set up a vast number of marketplaces to be
          sure, but that was so as to set up whorehouses in them. The
          bathhouses were for your own pleasure. Silver and gold belong to
          me anyhow: "Mine is the silver and mine is the gold, says the Lord
          of hosts" (Hag. 2:8). Are there any among you who have been
          telling of "this," and "this" is only the Torah: "And this is the Torah

that Moses set before the children of Israel" (Deut. 4:44).' So they will make their exit, humiliated.

K. "When the kingdom of Rome has made its exit, the kingdom of Persia enters afterward."

L. *How come? Because they are second in importance. And how do we know it on the basis of Scripture? Because it is written, "And behold, another beast, a second, like a bear" (Dan. 7:5), and in this connection R. Joseph repeated as a Tannaite formulation, "This refers to the Persians, who eat and drink like a bear, are obese like a bear, are shaggy like a bear, and are restless like a bear."*

M. "The Holy One, blessed be He, will say to them, 'How have you defined your chief occupation?'

N. "They will say before him, 'Lord of the world, we have thrown up a vast number of bridges, we have conquered a vast number of towns, we have made a vast number of wars, and all of them we did only for Israel, so that they may define as their chief occupation the study of the Torah.'

O. "The Holy One, blessed be He, will say to them, 'Whatever you have done has been for your own convenience. You have thrown up a vast number of bridges, to collect tolls, you have conquered a vast number of towns, to collect the corvée, and, as to making a vast number of wars, I am the one who makes wars: "The Lord is a man of war" (Ex. 19:17). Are there any among you who have been telling of "this," and "this" is only the Torah: "And this is the Torah that Moses set before the children of Israel" (Deut. 4:44).' So they will make their exit, humiliated."

P. *But if the kingdom of Persia has seen that such a claim issued by the kingdom of Rome did no good whatsoever, how come they go in at all?*

Q. *They will say to themselves, "These are the ones who destroyed the house of the sanctuary, but we are the ones who built it."*

R. "And so it will go with each and every nation."

S. *But if each one of them has seen that such a claim issued by the others did no good whatsoever, how come they go in at all?*

T. *They will say to themselves, "Those two subjugated Israel, but we never subjugated Israel."*

U. *And how come the two conquering nations are singled out as important and the others are not?*

V. *It is because the rule of these will continue until the Messiah comes.*

W. "They will say to him, 'Lord of the world, in point of fact, did you actually give it to us and we did not accept it?'"

X. *But how can they present such an argument, since it is written, "The Lord came from Sinai and rose from Sier to them, he shined forth from Mount Paran" (Deut. 33:2), and further, "God comes from Teman" (Hab. 3:3). Now what in the world did he want in Seir, and what was he looking for in Paran? Said R. Yohanan, "This teaches that the Holy One, blessed be He, made the rounds of each and every nation and language and none accepted it, until he came to Israel, and they accepted it."*

Y. *Rather, this is what they say, "Did we accept it but then not carry it out?"*

Z.   *But to this the rejoinder must be, "Why did you not accept it anyhow!"*

AA.   Rather, "this is what they say before him, 'Lord of the world, did you hold a mountain over us like a cask and then we refused to accept it as you did to Israel, as it is written, "And they stood beneath the mountain" (Ex. 19:17).'"

BB.   And [in connection with the verse, "And they stood beneath the mountain" (Ex. 19:17),] said R. Dimi bar Hama, "This teaches that the Holy One, blessed be He, held the mountain over Israel ike a cask and said to them, 'If you accept the Torah, well and good, and if not, then there is where your grave will be.'"

CC.   "Then the Holy One, blessed be He, will say to them, 'Let us make known what happened first: "Let them announce to us former things" (Isa. 43:9). As to the seven religious duties that you did accept, where have you actually carried them out?'"

DD.   *And how do we know on the basis of Scripture that they did not carry them out? R. Joseph formulated as a Tannaite statement, "'He stands and shakes the earth, he sees and makes the nations tremble' (Hab. 3:6): what did he see? He saw the seven religious duties that the children of Noah accepted upon themselves as obligations but never actually carried them out. Since they did not carry out those obligations, he went and remitted their obligation."*

EE.   *But then they benefited – so it pays to sin!*

FF.   Said Mar b. Rabina, [3A] "What this really proves is that even when they carry out those religious duties, they get no reward on that account."

GG.   *And they don't, don't they? But has it not been taught on Tannaite authority:* R. Meir would say, "How on the basis of Scripture do we know that, even if it is a gentile, if he goes and takes up the study of the Torah as his occupation, he is equivalent to the high priest? Scripture states, 'You shall therefore keep my statutes and my ordinances, which, if a human being does them, one shall gain life through them' (Lev. 18:5). What is written is not 'priests' or 'Levites' or 'Israelites,' but rather, 'a human being.' So you have learned the fact that, even if it is a gentile, if he goes and takes up the study of the Torah as his occupation, he is equivalent to the high priest."

HH.   Rather, what you learn from this [DD] is that they will not receive that reward that is coming to those who are commanded to do them and who carry them out, but rather, the reward that they receive will be like that coming to the one who is not commanded to do them and who carries them out anyhow.

II.   For said R. Hanina, "Greater is the one who is commanded and who carries out the religious obligations than the one who is not commanded but nonetheless carries out religious obligations."

JJ.   [Reverting to AA:] "This is what the gentiles say before him, 'Lord of the world, Israel, who accepted it – where in the world have they actually carried it out?'

KK.   "The Holy One, blessed be He, will say to them, 'I shall bear witness concerning them, that they have carried out the whole of the Torah!'

LL.   "They will say before him, 'Lord of the world, is there a father who is permitted to give testimony concerning his son? For it is written, "Israel is my son, my firstborn" (Ex. 4:22).'

MM.   "The Holy One, blessed be He, will say to them, 'The heaven and the earth will give testimony in their behalf that they have carried out the entirety of the Torah.'

NN.   "They will say before him, 'Lord of the world, the heaven and earth have a selfish interest in the testimony that they give: "If not for my covenant with day and with night, I should not have appointed the ordinances of heaven and earth" (Jer. 33:25).'"

OO.   *For said R. Simeon b. Laqish, "What is the meaning of the verse of Scripture,* 'And there was evening, and there was morning, the sixth day' (Gen. 1:31)? This teaches that the Holy One, blessed be He, made a stipulation with all of the works of creation, saying to them, 'If Israel accepts my Torah, well and good, but if not, I shall return you to chaos and void.' *That is in line with what is written:* 'You did cause sentence to be heard from heaven, the earth trembled and was still' (Ps. 76:9). If 'trembling' then where is the stillness, and if stillness, then where is the trembling? Rather, to begin with, trembling, but at the end, stillness."

PP.   [Reverting to MM-NN:] "The Holy One, blessed be He, will say to them, 'Some of them may well come and give testimony concerning Israel that they have observed the entirety of the Torah. Let Nimrod come and give testimony in behalf of Abraham that he never worshiped idols. Let Laban come and give testimony in behalf of Jacob, that he never was suspected of thievery. Let the wife of Potiphar come and give testimony in behalf of Joseph, that he was never suspected of "sin." Let Nebuchadnessar come and give testimony in behalf of Hananiah, Mishael, and Azariah, that they never bowed down to the idol. Let Darius come and give testimony in behalf of Daniel, that he did not neglect even the optional prayers. Let Bildad the Shuhite and Zophar the Naamatite and Eliphaz the Temanite and Elihu son of Barachel the Buzite come and testify in behalf of Israel that they have observed the entirety of the Torah: "Let the nations bring their own witnesses, that they may be justified" (Isa. 43:9).'

QQ.   "They will say before him, 'Lord of the world, give it to us to begin with, and let us carry it out.'

RR.   "The Holy One, blessed be He, will say to them, 'World class idiots! He who took the trouble to prepare on the eve of the Sabbath [Friday] will eat on the Sabbath, but he who took no trouble on the eve of the Sabbath – what in the world is he going to eat on the Sabbath! Still, [I'll give you another chance.] I have a rather simple religious duty, which is called "the tabernacle." Go and do that one.'"

SS.   *But can you say any such thing? Lo, R. Joshua b. Levi has said,*
         "What is the meaning of the verse of Scripture, 'The ordinances that
         I command you this day to do them' (Deut. 7:11)? Today is the
         day to do them, but not tomorrow; they are not to be done
         tomorrow; today is the day to do them, but not the day on
         which to receive a reward for doing them."

TT.   Rather, it is that the Holy One, blessed be He, does not exercise
         tyranny over his creatures.

UU.   *And why does he refer to it as a simple religious duty? Because it*
         does not involve enormous expense [to carry out that religious duty].

VV.   "Forthwith every one of them will take up the task and go and
         make a tabernacle on his roof. But then the Holy, One, blessed be
         He, will come and make the sun blaze over them as at the summer
         solstice, and every one of them will knock down his tabernacle and
         go his way: 'Let us break their bands asunder and cast away their
         cords from us' (Ps. 2:3)."

WW.   But lo, you have just said, "it is that the Holy One, blessed be
        He, does not exercise tyranny over his creatures"!

XX.   *It is becuase the Israelites, too – sometimes* **[3B]** *the summer solstice*
         goes on to the Festival of Tabernacles, and therefore they are bothered
         by the heat!

YY.   But has not Raba stated, "One who is bothered [by the heat] is
         exempt from the obligation of dwelling in the tabernacle"?

ZZ.   *Granting that one may be exempt from the duty, is he going to go and*
         tear the thing down?

AAA.   [Continuing from VV:] "Then the Holy One, blessed be He, goes
        into session and laughs at them: 'He who sits in heaven laughs' (Ps.
        2:4)."

BBB.   Said R. Isaac, "Laughter before the Holy One, blessed be He,
        takes place only on that day alone."

CCC.   *There are those who repeat as a Tannaite version this statement*
        of R. Isaac in respect to that which has been taught on Tannaite
        authority:

DDD.   R. Yosé says, "In the coming age gentiles will come and
        convert."

EEE.   *But will they be accepted? Has it not been taught on Tannaite*
        authority: Converts will not be accepted in the days of the
        Messiah, just as they did not accept proselytes either in the
        time of David or in the time of Solomon?

FFF.   Rather, "they will make themselves converts, and they will
        put phylacteries on their heads and arms and fringes on
        their garments and a mezuzah on their doors. But when
        they witness the war of Gog and Magog, he will say to
        them, 'How come you have come?' They will say,
        '"Against the Lord and against his Messiah."' For so it is
        said, 'Why are the nations in an uproar and why do the
        peoples mutter in vain' (Ps. 2:1). Then each one of them
        will rid himself of his religious duty and go his way: 'Let
        us break their bands asunder' (Ps. 2:3). Then the Holy
        One, blessed be He, goes into session and laughs at them:
        'He who sits in heaven laughs' (Ps. 2:4)."

GGG.   Said R. Isaac, "Laughter before the Holy One, blessed be He, takes place only on that day alone."

HHH.   But is this really so? And has not R. Judah said Rab said, "The day is made up of twelve hours. In the first three the Holy One, blessed be He, goes into session and engages in study of the Torah; in the second he goes into session and judges the entire world. When he realizes that the world is liable to annihilation, he arises from the throne of justice and takes up a seat on the throne of mercy. In the third period he goes into session and nourishes the whole world from the horned buffalo to the brood of vermin. During the fourth quarter he laughs [and plays] with leviathan: 'There is leviathan, whom you have formed to play with' (Ps. 104:26)." [This proves that God does laugh more than on that one day alone.]

III.   Said R. Nahman bar Isaac, "With his creatures he laughs [every day], but at his creatures he laughs only on that day alone."

The next passages, to the end of this entire composition, go their own way. In order to justify my decision to classify the entirety of I.2 – which is to say, I.2-I.32, in a single way, I have to show that the entire composite is connected to I.2, and that the whole forms a secondary formation, brought together for the purpose of giving a full and complete exposition of the statement of I.2 and of the materials included within that statement. To what entirely objective criterion do I appeal? Time and again in what follows we shall see clearcut reference, to something stated in I.2, not merely allusion to a theme or some other aspect of "intertextuality." The initial composition, I.2, is quoted, not merely referred to, and the entirety of what follows then serves that initial passage. Since I conceive everything that follows to form either a footnote to I.2 or an appendix to a footnote to I.2, I have set the whole into wider margins than the foregoing. This underlines the fact that the whole augments a principal and primary statement.

I.3   A.   Said R. Aha to R. Nahman bar Isaac, "From the day on which the house of the sanctuary was destroyed, the Holy One, blessed be He, has had no laughter.

     B.   *"And how on the basis of Scripture do we know that he has had none? If we say that it is because it is written, 'And on that day did the Lord, the god of hosts, call to weeping and lamentation' (Isa. 22:12), that verse refers to that day in particular. Shall we then say that that fact derives from the verse, 'If I forget you, Jerusalem, let my right hand forget her cunning, let my tongue cleave to the roof of my mouth if I do not remember you' (Ps. 137:5-6)? That refers to forgetfulness, not laughter. Rather, the fact derives from this verse: 'I have long held my peace, I have been still, I have kept in, now I will cry' (Isa. 42:14)."*

The reference to God's laughing at GGG accounts for the addition of No. 3. Then we proceed to No. 4, a further reference to an item at No. 2. Nos. 5, 6 address the general theme of Torah study. Because these compositions introduce the theme of this world and the world to come, punishment now, reward then, or recompense then for evil deeds done now, we find secondary developments on these themes at Nos. 7, 8, 9, 10, 11, 12, 13, 14.

I.4   A.   [Referring to the statement that during the fourth quarter he laughs [and plays] with leviathon,] *[nowadays] what does he do in the fourth quarter of the day?*

        B.   He sits and teaches Torah to kindergarten students: "Whom shall one teach knowledge, and whom shall one make understand the message? Those who are weaned from the milk?" (Isa. 28:19).

        C.   *And to begin with [prior to the destruction of the Temple, which ended his spending his time playing with leviathan], who taught them?*

        D.   *If you wish, I shall say it was Metatron, and if you wish, I shall say that he did both [but now does only one].*

        E.   *And at night what does he do?*

        F.   *If you wish, I shall say that it is the sort of thing he does by day;*

        G.   *and if you wish, I shall say,* he rides his light cherub and floats through eighteen thousand worlds: "The chariots of God are myriads, even thousands and thousands [shinan] (Ps. 868:48). Read the letters translated as thousands, shinan, as though they were written, she-enan, meaning, that are not [thus: "the chariots are twice ten thousand less two thousand, eighteen thousand (Mishcon)].

        H.   *And if you wish, I shall say,* he sits and listens to the song of the Living Creatures [hayyot]: "By the day the Lord will command his lovingkindness and in the night his song shall be with me" (Ps. 42:9).

I.5   A.   Said R. Levi, "To whoever stops studying the words of the Torah and instead takes up words of mere chatter they feed glowing coals of juniper: 'They pluck salt wort with wormwood and the roots of juniper are their food' (Job 30:4)."

        B.   Said R. Simeon b. Laqish, "For whoever engages in study of the Torah by night – the Holy One, blessed be He, draws out the thread of grace by day: 'By day the Lord will command his lovingkindness, and in the night his song shall be with me' (Ps. 42:9). Why is it that 'By day the Lord will command his lovingkindness'? Because 'in the night his song shall be with me.'"

        C.   *Some say,* said R. Simeon b. Laqish, "For whoever engages in study of the Torah in this world, which is like the night – the Holy One, blessed be He, draws out the thread of grace in the world to come, which is like the day: 'By day the Lord will command his lovingkindness, and in the night his song shall be with me' (Ps. 42:9). [Supply: Why is it that 'By day the Lord will command his lovingkindness'? Because 'in the night his song shall be with me.']"

I.6   A.   Said R. Judah said Samuel, *"What is the meaning of the verse of Scripture,* 'And you make man as the fish of the sea and as the creeping things, that have no ruler over them' (Hab. 1:14)? Why are human beings compared to fish of the sea? To tell you, just as fish in the sea, when they come up on dry land, forthwith begin to die, so with human beings, when they take their leave of teachings of the Torah and religious deeds, forthwith they begin to die.

      B.   "Another matter: just as the fish of the sea, as soon as dried by the sun, die, so human beings, when struck by the sun, die."

      C.   *If you want, this refers to this world, and if you want, this refers to the world to come.*

      D.   *If you want, this refers to this world, in line with that which R. Hanina [said],* for said R. Hanina, "Everything is in the hands of Heaven except cold and heat: 'colds and heat boils are in the way of the froward, he who keeps his soul holds himself far from them' (Prov. 22:5)."

      E.   *and if you want, this refers to the world to come, in accord with that which was stated by R. Simeon b. Laqish.* For said R. Simeon b. Laqish, "In the world to come, there is no Gehenna, but rather, the Holy One, blessed be He, brings the sun out of its sheathe and he heats the wicked but heals the righteous through it. The wicked are brought to judgment by [4A] it: 'For behold, the day comes, it burns as a furnace, and all the proud and all who do wicked things shall be stubble, and the day that comes shall set them ablaze, says the Lord of hosts, that it shall leave them neither root nor branch' (Mal. 3:19).

      F.   "'it shall leave them neither root' – in this world; 'nor branch' – in the world to come.

      G.   "'but heals the righteous through it': 'But to you that fear my name shall the sun of righteousness arise with healing in its wings' (Mal. 3:19). They will revel in it: 'And you shall go forth and gambol as calves of the stall' (Mal. 3:20)."

      H.   [Continuing C, above:] "Another matter: just with as the fish of the sea, whoever is bigger than his fellow swallows his fellow, so in the case of human beings, were it not for fear of the government, whoever is bigger than his fellow would swallow his fellow."

      I.   *That is in line with what we have learned in the Mishnah:* **R. Hananiah, Prefect of the Priests, says, "Pray for the welfare of the government. For if it were not for fear of it, one man would swallow his fellow alive" [M. Abot 3:2A-B].**

I.7   A.   *R. Hinena bar Pappa contrasted verses of Scripture: "It is written,* 'As to the almighty, we do not find him exercising plenteous power' (Job 37:23), but by contrast, 'Great is our Lord and of abundant power' (Ps. 147:5), and further, 'Your right hand, Lord, is glorious in power' (Ex. 15:6).

       B.   "But there is no contradiction between the first and second and third statements, for the former speaks of the time of judgment [when justice is tempered with mercy, so God does not do what he could] and the latter two statements refer to a time of war [of God against his enemies]."

I.8   A.   *R. Hama bar Hanina contrasted verses of Scripture: "it is written,* 'Fury is not in me' (Isa. 27:4) but also 'The Lord revenges and is furious' (Nah. 1:2).

       B.   *"But there is no contradiction between the first and second statements,* for the former speaks of Israel, the latter of the gentiles."

       C.   R. Hinena bar Pappa said, "'Fury is not in me' (Isa. 54:9), for I have already taken an oath: 'would that I had not so vowed, then as the briars and thorns in flame would I with one step burn it altogether' (Isa. 54:9)."

I.9   A.   *That is in line with what R. Alexandri said, "What is the meaning of the verse,* 'And it shall come to pass on that day that I will seek to destroy all the nations' (Zech. 12:9) –

       B.   "'seek' – seek permission from whom?

       C.   "Said the Holy One, blessed be He, 'I shall seek in the records that deal with them, to see whether there is a cause of merit, on account of which I shall redeem them, but if not, I shall destroy them.'"

I.10   A.   *That is in line with what Raba said, "What is the meaning of the verse,* 'Howbeit he will not stretch out a hand for a ruinous neap though they cry in his destruction' (Job 30:24)?

       B.   "Said the Holy One, blessed be He, to Israel, 'When I judge Israel, I shall not judge them as I do the gentiles, for it is written, "I will overturn, overturn, overturn it" (Ezek. 21:32), rather, I shall exact punishment from them as a hen pecks.'

       C.   "Another matter: 'Even if the Israelites do not carry out a religious duty before me more than a hen pecking at a rubbish heap, I shall join together [all the little pecks] into a great sum: "although they pick little they are saved" (Job 30:24) [following Mishcon's rendering].'

       D.   "Another matter: 'As a reward for their crying out to me, I shall help them' (Job 30:24) [following Mishcon's rendering]."

I.11   A.   *That is in line with what R. Abba said, "What is the meaning of the verse, 'Though I would redeem them, yet they have spoken lies against me' (Hos. 7:23)?* 'I said that I would redeem them through [inflicting a penalty] on their property in this world, so that they might have the merit of enjoying the world to come, "yet they have spoken lies against me" (Hos. 7:23).'"

I.12   A.   *That is in line with what R. Pappi in the name of Raba said, "What is the meaning of the verse, 'Though I have trained [and] strengthened their arms, yet they imagine mischief against me' (Hos. 7:15)?*

      B.   "Said the Holy One, blessed be He, I thought that I would punish them with suffering in this world, so that their arm might be strengthened in the world to come, 'yet they have spoken lies against me' (Hos. 7:23)."

I.13   A.   *R. Abbahu praised R. Safra to the minim* [in context: Christian authorities of Caesarea], *saying that he was a highly accomplished authority. They therefore remitted his taxes for thirteen years.*

      B.   *One day they came upon him and said to him, "It is written, 'You only have I known among all the families of the earth; therefore I will visit upon you all your iniquities' (Amos 3:2). If one is angry, does he vent it on someone he loves?"*

      C.   *He fell silent and said nothing at all. They wrapped a scarf around his neck and tortured him. R. Abbahu came along and found them. He said to them, "Why are you torturing him?":*

      D.   *They said to him, "Didn't you tell us that he is a* highly accomplished authority, *but he does not know how to explain this verse!"*

      E.   *He said to them, "True enough, I told you that he was a master of Tannaite statements, but did I say anything at all to you about his knowledge of Scripture?"*

      F.   *They said to him, "So how come you know?"*

      G.   *He said to them, "Since we, for our part, spend a lot of time with you, we have taken the task of studying it thoroughly, while others [in Babylonia, Safra's place of origin] do not study [Scripture] that carefully."*

      H.   *They said to him, "So tell us."*

      I.   He said to them, "I shall tell you a parable. To what is the matter comparable? To the case of a man who lent money to two people, one a friend, the other an enemy. From the friend he collects the money little by little, from the enemy he collects all at once."

I.14   A.   *Said R. Abba bar Kahana, "What is the meaning of the following verse of Scripture: 'Far be it from you to do after this manner, to slay the righteous with the wicked' (Gen. 18:25)?*

B.   "Said Abraham before the Holy One, blessed be He, 'Lord of the world! It is a profanation to act in such a way [a play on the Hebrew letters, shared by the words 'far be it' and 'profanation'], 'to slay the righteous with the wicked' (Gen. 18:25)."

C.   But is it not [so that God might do just that]? And is it not written, "And I will cut off from you the righteous and the wicked" (Ezek. 21:8)?

D.   That speaks of one who is not completely righteous, but not of one who is completely righteous.

E.   And will he not do so to one who is completely righteous? And is it not written, "And begin the slaughter with my sanctuary" (Ezek. 9:6), in which connection R. Joseph repeated as a Tannaite version, "Read not 'with my sanctuary' but rather, 'with those who are holy to me,' namely, the ones who carried out the Torah beginning to end."

F.   *There, too,* since they had the power to protest against the wickedness of the others and did not do so, they were not regarded as completely righteous at all.

The preceding composite, made up of connected compositions, has made reference to God's forgiveness and also God's anger. So we now address, as a tertiary augmentation, the issue of God's anger: when it happens, how it affects judgment, why it is important to avoid God's wrath and the like. The whole is an appendix to an appendix, a strung together set of compositions, all of them related fore and aft, so that, in following the chain from the end to the beginning, we can always account for why a given composition has been made part of the composite before us. So we can account for the movement from one to the next, beginning at No. 15:

I.15   A.   *R. Pappa contrasted verses of Scripture: "It is written, 'God is angry every day' (Ps. 7:12) but also 'who could stand before his anger' (Nah. 1:6).*

B.   *"But there is no contradiction between the first and second statements, for the former speaks of the individual, the latter of the community."*

I.16   A.   *Our rabbis have taught on Tannaite authority:*

B.   "God is angry every day" (Ps. 7:12), and how long is his anger? It is for a moment. And how long is a moment? The portion 1/53,848th of an hour is a moment.

C.   And no creature can determine that moment, except for Balaam that wicked man, of whom it is written, [5A] "who knew the knowledge of the Most High" (Num. 24:16).

D.   How can it be that a man who did not know the mind of his animal could have known the mind of the Most High?

I.17	A.	*And what is the meaning of the statement that* he did not know the mind of his animal?
	B.	*When they saw him riding on his ass, they said to him, "How come you're not riding on a horse?"*
	C.	*He said to them, "I sent it to the meadow."*
	D.	Forthwith: "The ass said, Am I not your ass" (Num. 22:30).
	E.	*He said to it, "Just as a beast of burden in general."*
	F.	*She said to him, "Upon whom you have ridden"* (Num. 22:30).
	G.	*He said to it, "Only from time to time."*
	H.	*She said to him, "*ever since I was yours {Num. 22:30). And not only so, but I serve you for riding by day and fucking by night."
	I.	For here the word "I was wont" is used, and the same letters bear the meaning of bedmate: "...and she served him as a bedmate" (1 Kgs. 1:2).
I.18	A.	*And what is the meaning of the statement that* he could have known the mind of the Most High?
	B.	For he knew precisely that moment at which the Holy One, blessed be He, was angry.
	C.	*That is in line with what the prophet had said to them,* "O my people, remember now what Balak king of Moab consulted and what Balaam son of Beor answered him from Shittim to Gilgal, that you may know the righteousness of the Lord" (Mic. 6:5).
I.19	A.	["O my people, remember now what Balak king of Moab consulted and what Balaam son of Beor answered him from Shittim to Gilgal, that you may know the righteousness of the Lord" (Mic 6:5)]:
	B.	Said R. Eleazar, "Said the Holy one, blessed be He, to Israel, 'My people, see how many acts of righteousness I carried out with you, for I did not grow angry with you during all those [perilous] days, for if I had grown angry with you, there would not have remained from Israel a remnant or a survivor.'
	C.	"And that is in line with what Balaam says: 'How can I curse seeing that God does not curse, and how can I be wrathful, seeing that the Lord has not been wrathful' (Num. 23:8)."
I.20	A.	And how long is his wrath? It is for a moment. And how long is a moment? The portion 1/53,848th of an hour is a moment.
	B.	And how long is a moment?
	C.	Said Amemar – others say, Rabina – "So long as it takes to say the word 'moment.'"
	D.	*And how on the basis of Scripture do we know that his wrath lasts for only a moment?*

	E.	*As it is written,* "For his anger is for a moment, his favor is for a lifetime" (Ps. 30:6).
	F.	*If you prefer:* "Hide yourself for a brief moment, until the wrath be past" (Isa. 26:20).
I.21	A.	*When is he angry?*
	B.	*Said Abbayye,* "*In the first three hours of the day, when the comb of the cock is white.*"
	C.	*Isn't it white all the rest of the day?*
	D.	*At other times it has red streaks, but then it has none.*
I.22	A.	*R. Joshua b. Levi – a certain min would bother him about verses of Scripture. Once he took a chicken and put it between the legs of the bed and watched it. He reasoned,* "When that hour comes, I shall curse him."
	B.	*But when that hour came, he was dozing. He said,* "What you learn from this experience is that it is not correct to act in such a way: 'His tender mercies are over all his works' (Ps. 145:9), 'Neither is it good for the righteous to inflict punishment' (Prov. 17:26)."
I.23	A.	*It was taught as a Tannaite version in the name of R. Meir,* "[That time at which God gets angry comes] when the kings put their crowns on their heads and prostrate themselves to the sun. Forthwith the Holy One, blessed be He, grows angry."
I.24	A.	*Said R. Joseph,* "A person should not recite the Prayer of the Additional Service for the first day of the New Year [the Day of Judgment] during the first three hours of the day or in private, lest, since that is the time of judgment, his deeds may be examined, and his prayer rejected."
	B.	*If so, then the prayer of the community also should not be recited at that time?*
	C.	*The merit [accruing to the community as a whole] is greater.*
	D.	*If so, then that of the Morning Service also should not be recited in private?*
	E.	*Since at that time the community also will be engaged in reciting the Morning Prayer, the individual's recitation of the Prayer will not be rejected.*
	F.	*But have you not said,* "In the first three the Holy One, blessed be He, goes into session and engages in study of the Torah; in the second he goes into session and judges the entire world"?
	G.	*Reverse the order.*
	H.	*Or, if you prefer, actually do not reverse the order.* For when God is occupied with study of the Torah, called by Scripture "truth" as in "buy the truth and do not sell it" (Prov. 23:23), the Holy One, blessed be He, in any event will not violate the strict rule of justice. But when engaged in judgment, which is not called "truth" by

Scripture, the Holy One, blessed be He, may step across the line of strict justice [towards mercy].

The long process of glossing the glosses has come to an end, so we now refer back to another statement of No. 2, which we shall develop. That covers Nos. 25-27:

I.25 A. Reverting to the body of the prior text:

   B. *R. Joshua b. Levi has said, "What is the meaning of the verse of Scripture,* 'The ordinances that I command you this day to do them' (Deut. 7:11)? Today is the day to do them, but not tomorrow; they are not to be done tomorrow; today is the day to do them, but today is not the day on which to receive a reward for doing them":

   C. Said R. Joshua b. Levi, "All the religious duties that Israelites do in this world come and give evidence in their behalf in the world to come: 'Let them bring their witnesses that they may be justified, let them hear and say it is truth.'"

   D. "Let them bring their witnesses that they may be justified": this is Israel.

   E. "Let them hear and say it is truth": this refers to the gentiles.

   F. And said R. Joshua b. Levi, "All the religious duties that Israelites do in this world come and flap about the faces of gentiles in the world to come: 'Keep therefore and do them, for this, your wisdom and understanding, will be in the eyes of the peoples' (Deut. 4:6).

   G. "What is stated here is not 'in the presence of the peoples' but 'in the eyes of the peoples,' which teaches you that they will come and flap about the faces of gentiles in the world to come."

   H. And said R. Joshua b. Levi, "The Israelites made the golden calf only to give an opening to penitents: 'O that they had such a heart as this always, to fear me and keep my commandments' (Deut. 5:26)."

I.26 A. That is in line with what R. Yohanan said in the name of R. Simeon b. Yohai: "David was really not so unfit as to do such a deed [as he did with Beth Sheva]: 'My heart is slain within me' (Ps. 109:22) [Mishcon: David's inclinations had been completely conquered by himself]. And the Israelites were hardly the kind of people to commit such an act: "O that they had such a heart as this always, to fear me and keep my commandments' (Deut. 5:26). So why did they do it?

   B. "[5A] It was to show you that if an individual has sinned, they say to him, 'Go to the individual [such as David, and follow his example], and if the community as a whole has sinned, they say to them, 'Go to the community [such as Israel].'

   C. *And it was necessary to give both examples. For had we been given the rule governing the individual, that might have been supposed to be because his personal sins were not broadly known, but in the case of the community, the sins of which will be broadly known, I might have said that that is not the case.*

   D. *And if we had been given the rule governing the community, that might have been supposed to be the case because they enjoy greater mercy, but an*

individual, who has not got such powerful zekhut, might have been
thought not subject to the rule.

E.   *So both cases had to be made explicit.*

I.27   A.   *That is in line with what R. Samuel bar Nahmani said R. Jonathan said,*
"What is the meaning of the verse of Scripture, 'The saying of David,
son of Jesse, and the saying of the man raised on high' (2 Sam. 23:1)?

B.   "It means, 'The saying of David, son of Jesse, the man who raised
up the yoke of repentence.'"

Now that the expansion of the passage at No. 2 has been completed,
we proceed to the extension of that expansion. The reward for the
religious duty, the punishment for the sin – these themes are developed
at No. 28, which makes the point, critical in No. 2 as well, that our
accomplishment of religious duties is acknowledged, so, too, what sins
we have done.

I.28   A.   Said R. Samuel bar Nahmani said R. Jonathan, "Whoever does a
religious duty in this world – that deed goes before him to the
world to come, as it is said, 'And your righteousness shall go before
you' (Isa. 58:8).

B.   "And whoever commits a transgression in this world – that act
turns aside from him and goes before him on the Day of Judgment,
as it is said, 'The paths of their way are turned aside, they go up
into the waste and perish' (Job 6:18)."

C.   R. Eliezer says, "It attaches to him like a dog, as it is said, 'He did
not listen to her to lie by her or to be with her' (Gen. 39:10).

D.   "'To lie by her' in this world.

E.   "'Or to be with her' in the world to come."

No. 29 forms a gloss to No. 28, though, obviously, it also is free-
standing and makes its own autonomous point. What we now are given
is an account of the result of sin, which, in this world, is death, a
sustained and well-argued proposition, the whole an appendix to the
general theme of No. 2 but to the particular statements of No. 28: sin and
punishment, on the day of judgment.

I.29   A.   Said R. Simeon b. Laqish, "Come and let us express our
gratitude to our ancestors, for if it were not for their
having sinned, we for our part should never have been
able to come into the world: 'I said you are gods and all of
you sons of the Most High' (Ps. 82:6). Now that you have
ruined things by what you have done: 'you shall indeed
die like mortals' (Ps. 82:6)."

B.   *Does that statement then bear the implication, therefore, that if
they had not sinned, they would not have propagated? But has
it not been written,* "And you, be fruitful and multiply"
(Gen. 9:7)?

C.   *That applies up to Sinai.*

D.   *But in connection with Sinai it also is written,* "Go say to
them, Go back to your tents" (Ex. 19:15), meaning, to

marital relationships. *And is it not also written,* "that it might be well with them and with their children" (Deut. 5:26)?

E. That speaks only to those who were actually present at Mount Sinai.

F. *But has not R. Simeon b. Laqish stated, "What is the meaning of that which is written:* 'This is the book of the generations of Adam' (Gen. 5:1)? Now did the first Adam have a book? The statement, rather, teaches that the Holy One, blessed be He, showed to the first Adam each generation and its authoritative expositors, each generation and its sages, each generation and those that administered its affairs. When he came to the generation of R. Aqiba, he rejoiced in the master's Torah but he was saddened by the master's death.

G. "He said, 'How precious are your thoughts to me, O God' (Ps. 139:17)."

H. And said R. Yosé, "The son of David will come only when all of the souls that are stored up in the body will be used up: 'For I will not contend for ever, neither will I be always angry, for the spirit should fall before me and the spirits which I have made' (Isa. 57:16)." [Mishcon: In the face of the foregoing teachings, how could it be stated that had it not been for the sin of the golden calf, we should not have come into the world?]

I. *Do not, therefore, imagine that the sense of the statement is, we should have not come into the world [if our ancestors had not sinned], but rather, it would have been as though we had not come into the world.*

J. *Does that then bear the implication that, if they had not sinned, they would never have died? But have not been written the passages that deal with the deceased childless brother's widow and the chapters about inheritances [which take for granted that people die]?*

K. These passages are written conditionally [meaning, if people sin and so die, then the rules take effect, but it is not necessary that they take effect unless that stipulation is fulfilled].

L. *And are there then any verses of Scripture that are stated conditionally?*

M. *Indeed so, for said R. Simeon b. Laqish, "What is the meaning of that which has been written,* 'And it was evening and it was morning, the sixth day' (Gen. 1:31)? This teaches that the Holy One, blessed be He, made a stipulation with the works of creation and said, 'If the Israelites accept the Torah, well and good, but if not, I shall send you back to the condition of formlessness and void.'"

N. *An objection was raised:* "O that they had such a heart as this always, to fear me and keep my commandments, that it may be well with them and their children" (Deut. 5:26): it is not possible to maintain that the meaning here is that He would take away the angel of death from them, for the decree had already been made. It means that the Israelites accepted the Torah only so that no nation or tongue would rule over them: "that it might be well with them and their children after them." [Mishcon: How could R. Simeon b. Laqish hold that but for the golden calf worship Israel would have enjoyed physical deathlessness?]

O.   *[R. Simeon b. Laqish] made his statement in accord with the position of this Tannaite authority, for it has been taught on Tannaite authority:*

P.   R. Yosé says, "The Israelites accepted the Torah only so that the angel of death should not have power over them: 'I said you are gods and all of you sons of the Most High. Now that you have ruined things by what you have done you shall indeed die like mortals' (Ps. 82:6)."

Q.   *But to R. Yosé also must be addressed the question, has it not been written,* "O that they had such a heart as this always, to fear me and keep my commandments, that it may be well with them and their children" (Deut. 5:26)? *Goodness is what is promised, but there still will be death!*

R.   *R. Yosé will say to you,* "If there is no death, what greater goodness can there ever be?"

S.   *And the other Tannaite authority – how does he read the phrase,* "You shall indeed die"?

T.   *The sense of "death" here is "poverty,"* for a master has said, "Four classifications of persons are equivalent to corpses, and these are they: the poor man, the blind man, the person afflicted with the skin disease [of Lev. 13], and the person who has no children.

U.   "The poor man, as it is written: 'for all the men are dead who sought your life' (Ex. 4:129). *Now who were they? This refers to Dathan and Abiram, and they were certainly not then dead,* they had only lost all their money.

V.   "The blind man, as it is written: 'He has made me dwell in darkness as those that have been long dead' (Lam. 3:6).

W.   "The person afflicted with the skin disease, as it is written: 'Let her, I pray you, not be as one who is dead' (Num. 12;12).

X.   "And the person who has no children, as it is written: 'Give me children or else I die' (Gen. 30:1)."

What follows, at No. 30, is an appendix to the foregoing. I see no tight bonds that link No. 30 to No. 29, though Nos. 30, 31, 32, and 33 present a continuous discussion of their own. I treat the whole as an appendix, therefore, tacked on to a prior appendix. No. 32 clearly glosses No. 31.

I.30   A.   *Our rabbis have taught on Tannaite authority:*

       B.   "If you walk in my statutes" (Lev. 26:3) – the word "if" is used in the sense of supplication, as in the verse, "O that my people would hearken to me, that

Israel would walk in my ways...I should soon subdue their enemies" (Ps. 81:14-15); "O that you had listened to my commandments, then my peace would have been as a river, your seed also would have been as the sand" (Isa. 48:18).

I.31 A. *Our rabbis have taught on Tannaite authority:*

B. "O that they had such a heart as this always, to fear me and keep my commandments, that it may be well with them and their children" (Deut. 5:26).

C. Said Moses to the Israelites, "You are a bunch of ingrates, children of ingrates. When the Holy One, blessed be He, said to you, 'O that they had such a heart as this always, to fear me and keep my commandments, that it may be well with them and their children' (Deut. 5:26), they should have said, 'You give it.'

D. "They were ingrates, since it is written, 'Our soul loathes [5B] this light bread' (Num. 21:5).

E. "...the children of ingrates: 'The woman whom you gave to be with me, she gave me of the fruit of the tree and I ate it' (Gen. 3:12).

F. "So our rabbi, Moses, gave an indication of that fact to the Israelites only after forty years: 'And I have led you forty years in the wilderness...but the Lord has not given you a heart to know and eyes to see and ears to hear unto this day' (Deut. 29:3, 4)."

I.32 A. ["And I have led you forty years in the wilderness...but the Lord has not given you a heart to know and eyes to see and ears to hear unto this day" (Deut. 29:3, 4):]

B. Said Raba, "This proves that a person will fully grasp the mind of his master only after forty years have passed."

If I were responsible to choose a suitable conclusion to this mass of material, one that would both say something fresh but also present a reprise of the entire thematic conglomerate that has gone before, I doubt I could make a better choice than the following, which we must, therefore, see as a deliberate sign that we have come to the end of an enormous, but continuous and sustained, discussion of the general theme of Israel's loyalty and gentiles' idolatry. I center the passage to signal its function, which is, to write the word *finis*.

I.33 A. *Said R. Yohanan in the name of R. Benaah, "What is the meaning of the verse of Scripture, 'Happy are you who sow beside all waters, that send forth the feet of the ox and the ass' (Isa. 32:20)? 'Happy are you, O Israel, when you are devoted to the Torah and to doing deeds of grace, then their inclination to do evil is*

	handed over to them, and they are not handed over into the power of their inclination to do evil.
B.	"For it is said, 'Happy are you who sow beside all waters.' For what does the word 'sowing' mean, if not 'doing deeds of grace,' in line with the use of the word in this verse: 'Sow for yourselves in righteousness, reap according to mercy' (Hos. 10:12), and what is the meaning of 'water' if not Torah: 'Oh you who are thirsty, come to the water' (Isa. 55:1)."
C.	As to the phrase, "that send forth the feet of the ox and the ass":
D.	it has been taught by the Tannaite authority of the household of Elijah:
E.	"A person should always place upon himself the work of studying the Torah as an ox accepts the yoke, and as an ass, its burden."

Let me now summarize what we have before us. I.1 begins with a systematic inquiry into the correct reading of the Mishnah's word choices. The dispute is fully articulated in balance, beginning to end. I.2 then forms a footnote to No. 1. No. 3 then provides a footnote to the leitmotif of No. 2, the conception of God's not laughing. and No. 4 returns us to the exposition of No. 2, at III. Nos. 5, 6 are tacked on – a Torah study anthology – because they continue the general theme of Torah study every day, which formed the main motif of No. 2 – the gentiles did not accept the Torah, study it, or carry it out. So that theme accounts for the accumulation of sayings on Torah study in general, a kind of appendix on the theme. Then – so far as I can see, because of the reference to God's power – No. 7 begins with a complement to 6.I. The compositions, Nos. 7, 8, then are strung together because of a point that is deemed to link each to its predecessor. No. 7 is linked to the foregoing because of the theme of God's power; but it also intersects with 2.III and complements that reference; the entire sequence beyond No. 2 then in one way or another relates to either No. 2, theme or proposition, or to an item that is tacked on to No. 2 as a complement. Thus No. 8 is joined to No. 7 because of the shared method of contrasting verses. Then No. 9 is tacked on because it continues the proposition of No. 8. No. 10 continues the foregoing. No. 11 is tacked on to No. 10 for the reason made explicit: it continues what has gone before.

The same is so for No. 12. No. 13 continues the theme, but not the form or the proposition, of the prior compositions, namely, punishment little by little, for example, in this world, in exchange for a great reward later on. The established theme then is divine punishment and how it is inflicted: gently to Israel, harshly to the gentiles; the preferred form is the contrast among two verses. That overall principle of conglomeration – form and theme – explains the inclusion of Nos. 14, 15+16, which is tacked on to 15. But then the introduction of Balaam, taken as the prototype for the *min* or heretic, accounts for the inclusion of a variety of further sayings on the same theme, specifically, No. 17, a gloss on the foregoing; No. 18, a continuation of the foregoing process of glossing; No. 19, an amplification on the now dominant theme; No. 20, a reversion to No. 16; No. 21, a story on the theme of how difficult it is to define precisely the matter dealt with in the foregoing. Nos. 21, 22, 23 complete the discussion of that particular time at which God is angry, a brief moment but one that is marked by a just cause. No. 23 then introduces the theme of choosing the right time – that is, not the moment of divine wrath – for prayer. This seems to me a rather miscellaneous item, and it marks the conclusion of the systematic expansion begun much earlier. That that is the fact is shown by the character of No. 24, which cites 2.HHH, and by No. 25, which explicitly reverts to 2.SS, which justifies my insistence that the entire corpus of materials that follow No. 2 simply amplify and augment No. 2, and that is done in a very systematic way. Some of the sets were formed into conglomerates prior to insertion here, but once we recognize that all of the sets serve the single task at hand, we see the coherence of what on the surface appears to be run-on and miscellaneous. So these materials serve No. 2, some as footnotes, some as appendices, and some as footnotes or appendices to footnotes or appendices.

No. 26 is a fine case in point. It complements 25.H, and is tacked on for that reason. Then No. 27 complements No. 26's statements concerning David. Bearing a formal tie to No. 27, with the same authority, No. 28 fits in also because it reverts to the theme of No. 25, the power of the religious duties that one carries out. No. 29 continues the theme of No. 28, that is, death and the day of judgment. Simeon's statement defines the center of gravity of the passage, which obviously was complete prior to its inclusion here. The reason it has been added is its general congruence to the discussions of sin, penitence, death and forgiveness. No. 30 is attached to No. 31, and No. 31 is tacked on because it refers to the prooftext in the prior composition. No. 32 takes up the prooftext of No. 31. No. 33 writes a solid conclusion to the whole, addressing as it does the basic theme that Israel's actions define their fate, and that study of the Torah is what determines everything else. That is a thematic conclusion to a composite largely devoted, one way or another, to that one theme.

Lest we lose sight of the purpose of this rather protracted analysis of the connections between and among compositions, connections that make well-knit composites out of a selection of compositions, I remind the reader of what is at stake. It is not merely to show that a composite of compositions in fact forms a single literary entity, a complete and whole and, within the conventions of these authors, cogent and coherent statement. Nor is my purpose merely to justify my classifying the whole as a single unit, for purposes of setting forth the rules of composition: of making composites, of writing whole and complete statements, both. The whole of I.1-32 forms a single, continuous and uninterrupted statement, the entirety of which is to be classified within a single rubric. My claim is that before us in writing is the representation of a culture of connections. And I regard the passage at hand as probative evidence of that simple fact. I.1 assuredly forms a beautifully expounded exercise in criticism of the text of the Mishnah. Why then do I insist No. 2 follows in the wake of No. 1 and finds its place, therefore, within the same taxon? It is simply because No. 2 is clearly intended as a footnote to No. 1, and from there, in a precise and concrete sense, the rest follow – all thirty-two compositions formed into a single string of connected, if not continuous, compositions. Now, it goes without saying, these literary facts dictate the character of any inquiry into the givens of discourse.

What we have seen suffices to make the simple point that analysis of the premises and presuppositions of the two Talmuds requires a very different approach from that operative in the examination of any of the prior compilations taken up in this research report. The principles of conglomeration and agglutination represent a set of premises concerning how things fit together to make sense. It is our task to locate and define the kinds of principles that governed the work of compilation and composite making. For when people addressed compositions and considered how these might be formed into larger composites, more than a single purpose – the purpose dictated by the making of the Talmud – instructed them on what to choose and on how to join this to that.

Then shall we conclude that the premises come to us from the individual compositions, such as those I have identified? I think not. The compositions reveal premises of one kind, the composite over all, presuppositions of an equally important character. When we grasp the purpose in the following composite, we shall see that the framer of the whole had in mind to make a major statement, which only after the fact served for this enormous thing, this Talmud, that is served by the statement. We shall now see that the wandering composite that follows in point of fact addresses a single matter and sets forth a simple statement of public policy. To clarify what belongs, and what does not belong, to the principal composite – which is not the one that serves as our Talmud – I set off the composite under discussion from what clearly forms the Talmud for our Mishnah paragraph. These materials begin at No. 2.

1:7

	A.	They do not sell them (1) bears or (2) lions, or (3) anything which is a public danger.
	B.	They do not build with them (1) a basilica, (2) scaffold, (3) stadium, or (4) judges' tribunal.
II.1	A.	They do not build with them (1) a basilica, (2) scaffold, (3) stadium, or (4) judges' tribunal:
	B.	Said Rabbah b. Bar Hanna said R. Yohanan, "There are three classifications of basilicas: those belonging to gentile kings, those belonging to bathhouses, and those belonging to storehouses."
	C.	Said Raba, "Two of those are permitted, the third forbidden [for Israelite workers to build], and your mnemonic is 'to bind their kings with chains' (Ps. 149:8)."
	D.	And there are those who say, said Raba, "All of them are permitted [for Israelite workers to build]."
	E.	*But have we not learned in the Mishnah:* **They do not build with them (1) a basilica, (2) scaffold, (3) stadium, or (4) judges' tribunal?**
	F.	*Say that that rule applies in particular to* a basilica to which is attached an executioner's scaffold, a stadium, or a judge's tribunal.

II.1 accomplishes the same purpose, of harmonizing opinions. Because of II.1, II.2 is tacked on, and the entire mass of material on rabbis' martyrdoms, already in place, was kept together with the illustration of the tribune and why Israelite workers should not join in building such a thing. To appreciate how a large composite takes shape, let us now review all that follows and identify the compositions that have been joined together and why they serve as they do. As before, I indent what I classify as compositions that serve as footnotes, and I further indent what I deem to be appendices.

II.2	A.	*Our rabbis taught on Tannaite authority:*
	B.	When R. Eliezer was arrested on charges of minut [being a Christian], they brought him up to the judge's tribunal to be judged. The hegemon said to him, "Should a sage such as yourself get involved in such nonsense as this?"
	C.	He said to him, "I acknowledge the Judge."
	D.	The hegemon supposed that he was referring to him, but he referred only to his father who is in heaven. He said to him, "Since I have been accepted by you as an honorable judge, demos! You are acquitted."
	E.	When he got to his household, his disciples came to him to console him, but he did not accept consolation. Said to him R. Aqiba, "My lord, will you let me say something to you from among the things that you have taught me?"
	F.	He said to him, "Speak."
	G.	R. Aqiba said to him, "Perhaps some matter pertaining to minut has come into your domain [17A] and given you some sort of satisfaction, and on that account you were arrested?"

H.   He said to him, "Aqiba, you remind me! Once I was going into the upper market of Sepphoris, and I found a certain person, named Jacob of Kefar Sakhnayya, who said to me, 'It is written in your Torah, "You shall not bring the hire of a harlot...into the house of the Lord your God" (Deut. 23:19). What is the law as to building with such funds a privy for the high priest?' Now I did not say a thing to him.

I.   "So he said to me, 'This is what I have been taught [by Jesus of Nazareth], "For the hire of a harlot has she gathered them, and to the hire of a harlot they shall return" (Prov. 5:8). They have come from a filthy place and to a filthy place they may return.' And that statement gave me a good bit of pleasure, and on that account I was arrested on the charge of being a Christian, so I violated what is written in the Torah: 'Remove your way far from her' – this refers to minut; 'and do not come near to the door of her house' (Prov. 5:8) – this refers to the government."

II.3   A.   There are those who refer "Remove your way far from her," to Christianity and to the ruling power, and the part of the verse, "and do not come near to the door of her house" (Prov. 5:8)] they refer to a whore.

II.4   A.   And how far is one to keep away?

       B.   Said R. Hisda, "Four cubits."

II.5   A.   And how do rabbis [who do not concur with Jacob] interpret the verse, "You shall not bring the hire of a harlot..into the house of the Lord your God" (Deut. 23:19)?

       B.   *They interpret it in accord with R. Hisda, for* said R. Hisda, "In the end every whore who hires herself out will hire out a man, as it is said, 'And in that you pay a hire and no hire is given to you, thus you are reversed' (Ezek. 16:34)."

II.6   A.   [*Referring to 4.B] that measurement differs from the opinion of R. Pedat, for* said R. Pedat, "The Torah has declared forbidden close approach only in the case of incest: 'None of you shall approach to any that is near of kin to him to uncover their nakedness' (Lev. 18:6)."

II.7   A.   *When Ulla would come home from the household of the master, he would kiss his sisters on their hand.*

       B.   *Some say, "On their breast."*

       C.   *He then contradicts what he himself has said, for said Ulla, "Even merely coming near is forbidden, as we say to the Nazirite, 'Go, go around about, but do not even come near the vineyard.'"*

II.8   A.   *When Ulla would come home from the household of the master, he would kiss his sisters on their hand.*

       B.   *Some say, "On their breast."*

       C.   *He then contradicts what he himself has said, for said Ulla, "Even merely coming near is forbidden, as we say to the Nazirite, 'Go, go around about, but do not even come near the vineyard.'"*

II.9   A.   "The horse leech has two daughters: Give, give" (Prov. 30:15) –

	B.	*What is the meaning of* "Give, give"?
	C.	Said Mar Uqba, "It is the voice of the two daughters who cry out from Gehenna, saying to this world, 'Bring, bring.' *And who are they? They are minut and the government.*"
	D.	There are those who say, said R. Hisda said Mar Uqba, "It is the voice of Gehenna that is crying out, saying, 'Bring me the two daughters who cry out from Gehenna, saying to this world, "Bring, bring."'"
II.10	A.	"None to her return, nor do they attain the paths of life" (Prov. 2:19):
	B.	Now since they never return, how are they going to attain the paths of life anyhow?
	C.	*This is the sense of the passage,* "But if they return, they will not attain the paths of life."
	D.	*Does that then bear the implication that whoever departs from minut dies? And lo, there is the case of a certain woman who came before R. Hisda and said to him,* "The lightest sin that she ever committed was that her younger son is the child of her older son."
	E.	*And R. Hisda said to her,* "So get busy and prepare shrouds."
	F.	*But she did not die. Now since she had said that her lightest sin was that her younger son is the child of her older son, it must follow that she had also gone over to minut [but she didn't die].*
	G.	*That one did not entirely revert, so that is why she did not die [in this world, leaving her to suffer in the world to come].*
	H.	*There are those who say, is it only from minut that one dies if one repents, but not from any other sin? And lo, there is the case of a certain woman who came before R. Hisda, who said to her,* "So get busy and prepare shrouds." *And she died.*
	I.	*Since she said that that was the lightest of her sins, it follows that she was guilty also of minut.*
II.11	A.	*And if one renounces sins other than minut, does one not die? And has it not been taught on Tannaite authority:*
	B.	They say concerning R. Eleazar b. Dordia that he did not neglect a single whore in the world with whom he did not have sexual relations. One time he heard that there was a certain whore in one of the overseas towns, and she charged as her fee a whole bag of denars. He took a bag of denars and went and for her sake crossed seven rivers. At the time that he was with her, she farted, saying, "Just as this fart will never return to its place, so Eleazar b. Dordia will never be accepted in repentence."

C. He went and sat himself down between two high mountains and said, "Mountains and hills, seek mercy in my behalf."

D. They said to him, "Before we seek mercy for you, we have to seek mercy for ourselves: 'For the mountains shall depart and the hills be removed' (Isa. 54:10)."

E. He said, "Heaven and earth, seek mercy for me."

F. They said to him, "Before we seek mercy for you, we have to seek mercy for ourselves: 'The heavens shall vanish away like smoke, and the earth shall wax old like a garment' (Isa. 51:6)."

G. He said, "Sun and moon, seek mercy for me."

H. They said to him, "Before we seek mercy for you, we have to seek mercy for ourselves: 'Then the moon shall be confounded and the sun ashamed' (Isa. 24:23)."

I. He said, "Stars and constellations, seek mercy for me."

J. They said to him, "Before we seek mercy for you, we have to seek mercy for ourselves: 'All the hosts of heaven shall moulder away' (Isa. 34:4)."

K. He said, "The matter depends only on me." He put his head between his knees and he wept a mighty weeping until his soul expired. An echo came forth and said, "R. Eleazar b. Dordia is destined for the life of the world to come."

L. *Now here was a case of a sin [other than minut] and yet he did die.*

M. *There, too, since he was so much given over to that sin, it was as bad as minut.*

N. [Upon hearing this story] Rabbi wept and said, "There is he who acquires his world in a single moment, and there is he who acquires his world in so many years."

O. And said Rabbi, "It is not sufficient for penitents to be received, even if they are called 'rabbi.'"

II.12   A. *R. Hanina and R. Jonathan were going along the way and came to a crossroads, with one road that led by the door of a temple of idol worship, the other by a whorehouse. Said one to the other, "Let's go by the road that passes the door of the temple of idol worship,* **[17B]** *for in any case the impulse that leads to that in our case has been annihilated."*

B.   The other said to him, "Let's go by the road that passes the door of the whorehouse and overcome our impulse, and so gain a reward."

C.   *[That is what they did.] When they came near the whorehouse, they saw the whores draw back at their presence. The other then said to him, "How did you know that this would happen?"*

D.   He said to him, "'She shall watch over you against lewdness, discernment shall guard you' (Prov. 2:11)."

II.13   A.   [As to the verse, "She shall watch over you against lewdness, discernment shall guard you' (Prov. 2:11),] said rabbis to Raba, "What is the meaning of the word translated 'lewdness'? Shall it be 'the Torah,' since the word translated 'lewdness' in the Aramaic translation is rendered, 'it is a counsel of the wicked' and Scripture has the phrase, 'wonderful is his counsel and great is his wisdom' (Isa. 28:29)?"

B.   "Then the word should have been written so as to yield 'lewdness.' Rather, this is the sense of the verse: 'against things of lewdness, discernment, the Torah, shall watch over you.'"

II.14   A.   *Our rabbis have taught on Tannaite authority:*

B.   When R. Eleazar b. Parta and R. Hanina b. Teradion were arrested, R. Eleazar b. Parta said to R. Hanina b. Teradion, "You are fortunate, for you have been arrested on only one count. Woe is me, that I have been arrested on five counts."

C.   Said to him R. Hanina, "You are fortunate, for you have been arrested on five counts but you will be saved, while woe is me, for although I have been arreted on only one count, I will not be rescued. For you have devoted yourself to the study of the Torah and also acts of beneficence, while I devoted myself only to the study of the Torah alone."

D.   *And that accords with R. Huna, for* said R. Huna, "Whoever devotes himself only to the study of Torah alone is like one who has no God, as it is said, 'Now for long seasons Israel was without the true God' (2 Chr. 15:3). What is the meaning of 'without the true God'? It means that whoever devotes himself only to the study of Torah alone is like one who has no God."

E.   But did he not engage in acts of beneficence as well? *And has it not been taught on Tannaite authority:*

F.   R. Eliezer b. Jacob says, "A person should not hand over his money to the charity box unless it is under the supervision of a disciple of sages such as R. Hanina b. Teradion."

G.   *While people did place their trust in him, he did not, in fact, carry out acts of beneficence.*

H. But has it not been taught on Tannaite authority, [R. Hanina b. Teradion, who was in charge of the community fund] said to [R. Yosé b. Qisma], "Money set aside for the celebration of Purim got confused for me with money set aside for charity, and I divided it all up for the poor [including my own funds]"?

I. *Well, while he did carry out acts of beneficence, he did not do so much as he was supposed to have done.*

J. *They brought R. Eleazar b. Parta and said to him, "How come you have repeated Mishnah traditions and how come you have been a thief?"*

K. *He said to them, "If a thief, then not a scribe, and if a scribe, then not a thief, and as I am not the one, so I am not the other."*

L. *"Then how come they call you 'rabbi'?"*

M. *"I am the rabbi of the weavers."*

N. *They brought him two coils of wool and asked, "Which is the warp and which is the woof?"*

O. *A miracle happened, and a she-bee came and sat on the warp and a he-bee came and sat on the woof, so he said, "This is the warp and that is the woof."*

P. *They said to him, "And how come you didn't come to the temple [literally: 'house of destruction']?"*

Q. *He said to them, "I am an elder, and I was afraid that people would trample me under their feet."*

R. *"And up to now how many old people have been trampled?"*

S. *A miracle happened, and on that very day an old man was trampled.*

T. *"And how come you freed your slave?"*

U. *He said to them, "No such thing took place."*

V. *One of them was about to get up to give testimony against him, when Elijah came and appeared to him in the form of one of the important lords of the government and said to that man, "Just as miracles were done for him in all other matters, a miracle is going to happen in this one, and you will turn out to be a common scold."*

W. *But he paid no attention to him and got up to address them, and a letter from important members of the government had to be sent to the Caesar, and it was through that man that it was sent; on the road Elijah came and threw him four hundred parasangs, so he went and never came back.*

X. *They brought R. Hanina b. Teradion and said to him, "How come you devoted yourself to the Torah?"*

Y. *He said to them, "It was as the Lord my God has commanded me."*

Z. Forthwith they made the decree that he was to be put to death by burning, his wife to be killed, and his daughter to be assigned to a whorehouse.

AA. He was sentenced to be burned to death, for he [18A] had pronounced the divine name as it is spelled out.

BB. *But how could he have done such a thing, and have we not learned in the Mishnah:* **All Israelites have a share in the world to come, as it is said, "Your people also shall be all righteous, they shall inherit the land forever; the branch of my planting, the work of my hands, that I may be glorified" (Isa. 60:21). And** these are the ones who have no portion in the world to come: (1) He who says, the resurrection of the dead is a teaching which does not derive from the Torah, (2) and the Torah does not come from heaven; and (3) an Epicurean. R. Aqiba says, "Also: He who reads in heretical books, and he who whispers over a wound and says, 'I will put none of the diseases upon you which I have put on the Egyptians, for I am the Lord who heals you' (Ex. 15:26)." Abba Saul says, "Also: he who pronounces the Divine Name as it is spelled out" [M. San. 10:1A-G]!

CC.	He did it for practice. *For so it has been taught on Tannaite authority:*
DD.	"You shall not learn to do after the abominations of those nations" (Deut. 18:9) – but you may learn about them so as to understand and to teach what they are.
EE.	*Then why was he subjected to punishment?*
FF.	It was because he repeated the Divine Name in public.
GG.	And why was his wife sentenced to be put to death?
HH.	*Because she did not stop him.*
II.	On that account they have said: Whoever has the power to prevent someone from sinning and does not do so is punished on account of the other.
JJ.	And why was his daughter sentenced to a whorehouse?
KK.	For said R. Yohanan, "One time his daughter was walking before the great authorities of Rome. They said, 'How beautiful are the steps of this maiden,' and she forthwith became meticulous about her walk.
LL.	*And that is in line with what R. Simeon b. Laqish said, "What is the meaning of that which is written, 'The iniquity of my heal compasses me about' (Ps. 49:6)? The sins that a person treads under heel in this world surround him on the day of judgment."*
MM.	When three of them went out, they accepted the divine decree. He said, "The rock, his work is perfect, for all his ways are justice" (Deut. 32:4).
NN.	His wife said, "A God of faithfulness and without iniquity, just and right is he" (Deut. 32:4).
OO.	His daughter said, "Great in counsel and mighty in deed, whose eyes are open on all the ways of the sons of men, to give everyone according to his ways and according to the fruit of his deeds" (Jer. 32:19).
PP.	Said Rabbi, "How great are these righteous. For it was for their sake that these verses, which justify God's judgment, were made ready for the moment of the acceptance of God's judgment."
II.15 A.	*Our rabbis have taught on Tannaite authority:*
B.	When R. Yosé b. Qisma fell ill, R. Hanina b. Teradion went to visit him. He said to him, "Hanina, my brother, don't you know that from heaven have they endowed this nation [Rome] with dominion? For [Rome] has destroyed his house, burned his Temple, slain his pious ones, and annihilated his very best –

and yet endures! And yet I have heard about you that you go into session and devote yourself to the Torah and even call assemblies in public, with a scroll lying before you in your bosom."

C.   He said to him, "May mercy be shown from heaven."

D.   He said to him, "I am telling you sensible things, and you say to me, 'May mercy be shown from heaven'! I should be surprised if they do not burn up in fire both you and the scroll of the Torah."

E.   He said to him, "My lord, what is my destiny as to the life of the age to come?"

F.   He said to him, "Has some particular act come to hand [that leads you to concern]?"

G.   He said to him, "Money set aside for the celebration of Purim got confused for me with money set aside for charity, and I divided it all up for the poor [including my own funds]."

H.   He said to him, "If so, out of the portion that is coming to you may be the portion that is coming to me, and may my portion come from your portion."

I.   They say: the days were no more than a few before R. Yosé b. Qisma died and all of the leading Romans went to bury him and they provided for him a splendid eulogy. And when they returned, they found R. Hanina b. Teradion in session and devoted to the Torah, having called assemblies in public, with a scroll lying before him in his bosom. So they brought him and wrapped him in a scroll of the Torah and surrounded him with bundles of branches and set them on fire. But they brought tufts of wool, soaked in water, and put them on his chest, so that he would not die quickly.

J.   Said to him his daughter, "Father, how can I see you this way?"

K.   He said to her, "If I were being burned all by myself, it would be a hard thing for me to bear. But now that I am being burned with a scroll of the Torah with me, he who will exact punishment for the humiliation brought on the scroll of the Torah is the one who will seek vengeance for the humiliation brought on me."

L.   Said to him his disciples, "My lord, what do you see?"

M.   He said to them, "The parchment is burned, but the letters fly upward."

N.   "You, too – open your mouth and let the fire in [so that you will die quickly]."

O.   He said to them, "It is better that the one who gave [life] take it away, but let a person not do injury to himself."

P.   The executioner said to him, "My lord, if I make the flames stronger and remove the tufts of wool from your chest, will you bring me into the life of the world to come?"

Q.   He said to him, "Yes."

R.   He said to him, "Will you take an oath to me?"

S.   He took an oath to him. Forthwith he made the flames stronger and removed the tufts of wool from his chest, so his soul rapidly departed. Then the other lept into the flames. An echo

		came forth and said, "R. Hanina b. Teradion and the executioner are selected for the life of the world to come."
	T.	Rabbi wept and said, "There is he who acquires his world in a single moment, and there is he who acquires his world in so many years."
II.16	A.	*Beruriah, the wife of R. Meir, was the daughter of R. Hanina b. Teradion. She said to him, "It is humiliating for me that my sister should be put into a whorehouse."*
	B.	*He took a tarqab full of denars and went. He said, "If a prohibited act has not been done to her, then a miracle will happen, and if she has done something prohibited, no miracle will happen to her."*
	C.	*He went and took on the guise of a horseman. He said, "Submit to me."*
	D.	*She said to him, "I am menstruating."*
	E.	*He said to her, "I'll wait."*
	F.	*She said to him, "There are plenty of girls here who are prettier than I am."*
	G.	*He said, "That means the woman has not done anything prohibited, that's what she says to everybody."*
	H.	*He went to her guard and said to him, "Give her to me."*
	I.	*He said to him, "I'm afraid of the government."*
	J.	*He said to him, "Take this tarqab of denars, half as a bribe, the other half for you."*
	K.	*He said to him, "What shall I do when these are used up?"*
	L.	*"Just say, 'Let the God of Meir answer me,' and you'll be saved."*
	M.	*He said to him, [18B] "And who will tell me that that's so?"*
	N.	*He said to him, "You'll now see." There were these dogs, who would bite people. He took a stone and threw it at them, and when they were going to bite him, he said, "God of Meir, answer me," and they left him alone.*
	O.	*So he handed her over to him. But eventually the matter became known at government house, and when the guard was brought and taken to the gallows, he exclaimed, "God of Meir, answer me."*
	P.	*They took him down from the gallows and asked him, "What's going on?"*
	Q.	*He told him, "This is what happened."*
	R.	*They then incised the likeness of R. Meir at the gate of Rome, saying, "Whoever sees this face, bring him here."*
	S.	*One day they saw him and pursued him. He ran from them and went into a whorehouse. Some say he just happened then to see food cooked by gentiles and dipped in one finger and then sucked another [pretending he was a gentile]. Others say that Elijah the prophet appeared to them as a harlot and embraced him (God forbid). So they said, "If this were R. Meir, he would never have done such a thing."*
	T.	*He went and fled to Babylonia. Some say, it was because of that incident that he fled to Babylonia, others, it was because of the incident with Beruriah [who committed adultery with one of his disciples].*

Nos. 3, 4, 5, 6 form footnotes to No. 2 or to one another. No. 7 is a footnote to No. 6. No. 8 then reverts to the general theme of the interplay of the government and minut. No. 9 then continues the theme of No. 8, which is the return of those who have gone over to minut and ended up in Gehenna. No. 11 goes forward along the same theme, though with a fresh composition. The issue once more is whether or not one may atone and so die and enter the world to come for the sin of minut, or whether one has to live out his years and then go to Gehenna. This forms part of a large-scale set of compositions on the common theme at hand. No. 12 proceeds along the line of the established theme: the sin of idolatry compared with other sins. No. 13 is a footnote to No. 12. The general theme of rabbis' arrests by the Romans explains why the next composition has been included; this brings us back to the interest of No. 2 and marks the end of the secondary expansion of the story about Eliezer. So each large-scale composite that forms a subdivision of the whole commences with a Tannaite formation, followed by a collection of secondary expansions of various kinds. The inclusion of No. 14 then makes sense within the framework of discourse established by No. 2. Nos. 15, 16 provide yet other stories involving Hanina b. Teradion and belong to the same prepared sequence of stories about him.

Here is then a splendid example of the forming of a composite for one clearly indicated purpose, and its utilization – quite tangentially – for another. II.2 forms the beginning of a large and beautifully crafted set of materials on a general theme, bearing a specific proposition. Any inquiry into the premise of a composite will yield some obvious results. The general theme is the relationship of sages to the Roman government. The specific proposition is that there are two sources of danger to one's immortal soul: dealing with minut (not defined, but in this context, certainly some Christianity or other), dealing with the government. The composite then forms a set of variations on the theme: dealing with gentiles is dangerous, but getting involved in heresy is still more threatening. Putting all of these materials together has served the purpose of making those points, which is to say, expressing those givens.

The first part of the composite deals with the former, the second, the latter. There is no mixing the one with the other, but, of course, dealing with minut involves government sanctions, as much as rebellion against the government itself. No. 2, carrying in its wake Nos. 3, 4, 5, as glosses and extensions, and bearing as footnotes Nos. 6, 7, form one cogent subdivision. No. 9 then provides a transition to the next, which will draw our attention to the dangers involved in dealing with the government. Is there a unifying theme throughout? Of course there is, and it involves the proposition that dealing with minut endangers one's soul, while, if one violates the policy of the government, one may lose his life, but thereby, in any event, gains the life of the world to come. No. 11 shows us a fully articulated composition, obviously completed in its own terms and for its author's own purpose, which has been inserted, with good reason. Nos. 14, 15, and 16, another obviously well-crafted set of stories, each made up in its own terms, but all of them working together in common cause, then form the conclusion, balancing the opening units.

This long presentation shows us the difference between composites and the compositions of which they are comprised. At the same time it permits us to experiment in the identification of the givens of a composite, as these come to expression through the selection of compositions and the arrangement of said compositions in a large-scale, sustained construction. Our inquiry necessitates our examining Talmudic composites from two distinct angles of vision. I maintain that compositions must be examined in their own terms, so that an account of their premises must emerge, as much as a picture of the premises of the composite of which they form part. The proof derives from the answer to a simple question. In the large sample before us, can we maintain that all of these materials have been made up merely to amplify a reference to the judge's tribunal? Obviously not. What challenge to the ingenuity of a compositor would such a purpose have presented? Mere amplification on a theme is too easy, too trivial a task. So compositions must be seen in their terms, composites in theirs.

We have here a variety of compositions, some of them bearing their own burden of secondary expansion, clarification, and complement, others not. If we were to ask, have these compositions been made up for the purposes of a composite of such materials? the obvious answer is, probably yes, but not for this composite in particular! The probability is that authors wrote up stories for collections meant to make a given point, serve a given purpose. To say that these formed "biographical collections," or "biographies" seems to me to make a rather banal statement. So we readily recognize the two dimensions of any given piece of writing that is wholly comprehensible within its own limits: [1] the purpose of the writer of a composition, therefore his premises and presuppositions; [2] the purpose of the compiler of a composite, therefore his premises and presuppositions. We now recognize that these scarcely intersect – which accounts for the striking difference between Chapters Two and Six, on the one side, and Chapters Three through Five, on the other.

The composite transcends the precipitating cause for the formation of the composite: it makes a much larger point, and in connecting this to that to the other thing to make that point, the framers have signalled a still larger and more important judgment on the nature of things. What begins as a fairly technical statement on the furniture of the courtroom rapidly expands into a complex and subtle formation of discrete but intersecting themes. Let us specify the premises on which the composite is constructed.

We start with a catalogue of things we do not sell the gentiles, meaning in this case, their governments. Israel is not to help the nations build the instruments of power, encompassing those for the governance of the social order: scaffold, stadium, judges' tribunal, for instance. Now if we ask ourselves what general theme is introduced in these details, it is Israel's corporate relationship to the corporate being of gentile society. Then what of the story of Eliezer? It is not so much an explanation of the detail about the judge's tribunal, as it is an extreme claim that even good things that gentiles (here: Christians) know, even legitimate learning in the Torah that they may have in hand, is to be shunned. The near-at-hand enemy, the brother, presents the greatest threat, and a long sequence of stories about minut then follows. The next major initiative, commencing at No. 14, explains how Israelites are to conduct themselves when facing the sanctions of the gentile state (clearly: not a Christian government here, since that is no longer a major motif).

What may we say in conclusion, meaning, what premises characterize the composite as a whole? The powerful formulation of the choices in public policy facing Israel – [1] don't you know that from heaven have they endowed this nation [Rome] with dominion? For [Rome] has destroyed his house, burned his Temple, slain his pious ones, and annihilated his very best – and yet endures!, or [2] may mercy be shown from heaven, meaning, God will resolve such matters – sets forth the alternatives. So a long and complex formation in fact holds together to treat a single problem and to make only a few points about that subject. The palimpsest in the end is subject to a single reading: the bore, top to bottom, brings up not mere detritus, the random sediment of passing ages, but a single solid rock. But it will take much work to locate that rock and to describe it. I see no difficulty in specifying the presuppositions upon which all rests – but, also, no need to do so.

Having established the fact that the Talmuds comprise compositions and composites, let me now answer the question: How are we to identify the premises and presuppositions of the framers of composites? That is a far more difficult problem than the one that defines the work of the shank of the book, the analysis of the givens of compositions. We now take up a single example of how the compositors make their statement, telling us what they wish to say through their selection and arrangement of compositions, showing us, therefore, the premises of their thought and argument. One case suffices to make the point.

2

The Premises of the Framers of Composites: A Single Case

Now that we recognize the difference between the Talmuds' compositions and their composites and realize that the latter comprise the Talmuds' own contribution, we begin with the most difficult problem, identifying what the compilers of a composite – the Talmuds' own writers – wish to say, therefore defining the premise of their entire enterprise at a given point of compilation of existing composites. For the authorship of a composite articulates its statement only through a process of making connections that yield an inexorable conclusion. What the composite says, therefore in the nature of things also what it takes for granted, comes to the surface only when we ask why the framers have put one thing together with something else; in the connection we discern the fresh message, and in the logic of the connection, we identify the premise or presupposition that is in play.

This we see when we ask, how do two matters (in the Talmud, meaning whole compositions set in sequence) relate, and what conclusions are we to draw from their deliberate juxtaposition by the Talmud itself? Since, readers already have noticed, the Talmud's discipline requires us to follow the shifts and turnings of a protracted analytical argument, the very dialectics of the document to begin with requires us to ask the question: What has this to do with that? And if we do not ask that question, we know for certain we are not following the argument at all. Discerning what is at stake, or, as I said in the Introduction, what else we know if we know what our sages are saying in an articulate way, demands that we examine the very character of the Talmud as a work of critical reflection, writing, and redaction: what does it say about a fundamental question, how does it make the successive parts of its statement, and in what manner do the components of the statement link together to form a whole that exceeds the sum of the parts. One warning is necessary: the results of this chapter lead to expectations that the three chapters of text analysis do not meet. To the contrary, we find in the pages that follow a level of abstraction, on the one side, and an achievement of connection making and conclusion drawing, on the other, that the everyday Talmud passages – three huge passages – we consider in the shank of the book do not match.

This somewhat abstract formulation of the final problem will now take on specificity. To understand the case at hand, I have to proceed through a number of stages of argument. The reason is that, as in any composite, the givens of the compositions that comprise the composite require articulation; only then shall we identify the very particular point at which the framers of the composite enter into discourse. So we work from the components upward to the composition that is made of them.

The stages of analysis cover the following propositions that have in succession to be examined, after which the issue of connection is to be raised and conclusions may be drawn:

[1]   a Mishnaic rule is philosophical in its categorical structure; this matters in our context because what the framers of the composite do is move from the philosophical structure they have received toward a theological proposition that, in their minds, overrides the philosophical composition they have in hand;

[2]   the Talmud (in this chapter we deal only with the Talmud of Babylonia) examines that rule within the received Mishnaic categories; the composition contributed by post-Mishnah, pre-Talmud writers involves the systematic exegesis of the received Mishnah paragraph;

[3]   but there is a point at which the connection between one thing and something else requires elucidation, and that is the point at which, the Talmud (by definition) having fallen silent, we intervene. That intervention consists in our asking, what has one thing to do with another? And the answer to that question bears the recognition of the Talmud's premise or presupposition. In making connections that they draw, the framers of the Talmud's composite see points of contact that we should not otherwise have identified; they yield a point of their own, and as we shall see, it is a theological point introduced in the very center of a philosophical exposition – a rather complex composite in all. In this way, then, I show what is at stake in the distinction between the composition and the composite, and how the

framers of the Talmud – in this case, the Bavli – have made a statement extrinsic to the materials they have assembled and paramount in our reception of the whole. Here, then, is the premise at the foundations of the Bavli's treatment of one Mishnah unit – a premise uncovered after a fair amount of work;[1]

[4]   a Mishnaic rule is philosophical in its categorical structure.

A brief account of the matter of responsibility as set forth by Aristotle suffices to make the point that the Mishnah's category formation governing necessity, cause and blame conforms to the lines of structure, with special attention to the governing distinctions, set forth by Aristotle.[2] The issue of responsibility has to be set forth in two parts, first, in the context of Aristotle's general theory of causation – if we don't know that an act has caused a result, we cannot hold responsible the person who has done the act for the consequences he has brought about – and only then, second, in the setting of the specific, juridical position set forth by Aristotle. We have for our purpose to pay close attention to the distinctions that he makes, for it is by showing that the Mishnah's law makes exactly the same distinctions that I make part of my case.

First, as to causation in general: Aristotle discusses causation in the context of physics, not relationships or events in the social order. He finds, in accounting for changes in nature, four causes: [1] form, [2] matter [3] moving cause, and [4] final cause. These are explained by G.E.R. Lloyd as follows:

> Take first an example of artificial production, the making of a table. To give an account of this four factors must be mentioned. First matter, for the table is made out of something, usually wood. Secondly form, for the table is not just any lump of wood, but wood with a certain shape.

---

[1]It hardly needs saying that a single case does not make a rule, nor is a list comprised of one entry. In fact, it was when the matter at hand became fully clear to me, in the context of this inquiry into premises and presuppositions, that I recognized the necessary next step in my work, which is a systematic commentary on the Talmud of Babylonia, which, in the nature of things, has to be called *Making Connections and Drawing Conclusions. An Academic Commentary to the Talmud.*

[2]My choice of Aristotle as the model for philosophy in general is explained in detail in the three works on philosophy, economics, and politics, *Judaism as Philosophy, The Economics of the Mishnah,* and *Rabbinic Political Theory.* As I review the literature on Aristotle, I am struck that I have claimed far too little, not too much, correspondence between Mishnaic principles and Aristotelian ones; my entire discussion of the potential and the actual, in *The Philosophical Mishnah* (Atlanta, 1989: Scholars Press for Brown Judaic Studies) I-IV, failed to point to the correspondence between the formulation of matters by our sages and that of Aristotle. That is a separate study, awaiting attention.

Thirdly, moving cause, for the table must be made by someone, the carpenter. Fourthly, the final cause, for when the carpenter made the table, he made it for a purpose.[3]

These same factors are taken into account in describing change from potentiality to actuality:

The seed of a tree is potentially the mature tree; it is potentially what the mature tree is actually. This doctrine draws attention to the continuity of natural change. The goals towards which natural changes are directed are the ends of continuous processes. But while the ideas of potentiality and actuality are obviously relevant in this way to natural growth, Aristotle generalizes the doctrine and applies it to other types of change as well. A hunk of wood in a carpenter's shop is potentially a table or a chair or a desk....[4]

Therefore Aristotle's interest in the four "causes" asks about "reason why," "through what," or "cause," in four senses:

He lists the From What, the Form, the Whence of the beginning of Change, and the End or For What.[5]

In analyzing the "why" of a thing or person or event, we have to take account of the material cause, the formal cause, the efficient cause, and the final cause.

Now we turn to what is to us the important classification of cause, the efficient cause, the point at which culpability will enter in when transactions of the social order come under consideration. The efficient cause is the "whence the change begins," the final cause, the "for-the-sake-of which," the goal.[6] In natural processes, Edel says,

the final cause is the mature development of the form itself in the particular materials: the acorn grows into an oak tree whose end is simply to express in its career what it is to be an oak tree....

---

[3]G.E.R. Lloyd, *Aristotle: The Growth and Structure of His Thought* (Cambridge, 1968: Cambridge University Press), pp. 58-9.

[4]My representation of the Mishnah as philosophical in classification, in *The Philosophical Mishnah* (Atlanta, 1989: Scholars Press for Brown Judaic Studies) I-IV, identified numerous Mishnah passages devoted to sorting out the issues of potentiality as against actuality, but I did not examine the Greco-Roman philosophical treatment of the same matter; I therefore claimed far less than I should have. And, I hasten to add, my close attention to Aristotle as the principal point of philosophical comparison for the Mishnah is not meant to close off reading of other philosophers, as my introduction, if very brief, of Middle Platonism into the discussion in *Judaism as Philosophy* will show.

[5]John Herman Randall, Jr., *Aristotle* (New York, 1960: Columbia University Press), p. 181.

[6]Abraham Edel, *Aristotle and His Philosophy* (Chapel Hill, 1982: University of North Carolina Press), pp. 61-2.

The efficient cause is

always some activity of the same type that the developed form exhibits.

At the same time, in the consideration of causation, we take up the matter of chance, when something happens "by accident." Randall explains, "Chance is the name given to all events caused by factors that are not relevant to the ends of natural processes, by all the nonteleological factors, the brute events interfering with the natural working out of a process, or achieving a quite different end incidentally...."[7] Chance will take its place in the grid to be placed over an event so as to affix responsibility. Any account of responsibility will have chance on the one side, total responsibility, based on volition expressed in wholly successful intention, on the other; but then, responsibility also will be modulated, with gradations from the one pole to the other.

These general remarks, of course, have a bearing upon responsibility in particular, only when we reach the question of responsibility for paying compensation for what one has caused. Then we have to assess degrees of culpability, from none to total, with close attention to the stages in between. And here is the point at which the category formation of Aristotle and that of the Mishnah will meet. It follows that, of the four causes, the one of greatest interest to us is efficient cause. From this point forward Sorabji provides the account upon which we shall rely; everything I say concerning category formation depends upon his exposition. As to the definition of efficient cause, Sorabji explains:

> The efficient cause is defined by reference to change; it is that whence comes the origin of change....[8]

And that is the point of intersection between the Mishnah's and Aristotle's treatment of the matter. Sorabji categorizes the treatment of efficient cause as the real point of Aristotle's contribution to legal theory. Concerning Aristotle's contribution as a whole he states:[9]

> It lies in his whole enterprise of trying to classify the different kinds of excuse and of culpability. This important step drew attention to whole classes of cause, not only to the general categories of voluntary and involuntary, but also to overwhelming external force, fear of a greater

---

[7]Randall, p. 183.
[8]Richard Sorabji, *Necessity, Cause and Blame. Perspectives on Aristotle's Theory* (London, 1980: Duckworth), p. 42. I submitted the descriptive part of this chapter to Professor Sorabji, who was kind enough to review the presentation and assure me of its accuracy. I obviously make no claim to competence in these philosophical matters, beyond choosing the reliable scholarship to reproduce.
[9]Sorabji, pp. 291ff.

evil, nonculpable ignorance of what one is doing, culpable ignorance, negligence, acts due to natural passion or to unnatural passion, acts due to deliberate choice....[10]

Sorabji further comments:

> [Aristotle] introduces the criterion of what is not contrary to reasonable expectation, and so he turns the category of mistakes into a category of negligence....
>
>   Aristotle further divides injustices into those that are merely voluntary, and ones that are in addition inflicted because of a deliberate choice.[11]

Aristotle's treatment of negligence is set forth by Sorabji in these terms, which at last lead us from the territory of metaphysical theory to incorporated society: issues of the social order, such as those with which the Mishnah is concerned:

> Aristotle starts by distinguishing two kinds of injury inflicted in ignorance (and therefore involuntarily). The first is a mere mishap; the second is called a mistake...a culpable mistake. It is distinguished by reference to two ideas. First, the injurious outcome is not contrary to reasonable expectation, as it would have been in a mere mishap. Second, the origin of the cause...lies within the agent, not outside, as it would in a mere mishap. Aristotle's remaining categories of injury are two kinds of injustice. They are distinguished from the first two categories by the fact that the agent acts knowingly.[12]

What makes important Aristotle's conception of responsibility as Sorabji spells it out is his attention to the classification of different kinds of "excuse and culpability," which corresponds to the matter of responsibility.

What this set of distinctions yields are these gradations between total culpability or blame, by reason of one's forming the efficient cause without mitigating considerations, and total absolution from culpability and blame, by reason of one's bearing no responsibility whatsoever for what has happened:

[1]   responsibility for all damages done, because the event that has caused loss and damage is voluntary and foreseeable, not the result of overwhelming external force; preventable; brought about by willful action; the result of culpable knowledge; deliberate choice, not mere negligence;

---

[10]Sorabji, p. 291.
[11]Sorabji, p. 293.
[12]Sorabji, pp. 278ff.

[2]   responsibility for the greater part of the damages that are done, because the damage is foreseeable; not the result of overwhelming external force; preventable; thus the ignorance is classified as culpable, but not voluntary;

[3]   responsibility for the lesser part of the damages that are done, because the damage is foreseeable, but the result of overwhelming external force and not preventable, thus: involuntary, but the result of culpable ignorance and negligence;

[4]   no responsibility at all, the event being involuntary, the result of overwhelming external force, not foreseeable, hence, inculpable ignorance; for example, pure chance.

I therefore identify three operative criteria – points of differentiation in the analysis of events and the actions that produce them[13] that form a cubic grid, with, in theory, nine gradations of blame and responsibility and consequent culpability:

[1]   an event produced by an action that is voluntary vs. involuntary;

[2]   an event that is foreseeable vs. not foreseeable, or an action the consequences of which are foreseeable vs. not;

[3]   an event that is preventable vs. not preventable; or an action that is necessary and therefore blameless, or one that is not.

Thus we may construct a grid of three layers or dimensions, one grid formed of considerations of what is voluntary vs. involuntary, the second, of what is foreseeable vs. not foreseeable, the third, of what is preventable vs. not preventable: a cube, with lines at each of the three intersecting levels drawn by the vertical of voluntary and the horizontal of involuntary, so, too, at the other layers, the whole then corresponding to the three categories just now given. One such mixed grid then will permit us to adjudicate complex cases of culpability and therefore compensation along lines projected at each of the layers. That permits us to identify an efficient cause that is voluntary, foreseeable, and preventable; voluntary, foreseeable, and not preventable; involuntary, foreseeable, and preventable; involuntary, not foreseeable, and not preventable; and so on for the rest. The nine possible combinations then

---

[13]That is in the assumption that the action is commensurate to the event, a problem that can be addressed but will be sidestepped to keep the matter economical. Commensurability is certainly a serious concern of the philosophers of the Mishnah, as their reading of the Written Torah's law of the manslayer shows.

allow us to sort out all situations that can arise; that is the compelling claim of philosophy that is "generalizable" or "universalizable."

The cubic grid will yield a set of consequences, each made up of its variables. These different classifications will contain their own calculations of culpability, on the one side, and their own corresponding levels of compensation, on the other; these range from total compensation for what is the result of voluntary action, the results of which are foreseeable, and in no way the result of overwhelming external force but preventable; to no liability at all for an event that is pure chance and not foreseeable, still the result of overwhelming external force, in no way intended. I need not elaborate to make the simple point that the lines of structure flow from the three categories enumerated just now. A treatment of the matter of cause and blame will then qualify as philosophical if it makes the same generalizing distinctions.

Now to point to the philosophical character of the Mishnah's statement on responsibility, we ask how the Mishnah's law classifies responsibility and sorts out questions of negligence. At issue is the categorical structure yielded by the Mishnah's several rules: explaining the distinctions made by those rules by reference to the structure of differentiations implicit in them. We are interested in differentiation at levels of compensation, corresponding to differentiation at layers of responsibility, the whole an exercise in the applied reason and practical logic made possible by the distinctions yielding the category formation just now outlined. Then we shall return to the Talmud's treatment of part of the Mishnah statement, stipulating that the treatment of the rest is uniform. What we want to identify are the generative variables, to find out whether they correspond to the set of three that are six that yields the mixed grid described just now.

What we shall now see is that the same points of distinction operate; the same variables function to create, in very concrete terms, a grid of cause and blame and responsibility. When these are fully exposed, they produce the same process of sorting out as does Aristotle's distinctions as laid out by Sorabji; and they therefore are to be classified as philosophical in character: abstract, generalizing, extending to all possible cases, subject to criticism in abstract terms as well – not limited to cases, not qualified by episodic considerations, not a matter of anecdotal or casuistic formulation or conception. The negatives are important in differentiating the Mishnah's from Scripture's formulation, classifying the former's as philosophical, the latter's not.[14] The Mishnah's

---

[14]One of the principal exercises of the earliest Midrash formulations is to demonstrate that Scripture's rules in fact convey principles that extend to a variety of cases; or can be expressed as generalizations. That is the principal

formulations on the subject of responsibility yield in terms of blame and culpability precisely the categorical results to be anticipated from a recapitulation of Aristotle's variables in a jurisprudential formulation.

Of the Mishnah chapters that pertain – Mishnah-tractate Baba Qamma Chapters One through Four[15] – I give only part of the pertinent chapters, so as to outline what is essential for our inquiry. That is merely formal proof that the same pattern of distinctions that Aristotle portrays in his philosophy also operates in the Mishnah's presentation of the matter of cause and blame: culpability and compensation, in juridical terms. The first deals with what is logically critical: the matter of responsibility, its levels or degrees:[16]

A. [There are] four generative classifications of causes of damages: (1) ox [Ex. 21:35-36], (2) pit [Ex. 21:33], (3) crop-destroying beast [Ex. 22:4], and (4) conflagration [Ex. 22:5].

B. [The indicative characteristic] of the ox is not equivalent to that of the crop-destroying beast;

C. nor is that of the crop-destroying beast equivalent to that of the ox;

D. nor are this one and that one, which are animate, equivalent to fire, which is not animate;

E. nor are this one and that one, which usually [get up and] go and do damage, equivalent to a pit, which does not usually [get up and] go and do damage.[17]

F. What they have in common is that they customarily do damage and taking care of them is your responsibility.

G. And when one [of them] has caused damage, the [owner] of that which causes the damage is liable to pay compensation for damage out of the best of his land [Ex. 22:4].

Mishnah-tractate Baba Qamma 1:1

---

polemic of Sifré to Deuteronomy in respect to Deuteronomy Chapters Twelve through Twenty-Six.

[15]We could have considered the Mishnah's reading of Scripture's law of the manslayer in Mishnah-tractate Makkot, but the pertinence to Sorabji's account of Aristotle's variables is hardly so immediate. Not only so, but problems of causation in the Mishnah vastly transcend the issue of legal or moral responsibility. As with Aristotle, so in the Mishnah, causation generates problems of metaphysics, not only ethics and jurisprudence.

[16]That commensurability also is in play here will strike the reader as self-evident, but I do not deal with that matter. I may have erred in limiting myself to a cubic grid, but for the purpose of my argument in this book, it did not strike me as necessary, and the argument is sufficiently complex as is. As always, the best is enemy of the good.

[17]This exercise of polythetic taxonomy has an interest in its own right, and I suspect adequate knowledge of Aristotelian method in natural history – the rules of taxonomy in particular – will show us counterpart exercises, but for the present purpose, we shall fix our attention on causation and blame alone.

The important point comes at G: establishing responsibility for four damages done by four distinctive types of causes of damage. Then we shall have to know the traits of each, before we can assess responsibility and consequent compensation: what each is likely to do, for which I bear full responsibility, as against what each is unlikely to do, which I therefore cannot foresee and prevent. First comes the governing rule, stating the definition and consequence of responsibility:

1:2   A.   In the case of anything of which I am liable to take care, I am deemed to render possible whatever damage it may do.

      B.   [If] I am deemed to have rendered possible part of the damage it may do,

      C.   I am liable for compensation as if [I have] made possible all of the damage it may do.

Now comes the distinction that is critical to the Mishnaic system, deriving as fact from the Written Torah but formulated by the Mishnah as a general rule.

What is assumed to be harmless but does damage produces culpability different from what is assumed to be an attested danger; the difference then is in the compensation. So here comes the issue of whether or not an outcome is foreseeable. And, intrinsic to foresight, of course, is the possibility of preventing the damage. So the two form a single case, though the principles are distinct in theory. If I can have foreseen the damage and did not prevent it, I am responsible for full damages; if I cannot, I pay only half of the total damages. In what follows we carefully delineate the specific aspects in which a danger from a given classification of danger in fact produces damage; damage produced in some other than the foreseeable manner is null:

1:4   A.   [There are] five [deemed] harmless, and five [deemed] attested dangers.

      B.   A domesticated beast is not regarded as an attested danger in regard to (1) butting, (2) pushing, (3) biting, (4) lying down, or (5) kicking.

      C.   (1) A tooth is deemed an attested danger in regard to eating what is suitable for [eating].

      D.   (2) The leg is deemed an attested danger in regard to breaking something as it walks along.

      E.   (3) And an ox which is an attested danger [so far as goring is concerned];

      F.   (4) and an ox which causes damage in the domain of the one who is injured;

      G.   and (5) man.

      H.   (1) A wolf, (2) lion, (3) bear, (4) leopard, (5) panther, and (6) a serpent – lo, these are attested dangers.

      I.   R. Eliezer says, "When they are trained, they are not attested dangers. But the serpent is always an attested danger."

J. What is the difference between what is deemed harmless and an attested danger?

K. But if that which is deemed harmless [causes damage], [the owner] pays half of the value of the damage which has been caused,

L. [with liability limited to the value of the] carcass [of the beast which has caused the damage].

M. But [if that which is] an attested danger [causes damage], [the owner] pays the whole of the value of the damage which has been caused from the best property

N. [he may own, and his liability is by no means limited to the value of the animal which has done the damage].

So much for the systematic presentation of the matter of foresight in interplay with responsibility. Let me give a single example of how the distinction between the damage that can be foreseen and the damage that cannot be foreseen is worked out for a single classification:

2:1 A. How is the leg deemed an attested danger in regard to breaking something as it walks along [M. 1:4D]?

B. A beast is an attested danger to go along in the normal way and to break [something].

C. [But if] it was kicking,

D. or if pebbles were scattered from under its feet and it [thereby] broke utensils –

E. [the owner] pays half of the value of the damages [caused by his ox].

F. [If] it stepped on a utensil and broke it,

G. and [the utensil] fell on another utensil and broke it,

H. for the first [the owner] pays the full value of the damage.

We have now covered distinctions of Aristotle between responsibility for all damages done, because the damage is [1] foreseeable and [2] preventable, and responsibility for the greater part of the damages that are done, because the damage is not the result of overwhelming external force but preventable. The distinctions that flow then depend on the distinction between what is foreseeable – damage done by an attested danger in the ordinary course of events – therefore preventable, and what is not foreseeable – damage done by an attested danger but not in the ordinary way in which that source of danger produces damage – but what is still preventable, for which partial compensation is paid.

Now in light of the foregoing, we revert to the conception of efficient cause. In what follows, we have an attested danger; full compensation is then required. Why? Because the accident is subject to foresight, it could have been prevented, and I am therefore fully responsible. But there is the matter of efficient cause that now intervenes: direct vs. indirect causation has to be worked out. That is to say, a cause that is necessary but not sufficient and a cause that is necessary and sufficient produce different assessments of responsibility. One is responsible for the damages that a dog directly does in the normal manner; one bears less responsibility for damage that is the result of overwhelming external force and not preventable, but still derives from culpable ignorance, my class three above.

2:3   A.   The dog or the goat which jumped from the top of the roof and broke utensils –
      B.   [the owner] pays the full value of the damage [they have caused],
      C.   because they are attested dangers.
      D.   The dog which took a cake [to which a cinder adhered] and went to standing grain, ate the cake, and set the stack on fire –
      E.   for the cake the owner pays full damages,
      F.   but for the standing grain he pays only for half of the damages [his dog has caused].

Here we see a fine example of the difference between Aristotle's classification [1] and Aristotle's classification [3]. Now the cause is necessary but not sufficient; the damage done to the standing grain is not preventable, in the way in which the damage done to the utensils is. The dog should have been tied up. Once the dog was not tied up and did the foreseeable damage, the owner is culpable for full responsibility. But if the dog has gone on and done damage that cannot have been foreseen, that is, to the standing grain, and that was not preventable, the owner is culpable only for half-damages.

The Mishnah of course is not a philosophical work, only a work that expresses philosophical concerns by building upon philosophical distinctions. An important jurisprudential distinction now intervenes, particular to the Mishnah but relevant to assessing responsibility. This distinction addresses the location at which the damage takes place. We distinguish damage [1] done in the domain of the injured party, for which full damages are paid, and that [2] done in public domain, where the ox had every right to walk, where only half-damages are done. Here we have damage that is not the result of overwhelming external force – no one pushed the ox into the domain of the injured party – but chance; but culpability is incurred, since the mitigating power of chance (what is totally unforeseeable) is weighed against the incriminating power of foreknowledge: the attested danger. Still, there are diverse dimensions of responsibility that are defined by circumstance: I am responsible for what happens in public domain, where I have to take extra precautions, but not for what happens in my own property, where I have to take only normal precautions:

2:5   A.   An ox which causes damage in the domain of the one who is injured [M. 1:4F] – how so?
      B.   [If] it gored, pushed, bit, lay down, or kicked [M. 1:4B],
      C.   in the public domain,

    D.   [the owner] pays half of the value of the damages [the ox has caused].

Now we come to the human being. Here we deal with a judgment of theological anthropology, expressed in a simple way: human beings are always, everywhere, under all circumstances, fully responsible for what they do. What they do is voluntary and foreseeable, preventable, willful, the result of deliberate choice. Chance is then to be held in the balance against total responsibility, and that forms the basis for the following:

2:6   A.   Man is perpetually an attested danger [cf. M. 1:4G] –
        B.   whether [what is done is done] inadvertently or deliberately,
        C.   whether man is awake or asleep.
        D.   [If] he blinded the eye of his fellow or broke his utensils, he pays the full value of the damage he has caused.

So much for the basic fact. Now to the sorting out of the relationship between chance and willful action, the point where the Mishnah becomes very specific in its assessment of responsibility:

3:1   A.   He who leaves a jug in the public domain,
        B.   and someone else came along and stumbled on it and broke it –
        C.   [the one who broke it] is exempt,
        D.   And if [the one who broke it] was injured by it, the owner of the jug is liable [to pay damages for] his injury.
        E.   [If] his jug was broken in the public domain,
        F.   and someone slipped on the water,
        G.   or was hurt by the sherds,
        H.   he is liable.

The owner of the jug bears full responsibility for whatever the jug has caused; we make no distinction between direct and indirect causation (an efficient cause that is necessary but not sufficient, in my language earlier). Here is where the Mishnah's formulation expresses in its familiar, concrete idiom the category formation that Aristotle (as read by Sorabji) sets forth in entirely abstract ways.

    What about damages done by accident? We have to assess the liabilities, which means, assign responsibility: the one party is negligible, therefore culpable; but the other has not taken adequate precautions, therefore also culpable – showing how, in my terms, the mixed grid helps to sort things out:

3:4   A.   Two pot sellers who were going along, one after another,
        B.   and the first of them stumbled and fell down,
        C.   and the second stumbled over the first –
        D.   the first one is liable [to pay compensation for] the injuries of the second.
3:5   A.   This one comes along with his jar, and that one comes along with his beam –
        B.   [if] the jar of this one was broken by the beam of that one,

C. [the owner of the beam] is exempt,
D. for this one has every right to walk along [in the street], and that one has every right to walk along [in the same street].
E. [If] the one carrying the beam was coming first, and the one carrying the jar was following behind,
F. [if] the jar was broken on the beam,
G. (1) the one carrying the beam is exempt.
H. (2) But if the one carrying the beam stopped short, he is liable.
I. (3) And if he said to the one carrying the jar, "Wait up!" he is exempt.

3:6 A. Two who were going along in the public domain,
     B. one was running, the other ambling,
     C. or both of them running,
     D. and they injured one another –
     E. both of them are exempt.

Enough has been set forth to validate the claim that the category formation set forth by Sorabji in behalf of Aristotle corresponds to the category formation set forth by the Mishnah. For we distinguish in both structures between entire responsibility, therefore blame and obligation to pay total damages, and partial responsibility; we distinguish between damage that is voluntary and foreseeable and damage that is involuntary but foreseeable, damage that is the result of overwhelming external force and damage that is preventable; so producing two intermediate categories; and onward to the end. So the Mishnah and Aristotle explore the domain of the efficient cause, finding appropriate charts to divide the territory. The lines of structure and order are then the same: [1] voluntary; [2] foreseeable; [3] preventable as against [1] involuntary; [2] not foreseeable; [3] not preventable. In the several combinations of those three distinct but intersecting categories, we form the grid that yields the generalizations of Sorabji's picture of Aristotle – mishap as against mistake; cause by the agent or cause not solely by the agent; knowing versus inadvertent knowledge.

[2]   the Talmud examines that rule within the received Mishnaic categories (cf. page 50);

What makes the Talmud philosophical is simply that it carries forward the Mishnah and analyzes its results. So far as the category formation that the Mishnah lays out governs the analytical work of the Talmud, the entire result – that is, the Mishnah as the Talmud wants it read – is to be classified as philosophy in the precise sense at hand; and that, I repeat, is why we can understand the Talmud without mediation other than a sage's instruction on its semiotics. To remind readers of my basic point: we can join in the thought process that has produced these results, because our thought process, shaped as it is within the philosophical heritage of the West, and that of the Talmud cohere.

The Talmud's representation of the Mishnah's philosophical laws preserves the received category formation of the Mishnah. To address the Talmud's treatment of the topic at hand, we turn to Bavli Baba Qamma Chapter Three. I take up the reading of Mishnah paragraph 3:1 and give the larger part of the Talmud's treatment of that pericope.[18]

A. He who leaves a jug in the public domain,
B. and someone else came along and stumbled on it and broke it –
C. [the one who broke it] is exempt.
D. And if [the one who broke it] was injured by it, the owner of the barrel is liable [to pay damages for] his injury.

> Bavli Baba Qamma 3:1 [27A]
> 3:1A-D

The Talmud has identified a few sentences for analysis, and it begins with a pretheological study of the language at hand, showing by consequence the fundamental theological dogma, the perfection of the Mishnah, as evidenced by the absence of flaws of formulation. To ease the burden on the reader, I skip that passage and turn directly to the matter of substance: whether the victim has exercised the necessary precautions. If he has not, then the person who broke the jug, not the one who put it in public domain, should be liable. The event is preventable and foreseeable – and borders on the willful.

II.1 A. and someone else came along and stumbled on it and broke it – [the one who broke it] is exempt:
B. Why should he be exempt? He should have opened his eyes as he walked along!
C. They said in the household of Rab in the name of Rab, "We deal with a case in which the whole of the public domain was filled with barrels."
D. Samuel said, "We deal with a case in which the jugs were in a dark place."
E. R. Yohanan said, "We deal with a case in which the jug was at a corner."

The question is answered in terms characteristic of the Mishnah: concrete and immediate; but the upshot is an abstract amplification of the law. The one who broke the jug would be exempt because the event of which the one who placed the jug in the street was the cause was by him rendered unavoidable (C), or preventable through the taking of proper precautions (D, E). It was not the result of overwhelming external force,

---

[18]A huge labor of rereading the Bavli with close attention to how it makes connections between, and draws conclusions from, its large-scale compositions and composites, will be required to make this point stick. That once more is the goal of *Making Connections and Drawing Conclusions. An Academic Commentary to the Talmud.*

and it also is not the consequence of anything the person who broke the jug has done or his failure to do something to prevent what was foreseeable to him. So the one who placed the jug is the necessarily efficient cause (absent the jug, no breakage!), and also the sufficient cause, there being no other participant to the incident, even though the one who actually broke the jug is the actual cause. That is the point at which responsibility parts company from the (mere) facts of the case. The hermeneutic of the Talmud requires dispute concerning the reading of the Mishnah; the result is clarification of the operation of the principles of the Mishnah. The theology that emerges once more affirms the flawless character of the Mishnah: its conformity to the abstract principle of justice, worked out through the concrete application of fair and reasonable rules.

We recall that a further characteristic of the Talmud's hermeneutic, and the dynamic of its thought, is the spinning out of a dialectic argument. We shall now pursue the argument wherever it leads, and the close reading of the Mishnah's language vastly expands our understanding of the principles and how they apply:

> F.   Said R. Pappa, "A close reading of our Mishnah rule can accord only with the view of Samuel or R. Yohanan. For if it were in accord with the position of Rab, then what difference does it make that exemption is accorded only if the man stumbled over the pitcher? Why not rule in the same way even if he deliberately broke the pitcher?"
>
> G.   Said R. Zebid in the name of Raba, "In point of fact, the same rule really does apply even if the defendant deliberately broke the jug. And the reason that the language, 'and stumbled on it,' is used, is that the later clause goes on to say, 'And if [the one who broke it] was injured by it, the owner of the jug is liable [to pay damages for] his injury.' But that would be the case only if he stumbled on it, but not if he deliberately broke the jug. How come? The man has deliberately injured himself. So that is why, to begin with, the word choice was 'and stumbled on it.'"
>
> II.2   A.   Said R. Abba to R. Ashi, "This is what they say in the West in the name of R. Ulla: 'The reason is that people do not ordinarily look out when they walk along the way.'"

Now we have a considerable extension of the Mishnah's rule, effected through clarification. The one who broke the jug bears no responsibility whatsoever, even though he did so deliberately. The action of the one who put the jug in the street forms the entire, sufficient, efficient cause; nothing that happens by consequence of that action is assigned to any other party. No. 2 then explains why: the ordinary rule is that people amble along without looking; they are not expected to watch their step, taking account of irregular actions; hence the placing of the jug by the jug owner accounts for everything that follows.

That lays the stress upon what is voluntary, as against what is foreseeable and preventable. Once an action is voluntary, the considerations of foresight – the one who broke the jug should have watched his step – and preventability (a variation of the foregoing) pertain. So as against a repertoire of considerations, the Talmud has identified only one that governs. How has the Talmud continued the Mishnah's philosophical analysis of the issue of responsibility? It has not only amplified the sense and identified the operative considerations of the Mishnah's rendition of the category formation comprising voluntarism, foresight, and preventability and their varying combinations; it has selected one for a position of priority. Here the hermeneutics of the dispute and the dialectic has led to a concrete position at the outer limit of the Mishnah's case. Once we challenge the rule of the Mishnah, we are led by degrees to a reformulation of matters.

The next entry simply provides illustrative cases, a commonplace part of the hermeneutics of the Talmud, yielding the familiar conception that the conduct of the everyday is organized along the rational lines of the Torah:

II.3　A.　　There was a case in Nehardea, and Samuel imposed liability [for the broken utensil]. In Pumbedita, and Rabbah imposed liability as well.

　　　B.　　Now there is no problem in understanding Samuel's ruling, since he acted in accord with his own tradition [if the pitcher was visible, there would be liability]. But shall we then say that Rabbah concurred with Samuel?

　　　C.　　Said R. Pappa, "The damage was done at the corner of an oil factory, and, since it is entirely permitted to store barrels there, the defendant should have walked along with his eyes wide open."

So much for the exposition of the Mishnah and its rule. We now identify an initiative that goes its own way, connected to the Mishnah rule only because at issue is damage done by an object, for example, the blade of a hoe or the handle of a hoe, rather than by a person's own hand. At 4R, our own case is introduced in one of its formulations, and – superficially – that accounts for the introduction of the entire composite, formulated on its own terms.

And yet, if we take a deeper look, we see that the issue is entirely relevant to the large question of responsibility. Indeed, whether or not one has the right to take the law into his own hands introduces a fundamental variable into the issue of responsibility. For if one has a right to take the law into his own hands, then damage done to another party, while voluntary, foreseeable, and preventable, still is not culpable. Responsibility ends where just cause intervenes. If one has just cause, then the other considerations of responsibility – foreseeability, preventability – fall away; a voluntary action that is right bears no consequences, just as one that is wrong (putting a jug in the street) imposes all liability. Will in the end gives way before right (one way or the other). And that represents a profound statement that is far more than an amplification.

So what the Talmud now contributes through an initiative of redaction – the insertion of a set of compositions formed into a coherent composite – in fact constitutes a vast expansion on the principle of responsibility. The inquiry itself clearly links responsibility for damages down to another party and the reason for one's action:

II.4   A.   R. Hisda sent word to R. Nahman, "Lo, they have said, 'For kicking with the knee, three selas; for kicking with the foot, five; for a blow with the saddle of an ass, thirteen.' What is the penalty for wounding with the blade of a hoe or the handle of a hoe?"

        B.   He sent word, "Hisda! Hisda! Are you really imposing in Babylonia such extrajudicial fines as these [which you have no right to do over there]? Tell me the details of the case as it happened."

        C.   He sent word, "There was a well that belonged to two people, who used it on alternate days. One of them then went and drew water on a day that was not assigned to him. The other said, 'This is my day.' The latter ignored him. So the other took the blade of a hoe and struck him with it."

        D.   R. Nahman sent word, "Even if he hit him a hundred times with the blade of the hoe [it would not have mattered]. For even in the opinion of one who says, 'Someone may not take the law into his own hands,' where there will be a loss, he has every right to do so."

Clearly, the composition, 4A-D, is complete in itself; we require nothing more fully to understand all of its components. But, of course, in its own terms, the composition in no way accounts for its present location, in a way that Nos. 1-3 clearly do; they depend upon their position in context; No. 4 does not.

But the expansion shows how the issue of responsibility is profoundly restated by introduction of the principle that someone does (or does not) have the right to take the law into his or her own hands. What this has to do with causation and culpability has to be analyzed; the passage is the critical point in the entire analysis, and we read the whole of it:

        E.   For it has been stated:
        F.   R. Judah said, "A man has not got the right to take the law into his own hands."
        G.   R. Nahman said, "A man has got the right to take the law into his own hands where there will be a loss."

Now the issue has been joined. But we are not told why the issue has to be raised at just this point. In the assumption that the document before us is purposive and not a mere scrapbook, however, we have to ask ourselves why this discussion is juxtaposed to the foregoing: what the issue of taking the law into one's own hands has to do with the matter of necessity, cause, and blame. When we ask that question, we move beyond the Talmud's boundaries; in the Talmud, what is juxtaposed is assumed to cohere, that is why the juxtaposition has taken place. But we are not bound by the facts to silence. The silence of the Talmud, on what its framers take for granted, invites our intervention; that is where we join the conversation. Let us see how the topic is explored in the dialectics:

H. Now all parties concur that where there will be a loss, someone may take the law into his own hands. Where there is an argument, it concerns a case in which there will be no loss. R. Judah said, "A man has not got the right to take the law into his own hands." Since there will be no loss, he can go to court. But R. Nahman said, "A man has got the right to take the law into his own hands where there will be a loss." Since he is acting in accord with the law anyhow, why take the trouble to go to court?

I. Objected R. Kahana [to R. Judah's view], "Ben Bag Bag says, 'A person should not go and retrieve his own property from the household of someone else, lest he appear to be a thief. But he should be ready in public to break his teeth and you may say to him, "I am seizing what is my own from the thief's possession"' [T. B.Q. 10:38]." [This then would contradict Judah's position.]

J. [Judah] said to him, [28A] "True enough, Ben Bag Bag is on your side. But his is a dissenting view, differing from rabbis."

K. R. Yannai said, "What is the meaning, anyhow, of 'break his teeth'? It is, in court."

L. If so, the language, you may say to him, is inappropriate. Rather it should be, they [the court] may say to him! So, too, the language, 'I am seizing what is my own,' is inappropriate. Rather, it should be, he is seizing what is his own!

M. So that's a problem.

N. Come and take note: in the case of an ox that climbed up on another one to kill it, and the owner of the one on the bottom came along and pulled out his ox, so that the one on the top fell and was killed – the owner of the bottom ox is exempt from having to pay compensation. Does this ruling not pertain to an ox that was an attested danger, in which case there is no loss to be expected?

O. No, it speaks of an ox that was deemed innocent, and there is a considerable loss to be expected.

P. If so, then look what's coming: If he pulled off the ox on top and it died, he is liable to pay compensation. But if the ox was deemed innocent, why should he have to pay compensation?

Q. Because he should have pulled his ox out from underneath, and he did not do that. [Kirzner: He had no right to push the ox on top.]

We now come to our particular case. From here to the end, the Talmud speaks for itself, without my explanation, so that we may follow the twists and turns of what is an entirely continuous and cogent analytical argument: dialectics at its most compelling.

R.   Come and take note: He who filled the courtyard of his fellow with jugs of wine and jugs of oil – the owner of the courtyard has every right to break the jugs in order to get out or break the jugs in order to get in.

S.   Said R. Nahman bar Isaac, "He breaks the jugs to get out only if a court says he may do so; he may break the jugs to get in only to get whatever documents he needs to prove his case in court."

T.   Come and take note: How on the basis of Scripture do we know that in the case of a slave whose ear had been bored [as an indication that he was in perpetual service, to the Jubilee Year], the term of service of which has come to an end [with the Jubilee], the owner of which has been urging him to leave, and, in the process, injured him and done him damage, the owner is exempt from having to pay compensation? Scripture states, "You shall not take satisfaction for him who is...come again..." (Num. 35:12), meaning, for one who is determined to come again [as a slave, continuing his service], you will not take a ransom.

U.   Here with what sort of a case do we deal? It is a slave who was a thief [Kirzner: so the owner is protecting himself from a genuine loss].

V.   Well, up to now he hasn't stolen anything, but now he's expected to go and steal?

W.   Yes, that's quite plausible, since up to now he was afraid of his master, but now that he is about to go free, he isn't afraid of his master anymore.

X.   R. Nahman bar Isaac said, "At issue is a slave to whom his master gave a Canaanite serving girl as a wife. Up to this time it was a legitimate relationship, but once he is freed, it is not legitimate" [Kirzner: so the master may use force to eject him].

Y.   Come and take note: He who leaves a jug in the public domain, and someone else came along and stumbled on it and broke it – [the one who broke it] is exempt. So the operative consideration is that he stumbled on it. Lo, if he had deliberately broken it, he would have been liable. [This is contrary to Nahman's view.]

Z.   Said R. Zebid in the name of Raba, "In point of fact, the same rule really does apply even if the defendant deliberately broke the jug. And the reason that the language, 'and stumbled on it,' is used, is that the later clause goes on to say, 'And if [the one who broke it] was injured by it,' the owner of the jug is liable [to pay damages for] his injury. But that would be the case only if he stumbled on it, but not if he deliberately broke the jug. How come? The man has deliberately injured himself. So that is why, to begin with, the word choice was 'and stumbled on it.'"

AA.   Come and take note: "Then you shall cut off her hand" (Deut. 25:12) – that refers to a monetary fine equivalent in value to the hand. Does this not speak of a case in which the woman has no other way of saving her husband but doing what she did [proving one may not take the law into one's own hands]?

BB. No, it involves a case in which she can save her husband in some other way.

CC. Well, if she cannot save her husband in some other way, would she be free of all liability? Then why go on to say, "And puts forth her hand" (Deut. 25:11) – excluding an officer of the court [from liability for humiliation that he may cause when acting in behalf of the court]? Rather, why not recast matters by dealing with the case at hand, thus: Under what circumstances? When she can save her husband by some other means. But if she cannot save him by some other means, then she is exempt.

DD. This is the sense of the passage: Under what circumstances? When she can save her husband by some other means. But if she cannot save him by some other means, then her hand serves as the agency of the court and she is indeed exempt.

EE. Come and take note: He who had a public way passing through his field, and who took it away and gave [the public another path] along the side, what he has given he has given. But what is his does not pass to him [M. B.B. 6:7A-D]. Now if you maintain that someone may take the law into his own hands, then let the man just take a whip and sit there [and keep people out of his property]!

FF. Said R. Zebid in the name of Raba, "It is a precautionary decree, lest he assign to the public a crooked path."

GG. R. Mesharshayya said, "It is a case in which he gives them a crooked path."

HH. R. Ashi said, "Any path that is over off to the side is classified as a crooked path to begin with, since what is nearer for one party will be farther for another."

II. If that's so, then why specify, But what is his does not pass to him? Why can't he just say to the public, "Take what is yours and give me what is mine?"

JJ. That is because of what R. Judah said, for said R. Judah, "A path that the public has taken over is not to be disrupted."

KK. Come and take note: a householder who designated peah at one corner of the field, and the poor come along and take the peah from another side of the field – both this and that are classified as peah. Now if you maintain that a person may take the law into his own hands, why should it be the fact that both this and that are so classified? Just let the man take a whip and sit there [and keep people out of his property]!

LL. Said Raba, "What is the meaning of the phrase, 'both this and that are so classified'? It is for the purpose of exempting the designated produce from the requirement of separating tithes. For so it has been taught on Tannaite authority: He who declares his vineyard to be ownerless and then gets up early in the morning and harvests the grapes is liable to leave for the poor the grapes that fall to the ground, the puny bunches, the forgotten ones, and the corner of the field, but is exempt from having to designate tithes."

The dialectical argument runs its course; I have not interrupted it, because a clear picture of how the Talmud makes its statement is required, lest a précis deny the reader access to the notes at hand in all their specificity. Now to the heart of matters: at no point does the discussion say what I say it says; the theological message is not expressed – except at the important turnings in the argument. But there, when we ask the right questions – questions of composition and context in particular – we see that someone has deliberately put together free-standing composites, themselves made up of sizable compositions, so as to yield a point that vastly recasts the original statement of the Mishnah.

[3]   but there is a point at which the connection between one thing and something else requires elucidation (cf. page 50):

This brings us to the premise that holds together the Talmud's discussion of the Mishnah. The Mishnah, continued by the Talmud, has set forth a philosophical category formation that held in the balance three equally pertinent criteria of responsibility: the intersection of lines covering what is voluntary, foreseeable, and preventable, and the opposites. The Talmud has contributed two points. First of all, the criterion of what is done voluntarily outweighs all else; but, second and entirely new, the Talmud sets forth and elaborates the criterion not introduced in the Mishnah at all. I state it with emphasis: doing what one has the right to do sets aside even the criterion of deliberation. The law of the Torah is now recast; the Oral Torah has announced three components to a decision on responsibility; the Talmudic re-presentation has selected one of those components, then contrasted it with a consideration external to the initial program and subordinated it to that consideration.

That new point is not continuous with the other. It is where the compositors take over, it is their shift in the exposition that expresses both what they wish to say and also what they take for granted. Indeed, the connection between the exposition of the received categories of the Mishnah and the introduction of an entirely new consideration has to be established, meaning, rationally explained. If we can draw a rational conclusion, a theological conclusion, from that odd juxtaposition, the adventitious intersection of two distinct compositions – "can one take the law into one's own hands" standing separate from issues of cause, blame, and responsibility – becomes a deliberate statement, and imposes upon us the task of reasoned inquiry into the substance of that statement. Here we shade over into a theological issue.

The substantive, theological statement proclaims that what is right overrides considerations even of will. If (within one theory of matters) one may take the law into his own hands, then even though the event is voluntary, foreseeable, and preventable, one still bears no responsibility for the resulting damage. If not, of course, then the body that does have the right to enforce the law obviously bears no responsibility. The upshot is the same: we have now subordinated issues of causation – cause and blame, in Sorabji's terms – to another matter altogether. Since, we recognize, the category formation that guides the analysis of responsibility treats responsibility as a consequence of causation, we find the theological re-presentation in fact stunningly fresh.

For the upshot of the juxtaposition of the several compositions and the two distinct composites and the sequence of their messages may be stated very simply:

[1]   responsibility is adjudicated not by causation in the philosophical reading of causation (such as the Mishnah has given us)

[2]   but by appeal to a higher criterion: what is right by the law of the Torah.

Exactly how does this work? It is at the specific point of discontinuity – the boundary marked by the conclusion of the Mishnah exposition by the Talmud, followed by the turning toward what is jarring and discontinuous – that our particular entry point opens up. There we are thrown into the depths of the compositors' thinking, and there we identify their premise. Then we ask, what has this got to do with that? And we answer the question for ourselves. Our task is to make sense of the juxtaposition before us, and that we do by explaining the connection between what is merely juxtaposed but superficially discontinuous.

Let me spell out this claim of mine by specifying the completed compositions and the point at which they are merely juxtaposed but by no means continuous. An example of the completed composition is at II.1A-E, complete in itself; proved by the fact that, without anything added, read along with the Mishnah paragraph, the passage is fully accessible. A composite is made up of II.1A-E joined by F-G, which make sense only when joined to the foregoing; but which then richly amplify the prior passage; and of course No. 2. Another completed composition of course is No. 3A, which provides us with everything we need to know to understand its point; but then 3B, C join A to the larger, now established context.

We have now identified the point at which compositors speak for themselves, and, further, we have specified what they wish to say through the words that express the specificities of their statement. The compositors' statement emerges when I ask how [1] the Mishnah, then [2] two massive composites, have been juxtaposed. This procedure calls our attention to the Mishnah's presentation of issues of responsibility in terms of causation (the point at which we started). Then the Talmud dealt with, first, the sorting out, in priority, of the criteria of causation

(Nos. 1-3), and, second, the free-standing exposition of the matter of taking the law into one's own hands (No. 4). In context, in sequence, No. 4 imposes a judgment upon the results of the Mishnah and Nos. 1-3. In these simple, entirely literary facts – the discontinuity of No. 4 to Nos. 1-3 – the work of the compositors emerges. By joining a free-standing composite, itself made up of composites that hold together compositions, the Talmud's composition sets forth the point that it makes concerning responsibility – all considerations of responsibility are subordinate to what is right; the issues of causation are declared instrumental and derivative; in this setting then, right overrides even will.

The premise of this search of mine for compositors' premises requires specification. It is that the Talmud is the way its framers wanted it to be. The document conforms to its teleology; then we may seek out the connections between this and that and draw rational conclusions from those connections. This we do by explaining how what is juxtaposed in fact interrelates. So if the compilation of the Talmud is deliberate and not simply the juxtaposition without purpose of thematically congruent materials, then the Talmud makes a powerful statement not only through the contents of its compositions (which really form the nouns of its sentences) nor the context defined by its composites (the verbs of the sentences) but through the selection, formulation, and presentation of the whole. I have given only a single example of that fact, but it suffices to establish that an account for the two Talmuds' working presuppositions must pay close attention to issues of juxtaposition, the making of connections, the drawing of conclusions. These conclusions then reveal to us some of those premises that we have undertaken to identify. Now we proceed to the analysis of a sequence of compositions – a more conventional inquiry, following the lines of thought familiar from the prior four volumes of this study. What we shall see does not match the results of this chapter, raising the question of whether premises and presuppositions that form the substrate of thought move from document to document. The result of this chapter can leave no doubt on that score: it is highly particular to the discussion at hand.

3

The Premises of the Authors of Compositions: Qiddushin 1:1 in Yerushalmi and Bavli

The opening chapter will deal at length with the issues at hand, and the next two chapters will draw on the results, providing a somewhat abbreviated account of matters.

1:1

A.   A woman is acquired [as a wife] in three ways, and acquires [freedom for] herself [to be a free agent] in two ways.

B.   She is acquired through money, a writ, or sexual intercourse.

C.   Through money:

D.   The House of Shammai say, "For a denar or what is worth a denar."

E.   And the House of Hillel say, "For a perutah or what is worth a perutah."

F.   And how much is a perutah?

G.   One eighth of an Italian issar.

H.   And she acquires herself through a writ of divorce or through the husband's death.

I.   The deceased childless brother's widow is acquired through an act of sexual relations.

J.   And acquires [freedom for] herself through a rite of removing the shoe or through the levir's death.

The premise before us is that title to a woman ("sanctification") passes, as does that to property of various classifications, through diverse, routine media of exchange.

I. The Talmud of the Land of Israel to M. Qiddushin 1:1

· [I.A]   The meaning of the language of the Mishnah [at M. 1:1B] is [that a woman is acquired] either through money, or through a writ, or

73

through sexual intercourse, [but all three are not required for such a transaction].

[B]   And so, too, did R. Hiyya teach, "It is not the end of the matter that all three are involved, but even through any one of them [the transaction is carried out]."

[C]   Through money: How do we know [that item on the basis of Scripture] ?

[D]   "If any man takes a wife" (Deut. 22:13) tells us that a woman is acquired through money.

[E]   Through sexual relations: How do we know [that item on the basis of Scripture]?

[F]   "And goes in to her [having sexual relations with her]" (Deut. 22:13) tells us that a woman is acquired through sexual relations.

[G]   I should then have reached the conclusion that the transaction is effected both through this means and through that [together].

[H]   How do I know that money effects acquisition without sexual relations, or that sexual relations effect acquisition without money?

[I]   R. Abbahu in the name of R. Yohanan: "It is written, 'If a man is found lying with a woman who has had sexual relations with her husband' (Deut. 22:22).

[J]   "Now take note: Even if the man has acquired her only through sexual relations, the Torah has decreed that he who has sexual relations thereafter is [guilty of having sexual relations with a married woman and is subject to the death penalty through] strangling."

[K]   [No, J's reading will not suffice. For] it is not the end of the matter that [the sexual relations take place] in the normal manner. But even [if the husband had sexual relations] not in the normal manner, [the woman is deemed fully wed to him].

[L]   [The following statement will indicate that the cited verse serves the purpose of proving that sexual relations not in the normal manner have the same effect. Consequently, the proof for H remains to be adduced.] R. Abbahu in the name of R. Yohanan: "The verse is required to indicate that sexual relations not in the normal manner effect acquisition of the woman. If you maintain [to the contrary] that the verse refers to a relationship effected through sexual relations in the normal manner, why should Scripture refer to a woman 'who has had sexual relations with her husband'? Even someone else [than the husband] may [through an act of normal sexual relations] render her 'a woman who has had sexual relations.'"

[M]   As to what we have learned there:

[N]   If two men had sexual relations with a betrothed girl in succession, the first is liable to be put to death by stoning, and the second by strangling [M. San. 7:9]. [The latter has had sexual relations with a nonvirgin who has the legal status of one "who has had sexual relations with her husband," although it is not her husband. See M. San. 11:1.]

[O]   Thus we have learned that sexual relations without payment of a money fee [effect acquisition of the woman].

[P]   Payment of money without sexual relations, whence?

[Q]   "And if he does not do these three things for her, she shall go out for nothing, without payment of money" (Ex. 21:11). "If he takes another wife to himself..." (Ex. 21:10).

[R]   Just as the woman [slave girl] mentioned first involves a money payment, so the woman [wife] mentioned second involves a money payment. [That is, in context the acquisition is through payment of money.]

[S]   "[When a man takes a wife and marries her, if then she finds no favor in his eyes because he has found some indecency in her,] and he writes her a bill of divorce and puts it in her hand and sends her out of his house, and if she goes and becomes another man's wife..." (Deut. 24:1, 2).

[T]   The "becoming" [another man's wife] is so joined to the sending forth. Just as the sending forth is through a writ, so the "becoming" [another man's wife] is through a writ.

I see as the premise of the Talmud of the Land of Israel the obvious one that Mishnah law rests upon Scripture's rules, and that the task of Mishnah exegesis is to identify the scriptural foundation for the Mishnah's rules. I shall not comment on this matter further, and when the Talmud presents compositions along these lines, I shall give only the opening lines, to indicate what is present.

[II.A]   [Having proved the rules through scriptural exegesis, we now turn to the experiment of proving the same rules through logical argument.] Said R. Abin, "And Hezekiah taught: 'When a man takes a wife' (Deut. 24:1) tells us that a woman is acquired through a money payment.

[B]   "Now, it is a matter of logical argument, if a Hebrew slave girl. who is not acquired through sexual relations, is acquired through a money payment [Ex. 21:7: 'When a man sells his daughter'], this one, who may be acquired through sexual relations, is it not reasonable to suppose that she should be acquired through a money payment?

[C]   "The childless brother-in-law's widow will prove [to the contrary], for she indeed is acquired through an act of sexual relations, but she is not acquired through a money payment.

[D]   "This one, too, should cause no surprise, that even though she is acquired through sexual relations, [on the analogy with the childless sister-in-law] she still is not acquired through a money payment.

[E]   "Accordingly, Scripture is required to state, 'When a man takes a wife' – indicating that she is acquired through a money payment.

[F]   "'And has sexual relations with her' – indicating that she is acquired through an act of sexual relations.

[G]   "Now is it not logical to argue as follows: If the childless widow, who is not acquired through a money payment, is acquired through an act of sexual relations, this one, who is acquired through a money payment, is it not logical that she should also be acquired through an act of sexual relations?

[H]   "The Hebrew slave girl proves to the contrary. For she is acquired through a money payment and is not acquired through an act of sexual relations.

[I]   "This one, too, should cause no surprise, for even though she is acquired through a money payment, she is not to be acquired through an act of sexual relations.

[J]   "Accordingly, Scripture is required to state, 'When a man takes a wife' – indicating that she is acquired through a money payment.

[K]   "'And has sexual relations with her' – indicating that she is acquired through an act of sexual relations.

[L]   "As to a writ: Now if a payment of money, which does not have the power to free the woman from her husband, has the power to bring her under the domain of her husband, a writ, which does have the power to take her out of his domain – is it not logical that it should also have the power to bring her into his domain?

[M]   "No, if you have stated that rule in regard to a money payment, which has the power to remove what has been sanctified from consecrated status through redemption [substitution], will you say the same of a writ, which does not have the power to redeem what has been consecrated and so remove it from its consecrated status?

[N]   "The argument a fortiori has been shattered, and, accordingly, you must return to Scripture.

[O]   "So it was necessary for Scripture to state: 'When a man takes a wife and marries her, if then she finds no favor in his eyes because he has found some indecency in her, and he writes her a bill of divorce and puts it in her hand and sends her out of his house, and she departs out of his house, and if she goes and becomes another man's wife...' (Deut. 24:1, 2).

[P]   "The 'becoming' [another man's wife] thus is joined to the sending forth. Just as the sending forth is through a writ, so the becoming another man's wife is through a writ."

The premise is that Scripture alone provides the necessary foundations for the Mishnah's rules. Logic unguided by Scripture has no bearing. This again is routine in both Talmuds and will not elicit comment any further. The extension of the matter follows.

[III.A]   Said R. Yudan, "It is possible to construct an argument a fortiori that a free woman may be acquired through an act of usucaption [in this context: through performing an act of service that a wife is expected to perform for the husband].

[B]   "[The argument rests upon the mode of acquisition of a Canaanite slave girl, which is through usucaption.] Now if, in the case of a Canaanite slave girl, who is not acquired through sexual relations, the girl is acquired through usucaption, this one, who is acquired through an act of sexual relations – is it not logical that she should be acquired through usucaption?

[C]   "Accordingly, Scripture is required to state, 'When a man takes a wife and has sexual relations with her' (Deut. 24:1), meaning, it is through sexual relations that this one is acquired, and she is not acquired through usucaption.

[D]   "[Similarly] we may construct an argument a fortiori in the case of a Canaanite slave girl that she should be acquired through an act of sexual relations.

[E]   "Now it is a matter of logic. If a free woman, who is not acquired through usucaption, is acquired through an act of sexual relations, this one, who is acquired through usucaption, is it not logical that she should be acquired through an act of sexual relations?

[F]   "Accordingly, Scripture is required to state, 'As for your male and female slaves whom you may have, you may buy male and female slaves from the nations that are round about you.... You may bequeath them to your sons after you, to inherit as a possession forever' (Lev. 25:46).

[G]   "It is through usucaption that a Canaanite slave girl is acquired, and she is not acquired through an act of sexual relations."

The next point of exegesis takes for granted that one law applies to Israelites, another to gentiles, and that requires that we derive from Scripture the law that pertains to outsiders:

[IV.A]   Lo, we have now proved that a woman is acquired as a wife in three ways...through money, writ, or sexual intercourse [see M. I:1B].

[B]   Up to now we have dealt with Israelites. [What is the law as to] gentiles?

[C]   R. Abbahu in the name of R. Eleazar: "It is written 'Behold, you are a dead man, because of the woman whom you have taken; for she has had sexual relations with her husband' (Gen. 20:3).

[D]   "For those who are acquired through sexual relations are they liable [for having sexual relations with a married woman], but they are not liable [for having sexual relations with] those who are [merely] betrothed."

[E]   The following statement of R. Eleazar [H-L] implies that that rule applies only when in the act of sexual relations the man has had the intention of effecting acquisition of the woman, while the following statement of Samuel [F-G] implies that that rule applies even when the man did not have the intention of effecting acquisition of the woman.

[F]   For R. Jonah said in the name of Samuel, "If a whore is standing at the window, and two men had sexual relations with her, the first is not put to death, while the second is put to death on account of the first [who through the act of sexual relations has acquired the woman as his wife, even though he did not intend to do so]."

[G]   Now did the former party actually intend through his act of sexual relations to acquire the whore as his wife? [Obviously not!]

[H]   "No man of you shall approach any one near of kin to him to uncover a nakedness" (Lev. 18:6).

[I]   Why does Scripture say, "No man ['man,' appearing twice in the verse]?"

[J]   It is to place under the jurisdiction of the laws of the nations gentiles who have had sexual relations with the connections prohibited to gentiles, and to place under the jurisdiction of the laws of Israel

[58c] gentiles who have had sexual relations with the connections prohibited to Israelites.

[K]   Said R. Eleazar, "Among all of them, you have only a betrothed Israelite woman [for whom a gentile is liable].

[L]   "[That is to say,] if a gentile had sexual relations with an Israelite woman who is betrothed, he is liable. If he had sexual relations with a gentile woman who was betrothed, he is exempt."

[M]   Now if he had sexual relations with a betrothed Israelite woman, on what count is he liable? Is it under their laws or under the laws of Israel?

[N]   If you say that they are tried under Israelite law, then they must be subject to the testimony of two witnesses, to the judgment of twenty-three judges, to appropriate admonition, and, if guilty, to execution through stoning.

[O]   If you say that they are tried under gentile law, then they must be subject to the testimony of only one witness, to the judgment of only one judge, to no admonition, and, if guilty, to execution through decapitation by a sword.

[P]   R. Judah bar Pazzi adds, "[They are put to death] through strangulation, by reason of that very verse [cited at Q]."

[Q]   "What is the scriptural basis for this position? 'Whoever sheds the blood of man, by man his blood shall be shed' (Gen. 9:6) – [and this is through strangulation]."

[R]   [As to further differences, along the lines of N-O,] if you say that they are tried under Israelite law, then if he converted, he remains liable.

[S]   If you say that they are tried under gentile law, then if he converted he becomes exempt.

[T]   For R. Haninah said, "If a Noahide cursed [God] and converted he is exempt, because his status under the law has changed."

[U]   R. Eleazar in the name of R. Haninah said, "How do we know that Noahides are subject to admonition to avoid prohibited connections as are Israelites?

[V]   "'Therefore...a man cleaves to his wife' (Gen. 2:24) – and not to his fellow's wife.

[W]   "'Therefore...a man cleaves to his wife' – and not to a male, or to a beast."

[X]   R. Samuel, R. Abbahu, R. Eleazar in the name of R. Haninah: "A Noahide who had sexual relations with his wife not in the usual way is put to death.

[Y]   "What is the scriptural basis for that view? 'Therefore...a man cleaves to his wife and they become one flesh' (Gen. 2:24) –

[Z]   "It is to be at the place at which the two of them become one."

[AA]   R. Yosé raised the question, "Sexual contact with a male – what is the law?

[BB]   "Sexual contact with a beast – what is the law?

[CC]   "Now all prohibited sexual relations were derived from the prohibition of having sexual relations with a menstruating woman. That covering a male or a beast likewise derives from the same analogy."

[DD] Now up to now we have raised the question concerning Israelites. What is the law regarding gentiles?

[EE] Said R. Mana, "Is it not from [the exegesis of the verse,] 'And he will cleave to his wife' – and not to the wife of his fellow? [That is, 'cleaving'] in any manner [is forbidden]."

[FF] Similarly, [there is also a prohibition of any sexual contact] with a male or an animal.

The same premise, that gentiles are subject to their own rules, generates the next discussion as well:

[V.A] Lo, we have learned that gentiles are not subject to the laws of consecrating a woman as betrothed [through money, IV.A-D]. What about their being subject to the laws of divorce?

[B] R. Judah b. Pazzi and R. Hanin in the name of R. Huna the Great of Sepphoris: "Either they are not subject to the law of divorce at all, or [unlike Israelite practice] each issues a writ of divorce to the other."

[C] R. Yohanan of Sepphoris. R. Aha, R. Hinena in the name of R. Samuel bar Nahman: "'For I hate divorce, says the Lord, the God of Israel' (Mal. 2:16).

[D] "Among Israelites I have framed the law of divorce, and I have not given the law of divorce to the nations of the world."

[E] R. Hananiah in the name of R. Pinhas: "The entire pericope makes use of the language 'the Lord of Hosts,' while here it uses the language 'the God of Israel.'

[F] "This is to teach you that the Holy One, blessed be He, has designated the use of his name in regard to divorces only with respect to Israelites alone."

[G] A statement of R. Hiyya the Elder implies that [in his view] gentiles are not subject to the law of divorce.

[H] Rather: For R. Hiyya taught, "A gentile...who divorced her, and the both of them [the first husband and the woman] converted to Judaism, I do not invoke the rule, 'Then her former husband, who sent her away, may not take her again [to be his wife]' (Deut. 24:4). [The rule is not applied because she is not regarded as having been divorced by him to begin with, when they both were gentiles]."

[I] And so, too, it has been taught: A case came before Rabbi, and he declared it valid for [the husband to remarry her].

The exposition of the omitted category, gentiles, concludes. We proceed to the next clause of the Mishnah paragraph:

[VI.A] With a writ: That is to say, with a writ that is not worth a perutah.

[B] But as to a writ that is worth a perutah, it is tantamount to money.

[C] This is in line with what R. Hiyya taught:

[D] **By a writ [– how so?]**

[E] **One must say that it is a writ worth a perutah.**

[F] **But is a woman consecrated with anything worth a perutah? Rather, even if one wrote it on a shard or on wastepaper [both of which have a value less than a perutah], and he gave it to her,**

[G] **lo, this one is consecrated [T. Qid. 1:2].**

[H]   If he wrote [a writ of divorce] on something from which one may not derive benefit at all, [what is the law]?

[I]   Is one deemed divorced or not?

[J]   R. Eliezer said, "She is not divorced."

[K]   [Now as to the use of such a thing for a writ of betrothal,] said R. Zeira, "Rabbis were at variance on this issue.

[L]   "The one who said 'She is not betrothed with such a thing' maintains that she also may not be divorced with such a thing.

[M]   "And the one who said 'She may be betrothed' also maintains that she may be divorced therewith."

[N]   Colleagues say [that such an analogy is null, for you cannot compare the law governing betrothal with the law governing divorce, and so they rule] to the strict side.

[O]   R. Yosé raised the question, "What is the meaning of 'ruling to the strict side'?

[P]   "[Shall we say that] she will not be betrothed [by such a writ] but she may be divorced by such a writ, and that is the meaning of 'rule to the strict side'?

[Q]   "Or do we maintain that she is not divorced [by such a writ] but she may be betrothed [by it], and that is 'ruling to the strict side'?" [This is not worked out.]

[R]   What is the law in the present matter [of betrothals]?

[S]   The rabbis of Caesarea in the name of R. Jacob bar Aha [maintain that there really is no dispute at all:] "The one who said that she may be divorced is of the opinion that it is permitted to betroth with a document written on material from which the scribes prohibited benefit.

[T]   "The one who said that she may not be divorced is of the opinion that it is prohibited to betroth with a document written on material from which the Torah prohibited benefit, but the scribes permitted such betrothal."

[U]   If you say so, does this statement not stand at variance with what Rab has said?

[V]   For Rab said, "In the view of R. Meir, 'He who effects a betrothal by handing over leaven [worth a perutah] from the sixth hour and onward [on the fourteenth of Nisan when, in point of fact. Israelites no longer may derive benefit from leaven, but this by ruling of scribes, not by the Torah's law] has done nothing whatever.'" [Now if the prohibition is merely on the basis of scribes' ruling, then the betrothal should be valid.]

[W]   There [in the case of handing over leaven] it is with the object itself that the man effects betrothal. Now leaven from the sixth hour and onward is worthless, [and that is why the betrothal is null].

[X]   But here it is with the conditions stated in the writ that the man has effected the betrothal.

[Y]   If that is the case, then even if it is with something from which benefit is prohibited by the Torah, [why] should the woman [not] be betrothed?

[Z]   What difference is there between such a thing and a writ that is not worth a perutah?

[AA]　There [in the case of a writ composed on something that may not be utilized at all] the material is not suitable for completing the value of the perutah, [for it is totally worthless,]

[BB]　while here [in the case of something not worth a perutah but with some slight value] the material is suitable for completing the value of the perutah. [It is offensive to give a woman something with no worth whatever, and on that account the materials forbidden for Israelite use or enjoyment may not be used at all.]

I discern in the foregoing nothing more than a secondary expansion of the Mishnah's rule. We proceed to the comparison of the views of Mishnah authorities on distinct, but parallel, topics, with an interest in finding out whether these views are consistent throughout. The premise is that authorities' views are coherent; whether that appears not to be the case, we have to find out why, or make the effort to show their inner consistency, for example, by a relevant distinction between two rulings on parallel matters that appear contradictory:

[VII.A]　There we have learned: **An oath imposed by judges is imposed if the claim is at least for two pieces of silver, and the concession on the part of the defendant is that he owes at least a perutah's worth [M. Shebu. 6:1A].**

[B]　**As to the claim:**

[C]　**The House of Shammai say. '[Money means] a maah."**

[D]　**And the House of Hillel say, "Two maahs."**

[E]　The opinions assigned to the House of Shammai are at variance with one another.

[F]　For there [at M. Qid. 1:1] the House of Shammai maintain that "money" means a denar, and here they say it means a maah.

[G]　The opinions assigned to the House of Hillel are at variance, for there [at M. Qid. 1:1] they say "money" means a perutah, and here they say that it means two maahs.

[H]　R. Jacob bar Aha in the name of R. Haninah: "The House of Shammai derive [their position] from the rule governing the selling of a Hebrew slave girl. Just as the operative price at the original sale of such a girl is a denar, so betrothal affecting her is for a denar.

[I]　"The House of Hillel derive their position from the law governing the payoff [in redeeming such a girl]. Just as the operative price at the payoff [in redeeming] her is a perutah, so betrothal affecting her is for a perutah."

[J]　What is the scriptural basis for the position of the House of Shammai?

[K]　It is said, "[And if he does not do these three things for her,] she shall go out for nothing, without payment of money."

[L]　Now do we not know that it is without payment of money? Why then should Scripture state, "Without payment of money"?

[M]　It is on the basis of this that we learn that she is sold for a sum of money greater than the minimum sum understood by the word "money." And how much is that? It is a denar.

[N]   Or perhaps "money" refers to a perutah, and "more than a minimum sum of money" would then mean two perutahs?

[O]   The smallest value of a minted coin is a maah.

[P]   In that case, let it be a maah?

[Q]   R. Bun in the name of R. Judah bar Pazzi: 'The reason is that if she wishes to work off what she owes, she deducts [from the debt] at the rate of a maah a year and goes free."

[R]   And let her deduct at the rate of a perutah.

[S]   Said R. Bun, "Take note. If she wanted to deduct what is owing on her debt at the beginning of the sixth [and final] year of service, then the sum owing at the beginning of her calculation would be a perutah, and the sum owing at the end of that same process of deducting from the debt will be a perutah. [That anomaly must be avoided.]

[T]   "Rather at the beginning of the last year, her debt will be a maah, and at the end she will deduct a perutah."

[U]   What is the basis for the position of the House of Hillel?

[V]   On the basis of the fact that at the end of the process of deduction from the original debt, a perutah remains, so you know that the sum required for betrothing her also is a perutah.

[W]   If at the end [of the process of working off the debt over a six-year period], there remains only what is worth a perutah, is it possible to suppose that she does not deduct that amount and go forth free? [Obviously not.]

[X]   Accordingly, just as the sum owing at the end of the six-year period of deduction is a perutah, so the sum required for betrothing her is a perutah.

[Y]   The opinions imputed to the House of Hillel are at variance.

[Z]   It is written, "If a man delivers to his neighbor money or goods to keep [and it is stolen out of the man's house...if the thief is not found the owner of the house shall approach the judges to show whether he has put his hand to his neighbor's goods]" (Ex. 22:7-8).

[AA]   Now if [the language, "money or goods"] is used to indicate that a court need not trouble with a claim of less than a perutah in value, it already is stated, "and thereby become guilty" (Lev. 6:7) – excluding what is worth less than a perutah.

[BB]   Accordingly, why does Scripture specify "money"?

[CC]   On the basis of that statement we derive the fact that at issue is more than a minimum sum of money. And how much is more than a minimum sum of money? It is two maahs.

[DD]   Or perhaps a minimum sum of money is a perutah, and more than a minimum sum of money would be two perutahs?

[EE]   The smallest minted coin is a maah.

[FF]   So let it be a maah.

[GG]   "Or goods" [stated in the plural] means two. So in the case of "money" it must be two [coins].

[HH]   How do the House of Shammai interpret the passage, "or goods"?

[II]   It is in line with the following, as it has been taught: R. Nathan says, "'or goods' seems to encompass under the law even clay pots."

[JJ]   Samuel said, "If one has laid claim for two needles, and the bailee confesses that he received one of them, he is liable for an oath."

[KK]   Said R. Hinena, "And that ruling applies if the two were worth two perutahs, so that the claim should be for at least a perutah, and the concession should cover an object worth at least a perutah."

[LL]   And this accords with the position of the House of Shammai, who do not derive the rule governing "money" from that governing "goods."

[MM]   But in accord with the view of the House of Hillel, who do derive the rule governing "money" [58d] from that governing "goods," just as "goods" must be two, so "money" must be two.

[NN]   Along these same lines, just as "money" refers to two maahs, so "goods" refers to what is worth two maahs.

We proceed to another secondary expansion of the Mishnah rule. In what follows, we introduce a Mishnah paragraph that intersects with the present one, that is, at the dispute on the amount of money required to effect a transfer of title to the betrothing party; this yields a broader issue of how the Houses in practical terms related to one another, since the rules governing valid marriages differ. The discussion is not particular to our Mishnah paragraph.

[VIII.A]   **Even though the House of Shammai and the House of Hillel disputed concerning the co-wives, concerning sisters, concerning the married woman, concerning a superannuated writ of divorce, concerning the one who betroths a woman with something of the value of a perutah, and concerning the one who divorces his wife and spends a night with her in an inn,**

[B]   **the House of Shammai did not refrain from taking wives among the women of the House of Hillel, and the House of Hillel from the House of Shammai [M. Yeb. 1:41].**

[C]   **But they behaved toward one another truthfully, and there was peace between them,**

[D]   **since it is said, "They loved truth and peace" (Zech. 8:19) [T. Yeb. 1:10].**

[E]   There is the matter of the genealogically illegitimate status of children between them, and yet you say this? [Incredible!]

[F]   What would be a practical case?

[G]   If a girl was betrothed to the first man with what is worth a perutah, and to the second with what is worth a denar, in the opinion of the House of Shammai, she is betrothed to the second man, and any offspring she has by the first are deemed illegitimate.

[H]   In the opinion of the House of Hillel, she is betrothed to the first man, and any offspring she has by the second are deemed illegitimate.

[I]   R. Jacob bar Aha in the name of R. Yohanan: "The House of Shammai concede to the House of Hillel as to the stringent side of things."

[J]   On the strength of that concurrence, the House of Shammai may marry women from the House of Hillel, for [the latter] concede [the position of the former].

[K]   But the House of Hillel should not marry women from the House of Shammai, for [the latter indeed still] do not concede [their position].

[L]   R. Yohanan in the name of R. Yannai: "Both these and these behaved in accord with the law. [That is why they could intermarry.]"

[M]   If they behaved in accord with the law, then note the following:

[N]   [Said R. Judah b. Betera, "There is the following precedent: A trough of Jehu was in Jerusalem, and it was perforated with a hole as large as the spout of a water skin. And everything that required preparation in conditions of cleanness in Jerusalem was prepared depending upon it for immersion.] And the House of Shammai sent and broke it down. For the House of Shammai say, 'Until the greater part of the object is broken down, it still is regarded as a utensil'" [M. Miq. 4:5P-S].

[O]   [The story, cited to indicate that the House of Hillel did not indeed adopt the stringent position of the House of Shammai in the conduct of the law, does not prove its point. For] R. Yosé b. R. Bun said, "Before the case came to the House of Hillel, the House of Shammai [had reason to] object [to the condition of the trough]. Once the case came to the House of Hillel, the House of Shammai had no [further reason to] object. [That is, once the matter was brought to the attention of the house that took the less stringent position, it changed its ways.]"

[P]   Said R. Abba Meri, "And that is right. What do we learn? That they declared unclean all the clean things prepared relying on the purification power of the trough in the past. But not from this time onward [that is, once the case came to the House of Hillel]."

[Q]   R. Yosé b. R. Bun said, "Rab and Samuel differed. One of them said, 'These and those conducted themselves in accord with the law,' and the other one said, 'These conducted themselves in accord with their view of the law, and those conducted themselves in accord with their view of the law.'"

[R]   [As to this latter view,] there is the matter of the genealogically illegitimate status of children between them, and yet you say this [that they both intermarried and also followed diverse views of the law]? [Incredible!]

[S]   The Omnipresent watched out for them, and a practical case [involving illegitimacy] never actually took place.

[T]   It has been taught: [Under all circumstances the law is in accord with the House of Hillel.]

[U]   To be sure, he who wants to impose a stricter rule on himself, to follow the law in accord with the opinion of the House of Shammai and in accord with the House of Hillel – concerning such a one, Scripture says, 'The fool walks in darkness" (Qoh. 2:1).

[V]   He who holds by the lenient rulings of the House of Shammai and the lenient rulings of the House of Hillel is out-and-out evil.

[W]   But if it is to be in accord with the teachings of the House of Shammai, then let it be in accord with both their lenient rulings and their strict rulings.

[X]   And if it is to be in accord with the teachings of the House of Hillel, then let it be in accord with both their lenient rulings and their strict rulings [T. Suk. 2:3K-O].

[Y] What you have stated [about following the opinions of both houses one way or the other] applies before the echo went forth [and declared the law to accord with the House of Hillel].

[Z] Once the echo had gone forth [saying,] "In all circumstances the law accords with the position of the House of Hillel, and whoever violates the position of the House of Hillel is liable to the death penalty," [that statement no longer applied].

[AA] It was taught: The echo went forth and declared, "These and those are both the words of God. But the law still accords with the position of the House of Hillel."

[BB] Where did the echo go forth?

[CC] R. Bibi in the name of R. Yohanan: "In Yavneh did the echo go forth."

We go forward with the exposition of another clause in the Mishnah paragraph; now we introduce Tosefta's secondary expansion of the same matter:

[IX.A] And how much is a perutah? One-eighth of an Italian issar [M. 1:1F-G].

[B] It is taught [A perutah of which they have spoken is one out of eight perutahs to an issar];

[C] an issar is one twenty-fourth of a denar [T. B.B. 5:11].

[D] A silver denar is one twenty-fourth of a gold denar.

[E] R. Hiyya taught [in the Tosefta's version,] "A sela is four denars.

[F] "Six silver maahs are a denar.

[G] "A silver maah is two pondions.

[H] "A pondion is two issars.

[I] "An issar is two mismasin.

[J] "A mismas is two quntronin.

[K] "A quntron is two perutahs."

[L] Said R. Zeira, "In the days of R. Simai and our rabbis, they declared that the perutah was one out of twenty-four to a maah."

[M] Rabban Simeon b. Gamaliel says, "The perutah of which they have spoken is one of six perutahs to the issar.

[N] "There are three hadrasin to a maah,

[O] "two hanassin to a hadras,

[P] "two shemanin to a hannas,

[Q] "two perutahs to a shemen" [T. B.B. 5:1].

[R] So it comes out that there are one out of twenty-four to a maah.

[S] R. Haninah and R. Mana: R. Haninah says, "As to copper perutahs, they stand at their assigned value [without rising or falling, contrary to the views given just now that Simai and our rabbis added to their value]. But silver [issars] may decrease or increase in value."

[T] R. Mana says, "[Issars made out of] silver stand in their assigned value. [Perutahs made out of] copper may increase or decrease in value."

[U] In the view of R. Haninah, in all circumstances six women may be betrothed with a single issar [since it is worth six perutahs at all times].

[V]   In the opinion of R. Mana, sometimes it will be six, sometimes eight.

[W] Hilpai said, "Set me down at the shore of the river; if I cannot demonstrate that whatever is said in the Mishnah of R. Hiyya [the Tosefta] may in fact be derived from our Mishnah, then throw me into the river."

[X]   They said to him, "And lo, R. Hiyya taught, 'A sela is four denars.'"

[Y]   He said to them, "So, too, have we learned: How much may a sela be defective and still not fall under the rule of fraud? R. Meir says, "Four issars at an issar to a denar [M. B.M. 4:5A-B]. [That is one twenty-fourth of a sela, for a denar is six maahs, and a maah is four issars, so it is one twenty-fourth. Four denars make up a sela.]"

[Z]   They said to him, "And has not R. Hiyya taught: 'Six maahs are a denar'?"

[AA] He said to them, "So we learn in our Mishnah: **Overreaching is an overcharge of four pieces of silver out of twenty-four pieces of silver to the sela, one sixth of the purchase price [M. B.M. 4:3A-B].** [So a denar is six maahs.]"

[BB] They said to him, "And has not R. Hiyya taught: 'Two pondions make up a maah'?"

[CC] He said to them, "**So we learn in our Mishnah: If one sanctified a field two or three years before the Jubilee, he gives a sela and a pondion for each year [M. Ar. 7:11].** [There are forty-eight pondions to a sela, twenty-four maahs to a sela. so two pondions to a maah.]"

[DD] They said to him, "And has not R. Hiyya taught: 'Two issars make up a pondion'?"

[EE] He said to them, 'So we learn in our Mishnah: **He who sets aside an issar [in the status of second tithe and takes it to Jerusalem] and ate [as second-tithe produce purchased] against half of its value, and then went to another area [in Jerusalem], and lo, [an issar] is worth a pondion. [That is, twice its previous value, so that the money remaining is worth a full issar of produce he eats against its value as second-tithe produce worth another issar (M. M.S. 4:6A-C).]** [So an issar is worth two pondions.]"

[FF] They said to him. "And has not R. Hiyya taught: 'Two mismasin are an issar; two quntronim are a mismas; two perutahs are a quntron'?"

[GG] He said to them, "So we learn in our Mishnah: **And how much is a perutah? One-eighth of an Italian issar [M. Qid. 1:1F-G].**"

The premise of the following is the familiar one that Scripture must be shown to sustain the Mishnah's rulings:

[X.A] **And she acquires herself through a writ of divorce [M. 1:1H].**

[B]   This is in line with what is written, "and he writes her a bill of divorce" (Deut. 24:2).

[C]   **Or through the death of the husband [M. 1:1H].**

[D]   This is in line with what is written, "or if the latter husband dies, who took her to be his wife" (Deut. 24:3).

[E]   That proves that the death of the second husband [frees her to remarry]. How do we know that the death of the first husband does so as well [in context]?

[F]   Now if in the case of the second husband, whose [death] does not constitute an ample release [of the woman, since she still may not remarry the original husband, who had divorced her], you say that death permits [her to remarry] the first husband, who has the power to release her more fully – is it not a matter of logic that his death should also permit her to remarry?

[G]   Said R. Huna, "Scripture itself has said that the death of the husband permits the wife to remarry,

[H]   "for it is written, 'If brothers dwell together, and one of them dies and has no son, the wife of the dead shall not be married outside the family to a stranger' (Deut. 25:5). Lo, if he does have a son, his death frees [the wife to marry anyone she wants]."

[I]   Said R. Yosé b. R. Bun, "If you say that death does not permit the wife to remarry, then how shall we declare that a widow is prohibited [only] to a high priest, or a divorcée or a woman who has undergone the rite of removing the shoe [Deut. 25:1ff.] to an ordinary priest? [For lo, the widow would be prohibited from marrying anyone, not merely a high priest, as Scripture specifies.]"

[J]   [Objecting to this argument regarding the widow and the high priest,] said R. Yohanan bar Mareh, "Interpret [the rule of the widow's not marrying the high priest] to apply [solely] to the case of a deceased childless brother's widow. [That is, such a childless widow may not marry her brother-in-law when he is high priest. She is permitted to the other levirate brothers and prohibited to all others. Accordingly, the attempted proof need not stand.]"

The premise remains the same. But a further proposition enters, which is, the various ways in which marital bonds are effected and severed are parallel to one another, since they produce a single effect. That leads to a comparison of betrothal through sexual relations and betrothal on the part of the levirate brother-in-law, with special attention to the comparability of the act of betrothal and the act of "bespeaking," meaning, the levir's declaring his intent of entering into levirate marriage:

[XI.A]   With regard to M. 1:1, **The deceased childless brother's widow is acquired through an act of sexual relations,** we turn to the exegesis of Deut. 25:5: "Her husband's brother shall go in to her, and take her as his wife, and perform the duty of a husband's brother to her."] "Her husband's brother shall go in to her" – this is the act of sexual relations.

[B]   "And he shall take her as his wife" – this refers to the act of bespeaking [that is, he says to her, "Behold you are sanctified to me."] [For the levirate marriage, bespeaking is the equivalent to an act of betrothal in an ordinary marriage.]

[C]   May one say that, just as the act of sexual relations completes the transaction of acquiring her as a wife, so the act of bespeaking [by itself] also will accomplish the thing [so that the levir inherits his brother's property]?

[D]   Scripture states, "[take her as his wife] and perform the duty of a husband's brother to her" [meaning, even after he has taken her as his wife through betrothal, he remains in the status of the husband's brother and must have sexual relations and does not accomplish the marriage merely by an act of betrothal].

[E]   The entire passage, therefore, indicates that, as to the levir, the act of sexual relations completes acquisition of the widow as his wife, and mere bespeaking does not complete the acquisition of the woman as his wife.

[F]   If so, what value is there in the act of bespeaking at all?

[G]   It serves to betroth her, as against the claim of the other brothers.

[H]   R. Simeon says, "Bespeaking either fully effects acquisition or does not." [Thus the foregoing position is rejected.]

[I]   What is the scriptural basis for R. Simeon's position?

[J]   "Her husband's brother shall go in to her" – this refers to an act of sexual relations.

[K]   "And take her as a wife" – this refers to an act of bespeaking.

[L]   [So the two are comparable, with the result that] just as an act of sexual relations effects complete possession of her as his wife, so does the act of bespeaking completely effect her acquisition as his wife.

[M]   Or "her husband's brother shall go in to her" and lo, "he takes her as a wife," with the result that the act of bespeaking has no standing in her regard at all.

[N]   R. Eleazar b. Arakh said, "The act of bespeaking effects a complete acquisition in the case of the childless brother's widow."

[O]   What is the scriptural basis for R. Eleazar b. Arakh's position?

[P]   "And take her as his wife" – lo, it is tantamount to the act of betrothing a woman.

[Q]   Just as in the case of betrothing a woman, one effects total possession, so in the case of a deceased childless brother's widow, also the act of bespeaking [which is the parallel, as explained above] effects total possession.

[R]   **What is "bespeaking"?**

[S]   **If the brother says, "Lo, you are sanctified to me by money," or "by something worth money"** [T. Yeb. 2:1].

Mishnah exegesis resumes in the following:

[XII.A]   [M. 1:1]: **The deceased childless brother's widow acquires freedom for herself through a rite of removing the shoe** omits reference to the act of a co-wife. Yet if the co-wife goes through the rite, the other co-wives are exempt. Accordingly,] R. Isaac asked, "And why do we not say that that is the case, whether it is the act of removing the shoe done by herself or by her co-wife?"

[B]   He reverted and said, "We learn, 'through a rite of removing the shoe,' and not 'through her rite of removing the shoe.' So here the meaning is that it is sufficient whether it is her rite of removing the shoe or whether it is the rite performed by her co-wife."

[C] And lo, we have learned, The deceased childless brother's widow is acquired through an act of sexual relations [M. 1:2].

[D] Now do you have the possibility of ruling that that is the case whether it is an act of sexual relations with her or an act of sexual relations with her co-wife? [Obviously not!]

[E] The Mishnah pericope speaks [only] of the case where there is only one surviving childless widow.

[F] "Why did [R. Isaac] ask about a case of two surviving childless widows [when our Mishnah deals with only one]?"

We turn to secondary and interstitial problems, having completed the exposition of the Mishnah paragraph. Now we want to know about the betrothed slave girl and how, in particular, she acquires ownership of herself, as a woman does through a writ of divorce:

[XIII.A] R. Samuel bar R. Isaac asked, "As to a betrothed slave girl ['If a man lies carnally with a woman who is a slave, betrothed to another man and not yet ransomed or given her freedom, an inquiry shall be held [an inquiry is also understood to mean that a flogging takes place]. They shall not be put to death, because she was not free; but he shall bring a guilt-offering for himself to the Lord' (Lev. 19:20-21)], by what means does she acquire full ownership of herself, to be exempt from a flogging, and her lover from a guilt-offering?"

[B] It is self-evident that she does not go forth by means of a writ of divorce.

[C] For R. Hiyya in the name of R. Yohanan said, "He who is half-slave and half-free – if he betrothed a woman, they do not scruple as to his act of betrothal, and, along these same lines, if he divorced a woman, they do not scruple as to his act of divorce. [Accordingly, an act of divorce is meaningless in this case.]"

[D] It is self-evident that she goes forth when her husband dies.

[E] This is in line with what R. Yosé said in the name of R. Yohanan, "Aqilas the proselyte translated before R. Aqiba, 'and she is a slave, betrothed to another man' as 'laid by a man' [hence the act of sexual relations has made the owner into her husband, and therefore when he dies she no longer is subject to flogging and the like]."

[F] This is in line with what you say, "[And the woman took and spread a covering over the well's mouth and scattered grain" (2 Sam. 17:19).

[G] [Along these same lines] said R. Hiyya in the name of R. Yohanan, "So, too, did R. Eleazar b. R. Simeon explain the matter before sages: 'and she is a slave, betrothed to another man' as 'laid by a man.'

[H] "This is in line with what you say, '[Crush a fool in a mortar with a pestle] along with crushed grain.'"

[I] What is the law as to her acquiring ownership of herself at the death of her master or at the completion of the six years?

[J] What is the force of this question?

[K] Is it in accord with the view of R. Aqiba? [Surely not.]

[L]   For R. Aqiba said, "Scripture speaks of a case in which she is half-slave and half-free, betrothed to a free boy. [In such a case what bearing does the death of the master have upon her status?]"

[M]   But in the view of R. Ishmael, it is a serious question.

[N]   For R. Ishmael said, "Scripture speaks of a Canaanite slave girl married to a Hebrew slave."

[O]   The issue then is whether the marriage has standing under the law of the Torah.

[P]   "If his master gives him a wife" (Ex. 21:4) [indicates that the marriage most certainly does have standing under the law of the Torah].

[Q]   No, the question remains pressing: What is the law as to her acquiring full ownership of herself when her master dies or the six years are fulfilled, in accord with the view of him who said that a Hebrew slave does not serve the heir [of his original master]?

A brief summary of the foregoing suffices. Unit I takes up the exegetical basis for the Mishnah's law, and, as we have noted, unit II, continuous with the foregoing, asks whether logic alone might have provided the foundation for the same facts. The consistent result is negative. Unit III takes up a further possibility of a mode of acquisition outside of the ones listed in the Mishnah and proves through Scripture that that mode is not valid. Unit IV then turns to the status of gentiles, asking (in the main) whether they are subject to the same rules. As to betrothing a woman, they are not. Unit V introduces the issue whether gentiles are subject to the rules of divorce. Unit VI distinguishes a writ from something worth a perutah, since the monetary requirement is such that the former may well be worth a perutah. The argument unfolds in terms of something totally without value; its logical potentialities are fully realized. Unit VII takes up M. 1:1C-D and accounts for the positions of the houses, at the same time comparing what they say here with a relevant position at M. Shebu. 6:1 . The main point is that the minimum sum at issue in a case in which the judges impose an oath, so far as the two houses are concerned, is different from the minimum sum to serve as betrothal money. Unit VIII amplifies unit VII. Unit IX proceeds to M. 1:1F-G. Its purpose is to introduce the Tosefta's materials and then to show that the Mishnah and Tosefta accord on the details of coinage. I present the Tosefta's version of the matter of what is assigned to Hiyya. Unit X proceeds to M. 1:1H, supplying its scriptural base. Units XI and XII take up the concluding materials of the Mishnah. Only unit XIII moves entirely beyond the limits of the Mishnah's language and problems. So what we have is a sustained analysis of the Mishnah and a rich anthology of relevant materials. For this inquiry into premises and presuppositions, the results prove trivial. What we learn is that the Talmud of the Land of Israel takes Mishnah exegesis to be its principal task; and that that Talmud finds a considerable hermeneutical challenge in showing the scriptural foundations for the Mishnah's laws. The quest for the Judaism behind the texts here yields no surprises. It also produces no considerable results. So far as the Talmud of the Land of Israel devotes itself to Mishnah exegesis, it rests upon premises of no broad generality or far-reaching relevance.

II. The Talmud of Babylonia to M. Qiddushin 1:1

The premise of the opening unit is that the language used throughout the Mishnah is uniform, so that variations in word choices or in the gender assigned to words are noteworthy and require harmonization. Here we vary the focus of discussion, the woman appearing here, the man who does the act defining the subject elsewhere:

I.1   A.   **A woman is acquired [as a wife]:**

        B.   *What differentiates the present passage, in which case the Tannaite formula commences,* **A woman is acquired [as a wife]**, *from the passage to come, in which case the Tannaite formula uses the language,* **A man effects betrothal [lit.: consecrates] on his own or through his agent [M. 2:1A]**? *[Why not say, a woman is betrothed, rather than, is acquired?]*

        C.   *Since the Tannaite framer of the Mishnah passage planned to introduce the matter of acquiring through money [he used language appropriate to a monetary transaction]. For how do we know that a monetary token serves to effect betrothal?* The fact derives from the verbal analogy established by the use of the word "purchase" [or take] with reference to the field of Ephron. Here we have, "if any man take a wife" (Deut. 22:13), and there, "I will give you money for the field, take it from me" (Gen. 23:13). [Freedman: Just as 'take' in the latter verse refers to money, so in the former, too, the wife is taken, betrothed, by money.] *And "taking" is referred to as acquisition, in line with the verse,* "The field that Abraham acquired" (Gen. 49:30). Or, also, "Men shall acquire fields for money" (Jer. 32:44). Therefore the framer of the Mishnah passage has used the word choice: **A woman is acquired [as a wife].**

        D.   *Well, then, why not use the same word choice in that other passage [at M. 2:1A], namely, A man acquires...?*

        E.   *To begin with, the Tannaite framer of the whole makes uses of the language of the Torah, and then, the language of rabbis.*

        F.   *And what is the meaning of the rabbinical word choice?*

        G.   *Through the act of betrothal the husband forbids the woman to everyone else in the world as that which has been consecrated is forbidden to everyone else in the world [but the Temple].*

        H.   *And why not use the Tannaite formulation here,* a man acquires [just as M. 2:1 uses the language, a man acquires]?

        I.   *The reason is that the framer of the passage planned at the end to present as the Tannaite formulation the rule,* **And she acquires herself through a writ of divorce and through the husband's death.** *Now* this refers to her, so the Tannaite framer likewise refers in the opening clause to her.

J.   Well, then, why not commence, a man acquires and also transfers ownership [of the woman to herself]?

K.   *The reason is that there also is the matter of the death of the husband, which restores the woman's title to herself, and that is not a transfer of title that the husband carries out! That is a transfer of title that is carried out by Heaven.*

L.   *And if you prefer, I shall say, had the Tannaite framer used the language, [the man] acquires, I might have supposed that that is even against the woman's will. In using the Tannaite formulation,* **A woman is acquired**, *he has implied, that is only with her knowledge and consent, but otherwise, not.*

The same premise, concerning linguistic harmony throughout, provokes the next discussion. It is then taken for granted that the Mishnah is a single, unitary document, governing throughout by the same preferences and rules of grammar and vocabulary:

I.2   A.   *And how come the Tannaite framer of the passage uses the feminine form of the word* three, *rather than the masculine form?*

B.   *The reason is that he will use the word* way, *which is feminine, too, in the following verse of Scripture:* "And you shall show them the way wherein they must walk" (Ex. 18:20).

C.   *Well, what about that which is taught on Tannaite authority, where the word* three *is used in the masculine form:* **In seven ways do they examine the Zab before he is confirmed as to flux [M. Zab. 2:2A]?** *Why not use the feminine form?*

D.   *The reason is that he proposes to speak of* way, *which appears in the masculine form in the following verse:* "They shall come out against you in one way and flee before you in seven ways" (Deut. 28:27).

E.   *Well, then, the two verses prove contradictory, and the Mishnah passages are likewise contradictory!*

F.   *The two verses are not contradictory. Where we find the feminine form, the reference point is the Torah, which is feminine in the verse,* "The torah of the Lord is perfect, restoring the soul" (Ps. 19:8), *and hence the feminine form is employed. There, the reference is to war making, which men, not women, do, so the masculine form is used. The Mishnah passages are not contradictory: since the reference here is to a woman, the word is given the feminine form; the reference in the intersecting passage is to a man, for a man is examined, but a woman isn't; a woman contracts that form of uncleanness even though there is no external cause [so no examination is necessary]. Hence the masculine form is used.*

I.3   A.   *Well, then, the Tannaite formulation uses* three? *It is because the word* ways *is to be used in the feminine? Then let the Tannaite formulation make reference to* things, *which is a masculine noun, and use the masculine form of the word for* three?

B.   *The reason is that the framer of the passage wanted to formulate the Tannaite rule with reference to sexual relations, and sexual relations is called* way, *in the verse,* "And the way of a man with a maid...such is the way of an adulterous woman" (Prov. 30:19-20).

I.4 A. *So there is no problems with respect to betrothal through sexual relations. What is to be said about betrothal through a monetary token or a document of betrothal?*

B. *They are formulated as they are in conjunction with the formulation on sexual relations.*

C. *And will two items be so formulated because of one?*

D. *These, too, are preliminaries to the sex act.*

E. *And if you like, I shall say, who is the authority behind the unattributed passage? It is R. Simeon, as has been taught on Tannaite authority:*

F. *R. Simeon says, "How come the Torah has said, 'If a man take a wife' (Deut. 22:13), and not, 'when a woman is taken by a man'? It is because it is the way of a man to go looking for a woman, but it is not the way of a woman to go looking for a man. The matter may be compared to the case of someone who has lost something: who looks for whom? The owner of the lost object looks for what he has lost."*

G. *Well, then, we have learned in the Mishnah:* **In seven ways do they examine the Zab before he is confirmed as to flux [M. Zab. 2:2A].** *Why not use the language,* things, *there?*

H. *In using the language they do there, we are informed that it is the way of gluttony to cause a flux, and it is the way of drunkenness to cause a flux.*

I. *But lo, we have learned in the Mishnah:* **A citron [tree] is like a tree in three ways, and like a vegetable in one way [M. Bik. 2:6A].** *Why not use the language,* things, *there?*

J. *It is because he wants to go onward,* **and like a vegetable in one way.**

K. *Big deal – so use the language,* things, *there, too!*

L. [3A] *There we are informed that* it is the ways of a citron to be like that of vegetables. Specifically, just as it is the way of vegetables to grow through any sort of water [even artificial irrigation, which cannot be done for wheat and vines], and when it is picked it is to be tithed, so it is the way of the citron to grow through any sort of water [even artificial irrigation, which cannot be done for wheat and vines], and when it is picked it is to be tithed.

M. *And lo, as we have learned in the Mishnah [using the word* way *rather than* thing *or aspect]:* **A koy [a beast that falls into the taxon of a wild beast and also into that of a domesticated beast] – There are ways in which it is like a wild animal, and there are ways in which it is like a domesticated animal; and there are ways in which it is like [both] a domesticated animal and a wild animal; and there are ways in which it is like neither a domesticated animal nor a wild animal [M. Bik. 2:8].** *Why not use the word* thing *here, too? And furthermore we have learned in the Mishnah [using the word* way *rather than* thing *or aspect]:* **This is one of the ways in which writs of divorce for women and writs [M. Git. 1:4C].** *Why not use the word* thing *here, too? Rather, in any passage in which there is a point of differentiation, the word* ways *is used as the Tannaite formulation, and in any passage in which there is no point of differentiation, the word* things *is used. The formulation of the Mishnah, closely examined, sustained that view:* **R. Eliezer says, "It is like a tree in every thing" [M. Bik. 2:6E].**

I.5   A.   *What exclusionary purpose – three, no more – is served by specifying the number at the opening clause and at the consequent one?*

       B.   *The exclusionary purpose of specifying the number at the opening clause serves to eliminate as a means of betrothal the marriage canopy [and its rite of consummating the marriage] itself.*

       C.   Well, then, from the perspective of R. Huna, who has said, "The marriage canopy effects acquisition of title to the woman, on the strength of an argument a fortiori," *what is eliminated by the specification of the number of modes of betrothal?*

       D.   *It serves to exclude the possibility of barter [trading the betrothal of a woman in exchange for an object]. It might have entered your mind to say, since we have derived the use of the word* take *from the use of the word* take *in connection with the field of Ephron, just as the title of a field may be acquired through barter, so title to a woman may be acquired through barter. Thus we are informed that that is not the case.*

       E.   *Yeah, so maybe it is the case?*

       F.   *There is the possibility of an act of barter of something worth less than a penny, but through something worth less than a penny* [3B] *a woman cannot be acquired.*

I.6   A.   *The exclusionary purpose of specifying the number at the concluding clause serves to eliminate the rite of removing the shoe. For it might have entered your mind to suppose that the possibility of the rite of removing the shoe should derive by an argument a fortiori from the case of the levirate wife. If a levirate wife, who is not freed by a divorce, is freed by the rite of removing the shoe, then this one [the levirate wife] who is freed by divorce surely should be freed by a rite of removing the shoe. Thus we are informed that that is not the case.*

       B.   *Yeah, so maybe it is the case?*

       C.   Scripture is explicit: "Then he shall write her a writ of divorce" (Deut. 24:1) – through a writ he divorces her, but he doesn't divorce her in any other way.

We proceed to the next, entirely familiar premise: Scripture provides the source for the Mishnah's rules:

II.1   A.   **She is acquired through money:**

       B.   *What is the scriptural source of this rule?*

       C.   And furthermore, we have learned in the Mishnah: **The father retains control of his daughter [younger than twelve and a half] as to effecting any of the tokens of betrothal: money, document, or sexual intercourse [M. Ket. 4:4A]** – *how on the basis of Scripture do we know that fact?*

       D.   Said R. Judah said Rab, "Said Scripture, 'Then shall she [the Hebrew slave girl] go out for nothing, without money' (Ex. 21:11). No money is paid to this master, but money is paid to another master, and who would that be? It is the father."

       E.   *But might one say that it goes to her?*

       F.   *But how can you suppose so? Since the father has the power to contract her betrothal, as it is written, "I gave my daughter to this man" (Deut. 22:16), can she collect the money? [Obviously she cannot, so the father gets the money.]*

G. *But maybe that is the case only for a minor, who has no domain ["hand," with which to effect acquisition], but in the case of a girl, who has a domain for the stated purpose, she may contract the betrothal and also get the money paid for the betrothal?*

H. Said Scripture, "Being in her youth, in her father's house" (Num. 30:17) – every advantage accruing to her in her youth belongs to her father.

I. *Then what about what* R. Huna said Rab said, *"How on the basis of Scripture do we know that the proceeds of a daughter's labor go to the father? 'And if a man sell his daughter to be a maidservant' (Ex. 21:7) – just as the proceeds of the labor of a maidservant go to the master, so the proceeds of the labor of a daughter go to the father"? What need do I have for such a proof, when the same proposition may be deduced from the phrase, "Being in her youth, in her father's house"* (Num. 30:17)?

J. *Rather, that verse refers to releasing her vows [and not to the matter at hand, as the context at Num. 30:17 makes clear].*

K. *And, furthermore, should you say, so let us derive the rule covering money from the rule covering other propositions, in fact, we do not ever derive the rule covering money from the rule covering other propositions!*

L. *And, furthermore, should you propose, so let us derive the rule governing the disposition of monetary payments from the rule governing fines; it is the simple fact that the rule governing monetary payments is not to be derived from the rule governing the disposition of fines.*

M. *Then here is the reason that compensation for humiliation and damages is assigned to the father:* [add: *if he wanted, he could hand her over [for marriage] to an ugly man or to a man afflicted with boils*]. [Since he himself could subject her to indignity and benefit from it, he gets the compensation from someone who does that to her (Slotki).]

N. *Rather, it is more reasonable that, when the All-Merciful excluded another "exodus" [from the household],* [4A] *it was meant to be like the original.* [Slotki: As in the original, it is the master, not the slave girl, who would have received the money for her redemption, but a specific text states to the contrary, so in the implication it must be the father, corresponding to the master, who gets the money when she leaves his control at betrothal.]

O. *Yes, but the one "exodus" is not really comparable to the other. For in the case of the master, the slave girl entirely exits from his control, while in the exodus from the domain of the father, the exit to the bridal canopy has not yet been completed.*

P. *Nonetheless, so far as it concerns his power to remit her vows, she does entirely exit his domain, for we have learned in the Mishnah:* **A betrothed girl – her father and her husband annul her vows [M. Ned. 10:1A-B].**

II.2 A. *But does the verse, "She shall go out for nothing" serve the present purpose? Surely it is required in line with that which is taught on Tannaite authority, as follows:*

B. "And she shall go out for nothing" – this refers to the days of her puberty; "without money" refers to the days of just prior to puberty. [Freedman: Thus the verse merely teaches that something else, not money, frees her, but implies no other conclusion.]

C.   *Said Rabina, "If so, Scripture ought to have said, 'no money.' Why formulate matters as 'without money'?* It is to indicate, 'No money is paid to this master, but money is paid to another master, and who would that be? It is the father.'"

D.   *And on what basis do we perform such an exegesis? It is as has been taught on Tannaite authority:*

E.   "And have no children" (Lev. 22:13) – I know only that that pertains to her own child, what about her grandchild? Scripture says, "And have no child," meaning, any child whatsoever.

F.   So far I know that that is the case only of a valid offspring, what about an invalid one?

G.   Scripture says, "And have no child," meaning, "hold an inquiry concerning her."

H.   *But lo, that clause has yielded the deduction concerning the grandchild!*

I.   *In point of fact it is not necessary to present a verse of Scripture to prove that* grandchildren are in the status of children. *Where a verse of Scripture is required is to deal with invalid offspring.*

J.   *And how does the Tannaite authority himself know that such an exegesis is undertaken?*

K.   *Say:* It is written, "Balaam refuses" and "my husband's brother refuses" (Num. 22:14, Deut. 25:7). In these instances, the words are written without the Y that they could have had. *Now here in the verses treated above, the Y is used, which proves that the Y, which is dispensable, is included for exegetical purposes.*

II.3   A.   *And it was necessary to provide a verse of Scripture to indicate that the minor daughter's token of betrothal is assigned to her father, and it also was necessary to find a verse of Scripture to indicate that her wages are assigned to her father. For if the All-Merciful had made reference to the assignment of the token of betrothal to her father, I might have supposed that that was because she has not labored for that item, but as to her wages, for which she has labored, I might have said that they are assigned to her. And if we had been informed of the matter of her wages, in which matter, after all, she is provided for by him, [I might have supposed that since he supports her, she gets her wages], but as to the matter of tokens of betrothal given to her from a third party, I might have supposed that these go to her. So both proofs were required.*

II.4   A.   *Reverting to the body of the foregoing:* "And she shall go out for nothing" – this refers to the days of her puberty; "without money" refers to the prepubescent time [days just prior to puberty].

B.   *But why should the All-Merciful simply make reference to the prepubescent time [days just prior to puberty], and it would not have been necessary to make reference to the time of her puberty?*

C.   Said Rabbah, "The one comes along to impart meaning to the other. *It may be comparable to the case of the words, a sojourner or a hired servant [Lev. 22:10: toshab, sakir,] as has been taught on Tannaite authority:*

D.   "'One word refers to a Hebrew slave acquired permanently, the other to one purchased for six years [at Lev. 22:10: "a slave purchased in perpetuity belonging to a priest or a slave purchased for six years shall not eat of the Holy Thing"]. If Scripture had referred to the former and not the latter, I would reason, if a slave acquired permanently may not eat Holy Things, how much more so is one acquired only for six years forbidden to do so! And if that were so, I would say, the former word refers to a slave purchased for a limited period, but one acquired in perpetuity may eat. So the word that refers to the slave purchased for a period of six years comes along and illuminates the meaning of the word for the one purchased in perpetuity, by contrast to the one purchased for a period of six years – and neither one may eat.'"

E. *Said to him Abbayye, "But are the cases truly parallel? In that case, they are two distinct classes of persons, so that, even if Scripture had made explicit reference to a sojourner whose ear had been pierced's not eating, and then made explicit reference to the other, then the hired hand might have been derived by an argument a fortiori. Such matters Scripture does take the trouble to spell out. But here, by contrast, the maidservant is one and the same person. Once she has left the prepubescent period, what business does she have to do with him when she becomes pubescent?"*

F. *Rather, said Abbayye, "It was necessary to make this point only to deal with the case of a woman who exhibits no signs of puberty even after she has reached the age of twenty years. It might have entered your mind to suppose that when she reaches pubescence, she goes free, but not merely by reaching her majority. So we are informed to the contrary."*

G. *Objected Mar bar R. Ashi to this proposition:* "But is this not attainable through an argument a fortiori? If the appearance of puberty signs, which do not remove the girl from the domain of the father, do remove the girl from the domain of the master, reaching maturity, which does remove her from the domain of the father, surely should remove her from the domain of the master!"

H. *Rather, said Mar bar R. Ashi, "The proof is required only to deal with the matter of the sale of a barren woman* [Freedman: a minor who shows symptoms of constitutional barrenness]. *It might have entered your mind to suppose that with one who will later on produce puberty signs, the sale is valid, but with one who won't, the sale is null.* **[4B]** *So we are informed by the verse, 'and she shall go out for nothing' that that is not the case."*

I. *But to Mar bar R. Ashi, who has said,* "But is this not attainable through an argument a fortiori?," *haven't we established the fact that something that can be proved through an argument a fortiori Scripture will nonetheless trouble to make explicit?*

J. *Well, that's true enough where there is no other possible reply, but if there is, we give that possible reply* [making the verse pertain to some other matter than the one under discussion (Freedman)].

II.5 A. *[That she is acquired through money] is derived by the following Tannaite authority on a different basis, as has been taught on Tannaite authority:*

B. "When a man takes a wife and has sexual relations with her, then it shall be, if she find no favor in his eyes, because he has found some unseemly thing in her" (Deut. 24:1) – the sense of "take" refers only to acquisition through a payment of money, in line with the verse, "I will give the money for the field take it from me" (Gen. 23:13).

C. But cannot the same be proven by an argument a fortiori: if a Hebrew slave girl, who cannot be acquired by an act of sexual relations, can be acquired by money, a wife, who may be acquired in marriage by an act of sexual relations, surely can be acquired by money!

D. A levirate wife proves the contrary, since she may be acquired by sexual relations but not by a money payment.

E. But what distinguishes the levirate wife is that she cannot be acquired by a deed, and can you say the same of an ordinary wife, who can be acquired by a deed? So it is necessary for Scripture to teach, "When a man takes a wife and has sexual relations with her, then it shall be, if she find no favor in his eyes, because he has found some unseemly thing in her" (Deut. 24:1) – the sense of "take" refers only to acquisition through a payment of money, in line with the verse, "I will give the money for the field take it from me" (Gen. 23:13) [Sifré Deut. 268:1.1].

F. But what need do I have for a verse of Scripture, *since it has been yielded by the argument a fortiori [the case of the levirate wife having been refuted]?*

G. *Said R. Ashi, "It is because one may raise the following disqualifying argument to begin with: whence have you derived proof for the matter? From the case of the Hebrew slave girl?* But what distinguishes the Hebrew slave girl is that she goes out from bondage with a money payment. Will you say the same in this case, in which she does not go forth through a money payment? So it is necessary for Scripture to teach, 'When a man takes a wife and has sexual relations with her, then it shall be, if she find no favor in his eyes, because he has found some unseemly thing in her' (Deut. 24:1) – the sense of 'take' refers only to acquisition through a payment of money, in line with the verse, 'I will give the money for the field take it from me' (Gen. 23:13)."

H. *And it was necessary for Scripture to deal with the case, "and she shall go out for nothing" and also "when a man takes." For had Scripture made reference to "when a man takes," I might have thought, the token of betrothal that the husband gives to her is her own; therefore Scripture states, "and she shall go out for nothing." And if Scripture had said only, "and she shall go out for nothing," I might have supposed, if the wife gives him the money and betroths him, it is a valid act of betrothal. Therefore Scripture stated, "when a man takes," but not, "when a woman takes."*

We ask now about the role of reason in discovering the law, once more insisting that reason unaided by Scripture yields uncertain results:

II.6   A. "...and possesses her [has sexual relations with her]":

B. This teaches that a woman is acquired through an act of sexual relations.

C. One might have reasoned as follows:

D. If a deceased childless brother's widow, who may not be acquired through a money payment, may be acquired through an act of sexual relations, a woman, who may be acquired through a money payment, logically should be available for acquisition through an act of sexual relations.

E.   But a Hebrew slave girl will prove the contrary, for she may be acquired through a money payment, but she is not acquired through an act of sexual relations. [On that account, you should not find it surprising for an ordinary woman, who, even though she may be acquired through a money payment, may not be acquired through an act of sexual relations] [Sifré Deut. 268:1.2].

F.   What characterizes the Hebrew slave girl is that she is not acquired for a wife. But will you say the same in this case, in which the woman is acquired for a wife?

G.   So Scripture states, "…and possesses her [has sexual relations with her]."

H.   But then why do I need a verse of Scripture [in light of F]? *Lo, the matter has been proven without it!*

I.   *Said R. Ashi, "Because there is the possibility of stating that at the foundations of the logical argument there is a flaw, namely, from whence do you derive the case? From the deceased childless brother's widow.* But what characterizes the levirate widow is that she is already subject to a relationship to the levir, but can you say the same in this instance, where the woman hardly is subject to any relationship whatever to this unrelated man? So it is necessary to state: '…and possesses her [has sexual relations with her]' – This teaches that a woman is acquired through an act of sexual relations."

The priority of Scripture in the determination of the law is repeated once more:

III.1   A.   [5A] And how on the basis of Scripture do we know that a woman may be acquired by a deed?

B.   It is a matter of logic.

C.   If a payment of money, which does not serve to remove a woman from a man's domain [as does a writ of divorce], lo, it has the power of effecting acquisition,

D.   a deed [namely, a writ of marriage or a marriage contract], which does [in the form of a writ of divorce] have the power to remove a woman from the domain of a man, surely should have the power of effecting acquisition.

E.   No, if you have made that statement concerning the payment of money, which does have the power of effecting acquisition of things that have been designated as Holy and of produce in the status of second tithe [there being an exchange of money for such objects, by which the objects become secular and the money becomes consecrated], will you make the same statement concerning a writ, which does not have the power of effecting acquisitions of Holy Things and produce in the status of second tithe, for it is written, "and if he who sanctifies the field will in any manner redeem it, then he shall add the fifth part of the money of your estimation, and it shall be assigned to him" (Lev. 27:19)?

F.   Scripture says, "and he writes her a bill of divorcement, hands it to her, and sends her away from his house; she leaves his household and becomes the wife of another man".

G.   Her relationship to the latter is comparable to her leaving the former. Just as her leaving the former is effected through a writ, so her becoming wife to the latter may be effected through a writ [Sifré Deut. 268:1.3].

H.   *Well, why not draw the comparison in the opposite direction, namely, the going forth from the marriage to the establishment of the marriage: just as the establishment of the marriage is through money, so the going forth from the marriage is through money?*

I.   Said Abbayye, "People will say, money brings the woman into the marriage and money takes her out of it? Then will the defense attorney turn into the prosecutor?"

J.   *If we accept that argument, then the deed of betrothal likewise will be subject to the saying, a writ removes her from the marriage, and a writ brings her into it? So will the prosecutor turn into the defense attorney?*

K.   *Yes, but the substance of this document is distinct from the substance of that document.*

L.   *Yeah, well, then, the purpose of this money payment is different from the purpose of that money payment!*

M.   *Nonetheless, all coins have the same mint mark! [So who knows the difference? But the documents contain different wordings.]*

III.2   A.   Raba said, "Said Scripture, 'And he shall write for her' (Deut. 24:1) – through what is in writing a woman is divorced, and she is not divorced through a money payment."

B.   *Why not say: through writing a woman is divorced, but she is not betrothed through what is in writing?*

C.   Lo, it is written, "And when she goes forth, then she may marry" so comparing divorce to marriage.

D.   Why choose that reading rather than the contrary one [excluding money for divorce but accept a deed for marriage? Why not reverse it?]

E.   *It stands to reason that when we deal with divorce, we exclude a conceivable means for effecting divorce; when dealing with divorce should we exclude what is a means of effecting a betrothal?*

F.   *Now how, for his part, does R. Yosé the Galilean attain that same principle, [since he interprets the language of the verse at hand for another purpose], how does he know that a woman is not divorced through a money payment?*

G.   *He derives that lesson from the language, "a writ of divorce," meaning, A writ is what cuts the relationship, and no other consideration cuts the relationship.*

H.   *And rabbis – how do they deal with the language, "a writ of divorce"?*

I.   *That formulation is required to indicate that the relationship is broken off through something that effectively severs the tie between him and her. For it has been taught on Tannaite authority:* [If the husband said], "Lo, here is your writ of divorce, on the condition that you not drink wine, that you not go to your father's house forever," this is not an act of totally severing the relationship. [If he said,] "... for thirty days...," lo, this is an act of severing the relationship. [The husband cannot impose a permanent condition, for if he could do so, then the relationship would not have been completely and finally severed.]

J.   And R. Yosé?

K.   *He derives the same lesson from the use of the language, "total cutting off" as against merely "cutting off."*

L.   And rabbis?

M.   *The rabbis do not derive any lesson from the variation in the language at hand.*

III.3 A.   *While it is not possible to derive the rule governing one mode of acquisition from another [the various arguments having failed], maybe it's possible to infer one from two others [so that if we can show that it is possible to effect acquisition through two modes that work elsewhere and also that work in respect to a betrothal, then a third, that works elsewhere, can work in this case, too]?*

B.   *Which two?*

C.   *Perhaps the All-Merciful should not make reference in Scripture to a deed, and that might be derived from the other two modes of acquisition [sexual relations, money payment]? But then one might argue that what characterizes these other two modes of acquisition is that a good deal of benefit derives from them, which is not the case for a mere piece of paper.*

D.   *Then perhaps Scripture should not make written reference to the mode of sexual relations, and that might be derived from the other two? But then one might argue that what is characteristic of the other two is that they serve to effect acquisition in a wide variety of matters, while that is not so in the instance of sexual relations!*

E.   *Then let Scripture not make reference to the matter of money, and let that derive from the other two? But what characterizes the other two is that they take effect even contrary to the woman's will, which is not the case of money [she must be willing to accept it]. And should you say that money, too, may take effect willy-nilly in the case of a Hebrew slave girl, nonetheless, in the matter of effecting a marriage, we find no such instance.*

III.4 A.   Said R. Huna, "The marriage canopy effects acquisition of title to the woman, on the strength of an argument a fortiori: if a money payment, which on its own does not confer the right to eat priestly rations, effects transfer of title to the husband over the woman, the marriage canopy, which does confer the right to eat priestly rations, surely should effect the transfer of title."

B.   But doesn't acquisition through a money payment confer the right to eat priestly rations? And hasn't Ulla said, "By the law of the Torah, a girl of Israelite caste who was betrothed to a priest is permitted to eat priestly rations: 'But if a priest buy any soul, the purchase of his money...' (Lev. 22:11) – *and this one also falls into the class of* 'purchased of his money.' And what is the reason that they have said that she may not eat priestly rations? Lest a cup of wine in the status of priestly rations be mixed for her in her father's house and she share it with her brother or sister [who are not in the priestly caste]"?

C.   *Then raise the following question:* what characterizes a money payment is that it does not effect the completion of the acquisition of the wife but nonetheless effects transfer of title; **[5B]** the marriage canopy, which does effect the completion of the acquisition of the wife, surely should effect transfer of title and hence betrothal!

D.   The particular trait of a money payment is that with it things that have been consecrated and second tithe may be redeemed.

E.   But sexual relations proves to the contrary [having no bearing on that matter].

F.   The distinguishing trait of sexual relations is that that is a means for acquiring a levirate widow as a wife.

G.   A money payment, inoperative there, proves the disqualifying exception.

H.   So we find ourselves going around in circles. The distinctive trait that pertains to the one is not the same as the distinctive trait that applies to the other, and the generative quality of the other is not the same as the generative quality of the one. But then, the generative trait that pertains to them all is that they effect transfer of title in general and they also effect transfer of title here. So I shall introduce the matter of the marriage canopy, which effects transfer of title in general and should also effect transfer of title here.

I.   But the generative quality that is characteristic of the set is that they produce a considerable benefit.

J.   A writ, a mere piece of paper, proves the disqualifying exception.

K.   The distinctive quality of the deed is that it can remove an Israelite woman from a marriage.

L.   A money payment and sexual relations provide the disqualifying exceptions.

M.   So we find ourselves going around in circles. The distinctive trait that pertains to the one is not the same as the distinctive trait that applies to the other, and the generative quality of the other is not the same as the generative quality of the one. But then, the generative trait that pertains to them all is that they effect transfer of title in general and they also effect transfer of title here. So I shall introduce the matter of the marriage canopy, which effects transfer of title in general and should also effect transfer of title here.

N.   But the generative quality that is characteristic of the set is that they serve under compulsion.

O.   And R. Huna?

P.   *In any event, we don't find any aspect of compulsion when it comes to the money payment.*

III.5   A.   [As to R. Huna's statement,] said Rabbah, "There are two refutations of what he has said: *first, we learn in the Mishnah the language,* **three**, *not* four; *and furthermore, isn't it the simple fact that the marriage canopy completes the relationship only in consequence of an act of betrothal? But can the marriage canopy complete the relationship not in the aftermath of an act of betrothal, so that we may deduce that, when it is not in consequence of an act of betrothal, there is the same result as the marriage canopy following such an act?"*

B.   *Said to him Abbayye, "As to what you have said, namely, first, we learn in the Mishnah the language,* **three**, *not* four, *the Tannaite authority makes explicit reference only to what is explicitly stated in Scripture, but not what is not explicitly stated [and we have shown that the media of money and deed derive from exegesis, if not from an explicit statement of*

> Scripture, but the validity of the marriage canopy is only derived by an argument a fortiori]. *And as to your statement, isn't it the simple fact that the marriage completes the relationship only in consequence of an act of betrothal? As a matter of fact, that is R. Huna's argument: if a money payment does not complete the relationship after a prior payment of a money payment, the marriage canopy, which does complete the relationship after a money payment, surely should effect transfer of title just as well!"*

We proceed to Tosefta's complement to our Mishnah rule; the operative premise, of course, is that the Mishnah is not the sole source of rules that enjoy Tannaite standing and sponsorship; other sources include Tosefta, and that document's materials will be subjected to the same exegetical process as shapes the Mishnah's rulings.

III.6   A.   *Our rabbis have taught on Tannaite authority:*
       B.   **With money, how so?**
       C.   **If he gave her money or what is worth money and said to her, "Lo, you are consecrated to me," "lo, you are betrothed to me," "lo, you are for me as a wife," lo, this one is consecrated. But if she gave it to him and said to him, "Lo, I am consecrated to you," "lo, I am betrothed to you," "lo, I am yours as a wife," she is not consecrated [T. Qid. 1:1B-D].**

III.7   A.   *Objected R. Pappa, "So is the operative consideration only that he gave the money and he made the statement? Then if he gave the money and she made the statement, she is not betrothed? Then note what follows:* **But if she gave it to him and said to him, "Lo, I am consecrated to you," "lo, I am betrothed to you," "lo, I am yours as a wife," she is not consecrated***! So the operative consideration is that she gave the money and she made the statement. Lo, if he gave the money and she made the statement, there would be a valid betrothal!"*
       B.   The opening clause describes precisely the details of the transaction, and the concluding one states them in more general terms.
       C.   *Yeah, well, then, can you make a statement in the second clause that contradicts the implications of the first!? But this is the sense of the statements before us:* if he gave the money and he made the statement, it is obvious that the betrothal is valid. If he gave the token and she made the statement, it is treated as a case in which she gave the money and made the statement, and there is no valid betrothal.
       D.   *And if you wish, I shall say,* if he gave the money and he made the statement, she is betrothed. If she gave the token and she made the statement, she is not betrothed. If he gave the token and she made the statement, *it is a matter of doubt, and, on the authority of rabbis, we take account of the possibility of a valid transaction.*

Samuel will now propose an extension of the law at hand, and this bears an implication concerning a broader issue altogether. Then that issue has to be exposed and discussed. It is the effect of the use of imprecise language, for example, inexplicit abbrevations; to what degree, we now want to know, must the formulation of language be precise? The premise, of course, is that language is effective in determining the status of things; what one says governs:

III.8   A.   Said Samuel, "In the matter of a betrothal, if he gave her money or what is worth money and said to her, 'Lo, you are sanctified,' 'lo you are betrothed,' 'lo, you are a wife to me,' lo, this woman is consecrated. 'Lo, I am your man,' 'lo, I am your husband,' 'lo, I am your betrothed,' there is no basis for taking account of the possibility that a betrothal has taken place. And so as to a writ of divorce: if he gave her the document and said to her, 'Lo, you are sent forth,' 'lo, you are divorced,' 'lo, you are permitted to any man,' lo, this woman is divorced. 'I am not your man,' 'I am not your husband,' 'I am not your betrothed,' there is no basis for taking account of the possibility that a divorce has taken place."

        B.   *Said R. Pappa to Abbayye, "Does this bear the implication that Samuel takes the view, 'Inexplicit abbreviations [such as the language that is used and then spelled out, for example, "I am forbidden by a vow from you" means, "I am not going to speak to you." "I am separated from you by a vow" means, "I am not going to do any business with you." "I am removed from you" means, "I am not going to stand within four cubits of you"] are null [and take effect only if they are made explicit]'? And have we not learned in the Mishnah:* **He who says, 'I will be [such],' – lo, this one is a Nazir [M. Naz. 1:1B]?** *And in reflecting on it, we stated: 'But maybe the sense of,* **I will be [such]**, *is "I will fast"?' And said Samuel, 'But that rule that the Mishnah states pertains to a case in which a Nazirite was walking by at just that moment.' So the operative consideration is that a Nazirite was walking by at just that moment. Lo, if that were not the case, it would not be the rule! [So Samuel maintains that inexplicit abbreviations are valid only if made explicit.]"*

        C.   *Here with what case do we deal? It is a case in which he said, "...to me."*
        D.   *If so, what's the point [that that we didn't already know]?*
        E.   *That* **[6A]** *is his position with respect to the latter formulations. Here it is written, "when any man takes a woman" (Deut. 24:5), not that he takes himself as a husband; and there "and when he sends her away" and not when he sends himself away.*

III.9   A.   *Our rabbis have taught on Tannaite authority:*
        B.   "Lo, you are my wife," "lo, you are my betrothed," "lo, you are acquired by me," she is consecrated.
        C.   "Lo, you are mine," "lo, you are in my domain," "lo, you are subject to me," she is betrothed.

III.10 A.   *So why not form them all into a single Tannaite statement?*
        B.   *The Tannaite had heard them in groups of three and that is how he memorized them.*

III.11 A.   *The question was raised: "If he used the language, 'Singled out for me,' '...designated for me,' '...my helpmate,' 'you are suitable for me,' 'you are gathered in to me,' 'you are my rib,' 'you are closed in to me,' 'you are my replacement,' 'you are seized to me,' 'you are taken by me,' [what is the consequence]?"*

B.   *In any event you can solve one of these problems on the basis of that which has been taught on Tannaite authority:* If he said, "You are taken by me," she is betrothed, in line with the language, "when a man takes a wife."

III.12 A.   *The question was raised, "If he said, 'You are my [betrothed] bondmaid,' what is the law?"*

B.   *Come and take note of what has been taught on Tannaite authority:*

C.   If he said, "You are my [betrothed] bondmaid," she is consecrated, for in Judea a betrothed woman is called a betrothed bondmaid.

D.   *So is Judah the majority of the world at large?*

E.   *This is the sense of the statement:* If he said, "You are my [betrothed] bondmaid," she is consecrated, for it is said, "that a betrothed bondman belonging to a man" (Lev. 19:20). Moreover, in Judea a betrothed woman is called a betrothed bondmaid.

F.   *So do I need to know a custom in Judah in order to sustain what Scripture says?*

G.   *This is the sense of the statement:* If in the territory of Judah he said, "You are my [betrothed] bondmaid," she is consecrated, for it is said, "that a betrothed bondman belonging to a man" (Lev. 19:20), for in Judea a betrothed woman is called a betrothed bondmaid..

III.13 A.   *With what situation do we deal [in the interpretation of the language just now cited as effective]? Should I say that it is a situation in which* he is not talking with her about business having to do with her writ of divorce or her betrothal? *Then how in the world should she know what he is talking about with her?! But rather, it is a case in which* he is talking with her about business having to do with her writ of divorce or her betrothal. *Then, even if he said nothing at all, but merely gave her money, she is still betrothed, for we have learned in the Mishnah:* [If] he was speaking to his wife about matters relevant to her divorce contract or her bride price and did not make it explicit – R. Yosé says, "It is sufficient for him [simply to give her the contract or bride price without a declaration." R. Judah says, "He must make it explicit" [M. M.S. 4:7]. And said R. Huna said Samuel, "The decided law accords with R. Yosé."

B.   *Say: in point of fact, it is a case in which* he is talking with her about business having to do with her writ of divorce or her betrothal. *If he had given her money and then shut up, that would indeed be the rule [she would be divorced or betrothed], but here with what situation do we deal? It is one in which he gave her the item and stated to her the language that has just now been set forth, and this is what is at issue here: when he used this language, was it for purposes of betrothal? Or was it for purposes of work? And that question stands over.*

III.14 A.   *Reverting to the body of the foregoing:*

B.   [If] he was speaking to his wife about matters relevant to her divorce contract or her bride price and did not make it explicit –

C.   R. Yosé says, "It is sufficient for him [simply to give her the contract or bride price without a declaration."

D.   R. Judah says, "He must make it explicit" [M. M.S. 4:7].

E.   Said R. Judah said Samuel, "And that is the case in which they were engaged in discussing that very same matter."

F. And so said R. Eleazar said R. Oshayya, "And that is the case in which they were engaged in discussing that very same matter."

G. *There is a Tannaite dispute on the same matter:*

H. **Rabbi says, "And that is the case in which they were engaged in discussing that very same matter."**

I. **R. Eleazar b. R. Judah says, "Even though they were not engaged in discussing that very same matter"** [cf. T. Qid. 2:8J].

III.15 A. *Well, if they were not engaged in discussing that very same matter, then how in the world should she know what he is talking about with her?*

B. Said Abbayye, "It is a case in which they moved from one topic to another in the same context."

III.16 A. Said R. Huna said Samuel, "The decided law accords with R. Yosé."

B. *Said R. Yemar to R. Ashi, "But what about what R. Judah said Samuel said, 'Whoever is not expert in the character of writs of divorce and betrothals should not get involved in dealing with them' – is that the case even if he has heard nothing of this ruling of R. Huna in Samuel's name?"*

C. He said to him, "Yes, indeed."

III.17 A. And so as to a writ of divorce: if he gave her the document and said to her, "Lo, you are sent forth," "lo, you are divorced," "lo, you are permitted to any man," lo, this woman is divorced.

B. *It is obvious that* if he gave her her writ of divorce and said to his wife, "Lo, you are a free woman," [6B] he has not said anything effective. If he said to his female slave, "Lo, you are permitted to any man," he has not said anything effective. If he said to his wife, "Lo, you are your own property," what is the law? *Do we say that he made that statement with respect to work? Or perhaps, he meant it to cover the entirety of the relationship?*

C. *Said Rabina to R. Ashi, "Come and take note of what we have learned in the Mishnah:* **The text of the writ of divorce [is as follows]: "Lo, you are permitted to any man."** R. Judah says, "[In Aramaic]: Let this be from me your writ of divorce, letter of dismissal, and deed of liberation, that you may marry anyone you want." **The text of a writ of emancipation [is as follows]: "Lo, you are free, lo, you are your own [possession]"** [cf. Deut. 21:14] [M. Git. 9:3]. *Now if, in the case of a Canaanite slave, whose body belongs to the master, when the master says to him,* **lo, you are your own [possession],** *he makes that statement covering the entirety of the relationship, when he makes such a statement to his wife, whose person he does not acquire as his possession, all the more so should it yield the same meaning!"*

III.18 A. Said Rabina to R. Ashi, "If he said to his slave, 'I have no business in you,' *what is the upshot? Do we say that the sense is,* I have no business in you in any way whatsoever? *Or perhaps he made that statement with respect to work?"*

B. *Said R. Nahman to R. Ashi, and others say, R. Hanin of Khuzistan to R. Ashi, come and take note:* **He who sells his slave to gentiles – the slave has come forth to freedom, but he requires a writ of emancipation from his first master. Said Rabban Simeon b. Gamaliel, "Under what circumstances? If he did not write out a deed of sale for him, but if he wrote out a deed of sale for him, this constitutes his act of emancipation"** [T. A.Z. 3:16A-C]."

C.   *What is a deed of sale?*

D.   *Said R. Sheshet, "He wrote for him the following language: 'when you escape from him, I have no claim on you.'"*

III.19 A.   Said Abbayye, "If someone effects a betrothal with a loan, the woman is not betrothed. If it is with the benefit of a debt, she is betrothed, but this is not to be done, because it constitutes usury accomplished through subterfuge."

B.   *What is the definition of the benefit of a debt? Should I say that he treated the interest as a loan, saying "I am lending you four zuz for five"? But that is actual usury. And it in fact is a debt.*

C.   *The rule pertains to a case in which he gave her extra time to pay the debt.*

III.20 A.   Said Raba, "If someone said, 'Take this maneh on the stipulation that you return it to me,' in regard to a purchase, he does not acquire title [for example, real estate would not be acquired if the money has to be returned]; in the case of a woman, she is not betrothed; in the case of redeeming the firstborn, the firstborn is not redeemed; in the case of priestly rations, he has carried out the duty of handing it over, but it is not permitted to do it that way, since it appears to be the case of a priest who assists in the threshing floor [in order to get the priestly rations, and that is not permitted because of the indignity]."

B.   *What is Raba's operative theory? If he maintains that a gift that is made on the stipulation that it will be returned is classified as a gift, then even the others, too, should be valid; and if he maintains that it is not a valid gift, then even in the case of priestly rations, it should not be valid. Not only so, lo, Raba is the one who* said, "A gift that is given on the stipulation that it is returned is classified as a gift," for said Raba, "'Here is this citron [as a gift to you] on condition that you return it to me' – if one has taken it and carried out his obligation and returned it to the other, he has carried out his obligation, but if he did not return it, he did not carry out his obligation." [So a conditional gift is entirely valid.]

C.   *Rather, said R. Ashi, "In all cases the gift that rests on a stipulation is valid, except the case of a woman, because* a woman is not acquired through barter."

D.   *Said R. Huna Mar b. R. Nehemiah to R. Ashi, "This is what we say in Raba's name, precisely as you have said it."*

III.21 A.   Said Raba, "If a woman said, 'Give a maneh to Mr. So-and-so [7A] and I shall be betrothed to you,' she is betrothed under the law of surety, *namely: even though a surety does not derive benefit from the loan, he obligates himself to repay it; so this woman, too, though she derives no benefit from the money, still obligates and cedes herself as betrothed.*

B.   "If someone said, 'Here is a maneh, and be betrothed to Mr. So-and-so' – she is betrothed under the law governing a Canaanite slave, *namely: in the case of a Canaanite slave, even though he himself loses nothing when someone else gives his master money to free him, nonetheless acquires ownership to himself, so even though this man personally loses nothing, he acquires the woman.*

C.   "If a woman said, 'Give a maneh to Mr. So-and-so, and I shall be betrothed to him,' she is betrothed on the basis of the law governing both classes of transactions; *as to a pledge, even though he personally* derives no benefit, he obligates himself, and this woman, too, though she gains nothing, cedes herself. Should you object, how are the cases parallel? In the case of a pledge he who acquires title loses money [paying off the debtor], but this man is acquiring the woman at no cost to himself – then the Canaanite slave proves the contrary, since he loses nothing but gains his freedom. And if you object, how are the cases parallel? In that case he who gives title acquires the money given for the slave, but here, does the woman cede herself and acquire nothing? Then the surety proves it, though he personally gets nothing, he still obligates himself."

III.22 A. Raba raised this question: "'Here is a maneh and I'll become betrothed to you' [Freedman: and the man accepted it saying, 'Be betrothed to me with it'], [what is the law?]"

B. Said Mar Zutra in the name of R. Pappa, "She is betrothed."

C. *Said R. Ashi to Mar Zutra, "If so, you have a case in which* property that is secured [real estate] is acquired along with property that is not secured [movables], *while in the Mishnah we have learned the opposite, namely:* **Property for which there is no security is acquired along with property for which there is security through money, writ, and usucaption. And property for which there is no security imposes the need for an oath on property for which there is security [M. 1:5C-D].**" [Freedman: A creditor could collect his debt out of the debtor's real estate, even if sold after the debt was contracted, but not out of movables, if sold; hence the former is termed property that ranks as security, the latter, not. Human beings are on a par with the former, and Ashi assumes that the woman is acquired in conjunction with the maneh.]

D. *He said to him, "Do you suppose that she said to him, '...along with...'? Here we deal with a person of high standing. In exchange for the pleasure that she derives from his accepting a gift from her, she has determined to give him title over her person."*

E. *So, too, it has been stated in the name of Raba: the rule is the same in monetary matters.* [Freedman: If A says to B, "give money to C, in return for which my field is sold to you," the sale is valid, by the law of surety.]

F. *And it was necessary for the rule to be stated in both instances. For if we had been informed of the rule only in connection with betrothals, it might have been thought that it is because the woman accepts the most meagre compensation, in line with what R. Simeon b. Laqish said, for said R. Simeon b. Laqish, "Better to live together than to live a widow," but as to a monetary transaction, I might have said that that is not the case. And if it had been only with respect to a monetary transaction that we had been informed of the law, that might have been because it is possible to remit a debt if one chooses, but that would not be the case with regard to a betrothal [in which instance a woman must receive a token of betrothal]. So it was necessary for the rule to be stated in both instances.*

III.23 A. Said Raba, "If a man said, 'Be betrothed to half of me,' she is betrothed;' 'half of you be betrothed to me,' she is not betrothed."

B. *Objected Abbayye to Raba, "What's the difference between the language, 'Be betrothed to half of me,' and the language, 'half of you be betrothed to me,' so that in the latter case she is not betrothed? Is it because Scripture has said, 'when a man take a wife' (Deut. 24:1) but* not half a wife? *Then Scripture also says, 'a man,' but not half a man!"*

C. *He said to him, "How are the cases parallel! In that case a woman cannot be assigned to two men, but can't a man be assigned to two or more women? So this is what he meant to say to her: 'If I want to marry another woman, I'll do just that.'"*

D. *Said Mar Zutra b. R. Mari to Rabina, "Why not consider that the betrothal spreads through the whole of the woman? Has it not been taught on Tannaite authority: 'if one says, "the foot of this animal shall be a burnt-offering," the whole becomes a burnt-offering'? And even in the opinion of him who says that* the whole of the beast is not then classified as a burnt-offering, that is the case in which one has sanctified a part of the beast on which life does not depend, but he who sanctifies a part of the beast on which life depends – the whole of it is indeed a burnt-offering!"

E. *But are the cases comparable? In that case, we deal with a mere beast. But in this case, we have a third-party opinion in play [so the woman would have to concur that the betrothal spread through the whole of her]. The matter is comparable only to the case of which R. Yohanan spoke, namely,* "In the case of a beast that belongs to two partners, if one of them consecrated his own half, and then he went and bought the half belonging to the other party and consecrated that part, it is indeed deemed consecrated, but it is not offered up. Still, it has the power to effect an act of substitution [with a secular beast with which it is exchanged], and the beast that is exchanged for it is in the same status. *Three rules are to be derived from this ruling* One may deduce, **[7B]** first of all, that a beast that is consecrated can be removed forever from sacred use [and even though later on they became fit to be offered, they cannot be offered, since they have prior been suspended from use on the altar for some reason]. And one may deduce, second, that if to begin with [at the point of its consecration] an animal is removed from sacred use, then the suspension remains valid forever. And you may deduce, third, that the consecration of animals that have been dedicated as to their value can be removed."

III.24 A. *Raba raised the question, "If one said, 'Half of you is betrothed with half of this penny, and half of you is betrothed with the other half,' what is the law? Once he said to her, 'a half penny,' he has divided the money [and there is no valid betrothal], or maybe what he was doing was just counting out the matter [betrothing her for the penny, half for half]? If, then, you should maintain that he was just counting the matter out, what if he said, 'half of you for a penny, and half of you for a penny,' what is the law? Since he has said, 'for a penny,' and 'for a penny,' he has divided his statement [and it is null], or maybe, if the procedure was on a single day, what he was doing was counting out the matter? And if you say that, if it was on the same day, he was counting out the matter, then what if he said, 'half of you for a penny today, and the other half of you for a penny tomorrow'? Since he said, 'tomorrow,' he has divided it up and the transaction is null, or perhaps this is what he meant: the betrothal starts right away but won't be finished until tomorrow? And if he said, 'both halves of you for a penny,' here he certainly has made* the entire proposition all together, or maybe a woman can't be betrothed by halves?"

B. The questions stand.

III.25 A. *Raba raised the question, "What if a man said, 'Your two daughters are betrothed to my two sons for a penny'?* Do we invoke as the operative criterion the one who gives and the one who receives, so there is a valid monetary transaction [one person gives and one person receives the penny], there is no transaction under that sum? Or perhaps we invoke the criterion of the one who betroths and the one who is betrothed, so there is no monetary transaction here?"

B. The question stands.

III.26 A. *R. Pappa raised the question, "What if a man said, 'Your daughter and your cow are mine for a penny'?* Do we interpret the language to mean, 'your daughter for a half-penny and your cow for a half-penny,' or perhaps 'your daughter for a penny, and ownership of title to your cow by the act of drawing it'?"

B. The question stands.

III.27 A. *R. Ashi raised the question, "What if a man said, 'Your daughter and your real estate are mine for a penny'?* Do we interpret the language to mean, 'your daughter for a half-penny and your property for a half-penny,' or perhaps 'your daughter for a penny, and ownership of title to your property through usucaption'?"

B. The question stands.

III.28 A. *There was a man who betrothed a woman with a token of silk. Said Rabbah, "It is not necessary to perform an act of valuation in advance [to inform the woman of its value]."*

B. *R. Joseph said, "It is necessary to perform an act of valuation in advance [to inform the woman of its value]."*

C. If he said to her, "Be betrothed for what is worth any piddling sum," all parties concur that it is not necessary to make an upfront valuation of the silk. If he said to her, "for fifty zuz," and this silk is not worth that much, then it isn't worth that [and the transaction is null]. Where there is a point of difference, it is a case in which he said, "Fifty...," and the silk is worth fifty.

D. *Rabbah said, "It is not necessary to perform an act of valuation in advance, since, after all, it is worthy fifty."*

E. *R. Joseph said, "It is necessary to perform an act of valuation in advance; since a woman is not necessarily an expert in the value of the silk, she will not depend on that, without an expert evaluation."*

F. *There are those who say, even in a case in which the transaction was for any piddling value there is a dispute.*

G. R. Joseph said, "The equivalent of cash must be treated like cash itself: just as a cash transaction must involve an articulated sum, [8A] so cash equivalent must involve an articulated sum."

III.29 A. *Said R. Joseph, "How do I know it? Because it has been taught on Tannaite authority:*

B. "'If there be yet many years, according to them he shall give back the price of his redemption out of the money with which he was acquired' (Lev. 25:51) – he may be acquired by money, not by produce or utensils.

C.   *[Joseph continues,] "Now what is the meaning of* 'produce or utensils'*? Should I say that there is no possibility of acquiring title through a transaction symbolized by these in any way at all? But Scripture has said,* 'he shall return the price of his redemption' (Lev. 25:51), *which serves to encompass a cash equivalent as much as actual cash. And if these are of insufficient value to add up to a penny, then why make reference in particular to produce or utensils, when the same is the rule governing ready cash? So does it not mean that they are worth a penny, but, since they do not add up to an articulated sum, they do not serve that purpose."*

D.   *And the other party?*

E.   *This is the sense of the matter:* he is acquired under the torah governing cash, but he is not acquired under the torah governing produce and utensils. *And what might that involve? Barter.* [Freedman: Whatever is given for a slave, whether money or cash equivalents, must be given in money; produce and utensils can be given in that way, but not as barter, in exchange for the slave, for barter can acquire only movables, but human beings rank as real estate.]

F.   *Well, then, from the perspective of R. Nahman, who has said, "Produce cannot effect a barter" [though a utensil can], what is to be said?*

G.   *Rather, in point of fact, these objects [produce, utensils] are worth at least a penny, and as to your question, then why make reference in particular to produce or utensils, when the same is the rule governing ready cash? The intent of the Tannaite framer is to make the point in the form of a statement, it goes without saying, thus: it is not necessary to make that point in respect to cash, for if it is worth a penny, the transaction is valid, and if not, it is not valid, but even with regard to produce and utensils, where I might argue, since the benefit from these is close at hand, the slave permits himself to be acquired – so we are informed that that is not the case.*

H.   *Said R. Joseph, "How do I know it? Because it has been taught on Tannaite authority:*

I.   **"[If someone said,] 'This calf is for the redemption of my firstborn son,' 'this cloak is for the redemption of my firstborn son,' he has said nothing whatsoever. '...this calf, worth five selas, is for the redemption of my son,' 'this cloak, worth five selas, is for the redemption of my son,' – his son is redeemed [T. Bekh. 6:13].**

J.   *[Joseph continues,] "Now what is the meaning of redemption? Should I say that the calf or cloak is not worth five selas? Then does he have the power to make such a decision [when that is what is owing]? So isn't it a case in which that is so even though they are worth the stated sum, but since there is no fixed value assigned to them that is made articulate, they are not acceptable?"*

K.   *Not at all. In point of fact it is a case in which they do not have the requisite value, but it is for example a case in which the priest accepted the object as full value for the redemption, as in the case of R. Kahana, who took a scarf in exchange for the redemption of the firstborn, saying to the father, "To me it's worth five selas."*

L. *Said R. Ashi, "Well, we make that rule only with someone such as R. Kahana, who is an eminent authority and needs a scarf for his head, but not of everybody in general."*

M. *That is like Mar bar R. Ashi, who bought a scarf from the mother of Rabbah of Kubi worth ten zuz for thirteen.*

III.30 A. Said R. Eleazar, "[If the man said,] 'Be betrothed to me for a maneh,' but he gave her a denar, lo, this woman is betrothed, and he has to make up the full amount that he has promised. *Why is that the rule? Since he referred to a maneh but gave her only a denar, it is as though he had said to her, '...on the stipulation...,' and said R. Huna said Rab, 'Whoever uses the language, "on the stipulation that...," is as though he says, "...as of now."'"* [Freedman: Thus it is as though he said, "be betrothed to me immediately for a denar, on condition that I give you a maneh later."]

B. *An objection was raised:* [If the man said,] "Be betrothed to me for a maneh," and he was continuing to count out the money, and one of the parties wanted to retract, even up to the final denar, he or she has every right to do so.

C. *Here with what situation do we deal? It is one in which he said, "...for this particular maneh...."*

D. *Lo, since the concluding clause makes reference to the language, "...for this particular maneh," it must follow that the introductory clause speaks of a case in which he made reference to a maneh without further specification. For the concluding clause goes as follows in the Tannaite formulation:* if he said to her, "Be betrothed to me for this maneh," and it turns out to be a deficient maneh coin, lacking a denar in value, or a denar of copper, she is not betrothed. If it was just a debased denar, she is betrothed, but he has to exchange it for a good one.

E. *Not at all, the opening clause and the concluding one both deal with a case in which he said, "With this maneh," and the sense is to spell out the transaction and its meaning thus:* if one of the parties wanted to retract, even up to the final denar, he or she has every right to do so. How so? For example, if he said to her, "Be betrothed to me for this maneh." *And that, in point of fact, stands to reason. For if you should imagine that the opening clause deals with a case in which he has not specified the maneh, if in the case in which he has referred to a maneh without further clarification, there is no valid betrothal, if he made reference to "this maneh," can there be any question?*

F. *If that's all you've got to say, then it is hardly a done deal; for the second clause may serve to clarify the first, so that you shouldn't maintain, the first clause deals with a case in which he said "this maneh," but if he did not specify the maneh, it would be a valid betrothal; so the second clause makes specific reference to his saying, "this maneh," from which it follows that the first case refers to an unspecified amount of money, and yet even here the betrothal is null.*

G. *R. Ashi said, "A case in which he is counting out the money is different, because in that case her intent concerns the whole of the sum."*

III.31 A. *As to this a denar of copper, with what sort of a case do we deal? If she knew about its character, well, then she was informed and accepted it!*

B.	*Not at all, the specific reference is required to deal with a case in which he gave it to her at night, or she found it among other coins.*
III.32 A.	*As to this a debased denar, with what sort of a case do we deal? If it is not in circulation, then isn't it in the same class as a copper denar?*
B.	*Said R. Pappa, "It would be one that circulates but only with difficulty."*
III.33 A.	Said R. Nahman, "If he said to her, 'Be betrothed to me with a maneh,' and he gave her a pledge for it, she is not betrothed. [8B] There is no maneh here, there is no pledge here. [Freedman: She neither received the maneh nor did he actually give her a pledge, since that has to be returned.]
B.	*Raba objected to R. Nahman, "If he betrothed her with a pledge, she is betrothed."*
C.	*That refers to a pledge belonging to a third party, in accord with what R. Isaac said, for* said R. Isaac, "How on the basis of Scripture do we know that the creditor acquires title to the pledge [while it is in his possession and so is responsible for any accident that occurs]? Scripture states, 'In any case you shall deliver the pledge again when the sun goes down...and it shall be righteousness for you' (Deut. 24:13). Now if he doesn't have title to the object, whence the righteousness? This proves that the creditor takes the title to the pledge." [Freedman: It is legally his while in his possession, therefore he may validly offer it for a token of betrothal.]
III.34 A.	*The sons of R. Huna bar Abin bought a female slave for copper coins. They didn't have the coins in hand, so they gave as a pledge a silver ingot. The slave's value increased. They came before R. Ammi. He said to them, "There are here neither coins nor an ingot" [and the transaction can be cancelled].*
III.35 A.	*Our rabbis have taught on Tannaite authority:*
B.	**"Be betrothed to me with a maneh," and she took it and threw it into the sea or fire or anywhere where it is lost – she is not betrothed [T. Qid. 2:8A-C].**
III.36 A.	*So if she threw it down before him, is it a valid betrothal? Lo, in so doing, she says to him, "You take it, I don't want it."*
B.	*The formulation means to say, it is not necessary to say..., thus: it is not necessary to say that if she threw it back before him, this is not a valid betrothal, but if she threw it into the sea or into the fire, I might have supposed that, since she now is liable for the money, she has most certainly allowed herself to be betrothed, and the reason that she did what she did is that she was thinking, "I'll test him to see whether he is temperamental or not." So we are informed that that is not the case.*
III.37 A.	*Our rabbis have taught on Tannaite authority:*
B.	**"Be betrothed to me with this maneh" –**
C.	**"Give it to my father or your father" –**
D.	**she is not betrothed.**
E.	**"...on condition that they accept it for me" –**
F.	**she is betrothed [T. Qid. 2:8D-E].**
III.38 A.	*The Tannaite formulation has made reference to "father" to show you the full extent of the application of the rule of the first clause [even then she is not betrothed], and the usage of "your father" shows how far we go in the second clause [that she is then betrothed].*
III.39 A.	**"Be betrothed to me with a maneh" –**

B. "Give them to Mr. So-and-so" –
C. she is not betrothed.
D. "...on condition that Mr. So-and-so accept the money for me," she is betrothed [T. Qid. 2:8D-G].

III.40   A.   *And it was necessary to specify both cases. For if we had been informed of the cases of her referring to her father or his father, it would be in such a case in which if she said, "on condition that they receive them for me," she would have accomplished a valid betrothal, for she would have relied on them, assuming that they would carry out her commission. But that would not be the case when she merely made reference to Mr. So-and-so. And had we been informed of her referring to Mr. So-and-so, it would be in this case in particular that the rule would apply, for if she said, "Give them to Mr. So-and-so," she would not be betrothed, for she would not have known the man well enough to give her the money as a gift. But as for her referring to her father or his father, with whom she is closely related, one might have supposed that her intent was to make a gift of the money to them. So both cases are required.*

III.41   A.   *Our rabbis have taught on Tannaite authority:*
B.   "Be betrothed to me for this maneh" –
C.   "Put it on a rock" –
D.   she is not betrothed.
E.   But if the rock belonged to her, she is betrothed.

III.42   A.   *R. Bibi raised this question:* "If the rock belonged to the two of them, what is the law?"
B.   *That question stands.*

III.43   A.   "Be betrothed for this loaf of bread" –
B.   "Give it to a dog" –
C.   she is not betrothed.
D.   But if the dog belonged to her, she is betrothed.

III.44   A.   *R. Mari raised this question:* "If the dog was running after her, what is the law? *In exchange for the benefit that she gets in being saved from the dog, she has determined to assign to him title over herself? Or perhaps she has the power to say, 'By the law of the Torah, you were obligated to save us?'"*
B.   *That question stands.*

III.45   A.   "Be betrothed to me for this loaf of bread" –
B.   "Give it to that poor man" –
C.   she is not betrothed, even if it was a poor man who depended on her.

III.46   A.   *How come?*
B.   *She can say to the man, "Just as I have an obligation to him, so you have an obligation to him."*

III.47   A.   *There was someone who was selling* **[9A]** *glass beads. A woman came to him. She said to him, "Give me one string."*
B.   *He said to her, "If I give it to you, will you become betrothed to me?"*
C.   *She said to him, "Give it to me, do."*
D.   *Said R. Hama, "Any case in which someone said, 'Give it to me, do,' means absolutely nothing."*

III.48   A.   There was someone who was drinking wine in a wine shop. A woman came. She said to me, "Give me a cup."
B.   *He said to her, "If I give it to you, will you be betrothed to me?"*

C. *She said to him, "Oh, let me have a drink."*

D. *Said R. Hama, "Any case in which someone said, 'Oh, let me have a drink,' means absolutely nothing."*

III.49 A. *There was someone who was throwing down dates from a date palm. A woman came along and said to him, "Throw me down two."*

B. *He said to her, "If I throw them down to you, will you become betrothed to me?"*

C. *She said to him, "Oh, throw them down to me."*

D. *Said R. Zebid, "Every usage such as, 'Oh, throw them down to me,' is null."*

III.50 A. *The question was raised: "What if she said, 'give me,' 'let me drink,' or 'throw them down'?"*

B. Said Rabina, "She is betrothed.

C. R. Sama bar Raqata said, "By the king's crown, she's not betrothed."

D. *And the decided law is, she's not betrothed.*

E. *And the decided law is, silk doesn't have to be evaluated.*

F. *And the decided law is in accord with R. Eleazar.*

G. *And the decided law is in accord with Raba as stated by R. Nahman.*

We now revert to the work of Mishnah exegesis. The task at the outset is clarifying the rule, and I see no premise in play here:

IV.1 A. [**a writ:**] *Our rabbis have taught on Tannaite authority:*

B. A writ: how so?

C. If one wrote on a parchment or on a potsherd, even though they themselves were of no intrinsic value, "Lo, your daughter is betrothed to me," "your daughter is engaged to me," "your daughter is a wife for me" – lo, this woman is betrothed.

D. *Objected R. Zira bar Mammel, "Lo, this writ is not comparable to a writ of purchase, for there, the seller writes, 'My field is sold to me,' while here, it is* the prospective husband who writes, 'Your daughter is consecrated to me.'"

E. *Said Raba, "There the formulation derives from the expression of Scripture, and here the formulation derives from the expression of Scripture. In reference to that other matter it is written,* 'and he sell some of his possessions' (Lev. 25:25), *so it is on the seller that the All-Merciful has made the matter depend. Here it is written,* 'when a man takes a woman' (Deut. 24:1), *so it is on the husband that Scripture had made the matter depend."*

F. *But in that other context, it is also written,* "Men shall buy fields for money" (Jer. 32:44).

G. *Read the letters as though they bore vowels to yield,* "Men shall transmit" [that is, sell].

H. *Well, then, if you read the word to yield "transmit," because it is written* "and he sell," *then here, too, read* "If a man be taken," *since it is written,* "I gave my daughter to this man for a wife" (Deut. 22:16)!

I. *Rather said Raba, "What we have is a law by decree, and our rabbis have then found support for the law in verses of Scripture. Or, if you prefer, I shall say, there, too, it is also written,* 'So I took the deed of the purchase' (Jer. 32:11)." [Freedman: This shows that Jeremiah, the purchaser, received the deed, which must have been drawn up by the vendor.]

IV.2 A. Said Raba said R. Nahman, "If one wrote on a piece of paper or a sherd, even though these were not worth a penny, 'Your daughter is consecrated to me,' 'your daughter is betrothed to me,' 'your daughter is mine as a wife,' whether this is effected through her father or through herself, she is betrothed by the father's consent. That is the case if she had not reached maturity. If one wrote for her on a piece of paper or a sherd, even though these were not worth a penny, 'You are consecrated to me,' 'you are betrothed to me,' 'you are mine as a wife,' whether this is effected through her father or through herself, she is betrothed by her own consent."

IV.3 A. R. Simeon b. Laqish raised the question, "As to a deed of betrothal that was not written for the purpose of betrothing this particular woman, what is the law? *Do we treat as comparable the formation of a marriage and its dissolution, so that,* **[9B]** *just as in the case of its dissolution, we require that the writ of divorce be written for the particular purpose of divorcing this woman, so in the case of the formation of the marriage, we require the writ of betrothal to be written for the particular purpose of betrothing this woman? Or do we treat as comparable the several modes for effecting a betrothal: just as the betrothal by a monetary token need not be accomplished by a token prepared for her sake in particular, so betrothal by a deed does not have to be through a deed prepared for this particular woman?"*

   B. *After he raised the question, he went and solved it: "We do indeed treat as comparable the formation of a marriage and its dissolution. For said Scripture,* 'and when she has gone forth...she may be another man's wife' (Deut. 24:1)."

IV.4 A. *It has been stated:*
   B. If someone wrote a deed of betrothal in her name but without her knowledge and consent –
   C. *Rabbah and Rabina say,* "She is betrothed."
   D. *R. Pappa and R. Sherabayya say,* "She is not betrothed."
   E. *Said R. Pappa,* "*I shall state their scriptural foundations and I shall state mine. I shall state their reason: it is written,* 'and when she has gone forth...she may be another man's wife' (Deut. 24:1). *Scripture treats as comparable the betrothal and the divorce: just as the writ of divorce must be written for the purpose of divorcing this particular woman, though it is written yet without her knowledge and consent, so the writ of betrothal must be written for her own sake, and without her consent. And I shall state the scriptural foundation of my position:* 'and when she has gone forth...she may be another man's wife' (Deut. 24:1). *This treats betrothal as comparable to divorce: just as in the divorce, the knowledge of the giver is required [the husband has obviously to concur], so in betrothal the giver's knowledge is essential [and it is the woman who gives herself].*"
   F. *An objection was raised:* **They write the documents of betrothal and marriage only with the knowledge and consent of both parties [M. B.B. 10:4A].** *Doesn't this mean literally, documents of betrothal and marriage?*
   G. *No, it means deeds of apportionment [designating how much the families are giving to the son and daughter], in accord with what R. Giddal said Rab said, for* said R. Giddal said Rab, "'How much are you going to give to your son?' 'Thus and so.' "How much are you going to give

to your daughter?" 'Thus and so.' If they then arose and declared the formula of sanctification, they have effected transfer of the right of ownership. These statements represent matters in which the right of ownership is transferred verbally."

The exegesis of the next clause once more reveals the presupposition that the Mishnah's rules rest upon Scripture's statements:

V.1 A. **or sexual intercourse:**
      B. *What is the scriptural source of this rule?*
      C. *Said R. Abbahu said R. Yohanan, "Said Scripture, 'If a man be found lying with a woman who had intercourse with a husband' (Deut. 22:22) – this teaches that he became her husband through an act of sexual relations."*
      D. Said R. Zira to R. Abbahu, and some say, R. Simeon b. Laqish to R. Yohanan, "Is then what Rabbi taught unsatisfactory, namely, '"and has intercourse with her" (Deut. 24:1) – this teaches that he became her husband through an act of sexual relations'?"
      E. *If I had to derive proof from that verse, I might have supposed that he first has to betroth her [with a monetary token] and only then have sexual relations with her. So we are informed that that is not the case.*
      F. *Objected R. Abba bar Mammel, "If so, then in the case of the betrothed maiden, where Scripture decrees stoning as the death penalty should she commit adultery, how can we find a concrete case in which that would be the upshot? If he first betrothed her and then had sexual relations, she is in the classification of a woman who has had sexual relations [and stoning is the death penalty for a virgin alone]; if he betrothed her but did not have sexual relations with her, then it is on this hypothesis null anyhow!"*
      G. *Rabbis stated the solution to this conundrum before Abbayye: "You would find such a case if the prospective groom had sexual relations with her through the anus."*
      H. *Said to them Abbayye, "But in point of fact, even Rabbi and rabbis conduct their dispute only with regard to an outsider; but as to the husband, all concur that if the prospective groom had sexual relations with her through the anus, she is classified as one who has had sexual relations."*
      I. *What is the pertinent passage? As has been taught on Tannaite authority:*
      J. **If ten men had intercourse with her and she remained yet a virgin, all of them are put to death by stoning.**
      K. **Rabbi says, "The first is put to death by stoning, and the others by strangulation"** [T. San. 10:9C-D].
      L. *Said R. Nahman bar Isaac, "You would find such a case, for instance, if he betrothed her with a writ.* Since a writ is wholly sufficient to sever the marital bond, it also is sufficient fully to effect it." [Freedman: Yet it might be that money betrothal must be followed by sexual relations.]
      M. And as to the clause, "and has intercourse with her" (Deut. 24:1), *how does R. Yohanan make use of that item?*
      N. *He requires it to show the following: a wife is acquired by sexual relations, but a Hebrew slave girl is not acquired by sexual relations. For it might have entered your mind to maintain that the*

contrary may be inferred by an argument a fortiori from the case of the levirate wife: if a levirate wife, who is not acquired by a money payment is acquired through an act of sexual relations, this woman, who is acquired by a money payment, surely should be acquired by an act of sexual relations!

O. [But the verse is not required for that purpose, for one may well respond:] what characterizes the levirate wife is that she is already subject to the bond to the husband [which obviously does not pertain to the slave girl].

P. *Well, it might have entered your mind to maintain:* since it is written, "If he take another wife" (Ex. 21:10) [in addition to the slave girl] – just as the other is acquired by intercourse, so a Hebrew slave girl would be acquired through an act of sexual relations. *So by this verse we are informed to the contrary.*

Q. *And how does Rabbi deal with this theoretical proposition?*

R. *If it is so [that verse yields only the proposition that sexual relations is a medium of betrothal], Scripture should have written, "and he have sexual relations." Why say, "and he have sexual relations with her"? That yields both points.*

S. *And from the perspective of Raba, who said, "Bar Ahina explained to me, '"When a man takes a woman and has sexual relations with her" (Deut. 24:1) – a betrothal that can be followed by sexual relations is valid, but a betrothal that cannot be followed by sexual relations is not valid,'" what is to be said?*

T. *If that were the sole point, Scripture could have written, "or has sexual relations with her." Why, "and has sexual relations with her"? This yields all the pertinent points.*

U. *And how does Rabbi deal with the phrase, "who had intercourse with a husband"?*

V. *He uses it to teach the following proposition:* a husband's act of anal intercourse renders her a woman who is no longer a virgin, but a third party's action does not.

W. *Well, now, is that Rabbi's position? Hasn't it been taught on Tannaite authority:*

X. **If ten men had intercourse with her and she remained yet a virgin, all of them are put to death by stoning.**

Y. **Rabbi says, "The first is put to death by stoning, and the others by strangulation" [T. San. 10:9C-D].**

Z. [10A] Said R. Zira, "Rabbi concedes that, in regard to the extrajudicial sanction, all have to pay the fine. *And how come this is different from the death penalty [in which case Rabbi classifies her as a virgin]? That is differentiated by Scripture itself:* 'Then the man alone that lay with her shall die' (Deut. 22:25)."

AA. *And rabbis – how do they deal with the word "alone"?*

BB. *They require it in line with that which has been taught on Tannaite authority:*

CC. "'Then they shall both of them die' (Deut. 22:22) means that a penalty is imposed only when the two of them are equal," the words of R. Josiah.

DD. R. Jonathan says, "'Then the man only that lay with her shall die' (Deut. 22:25)."

EE.   *And whence does R. Yohanan derive this thesis?*

FF.   *If it were so, Scripture should have said,* "who has had intercourse with a man." *Why say,* "who has had intercourse with a husband"? *That is to yield both matters.*

We now raise a theoretical question, bearing an explicit, practical consequence. But I cannot state a premise that generates the question, other than that a given action may be divided into beginning, middle, and end:

V.2   A.   *The question was raised:* is it the beginning of the act of intercourse that effects the acquisition of the woman, or the end of the act of sexual relations that does? *The practical difference would derive from a case in which* he performed the initial stage of sexual relations, then she put out her hand and accepted a token of betrothal from someone else; *or the case of whether a high priest may acquire a virgin through an act of sexual relations. What is the rule?*

      B.   Said Amemar in the name of Raba, "Whoever has sexual relations is thinking about the completion of the act of sexual relations [not only the commencement of the act]."

V.3   A.   *The question was raised:* do sexual relations effect a consummated marriage or merely a betrothal? *The practical difference would pertain to the question of* whether he inherits her estate, contracts uncleanness to bury her [if he is a priest], and abrogates her vows. *If you maintain that* sexual relations effect a consummated marriage, then he inherits her estate, contracts uncleanness to bury her [if he is a priest], and abrogates her vows. *If you maintain that* sexual relations effect only betrothal, then he does not inherit her estate, contract uncleanness to bury her [if he is a priest], and abrogate her vows. *What is the rule?*

      B.   Said Abbayye, "**The father retains control of his daughter [younger than twelve and a half] as to effecting any of the tokens of betrothal: money, document, or sexual intercourse. And he retains control of what she finds, of the fruit of her labor, and of abrogating her vows. And he receives her writ of divorce [from a betrothal]. But he does not dispose of the return [on property received by the girl from her mother] during her lifetime. When she is married, the husband exceeds the father, for he disposes of the return [on property received by the girl from her mother] during her lifetime. But he is liable to maintain her, and to ransom her, and to bury her [M. Ket. 4:4].** *Now there is a clear reference to sexual relations, and yet the Tannaite formulation also qualifies the matter,* **When she is married.**"

      C.   *But the clause,* **When she is married,** *may refer to other matters.*

      D.   *Said Raba,* "*Come and take note:* **A girl three years and one day old is betrothed by intercourse. And if a levir has had intercourse with her, he has acquired her. And they are liable on her account because of the law [prohibiting intercourse with] a married woman. And she imparts uncleanness to him who has intercourse with her [when she is menstruating] [10B] to convey uncleanness to the lower as to the upper layer. [If] she was** married to a priest, she eats heave-offering. [If] one of those who are unfit [for marriage] has intercourse with her, he has rendered her unfit to marry into the priesthood. [If one of all those who are forbidden in the Torah to have intercourse with her did so, they are put to death on her account. But she is free of responsibility. If she is younger than that age, intercourse with her is like putting a finger in the eye] [M. Nid. 5:4]. *Now there is a clear reference to sexual relations, and yet the Tannaite formulation also qualifies the matter,* **When she is married."**

E. *This is the sense of the passage: if this intercourse mentioned at the outset is with a priest, then she may eat priestly rations.*

F. *Come and take note:* It is the fact that Yohanan b. Bag Bag sent word to R. Judah b. Beterah in Nisibis, "I heard in your regard that you maintain, an Israelite woman who is betrothed to a priest may eat priestly rations." He replied, "And don't you concur? I have it on good authority in your regard that you are an expert in the innermost chambers of the Torah, knowing how to compose an argument a fortiori. So don't you know the following: 'if a Canaanite slave girl, upon whom an act of sexual relations does not confer the right to eat priestly rations, may eat priestly rations by reason of a money purchase of ownership to her, this one, upon whom an act of sexual relations does confer the right to eat priestly rations, surely should be permitted to eat priestly rations by means of the transfer of a token of betrothal!' But what can I do? For lo, sages have ruled: an Israelite girl betrothed to a priest may not eat priestly rations until she enters the marriage canopy." *Now how are we to understand the case here? If it is sexual relations after the marriage canopy and a betrothal through a monetary token followed by a marriage canopy, in both cases there is obviously no doubt that she may eat priestly rations. If it is intercourse with the marriage canopy or money without, then here there are two operative analogies, there, only one [and how can the rule governing money without a marriage canopy be deduced from the rules governing intercourse with]? So the passage surely must speak to both intercourse and money payment without a marriage canopy. If you maintain that intercourse brings about the consummated marriage, well and good; it is self-evident that sexual relations has a greater effect than money; but if you maintain that it effects only the betrothal, then what makes him certain in the one case and doubtful in the other?*

G. *Said R. Nahman bar Isaac, "In point of fact, I shall explain the matter to you to refer to sexual relations accompanied by the marriage canopy or monetary token without. And as to your objection, here there are two operative analogies, there, only one [and how can the rule governing money without a marriage canopy be deduced from the rules governing intercourse with]? Still there is an argument a fortiori that remains entirely valid. And this is what he sent to him by way of reply:* if a Canaanite slave girl, upon whom an act of sexual relations does not confer the right to eat priestly rations, even via the marriage canopy, may eat priestly rations by reason of a money purchase of ownership to her – without the intrusion of the rite of the marriage canopy, this one, upon whom an act of sexual relations does confer the right to eat priestly rations by means of the marriage canopy, surely should be permitted to eat priestly rations by means of the transfer of a token of betrothal – without the intrusion of the rite of the marriage canopy! But what can I do? For lo, sages have ruled: an Israelite girl betrothed to a priest may not eat priestly rations until she enters the marriage canopy. That is on account of what Ulla said ["By the law of the Torah, a girl of Israelite caste who was betrothed to a priest is permitted to eat priestly rations: 'But if a priest buy any soul, the purchase of his money...' (Lev. 22:11) – *and this one also falls into the class of* 'purchased of his money.' And what is the reason that they have said that she may not eat priestly rations? Lest a cup of wine in the status of priestly rations be mixed for her in her father's house and she share it with her brother or sister who are not in the priestly caste"]."

H.   *And Ben Bag Bag [doesn't he accept the argument a fortiori]?*

I.   *In the acquisition of the gentile slave girl, the man has left out nothing in acquiring her [once he pays the money, she is his], but here, he has left out part of the process of acquiring her [for only after the marriage canopy does he inherit her and so forth].*

J.   *Rabina said, "On the basis of the law of the Torah, [Ben Bag Bag] was quite certain that she may eat priestly rations, but it was only with respect to the position of rabbinical law that he sent word to him claiming that she is forbidden to do so, and this is the character of his inquiry:* 'I have heard in your regard that you maintain, an Israelite woman betrothed to a priest may eat priestly rations, thus disregarding the possibility of nullification' [for example, through discovery of an invalidating cause to nullify the betrothal; this then has no bearing on the question of status conferred by intercourse, since all concur that a betrothed girl may eat priestly rations so far as the law of the Torah is concerned (Freedman)]. And he sent word back, 'And don't you take it the same position? I have it on good authority in your regard that you are an expert in the innermost chambers of the Torah, knowing how to compose an argument a fortiori. So don't you know the following: if a Canaanite slave girl, upon whom an act of sexual relations does not confer the right to eat priestly rations, may eat priestly rations by reason of a money purchase of ownership to her, *and we don't take account of the possibility of nullification of the betrothal* – this one, upon whom an act of sexual relations does confer the right to eat priestly rations, surely should be permitted to eat priestly rations by means of the transfer of a token of betrothal – *and we shouldn't take account of the possibility of nullification of the betrothal.* But what can I do? For lo, sages have ruled: an Israelite girl betrothed to a priest may not eat priestly rations **[11A]** until she enters the marriage canopy, on account of what Ulla said ["By the law of the Torah, a girl of Israelite caste who was betrothed to a priest is permitted to eat priestly rations: 'But if a priest buy any soul, the purchase of his money...' (Lev. 22:11) – *and this one also falls into the class of* 'purchased of his money.' And what is the reason that they have said that she may not eat priestly rations? Lest a cup of wine in the status of priestly rations be mixed for her in her father's house and she share it with her brother or sister who are not in the priestly caste"].'"

K.   And Ben Bag Bag?

L.   *He does not concede that a possibility of invalidating the transaction can take place in the sale of slaves. For if these were defects that were visible, then he has seen them and accepted them; if it was on account of defects that were concealed, what difference does it make to him? He wants the slave for work, and it wouldn't matter to him. If the slave turns out to be a thief or a rogue, he still belongs to the purchaser [since most slaves are that way anyhow]. So what can you say, that he turned out to be a thug or an outlaw? These would be known defects.*

M.   *Now since both parties concur that a betrothed woman may not eat priestly rations, what's at issue?*

N.   At issue is a case in which the husband accepted the body defects; or the father handed her over to the husband's messengers to be taken to her husband's house; or if the father's messengers were en route with the husband's messengers. [In the first case, Ben Bag Bag lets her eat priestly rations; in Judah b. Batera's view, she cannot do so, by reason of Ulla's explanation; in the second, Ulla's consideration no longer pertains, there being no family around, but there can be nullification; and the third is governed by the same rule (Freedman).]

The inquiry into the next clause of the Mishnah's rule concerns the premise of the position of one of the parties to the dispute. They are assumed to impute to the woman a view of herself, which is articulated:

VI.1 A.   **Through money: The House of Shammai say, "For a denar or what is worth a denar":**

B.   *What is the operative consideration in the mind of the House of Shammai?*

C.   Said R. Zira, "For a woman is particular about herself and is not going to allow herself to become betrothed for less than a denar."

D.   *Said to him Abbayye, "Well, then what about the daughters of R. Yannai, who were so particular about themselves that they would not become betrothed for less than a tubful of denarii! If she should put out her hand and accept a coin from a stranger as a token of betrothal, is she then betrothed?!"*

E.   *He said to him, "Well, if she put out her hand and accepted the token, I don't take that position. I speak of a case in which he conducts the betrothal at night [so doesn't know what she got] or if she appointed an agent."*

F.   *R. Joseph said, "The operative consideration in the mind of the House of Shammai accords with what R. Judah said R. Assi said, for* said R. Judah said R. Assi, "Whenever 'money' is mentioned in the Torah, what is meant is Tyrian coinage; when rabbis speak of money, they refer to the coinage that circulates in the provinces. [The betrothal token is scriptural, so it must be a valuable coin, not a copper coin, hence a denar.]"

VI.2 A.   *Reverting to the body of the foregoing:* said R. Judah said R. Assi, "Whenever 'money' is mentioned in the Torah, what is meant is Tyrian coinage; when rabbis speak of money, they refer to the coinage that circulates in the provinces."

B.   *Is this a ubiquitous principle?* Lo, there is the case of a claim, concerning which Scripture states, "If a man shall deliver to his neighbor money or utensils to keep" (Ex. 22:6), *and yet we have learned in the Mishnah:* **The oath imposed by judges [is required if] the claim is [at least] two pieces of silver, and the concession [on the part of the defendant is that he owes] at least a penny's [perutah's] worth [M. Shebu. 6:1A].**

C.   *There the governing analogy is utensils:* just as utensils are two, so the coins must be two, just as money speaks of what has intrinsic worth, so utensils speak of something that is of worth.

D.   Lo, there is the case of a second tithe, concerning which Scripture states, "And you shall turn it into money and bind up the money in your hand," *and yet we have learned in the Mishnah:* **One who exchanges a [silver] sela [sanctified as] second tithe [for other coins] in Jerusalem – The House of Shammai say, "The whole sela [he receives must consist] of [copper] coins."** And the House of Hillel say, "[The sela he receives may consist] of one shekel of silver [coins] and one shekel of [copper] coins." The disputants before the sages say, "[The sela may consist] of three silver denars and [one] denar of [copper] coins." R. Aqiba says, "[The sela may consist] of three silver dinars and a quarter [of the fourth denar must consist of] [copper] coins." R. Tarfon says, "[The fourth denar may consist of] four aspers of silver [equal to four-fifths of the denar's value and the remaining asper must be of copper]." Shammai says, "Let him deposit it in a shop and consume its value [in produce]" [M. M.S. 2:9].

E.   Reference to "money" is inclusionary.

F.   What about what has been consecrated, concerning which it is written, "Then he shall give the money and it shall be confirmed in his ownership," in which regard Samuel said, "If what has been consecrated is worth a maneh and it is redeemed with what is equivalent in worth to a penny, it is validly redeemed"?

G.   *In that case, we deduce the meaning of "money" from the sense of the word when it is used in reference to tithes.*

H.   Lo, there is the case of a token of betrothal given to a woman, concerning which Scripture states, "When a man takes a wife and marries her," and we have deduced the meaning of "take" from the transaction of the field of Ephron, *and yet we have learned in the Mishnah:* **And the House of Hillel say, "For a perutah or what is worth a perutah"**! *Is the upshot, then, that we shall have to concede R. Assi has made his ruling in accord with the position of the House of Shammai?*

I.   *Rather, if such a statement was made, this is how it was made:* said R. Judah said R. Assi, "Whenever 'money' in a fixed amount is mentioned in the Torah, what is meant is Tyrian coinage; when rabbis speak of money, they refer to the coinage that circulates in the provinces."

J.   *Well, then, what does he tell us that we don't already know!? We have a Tannaite statement as follows:* **The five selas for redeeming the firstborn son are in Tyrian coinage. (1) The thirty for the slave [Ex. 21:32], and (2) the fifty to be paid by the rapist and seducer**

[Ex. 22:15-16, Deut. 22:28-29], and (3) the hundred to be paid by the gossip [Deut. 22:19] – all are to be paid in the value of sheqels of the sanctuary, in Tyrian coinage. And everything which is to be redeemed [is redeemed] in silver or its equivalent, except for sheqel-dues [M. Bekh. 8:7]!

K. *It is necessary to make that statement to cover the rule,* when rabbis speak of money, they refer to the coinage that circulates in the provinces, *which we have not learned in the Mishnah. For we have learned in the Mishnah,* **He who boxes the ear of his fellow pays him a sela** [M. B.Q. 8:6A]. *You should not suppose that the sela under discussion is four zuz, but it is half a zuz, for people call half a zuz a sela.*

VI.3 A. R. Simeon b. Laqish says, *"The operative consideration behind the ruling of the House of Shammai is in accord with Hezekiah, for* said Hezekiah, 'Said Scripture, "then shall he let her be redeemed" (Ex. 21:8) – this teaches that she deducts from her redemption money and goes out free.' *Now if you maintain that the master gives her a denar [when he buys her, which would be the counterpart to the token of betrothal], then there is no problem; but if you say it was a mere penny, then what deduction can be made from a penny?"*

B. But maybe this is the sense of what the All-Merciful has meant to say: in a case in which he gave her a denar, there is a deduction made until a penny is left; but if he gave her a penny, there is no deduction made at all?

C. [12A] *Don't let it enter your mind. For it is comparable to the act of designating a Hebrew handmaid [for betrothal, once the Hebrew slave girl has been purchased; there is no further token of betrothal required]: just as, in the case of such a designation, even though the master can designate her or refrain from doing so, as he prefers, where he doesn't designate her for marriage, the sale is invalid, so here, too, where we cannot make such a deduction, the sale is invalid. And the House of Shammai derive the rule governing the betrothal of a woman from the rule governing the Hebrew slave girl. Just as a Hebrew slave girl cannot be acquired for a penny, so a woman cannot be betrothed for a penny.*

D. *Well, why not say half a denar or two pennies?*

E. *Once the penny was excluded as a measure, the matter was set at a denar.*

VI.4 A. Raba said, *"This is the operative consideration for the position of the House of Shammai: so that Israelite women won't be treated as ownerless property."*

I discern no premise in what follows, only an exegetical program of limited dimensions:

VII.1 A. **And the House of Hillel say, "For a perutah or what is worth a perutah":**

B. *R. Joseph considered ruling, "A penny, of any sort [however debased]."*

C. *Said to him Abbayye, "But lo, there is a Tannaite clarification of this matter in so many words:* **And how much is a perutah? One-eighth of an Italian issar.** *And should you say, that ruling addresses the time of Moses, while at the present time, it is as generally valued, lo, when R. Dimi came,* he said, 'R. Simai estimated the value in his time to determine how much a penny is, and determined, an eighth of an

Italian issar,' *and when Rabin came,* he said, 'R. Dosetai, R. Yannai, and R. Oshayya estimated how much a penny is worth, and determined, a sixth of an Italian issar.' "

D. Said R. Joseph to him, "If so, then, that is in line with the following Tannaite statement: Go and estimate, how many pennies are there in two selas? More than 2000. *Now, since there are not even 2,000, can the Tannaite call it more than 2,000?"*

E. *Said to them a certain sage, "I have the Tannaite formulation as,* near two thousand."

F. *One way or the other, it is only 1,536.*

G. *Since it goes beyond half [which would be a thousand], it is classified as "close to 2,000."*

VII.2 A. *Reverting to the body of the foregoing: when R. Dimi came,* he said, "R. Simai estimated the value in his time to determine how much a penny is, and determined, an eighth of an Italian issar," *and when Rabin came,* he said, "R. Dosetai, R. Yannai, and R. Oshayya estimated how much a penny is worth, and determined, a sixth of an Italian issar."

B. *Said Abbayye to R. Dimi, "May we then propose that you and Rabin differ in the same way as the following Tannaite authority, as has been taught on Tannaite authority":*

C. **[Following Tosefta's version:] "A perutah [translated above: penny] of which they have spoken is one out of eight pennies [perutot] to an issar; an issar is one twenty-fourth of a denar; six silver maahs are a denar; a silver maah is two pondions; a pondion is two issars; an issar is two mismasin; a mismas is two quntronin; a quntron is two pennies [perutot].**

D. **"Rabban Simeon b. Gamaliel says, 'The perutah of which they have spoken is one of six pennies [perutot] to the issar; there are three hadrasin to a maah; two hannassin to a hadrash; two shemanin to a hannas; two pennies [perutot] to a shemen' [T. B.B. 5:11-12].**

E. *"So may we then say that the one authority concurs with the initial Tannaite authority, and Rabin accords with Rabban Simeon b. Gamaliel?"*

F. *He said to him, "Whether in accord with my view of that of Rabin, we concur with the initial Tannaite statement here, and there is nonetheless no contradiction; in the one case, the issar bears full value, in the other, it had depreciated. In the one case the issar bears full value, twenty-four being the equivalent to a zuz; in the other case it had depreciated, thirty-two for a zuz."*

VII.3 A. Said Samuel, "If one betrothed a woman with a date, even if a kor of dates were at a denar, she is deemed betrothed, *for we take account of the possibility that in Media it may be worth a penny."*

B. *But lo, we have learned in the Mishnah:* **And the House of Hillel say, "For a perutah or what is worth a perutah"**!

C. *No problem, the one speaks of a betrothal that is beyond all doubt, the other, a betrothal that is subject to doubt.*

VII.4 A. *There was someone who betrothed a woman with a bundle of tow cotton [Freedman]. In session before Rab, R. Shimi bar Hiyya examined the question: "If it contains the value of a penny, she would be betrothed, if not, not."*

B. *...if not, not? But didn't Samuel say, "for we take account of the possibility that in Media it may be worth a penny"?*

C. *No problem, the one speaks of a betrothal that is beyond all doubt, the other, a betrothal that is subject to doubt.*

VII.5 A. *There was someone who betrothed a woman with a black marble stone. In session, R. Hisda estimated its value: "If it contains the value of a penny, she would be betrothed, if not, not."*

B. *...if not, not? But didn't Samuel say, "for we take account of the possibility that in Media it may be worth a penny"?*

C. *R. Hisda does not view matters as does Samuel.*

D. *Said his mother to him, "But lo, on that day on which he betrothed her, it was worth a penny."*

E. *He said to her, "You don't have the power to prohibit her from marrying the other fellow [to whom in the interval she had been betrothed].* **[12B]** *For isn't this parallel to the case of Judith, wife of R. Hiyya? She suffered terrible pains in childbirth [and didn't want more children]. She said to him, 'Mother told me, "Your father accepted a token of betrothal on your behalf from someone else when you were a child."' He said to her, 'Your mother doesn't have the power to forbid you to me.'"*

F. *Said rabbis to R. Hisda, "Why not! Lo, there are witnesses in Idit who know as fact that, on that day, it was worth a penny."*

G. *"Well, anyhow, they're not here with us now! Isn't that in line with what R. Hanina said, for said R. Hanina, 'Her witnesses are in the north, but she is nonetheless forbidden.'"*

H. *Abbayye and Raba do not concur with that view of R. Hisda:* "If rabbis made a lenient ruling in the context of a captive woman [to which Hanina's statement referred], in which case the woman was humiliated in captivity of kidnappers, should we make an equivalently lenient ruling in the case of a married woman?"

I. *Members of that family remained in Sura, and rabbis kept away from them, not because they concurred with the position of Samuel, but because they concurred with the view of Abbayye and Raba.*

VII.6 A. *There was someone who in the marketplace betrothed a woman with a myrtle branch. R. Aha bar Huna sent word to R. Joseph, "In such a case, what is the ruling?"*

B. *He sent back, "Flog him in accord with the position of Rab, but require him to issue a writ of divorce in accord with the position of Samuel."*

C. *For Rab would flog someone who betrothed through an act of sexual relations, and one who betrothed in the marketplace, and one who betrothed without prior negotiation, one who nullified a writ of divorce, one who called into question the validity of a divorce, one who offends an agent of the rabbis, one who permitted a rabbinical ban of ostracism to remain upon him for thirty days without coming to the court to ask for its removal, and a son-in-law who lives in his father-in-law's house [prior to the consummation of the marriage].*

D. *If he actually lives there but not if he merely goes by there? And lo, there was someone who merely passed by the doorway of his father-in-law's house, and R. Sheshet ordered him flogged!*

E. *That man was suspect of illicit relations with his mother-in-law.*

F.   *The Nehardeans said, "In none of these cases did Rab order a flogging except in the case of the ones who betrothed through an act of sexual relations or did so without prior negotiations."*

G.   *There are those who say, "Even in the case of preliminary negotiation, on account of the possibility of licentiousness."*

VII.7 A.   *There was someone who in the marketplace betrothed a woman with a mat made of myrtle twigs. They said to him, "But it's not worth a penny!"*

B.   *He said to them, "Let her be betrothed for the four zuz that it contains [wrapped up in the mat]."*

C.   *She took the mat and shut up.*

D.   *Said Raba, "You have then a case of* silence following receipt of funds, and that kind of silence is null."

E.   *Said Raba, "How do I know it? Because it has been taught on Tannaite authority:*

F.   *"'Take* this sela as a bailment,' and then he said to her, 'Be betrothed to me with it' – if this was at the moment that he handed over the money, she is betrothed; if it was afterward, if she wanted, she is betrothed, but if she didn't want, she is not betrothed [T. Qid. 2:7A-D].

G.   *"Now what is the meaning of* if she wanted, *and what is the meaning of* if she didn't want? *Shall we say that the meaning of,* if she wanted, *is, she said yes, and the meaning of* if she didn't want *is, she said no? Then it would follow that the first clause bears the meaning,* [13A] *even if she said no, it is a valid act of betrothal. But why should that be the case? Lo, she has said no! Rather, is not the meaning of,* if she wanted, *she said yes, and would not the language,* if she didn't want, *mean, she remained silent? Then it would follow,* silence following receipt of funds is null."

H.   *The following challenge was raised at Pum Nahara in the name of R. Huna b. R. Joshua, "But are the cases truly comparable? In that other case, the man handed over the money under the torah that governs bailments, and she reasoned, 'If I throw it away and it is broken, I am liable for it.' But here he handed it over under the torah of betrothals, and if it were the fact that she didn't concur, she should throw the money away."*

I.   *R. Ahai objected, "So are all women such experts in the law? Here, too, she could have thought, 'If I throw it away and it is broken, I am liable for it.'"*

J.   *R. Aha bar Rab sent word to Rabina, "So in such a case, what's the law?"*

K.   *He sent word to him, "We have heard no objection such as what R. Huna b. R. Joshua has raised, but you, who have heard it, have to pay full attention to it."*

VII.8 A.   *There was a woman who was selling silk skeins [Freedman]. Someone came along and grabbed a piece of silk from her. She said to him, "Give it back to me."*

B.   *He said to her, "If I give it back to you, will you be betrothed to me?"*

C.   *She took it from him and shut up.*

D.   *And said R. Nahman, "She has every right to claim, 'Yes, I took it, but I took what was mine!'"*

E.   *Raba objected to R. Nahman, "* If someone betrothed a woman with stolen property, or with what was gained by violence or by theft, or if he grabbed a sela from her hand and betrothed her with it, she is betrothed [T. Qid. 4:5A-C]."

F. *"In that case, it was a situation in which there was negotiation about marriage."*

G. *"And how do you know that we differentiate between a case in which there had been negotiation on marriage and one in which there had not? As it has been taught on Tannaite authority:* If he said to her, 'Take this sela, which I owe you,' and then he said to her, 'Be betrothed to me with it,' if this was at the moment that he handed over the money, if she wanted, she is betrothed, and if she didn't want, she is not betrothed. If this was after the handing over of the money, even if she wanted, she is not betrothed. *Now what is the meaning of* if she wanted, *and what is the meaning of* if she didn't want? *Shall we say that the meaning of,* if she wanted, *is, she said yes, and the meaning of* if she didn't want *is, she said no? Then it would follow that if she kept silent, it would have been a valid betrothal? Then the Tannaite formulation should be simply,* she is betrothed, *without further specification, just as in the prior instance. So we must say, the language,* if she wanted, *means, she said yes, and the language,* if she wanted, *means, she kept silent. And the Tannaite rule is,* she is not betrothed. *How come? She has every right to claim,* 'Yes, I took it, but I took what was mine!' *Nonetheless, there is a problem in connection with the language,* with stolen property, or with what was gained by violence or by theft and betrothed her with it, she is betrothed. *So doesn't it follow that the one speaks of a case in which there had been prior negotiations about marriage, the other of a case in which there had been none?"*

VII.9 A. *When R. Assi died, rabbis assembled to collect his traditions. Said one of the rabbis, R. Jacob by name, "This is what R. Assi said R. Mani said,* 'Just as a woman may not be acquired with less than a penny, so real estate cannot be acquired for less than a penny.'"

B. *They said to him, "But hasn't it been taught on Tannaite authority:* Even though a woman may not be acquired with less than a penny, real estate can be acquired for less than a penny?"

C. *He said to them, "When that Tannaite ruling was set forth, it had to do with barter, for it has been taught on Tannaite authority:* Transfer of title may take place with a utensil even though the utensil is not worth a penny."

VII.10 A. *Further, in session they said, "Lo, in regard to what R. Judah said* Samuel said, 'Whoever doesn't know the essentials of writs of divorce and betrothals should not get involved in them,' said R. Assi said R. Yohanan, 'And such folk are more of a problem to the world than the generation of the flood, for it has been stated, "By swearing, lying, killing, stealing, and committing adultery, they spread forth and blood touches blood"' (Hos. 4:2)."

B. *How does that verse bear the alleged implication?*

C. *It is in line with the way in which R. Joseph interpreted the verse in his translation, "They beget children by their neighbors' wives, piling evil upon evil."*

D. [Reverting to A:] "And it is written, 'Therefore shall the land mourn and everyone who dwells therein shall languish, with the beasts of the field and the fowl of heaven, yes the fish of the sea also shall be taken away' (Hos. 4:3). By contrast, with respect to the generation of the flood, there was no decree against the fish of the sea: 'of all that was in the dry land died' (Gen. 7:22) – but not the fish in the sea; here even the fish in the sea are covered."

E. *But might one say that that penalty was inflicted only when all of the sins listed were committed [not only adultery]?*

F. *Don't imagine it! For it is written,* "For because of swearing the land mourns" (Jer. 23:10) [a single crime suffices (Freedman)].

G. *Well, maybe swearing stands on its own terms, and the others combined on theirs?*

H. **[13B]** Is it written, "and they spread forth"? What is written is, "they spread forth."

VII.11 A. *Further, in session they said, "Lo, in regard to what we have learned in the Mishnah,* **The woman who brought her sin-offering, and died – let the heirs bring her burnt-offering. [If she brought] her burnt-offering and died, the heirs do not bring her sin-offering [M. Qin. 2:5/O-Q),** and, in which regard, said R. Judah said Samuel, 'That rule applies to a case in which she had designated the offering while she was yet alive, but not otherwise,' *therefore taking the view that the obligation incurred by a debt is not based on the law of the Torah* [Freedman: if a man borrows money, we do not say that his property is automatically mortgaged for its repayment, so that in the event of his death, his heirs are liable on the law of the Torah, since they inherit mortgaged property unless the debtor explicitly mortgages his goods in a bond; here, too, the woman is under an obligation to God to bring a sacrifice, yet, since she did not designate an animal for it, no obligation lies on the heirs] – said R. Assi said R. Yohanan, 'That rule applies even though she had not designated the offering while she was yet alive, but not otherwise,' *therefore taking the view that the obligation incurred by a debt is based on the law of the Torah – in that context, lo, the dispute was set forth in another connection [and hardly required repetition].*

B. "*For Rab and Samuel both say,* 'A debt attested only orally cannot be collected from the heirs or the purchasers of the indentured property,' *and both R. Yohanan and R. Simeon b. Laqish say,* 'A debt attested only orally can be collected from the heirs or the purchasers of the indentured property.'"

C. *Well, as a matter of fact, both versions of the dispute had to be set forth. For if it had been stated in the latter case only, I should have supposed that it is only in that case that Samuel took the position that he did, because it is not a debt the type of which is set forth in the Torah, but in the other case, I might have said that he concurs with R. Yohanan and R. Simeon b. Laqish. And if it had been stated in the former case only, I should have supposed that it is only in that case that R. Yohanan took the position that he did, because a class of debt that is known in Scripture is equivalent to one that is written out in a bond, but in the latter case, I might have supposed that he concurs with Samuel. So both versions of the dispute had to be set forth.*

D.   Said R. Pappa, "The decided law is, 'A loan that is only verbal is collected from an estate but may not be collected from purchasers [of the property from the now deceased testator].

E.   "It is collected from an estate, *since the indenture derives from the Torah,* but it may not be collected from purchasers [of the property from the now deceased testator], *since it will not be widely known [so the purchasers cannot protect themselves].*"

VIII.1 A. **And she acquires herself through a writ of divorce or through the husband's death:**

B.   *Well, there is no problem identifying the source for the rule concerning divorce, since it is written, "And he shall write for her a writ of divorce"* (Deut. 24:1). *But as to the husband's death, how do we know it?*

C.   *It is a matter of reasoning:* he binds her [to himself, forbidding her to all other men] so he can free her.

D.   *Well, what about the case of consanguineous relations, from whom he forbids her, but for whom he cannot release her [even after he dies]?*

E.   *Rather, since the All-Merciful has said,* a levirate widow without children is forbidden, it must follow that, lo, if she has children [after the husband's death] she is permitted [to remarry].

F.   *Well, maybe, if she has no children, she is forbidden to everybody but not forbidden to the levir, and if she has children, she is forbidden to everybody without exception?*

G.   *Rather, since Scripture has said that a widow is forbidden to marry a high priest, lo, she is permitted to marry an ordinary priest [and any other man].*

H.   *Well, maybe, she is forbidden by a negative commandment to a high priest but to everyone else by a positive commandment?*

I.   *So what's this alleged positive commandment doing here? If her husband's death matters, she should be wholly free to remarry, but if not, let her stay as she was.* [Freedman: As a married woman, she is forbidden to others by a negative commandment, there are no grounds for supposing that her husband's death leaves the prohibition but changes its nature.]

J.   *Well, how come not? The husband's death can remove her from liability to the death penalty and place her under the prohibition involved in an affirmative commandment. It would then be comparable to the case of animals that have been consecrated but then rendered unfit for sacrifice. Before they were unfit, they would be subject to sacrilege and not sheared or worked with; when redeemed, they are no longer subject to the laws of sacrilege, but they still are not to be sheared or worked with.*

K.   Rather, Scripture said, "What man is there...his house, lest he die in battle and another man take her" (Deut. 20:7).

L.   *Objected R. Shisha b. R. Idi, "But might I then say, who is 'another man'? It is the levir."*

M.   Said R. Ashi, "There are two replies in this matter. *The first is, the levir is not classified as 'another.'* Furthermore, it is written, 'and if the latter husband hate her and write her a writ of divorce...or if the latter husband die...' (Deut. 24:3) – *so death is treated as wholly comparable to a writ of divorce; just as the writ of divorce leaves her completely free, so death leaves her completely free.*"

Mishnah exegesis once more reverts to the familiar question concerning the scriptural basis for the Mishnah's rule:

IX.1 A. **The deceased childless brother's widow is acquired through an act of sexual relations:**

B. *How do we know that she is acquired by an act of sexual relations?*

C. Said Scripture, **[14A]** "Her husband's brother shall go in to her and take her to him as a wife" (Deut. 25:5).

D. *Might I say that she is his wife in every regard [so that she can be acquired by money or a deed]?*

E. *Don't let it enter your mind, for it has been taught on Tannaite authority:* Might one suppose that a money payment or a writ serve to complete the bond to her, as much as sexual relations does? Scripture says, "Her husband's brother shall go in to her and take her to him as a wife" (Deut. 25:5) – sexual relations complete the relationship to her, but a money payment or a writ do not do so.

F. *Might I say, what is the meaning of* take her to him as a wife? *Even against her will he enters into levirate marriage with her?*

G. *If so, Scripture should have said, "and take her...." Why say, "and take her to wife? It bears both meanings just now under discussion.*

X.1 A. **And acquires [freedom for] herself through a rite of removing the shoe:**

B. *How do we know it?*

C. Said Scripture, "And his name shall be called in Israel, the house of him who has had his shoe removed" (Deut. 25:12) – once his shoe has been removed by her, she is permitted for all Israel.

D. *Is this the purpose of the word "Israel" in this context? Isn't it required in line with that which R. Samuel bar Judah taught as a Tannaite statement: "'In Israel' (Deut. 25:7) means that the rite of removing the shoe must be done in front of a court of Israelites by birth, not a court of proselytes"?*

E. *There are two references in context to "in Israel."*

F. *Nonetheless, it is required in line with that which has been taught on Tannaite authority:* said R. Judah, "Once we were in session before R. Tarfon, and a levirate woman came to perform the rite of removing the shoe, and he said to us, 'All of you respond: "The man who has had his shoe removed"' (Deut. 25:10)."

G. *That is derived from the formulation, "and his name shall be called" [with "in Israel" free for its own purpose].*

XI.1 A. **and through the levir's death:**

B. *How do we know it?*

C. It derives from an argument a fortiori: if a married woman, who, if she commits adultery, is put to death through strangulation, is released by the death of the husband, a levirate widow, who is forbidden merely by a negative commandment [from marrying someone else] all the more so should be freed by the death of the levir!

D. But what distinguishes a married woman is that she goes forth with a writ of divorce. Will you say the same of this woman, who does not go forth with a writ of divorce?

E.   But she, too, goes forth with the rite of removing the shoe [which is comparable to a writ of divorce].

F.   Rather: what is special about the married woman is that the one who forbids her to other men also frees her [which is not the case with the levirate widow, since she is forbidden to others because of her childless deceased husband, but that the death of the levir frees her has yet to be proved].

G.   *Said R. Ashi, "Lo, here, too, he who forbids her also frees her: the levir forbids her, the levir frees her"* [since if there were no levir, her husband's death alone would have freed her, so he really is responsible (Freedman)].

XI.2 A.   A married woman also should be freed through the rite of removing the shoe, by reason of an argument a fortiori based on the levirate widow, namely: If a levirate wife, who is not freed by a divorce, is freed by the rite of removing the shoe, then this one [the levirate wife] who is freed by divorce surely should be freed by a rite of removing the shoe. Thus we are informed that that is not the case. Said Scripture, "Then he shall write her a writ of divorce" (Deut. 24:1) – through a writ he divorces her, but he doesn't divorce her in any other way.

B.   Then a levirate widow should go forth through a writ of divorce, by reason of an argument a fortiori, namely: if a married woman, who does not go forth through the rite of removing the shoe, goes forth through a writ of divorce, this one, who does go forth through the rite of removing the shoe, surely should go forth with a writ of divorce. So Scripture says to the contrary, "Thus it shall be done" (Deut. 25:9) – *this is the only possible way, and in any circumstance in which there is a clear indication of what is indispensable, an argument a fortiori is not composed.*

C.   Then what about the case of the Day of Atonement, in connection with which there is clear scriptural reference to "lot" and "statute" (Lev. 16:9) [and "statute" is a sign of an indispensable detail], *and it has been taught on Tannaite authority:* "And Aaron shall present the goat upon which the lot fell for the Lord and make it a sin-offering" (Lev. 16:9) – the lot is what designates the goat as a sin-offering, and mere designation of the classification of the goat is not what turns it into a sin-offering, nor does the priest designate it as a sin-offering. For one might have argued to the contrary: is it not a matter of logic? If in a case in which the lot does not consecrate an offering for a particular purpose, the designation does consecrate the offering for a particular purpose, in a case in which the lot does consecrate the offering for a particular purpose, is it not a matter of logic that the designation for a given purpose serves also to designate what is offered for a given purpose? For that reason Scripture states, "And Aaron shall present the goat upon which the lot fell for the Lord and make it a sin-offering" (Lev. 16:9) – the lot is what designates the goat as a sin-offering, and mere designation of the classification of the goat is not what turns it into a sin-offering. *So the operative consideration is that Scripture is what excludes that possibility. Then if it were not for that, we should have composed an* argument *a fortiori*, even though the word "statute" is written in that connection!

D.   [There is another reason altogether, namely,] said Scripture, "Then he shall write her a writ of divorce" (Deut. 24:1), for her, not for a levirate widow.

E.   *But might one say, "for her," meaning, for her in particular?*

F.   *There are two Scripture references to "for her."*

G.   *Nonetheless, they are needed for another purpose, one reference to, "for her," means, for her sake in particular, and the other reference to "her" meaning, but not for her and another woman.*

H.   Rather, said Scripture, "The house of him that has had a shoe removed" *– a shoe alone permits her to remarry, nothing else.*

I.   *Well, is that the purpose served by the reference to shoe? Isn't it necessary in line with that which has been taught on Tannaite authority?*

J.   *"...pull the sandal off his foot":*

K.   **I know only that the rule speaks of a sandal belonging to him. How on the basis of Scripture do I know that it is all right if the sandal belongs to someone else?**

L.   **Scripture says, "pull the sandal" – under any circumstances.**

M.   **If so, why does Scripture say, "his sandal"?**

N.   **It excludes the case of a large shoe, in which one cannot actually walk, or a small one, which does not cover the larger part of his foot, [14B] or a slipper lacking a heel. [In such instances the act of removing the shoe is null.] [Sifré Deut. CCXCI:II.2].**

O.   *If so, Scripture should have said merely "shoe." Why "the shoe"? To yield both propositions.*

It is difficult for me to discern a rich and diverse corpus of premises and presuppositions. To the contrary, when we have completed the familiar program, [1] scriptural origins, and [2] the superiority of Scripture over logic, we find an exegetical program that rests upon practical logic and applied reason, but little evidence of deep layers of thinking upon which the structure is built. A brief review of what we have examined shows how little we derive when we address our question to this Talmudic discussion.

I.1 presents an exegetical question for clarifying the formulation of the commencement of the Mishnah tractate. Nos. 2-4, 5-6 follow suit. II.1+2-3, 4-5 work on the problem of the scriptural origins of the Mishnah's rule. III.1-2, 3, 4-5 go through the same exercise. No. 6, with its talmud at Nos. 7-8, and No. 9, with its talmud at Nos. 10-12, then move on to a Tannaite complement to the Mishnah paragraph. Nos. 13+14-17 then extend the discussion of the foregoing set of entries in more general terms. Nos. 18-19 proceed to a variety of important theoretical questions, well within the framework of the foregoing. Nos. 20-25 present a sequence of systematic theoretical problems in the name of a single individual. There follow further theoretical questions along the same lines, Nos. 26-27. Then comes a case, No. 28, which yields a further theoretical problem, extending beyond the range of our particular topic. No. 29 extends the foregoing. No. 30, with a talmud at Nos. 31-2, resumes the analysis of theoretical questions pertinent to the protracted thematic appendix at hand. No. 33 proceeds with another, related theoretical problem. No. 34 illustrates the foregoing. No. 35, with a talmud at No. 36, then No. 37, with its talmud at No. 38, No. 39, with a talmud at No. 40, No. 41, analyzed by No. 42, No. 43, analyzed by No. 44, No. 45, analyzed at No. 46, in a coherent pattern and following a cogent program, all provide Tannaite complements to the same general theme as has been under discussion. Then come a set of cases, Nos. 47-50. IV.1 starts back at the starting point, with the exposition of the Mishnah's rule. No. 2 then expands on the same theme. Nos. 3-4 raise secondary questions of refinement of the now established facts. V.1 finds the scriptural basis for the Mishnah's rule. Nos. 2, 3 proceed to theoretical questions, clarifying the fact given by the Mishnah rule. VI.1, with a footnote at No. 2, supplies an explanation of the Mishnah statement. Nos. 3, 4 continue the inquiry of No. 1. VII.1, with a footnote at No. 2, continues the exposition of the rule of the Mishnah. Nos. 3+4-8, 9+10-11 then move on to the elaboration and extension of the Mishnah's rule. VIII.1, IX.1, X.1, XI.1+2 ask about the sources of the rule of the Mishnah, whether scriptural, whether logical. The former is preferred. None of these compositions or composites refers to some deeper set of presuppositions for the definition of its work. I see in this Talmudic passage no considerable corpus of premises or presuppositions, only an ad hoc exploration of practical issues in light of certain established, broad based theoretical considerations of a familiar order.

III. Comparing the Two Talmuds' Programs

Let us now ask whether the two Talmuds may be differentiated as to their premises and presuppositions. For this purpose we compare the ways in which each Talmud reads the same Mishnah passage, with the Yerushalmi on the left, the Bavli on the right:

1:1 I A-B Gloss of the Mishnah sentence.	1:1 I.1 What differentiates the language of the present Mishnah passage from that of an adjacent one, which is formulated in a different way?
1:1 I C-F Citation of Mishnah + how on the basis of Scripture do we know that fact?	
	1:1 I.2 As above.
1:1 I G-L Conclusion & speculative question. I have the following proposition, how on the basis of Scripture do I know that that is not so?	1:1 I.3-4 Continuation of foregoing.
	1:1 I.5-6 What exclusionary purpose is served by the wording...?
	1:1 II.1 Citation of Mishnah clause +

1:1 I-II Citation of Scripture based fact, this is a matter of logic, why do we require Scripture to make that point?

1:1 III It is possible to prove through an argument based on hierarchical classification that a proposition is so.

1:1 IV A-D Up to now we have proved X, what about X's counterpart & opposite + Scriptural demonstration.

1:1 IV E-FF: dialectical exchange between two contradictory opinions.

1:1 V We have learned + proposition of unit IV, how about + further proposition generated in line with the foregoing.

1:1 VI A-C Citation of a clause of the Mishnah plus paraphrase, setting forth proposition: X, but as to Y..., with further expanion along the same lines.

1:1 VI H-BB Question and continuous argument answer.

1:1 VII Citation of Mishnah passage that intersects with and contradicts the rule before us. Harmonization.

1:1 VIII Same as above.

1:1 IX Citation of Mishnah clause plus gloss joined by a question.

1:1 X Citation of Mishnah clause plus "that is in line with this verse of Scripture."

1:1 XI Citation and systematic gloss of components of a verse of Scripture that stands behind Mishnah rule.

1:1 XII Question addressed to Mishnah clause, yielding a proposition for testing.

1:1 XIII Proposition plus secondary question.

what is Scriptural source of this rule?

1:1 II.2 Does the cited verse have to serve that purpose? Doesn't it serve this purpose?

1:1 II.3-4 It was necessary for Scripture to provide a verse for each purpose, because....

1:1 II.5 Tannaite composition to prove the point of the Mishnah; free-standing and inserted whole.

1:1 III.1 Same form as above.

1:1 III.2-3 As above.

1:1 III.4-5 Said X + free-standing statement, proposition of law that advances the theoretical inquiry.

1:1 III.6-7 Tannaite complement: citation of the Mishnah rule + how so + illustrative case.

1:1 III.8 Said X + free-standing statement, proposition of law that advances the theoretical inquiry.

1:1 III.9+10-16 Tannaite rule followed by a talmud, that is, secondary analytical inquiry into the problem introduced by that rule.

1:1 III.17-18 Free-standing statement of a rule, followed by secondary analysis, "it is obvious that...but what if..."

1:1 III.19 Said X + free-standing statement, proposition of law that advances the theoretical inquiry.

1:1 III.20, 21 As above.

1:1 III.22 Theoretical problem: X raised this question.

1:1 III.23-27 As above.

1:1 III.28 Case: there was a certain man who....

1:1 III.29 Said X, how do I know +.

1:1 III.30+31, 32 Said X + theoretical proposition.

1:1 III.33 As above.

1:1 III.34 Illustrative case.

1:1 III.35 Tannaite proposition.

1:1 III.36 Talmud to the foregoing.

1:1 III.37-8 Same pattern as above.

1:1 III.39-40 Same pattern as above [*And it was necessary to specify both cases...*].

1:1 III.41-42 Tannaite proposition + talmud.

1:1 III.43-44 As above.

1:1 III.45-46 As above.

1:1 III.47-49 Illustrative cases: There was someone who was.

1:1 III.50 Speculative question.

1:1 IV 1 Mishnah clause cited and glossed.

1:1 IV.2 Said + declarative sentence.

1:1 IV.3 X raised the question.

1:1 IV.4 It has been stated plus proposition plus dispute.

1:1 V.1 What is the scriptural basis for the Mishnah's rule.

1:1 V.2 The question was raised + theoretical issue, statement of practical consequences.

1:1 V.3 As above.

1:1 VI.1 *What is the operative consideration* behind a position taken in the Mishnah rule.

1:1 VI.2 Citation of and gloss on the foregoing.

1:1 VI.3, 4 continue No. 1.

1:1 VII.1 Citation of Mishnah clause plus X considered ruling....

1:1 VII.2 Citation of and gloss on the foregoing.

1:1 VII.3 Said X plus proposition.

1:1 VII.4-8 Illustrative cases.

1:1 VII.9-11 When X died..., plus citation of rulings in a given name and analysis thereof. Continued at Nos. 10-11.

1:1 VIII.1 Source in Mishnah, phrased slightly differently from the norm.

1:1 IX.1 Citation of Mishnah rule + how do we know that + said Scripture.

1:1 X.1 As above.
1:1 XI.1 Citation of Mishnah rule +
how do we know it + it derives
from + argument of comparison and
contrast. No. 2 continues the
foregoing.

We find in the second Talmud everything that is in the first, but important constructions lacking in the prior Talmud. That is to say, on the left-hand column we find the gloss form, the citation of a Mishnah clause with the question, "how do we know it," the proposal of the demonstration on the basis of an argument a fortiori, resting on hierarchical classification, in place of a Scripture proof, the dialectical exchange between two propositions, the paraphrase of the Mishnah leading to an exclusionary question: X but as to Y?, and so on. If I had to characterize the formal quality of the Yerushalmi, it would be simple: citation and gloss of Mishnah statements and secondary developments along some few, paramount lines. If, then, we had to proceed to specify the premises that generate the Yerushalmi's treatment of the Mishnah, they are the two that we noted at the very outset: priority accorded to Scripture over logic as the source for the Mishnah's rules; the critique of logic unaided by Scripture.

Where does the Bavli differ? First, we begin with a sizable inquiry into the language of the Mishnah passage, and this linguistic criticism bears no counterpart in the Yerushalmi. The study of the wording of the Mishnah is worked out at some length. The premise is that the Mishnah does not contain flaws or imperfections, it is harmonious and consistent in its usages. Then we take up the familiar program, citation of a Mishnah clause and inquiry into its scriptural foundations. But this yields a second interesting difference, namely, the secondary development: Does the verse have to serve this purpose? And this is completed by "it was necessary" to have a verse for each of two or more parallel cases. So there is a theoretical and dialectical level of inquiry that we did not discern in the earlier Talmud.

Third in sequence and certainly unique to the Bavli of our sample is the form, said X + theoretical inquiry. Fourth, and along the same lines, we find "X raised this question." Fifth, sequences of cases are adduced for analysis or for mere reenforcement of a point. Sixth, one of the Bavli's most interesting compositions is made up of a citation of a Tannaite statement (often marked with a TN-formula) followed by what I call "a talmud," which is to say, a secondary, systematic critical inquiry. In other words, for the Bavli, the Mishnah is not the sole received document to undergo the analysis of applied logic and practical reason; Tannaite statements now found, also, in the Tosefta, as well as others so marked but collected in no compilation now in our hands, also are treated in the same way. Mishnah analysis therefore overspreads the whole of the corpus classified as Tannaite. The sequence of 1:1 III.35-50 forms a wonderful example of this remarkable exercise. It follows that there are important points of differentiation between the two Talmuds. In common their authorships read and gloss the Mishnah and ask for scriptural bases for Mishnah rules. But the Bavli proves far more talmudic than the Yerushalmi, not because of its vastly greater dimensions, but because of a quality of mind.

IV. The Intellectual Programs of the Two Talmuds in Comparison and Contrast

Now we turn to the premises and presuppositions operative in the two Talmuds, once more trying to articulate the conceptions or problems that have precipitated the formulation of the specific compositions and composites we have examined:

1:1 I Clarification of the limitation of the Mishnah rule.
1:1 I C-T How on the basis of Scripture do we know that fact? How on the basis of Scripture do we know that a false proposition is false? This set links two distinct questions, the one of scriptural origin, the other, the application of the rule to a given circumstance.
1:1 II How on the basis of applied logic do we know the facts just now adduced on the strength of Scripture?
1:1 III It is possible on the basis of applied logic to prove the proposition, but in fact that possibility is null.
1:1 IV A-D Scripture shows what the Mishnah law maintains, how now do we know the law for a category of persons to which the Mishnah rule does not pertain + scriptural evidence to that effect.
1:1 IV E-FF Contrast between two statements that bear contradictory implications, set forth and resolved.
1:1 V We have learned plus the proposition of unit IV – how about

1:1 I.1 Comparison of the formulation of this Mishnah rule with a parallel one, explaining the difference in wording The word of the Mishnah analyzed.
1:1 I.2-4 The same problem considered, with new data.
1:1 I.5-6 The implications as to law of the wording of the Mishnah rule: what exclusionary purpose is served by this wording?
1:1 II.1-2+3 Scriptural foundations for the Mishnah rule; distinct verses are required for each case, which might be differentiated so that a single verse would not suffice for all cases.
1:1 II.4 Cited verse refers to such and such, but what is the case?
1:1 II.5 Tannaite proof of the proposition that the Mishnah rule presents, with stress on why reasoning alone is insufficient.

1:1 III.1-2 Same as above.
1:1 III.3 Even though monothetic taxi indicators fail, perhaps polythetic taxonomy succeeds: possibility considered and rejected.

the further proposition, generated in line with the foregoing? This continues the prior interest in complementary questions concerning the category not treated by the Mishnah; secondary speculation.

1:1 VI A-C Continuation of secondary expanion of the Mishnah rule: X not Y.

1:1 VI H-BB Speculative question, dialectically carried forth.

1:1 VII Intersecting Mishnah rule cited, contrasted, harmonized.

1:1 VIII Same as above.

1:1 IX Gloss of Mishnah clause.

1:1 IX A-B, C-D Scriptural support for a detail of the Mishnah; Scripture and reason make the same point.

1:1 IX Eff.: Further Tannaite materials that amplify the facts under discussion.

1:1 X Citation of Scripture demonstrates the facts of the Mishnah; this yields a secondary question, "that proves...but what about...."

1:1 XI Systematic exegesis of a verse of Scripture relevant to the Mishnah rule. (See below.)

1:1 XII Secondary question based on the rule of the Mishnah.

1:1 XIII Theoretical question deriving from an established fact.

1:1 III.4-5 Fresh proposition, which expands by applying the principle of the Mishnah to a new theoretical problem. This goes over the ground of No. 3: polythetic taxonomy and its limitations; only Scripture is reliable.

1:1 III.6-7 Case illustration of the rule of the Mishnah.

1:1 III.8 Proposition of law that expands the principle of the Mishnah to a new theoretical problem.

1:1 III.9-12: Tannaite rule, with a talmud, first dealing with the formulation of the rule, then asking a theoretical question that carries the rule forward, following by further theoretical problems attached to the initial statement. Then, No. 13, the theoretical situation to which reference has been made.

1:1 III.13 Clarification of foregoing: with what situation do we deal?

1:1 III.14-15 Footnote to the foregoing.

1:1 III.16 The decided law.

1:1 III.17 It is obvious that...but if...what is the law?

1:1 III.18 If he said...what is the law? Conflict of possibly applicable principles.

1:1 III.19 Said X plus a proposed proposition.

1:1 III.20 Same as above.

1:1 III.21 Same as above.

1:1 III.22 X raised the following theoretical question.

1:1 III.23 Said X + theoretical proposition, with a secondary debate.

1:1 III.24 X raised the following theoretical question.

1:1 III.25 As above.

1:1 III.26 As above.

1:1 III.27 As above.

1:1 III.28 Case in point.

1:1 III.29 How do I know + restatement of the proposition of the foregoing.

1:1 III.30 Said X + proposition.

1:1 III.31, 32 Gloss of the foregoing.

1:1 III. 33 Said X + proposition.

1:1 III.34 Case illustrative of foregoing.

1:1 III.35-36 Tannaite rule; secondary implications thereof explored.

1:1 III.37-38 Same pattern as above.

1:1 III.39-40 As above. *And it was necessary to specify both cases. For if we had been informed of....*

1:1 III.41-2 Tannaite rule plus talmud.

1:1 III.43-4 As above.

1:1 III.45-6 As above.

1:1 III.47, 48, 49 Illustrative cases.

1:1 III.50 Secondary theoretical question.

1:1 IV.1 Mishnah clause cited, then explained in terms of a concrete illustrative situation.

1:1 IV.2 Said + plus theoretical rule.

1:1 IV.3 X raised this question.

1:1 IV.4 It has been stated + dispute on a theoretical case.

1:1 V.1 Citation of the Mishnah clause + what is the scriptural source of this rule?

1:1 V.2 The question was raised.

1:1 V.3 As above.

1:1 VI.1 Mishnah clause cited + *What is the operative consideration...,* continued at Nos. 3, 4.

1:1 VI.2 Footnote to the foregoing.

1:1 VII.1 X considered ruling.

1:1 VII.2 Footnote to the foregoing.

1:1 VII.3 Said + proposition resting on a premise contradictory to the Mishnah's.

1:1 VII.4-8 Cases illustrative of the foregoing problem.

1:1 VII.9 Comparison of our rule with parallel rule on other topics. Continued at Nos. 10-11.

1:1 VIII.1 Secondary expansion of the rule, based on theoretical considerations and appeal to Scripture.

1:1 IX.1 How on the basis of Scripture do we know the Mishnah rule?

1:1 X.1 As above.

1:1 XI.1 How do we know the rule of the Mishnah + argument of applied reason based on hierarchical classification.

1:1 XI.2 Building on the result of the foregoing, a logical argument moving to a fresh problem.

Going over matters a second time has yielded familiar results. Can we specify with certainty the premises of the Talmuds' compositions and composites? We certainly can – indeed, we already have. The Yerushalmi's intellectual program corresponds to its formal plan: clarification of the Mishnah's statements through episodic, ad hoc gloss, on the one side, inquiry into the Mishnah's scriptural foundations, on the other. The latter initiative draws in its wake an interest in whether applied logic may do the work of Scripture. The program as a whole leads us to ask secondary questions, for example, if we know the rule for A, what about the opposite of A? What about classes of things or persons comparable to A but differentiated in some subordinate trait? A third important problem for the authors and compilers of the Yerushalmi draws attention to disharmony in statements of the law or their premises, and a labor of harmonization is invariably provoked when contradictions emerge, either on the surface or in the substrate of thought. A fourth interest (minor in our sample) is in the systematic exegesis of a verse of Scripture; this ordinarily focuses upon a verse of Scripture pertinent to a Mishnah statement. Theoretical questions are few and far between. So far as we may speak of a "Judaism behind the text," for the Yerushalmi it consists of two basic principles, on the one side, and a number of fairly obvious modes of logical analysis, on the other.

The Bavli's authorships and compilers concur on all these points of interest. They proceed along lines of their own. Specifically, the Bavli's interest is in the wording of the Mishnah, a correct reading in its own terms; in the Mishnah's word choices; in the implications for the law of one word choice over some other. So what we might now call "Mishnah criticism" forms an important point at which the Bavli differs from the Yerushalmi. Second, they will want to subject a Tannaite statement to a talmudic inquiry, even when said statement is not located in the Mishnah or the Tosefta. This is a systematic program and yields its own formal arrangements, as we have already noticed. The premises of this program lead us into the realm of formal logic; I find nothing of propositional consequence, such as would permit us to speak of "Judaism."

Third, the authors of the Bavli's compositions and framers of its sustained composites will entertain free-standing proposals, statements of the law pertinent in theme to what is under discussion but fresh in conception or problematic, for example, a case simply not addressed within the framework of the Mishnah rule or some other rule bearing a Tannaite classification. The fixed form, said X + generalization of a law followed by a sustained talmud, bespeaks an intellectual program of enormous ambition: to join in legislation through the inquiry into the practical implications of established theory, on the one side, or through the speculative analysis of secondary amplifications of said established theory, on the other. The two forms of speculation correspond, and, along with them, there is the third: the address to a theoretical question, formulated as such. B. 1:1 III.19-21 and 1:1 III.22 seem to me to differ only in form but in no material way. A fourth intellectual inquiry characteristic of the Bavli but not the Yerushalmi is the interest in composition, proportion, and balance expressed in the language: *it was necessary...*, always in Aramaic. These inquiries may explain why we require three or more statements in diverse cases of what appears to be a single principle; or they will tell us why two or more verses of Scripture are required to make the same point; or in some other way they will defend the integrity of a prior composition or even composite. Here, once more, what distinguishes the Bavli is a quality of mind, rather than a concrete propositional agendum.

The Bavli's authorships and framers have formulated a talmud that undertakes intellectual tasks beyond the ambition of those of the Yerushalmi. The differences between the Talmuds then adumbrate a more profound point of departure, taken by the second Talmud's writers, in the definition of the work of applied reason and practical logic brought to the form of writing. Since, as a matter of fact, the two Talmuds share in common a huge store of statements, made by the very same authorities about the very same subjects, the differences between them pertain wholly to the analytical program of the second of the two Talmuds – that program and its intellectual consequences. And to that program, the issue of premises of a propositional order is simply irrelevant. Only in Chapter Six shall we return to the problem of how an analytical project itself may bear propositional consequence and, it must follow, also rest upon prior presuppositions of a propositional order. We now carry forward this tedious work of examining the two Talmuds' treatment of the same Mishnah in quest of a clear account of the premises and presuppositions that form the foundations of each document.

4

The Premises of the Authors of Compositions: Qiddushin 1:2 in Yerushalmi and Bavli

We continue our detailed survey, looking for evidence that a premise of consequence has precipitated the writing of a composition or the formation of a composite.

1:2

A. A Hebrew slave is acquired through money and a writ.
B. And he acquires himself through the passage of years, by the Jubilee Year, and by deduction from the purchase price [redeeming himself at his outstanding value (Lev. 25:50-51)].
C. The Hebrew slave girl has an advantage over him.
D. For she acquires herself [in addition] through the appearance of tokens [of puberty].
E. The slave whose ear is pierced is acquired through an act of piercing the ear [Ex. 21:5].
F. And he acquires himself by the Jubilee and by the death of the master.

I. The Talmud of the Land of Israel to M. Qiddushin 1:2

[I.A] It is written. "If your brother, a Hebrew man, or a Hebrew woman, is sold to you, he shall serve you six years, and in the Seventh Year you shall let him go free from you" (Deut. 15:12).

[B] Scripture treats in the same context a Hebrew man and woman.

[C] Just as the Hebrew woman is acquired through money or a writ, so a Hebrew man is acquired through money or a writ.

[D] The proposition that that is through money poses no problems, for it is said, "she shall go out for nothing, without payment of money" (Ex. 21:11).

[E] But whence do we know that that applies also to a writ?

[F] We derive the rule for the Hebrew woman servant from a free woman, and the rule for a Hebrew manservant derives from that for a Hebrew woman servant.

[G] It turns out that what derives from one proposition serves to teach the rule for another.

The premise as to logic is that items in a single category follow the same rule, thus women, whether slave or free, are released from bondage or marriage in the same way. That principle is not universally held:

[H] To this point we have proved the proposition in accord with R. Aqiba, who indeed concurs that what derives from one proposition may then serve to teach the rule for another.

[I] But as to R. Ishmael, who does not concur that what derives from one proposition may then serve to teach the rule for another, [how do we prove that a Hebrew manservant is acquired through a writ]?

[J] The following Tannaite teaching is available: R. Ishmael teaches in regard to this statement, "freedom has not been given to her" (Lev. 19:20), "You shall let him go free from you" (Deut. 15:12). [The latter is interpreted in the light of the former.]

[K] Now in all [other] contexts R. Ishmael does not concur that what derives from one proposition may then serve to teach the rule for another, and yet here [at J] he does indeed hold that view.

[L] It [that is. the teaching at J] was taught in the name of a sage. "How does R. Ishmael prove [that a writ is applicable to the Hebrew manservant]?

[M] "'Sending forth' is stated at Deut. 15:2, and also 'sending' is stated at Deut. 24:1.

[N] "Just as 'sending forth' stated in regard to a divorce means that it is done through a writ, so the 'sending forth' stated in regard to the slave means that it is done through a writ."

[O] [But the issue is not the same.] The two cases are dissimilar. For in the case of the divorce of the woman, the writ serves to give her full possession of herself. But here the writ serves to give possession of the Hebrew slave to others. [The proposition is to prove that a Hebrew man is acquired through a writ, and that has not been proved.]

[P] Said R. Mattenaiah, "The use of the language of sale will prove the case. ['If your brother...is sold to you' (Deut. 15:12); 'If your brother becomes poor and sells part of his property' (Lev. 25:25).] Just as 'sale' stated in the latter case involves use of a writ, so the language of 'sale' used here involves use of a writ."

[Q] Or, perhaps may one argue, just as in the case of a field acquisition may be made through usucaption, so in the case of the slave, it may be through usucaption?

[R] [There is a better mode of proof of the besought proposition.] Said R. Hiyya bar Ada, "A Hebrew man and a Hebrew woman are subject to one and the same law."

In the following, I see only the manipulation of Scripture for the specified purpose:

[II.A] **Through money.** ["If there are still many years according to them he shall refund out of] the price paid for him [the price for his redemption]" (Lev. 25:51).

[B] Through the payment of money he is redeemed [from the owner, in line with the cited verse], and he is not redeemed through handing over grain or goods.

[C] In all other contexts you treat what is worth money as tantamount to ready cash, but here you do not treat what is worth money as tantamount to ready cash.

[D] Said R. Abba Meri, "The present case is to be treated differently, for Scripture itself twice mentioned 'price' (Lev. 25:51)."

[E] Said R. Hiyya bar Abba, "Abba will concur that, if the slave sought to deduct from the purchase price, he may do so and go forth free even by means of paying grain or goods."

[F] Said R. Yudan, father of R. Mattenaiah, "What you have stated [at A-D] applies to a case in which one has not estimated their value [grain, goods], but if one has estimated their value, they are deemed tantamount to money."

In the next items, III-IV, I see only a clarification of the rule of the Mishnah:

[III.A] **Through a writ:** Said R. Abbahu, "This is by means of a writ covering the money that has been paid over. Lo, it is not to be with a writ of gift [of himself to the master], lest the slave retract his gift of himself to the master."

[B] But if that is the case, then perhaps even in the case of a writ covering money that has been paid over, the slave has the power to retract.

[C] [What was said at A was actually,] "Perhaps a year of famine may come, and the master may retract [on the purchase]." [Consequently, a writ of sale covering funds paid over must be made out, to prevent the master from retracting at will.]

[IV.A] The language of sale is this: "I, Mr. So-and-so, have sold my daughter to Mr. Such-and-such."

[B] The language of betrothal is this: "I, Mr. So-and-so, have betrothed my daughter to Mr. Such-and-such."

[C] R. Haggai raised the question before R. Yosé: "[If] one reversed the language and said, 'I, Mr. So-and-so, have purchased the daughter of Mr. Such-and-such,' 'I, Mr. So-and-so, have betrothed the daughter of Mr. Such-and-such,' [what is the law]?"

[D] He said to him, "That means nothing. But if he used the language of sale for the language of betrothal, or the language of betrothal for the language of sale, he has done nothing whatever."

The pertinent verse of Scripture is now clarified:

[V.A] It is written. "When you buy a Hebrew slave, he shall serve six years, and in the seventh he shall go out free, for nothing" (Ex. 2:1).

[B] Is it possible to suppose that he goes forth at the end of the sixth year?

[C]   Scripture says, "And in the seventh he shall go out free."

[D]   Is it possible to suppose that he will go forth at the end of the Seventh Year?

[E]   Scripture says, "Six years shall he serve."

[F]   How then is this to be?

[G]   He works all six years and goes forth at the beginning of the seventh.

[H]   And as to this reference to the Seventh Year, he goes out at the Seventh Year of his own sale, not at the Seventh Year [the year of release] of the world at large.

[I]   You say that he goes forth at the Seventh Year of his own sale. But perhaps it is at the Seventh Year of the world at large?

[J]   When Scripture states, "He shall serve for six years," lo, six full years of service are specified.

[K]   How then am I to interpret "And in the seventh he shall go out"?

[L]   He goes forth in the Seventh Year of his own sale, but not in the Seventh Year of the world at large.

[M]   Might I say the very opposite [that Scripture really does refer to the Seventh Year, the year of release, and not the Seventh Year of the man's personal status as a slave]?

[N]   R. Zeira in the name of R. Huna, "'And in the Seventh Year' is written."

[O]   [As a separate argument for the same basic proposition,] said R. Huna, "If you maintain that it is the Seventh Year at large [and not the Seventh Year of service of the individual slave], then when the Jubilee Year comes along, what sort of slave is it going to release, [since all of them will be free in accord with the previous seven years of release, every Seventh Year]."

[P]   Said R. Yohanan bar Mareh, "That is in accord with the position of him who said, 'The Jubilee Year does not count among the years of the septennate' [but is in addition to them, thus it is the fiftieth year of the cycle].

[Q]   "But in accord with the position of him who said, 'The Jubilee Year does count among the years of the septennate' [serving as the first year of the coming seven-year cycle], there are times in which the Jubilee Year will come in the middle of the years of the septennate, [in which case the question raised at O is a valid one, since there will be slaves to free]."

[R]   The rabbis of Caesarea moreover point out, "Even in accord with the one who said, 'The Jubilee Year does not count among the years of the septennate,' we can still answer the argument [at O]. For the Seventh Year will serve to free ordinary slaves, and the Jubilee Year will serve to free slaves who have had their ears pierced and so remained permanently with their masters."

We proceed to a speculative question, which takes for granted the proposition that the Seventh Year operates in its own terms, ex opere operato, not in relationship to the number of years that have been served before its advent:

[VI.A] How do I know that one is freed in the Seventh Year even though he has not worked all six years?

[B] Scripture says, "And in the Seventh Year he shall go out free, for nothing."

[C] Is it possible to suppose that that applies even to a case in which he fled?

[D] Scripture says, "Six years he shall work."

[E] Why do you encompass this one [who fell ill, for he, too, is freed] and exclude that one [who fled]?

[F] After Scripture used encompassing language, it used exclusive language. Accordingly, I encompass this one [who fell ill] who remains in his domain and exclude that one who is not in the owner's domain."

[G] R. Bun bar Hiyya said R. Hoshaiah raised the question: "I see no problem in the case of one who was ill and later fled, that he serves out the required six years.

[H] "But if he fled and afterward he fell ill [what is the rule]? [Do we say that since he fled at the outset he must make up the years? Or perhaps he may claim that even if he were with the master, he would not have been able to work.]"

[I] Said R. Hiyya bar Ada, "Let us derive the answer from the following:

[J] "She who rebels against her husband [by declining to have sexual relations with him] – they deduct from her marriage contract seven denars a week [M. Ket. 5:7].

[K] "They write for him a writ of rebellion as a charge against her marriage contract.

[L] "In this regard R. Hiyya taught, '[Even in the case of] a menstruating woman, a sick woman, a betrothed girl, and a deceased childless brother s widow – they write for him a writ of rebellion as a charge against her marriage contract.'

[M] "Now how do we interpret this matter? If it was a case in which she rebelled against him [refusing to have sexual relations], and she is already in her menstrual period, it is the Torah that has required her to rebel against him.

[N] "But thus must we interpret the matter: It is a case in which she rebelled against him [refusing to have sexual relations] before her menstrual period had begun.

[O] "Now [the argument continues], when in fact she comes to her menstrual period, she is no longer in a position to rebel, and yet you say that [nonetheless] he writes such a writ of rebellion against her marriage contract.

[P] "Here, too, [by analogy], if the slave fled [when he was well] and afterward fell ill [as at O], he still must make up the years he has not served.

[Q] "For the master has the right to say to him, 'If you had been with me, you would not have gotten sick.'"

[R] Said R. Hinena, "Even in regard to the first case [in which the slave got sick, then fled], the same ruling applies. If the slave got sick and then fled, he must complete the six years, for the master has the right to say to him, 'If you had been with me, you would have been healed more rapidly.'"

We revert to Mishnah clarification:

[VII.A]   **And he acquires himself through the passage of years** [by the Jubilee Year, or by deduction from the purchase price, redeeming himself at his outstanding value]. [This is in line with Lev. 25:50-52: "He shall reckon with him who bought him from the year when he sold himself to him until the year of Jubilee, and the price of his release shall be according to the number of years; the time he was with his owner shall be rated as the time of a hired servant. If there are still many years, according to them he shall refund out of the price paid for him the price for his redemption. If there remain but a few years until the year of Jubilee, he shall make a reckoning with him; according to the years of service due from him he shall refund the money for his redemption."]

[B]   There is a Tannaite authority who teaches: "He may be sold for less than six years, but he may not be sold for more than six years."

[C]   There is a Tannaite authority who teaches: "He may not be sold either for [59b] less than six years or for more than six years."

[D]   Said R. Jeremiah, "The reason for the former Tannaite authority's view is that there are times that he is sold two or three years before the Jubilee Year, and the Jubilee Year comes along and removes him [from the domain of the master] willy-nilly."

[E]   By the Jubilee Year: As it is written, "He shall be released in the year of the Jubilee" (Lev. 25:54).

[F]   Or by deduction from the purchase price: As it is written, "If there are still many years, according to them he shall refund out of the price paid for him the price for his redemption. If there remain but a few years until the year of Jubilee, he shall make a reckoning with him; according to the years of service due from him he shall refund the money for his redemption" (Lev. 25:51-52).

[G]   Now do we not know that if there are many years, there are not a few remaining, and if there are few, there are not many? [Why does the same proposition require repetition?]

[H]   Said R. Hila, "There are times that the money owing on the years remaining is greater than the value of the man as a slave, and there are times that the money owing for the years remaining is less than the value of the man as a slave.

[I]   "How do you know that if the man was sold at the rate of a maneh [a hundred zuz] per year of service, and he has increased in value, so that lo, he now is worth two hundred zuz per year of service, how do you know that he reckons with him only at the rate of a maneh per year of service [as yet remaining]?

[J]   "Scripture states, 'out of the money that he was bought for.'

[K]   "How do you know that if the man was sold at the rate of two hundred zuz per year of service, and he fell in value, and now is worth a maneh, how do you know that he reckons with him only at the rate of a maneh per year of service [as yet remaining]?

[L] "Scripture states, 'according to his years of service due from him he shall refund the money for his redemption.'

[M] "We have thus derived the rule in the case of an Israelite sold to a gentile that, when he is redeemed, he has the upper hand."

[N] How do we learn that in the case of one sold to an Israelite, when he is redeemed, he also has the upper hand?

[O] The word "hired servant" is used in both contexts [sold to an Israelite: Lev. 25:40; to a gentile: Lev. 25:53], serving the purpose of establishing a common rule for both.

[P] Just as the use of the word "hired servant" stated in the context of gentile ownership means that, when he is redeemed, he has the upper hand, so the use of the word "hired servant" in the Israelite setting means that when he is redeemed, he has the upper hand.

[Q] Rabbi says, "Why does Scripture repeat the word 'He will redeem him' three times? It is to encompass all acts of redemption, requiring that each of them follow the same procedures, [thus proving that when the slave is redeemed from an Israelite he also has the upper hand]."

The scriptural formulation of the rule is itself expanded:

[VIII.A] "And if he is not redeemed by these [means, then he shall be released in the year of Jubilee, he and his children with him]" (Lev. 25:54).

[B] R. Yosé the Galilean says, "By these [relatives (Lev. 25:49ff.) it is for freedom, or [if he is redeemed] by anyone else it is for subjugation [purchased for further service]."

[C] R. Aqiba says, "By these [relatives] it is for subjugation, or by any one else it is for freedom."

[D] [What is at issue in this dispute?] R. Abbahu in the name of R. Yohanan: "Now both of them interpret a single verse of Scripture: 'And if he is not redeemed by these' –

[E] "R. Yosé the Galilean interprets the verse, 'And if he is not redeemed by these [relatives] but by others, then he remains in service [to the master until the Jubilee] and then goes free.'

[F] "R. Aqiba interprets the verse, 'But if he is not redeemed by (himself)' but by relatives he serves out the years until the Jubilee and then goes free."

[G] But as to the opinion of sages [in the same matter], R. Yosa in the name of R. Yohanan. "Whether he is redeemed by these [relatives] or by others, it is for freedom."

[H] And so, too, has it been taught: "or if his hand should turn up [sufficient funds], he will be redeemed" (Lev. 25:9) –

[I] "If his own hand turns up sufficient means for his redemption': Just as if his own hand turns up sufficient means, [he is freed and does not serve others], so if the hand of others [turns up sufficient means for his redemption], it is for his own benefit [and not so that he may then be subjugated to them].

[J] [Now to explain the position of those who say that he is redeemed in order to complete the term of service:] R. Jacob bar Aha in the name of R. Yohanan, "In the view of him who says, 'It is to subjugation,' [it is so that] he completes the original term of service and then goes forth [but does not serve another six years]."

[K] And has it not been taught: If after he has been redeemed [he is resubjugated], lo, it is as if he is sold to him? He is subjugated [for the six-year term of service] and then goes forth.

[L] R. Abba Meri said, "The proper reading here is not that he is subjugated [for the whole term of six years] and then goes free, but rather, 'He completes the original term of service and then goes free.'"

[M] If his relatives wanted to redeem him from the first purchaser, they have that right.

[N] [If he is redeemed from the first purchaser and] the relatives wanted to redeem him from the redeemer, they do not have that right.

[O] R. Yosa in the name of R. Yohanan, "That statement accords with the view of him who said, 'by these [relatives]' means that he is redeemed for freedom, but by any other person he is taken over into a new term of service."

The speculative question that follows develops the scriptural formulation; the advent of a speculative and secondary issue marks the end of Mishnah commentary:

[IX.A] Samuel bar Abba raised the question before R. Yosa, "Here [in regard to redeeming the slave] it is written, 'He shall reckon with him...from the year when he sold himself to him until the year of Jubilee' (Lev. 25:50) and [in regard to redeeming an inherited field that one has consecrated, it is written, 'Then the priest] shall reckon [the money value for it according to the years that remain until the year of Jubilee, and a deduction shall be made from your valuation]' (Lev. 27:23).

[B] "Now here [in the case of redeeming a slave] you take account of months as well as years, when he goes forth [so that if it is the middle of the year, half of the year is deemed to count as part of the term of service, but when the field is assessed by the priest, only whole years are taken into account (cf. M. Ar. 7:1)]. [What is the difference?]"

[C] He said to him, "The present case is different, for the Torah has treated the slave in the context of the hired hand. just as the latter reckons months and completes his term of service, so this one also reckons months as well as years and completes his term of service."

Once more, Mishnah commentary takes over, with a familiar procedure:

[X.A] **[The Hebrew slave girl has an advantage over him. For she acquires herself in addition through the appearance of tokens of puberty (M. 1:1C-D):]** "She shall go out for nothing, without payment of money" (Ex. 21:11).

[B] "For nothing" – refers to the time of pubescence.

[C] "Without payment of money" – refers to the tokens of maturity.

[D] And why should the law not refer to only one of them?

[E] If it had referred to only one of them, I might have maintained, "If she goes forth through the appearance of the signs of puberty, all the more so will she go forth at the time of pubescence."

[F] If so, I would have maintained, the time of pubescence is the only time at which she goes forth, and not the time at which she produces signs of puberty.

[G] Now logic would suggest as follows: Since she leaves the domain of the father and leaves the domain of the master, just as from the domain of the father she goes forth only when she has produced the signs of puberty, also from the domain of the master she should go forth only when she produces signs of puberty.

[H] On that account it was necessary to state:

[I] "For nothing" – refers to the time of pubescence.

[J] "Without a payment of money" – refers to the signs of puberty.

[K] And perhaps matters are just the opposite [so that "she will go forth for nothing" refers to the period of twelve and a bit more in which she is a girl, and "without a payment" refers to the time at which she has reached puberty]?

[L] R. Tanhuma in the name of R. Huna: "'Without money' – in any context in which the father receives money, the master does not receive money."

The relevant verse of Scripture is itself amplified:

[XI.A] "[If she does not please her master,] who has designated her for himself, then he shall let her be redeemed" (Ex. 21:8).

[B] "This teaches that he may not designate her for himself unless there is sufficient time left in the day for redeeming her. [That is, the labor on this very last day of her term of service must still be worth at least a perutah, so that she could be designated to him by means of the deduction of that amount of money.]

[C] "[The consequence is that] in the remaining labor to be done by her there must be a value of a perutah, so that in the deduction applying to her, there will be a value of a perutah," the words of R. Yosé b. R. Judah.

[D] And sages say, "He may designate her all day long, down to the very last rays of the sun."

[E] Said R. Hiyya bar Ada, "All concur in the case of [redeeming] a Hebrew slave that this may be done only so long as there remains the sum of a perutah [to be worked off]. [If such a sum is yet owing, he may be redeemed therefrom. Otherwise the process does not apply.]"

[F] Well did R. Yosé b. R. Judah rule [that betrothal takes place only if there is sufficient time left in the day for labor of a value of a perutah to be remitted by the owner, thus constituting the sum owing to the girl for her betrothal].

[G] What is the reason of the rabbis? [For what constitutes the sum of betrothal, on the strength of which the owner designates the girl as his betrothed?] There is no issue of money, nor is there an issue of the value of her labor [at the end of that last day]. So with what does the owner designate her [and betroth her]?

[H]   Said R. Zeira. "He designates her by a mere oral declaration, [which suffices]. '

[I]   R. Hoshaiah taught. "How does he designate her? He says to her before two witnesses, 'Lo, you are designated unto me [as my betrothed]."'

[J]   [We turn to the principle at issue at B-D.] In the opinion of R. Yosé b. R. Judah it is only at the end of the transaction that [whatever] money [is left over from the period of service] is given to her for the purposes or designation [as his betrothed].

[K]   In the opinion of the rabbis from the very beginning of the transaction [when the girl was sold by her father to the owner], the money was handed over for the purposes of designation [and hence betrothal]. [That is why, so far as they are concerned, whether or not there is sufficient time left in the day for her to work off a perutah, which is forgiven her in exchange for the designation as betrothed, the rabbis deem her betrothed. The betrothal money was paid out as the original price for the girl.]

[L]   What is the practical difference between the two?

[M]   It is ownership of the fruits of her labor.

[N]   The one who said that at the end the money is given over to her for the purposes of designation, [that is, R. Yosé b. R. Judah,] maintains that the usufruct of her labor belongs to the master [and not to her father]. [She is deemed married like any other woman.]

[O]   The one who said that from the very outset the money is given over to her for the purposes of designation maintains that the usufruct of her labor belongs to her father. [If the master designates her at the end of the six years, it does not matter, since the original sum paid to the father covered the money owing for the designation as the betrothed of the master. Whatever work she does after the six years are over produces benefit to the father, since she is not deemed normally wed to the master. She returns to the domain of the father and is not deemed wed to the master. The effect of the designation is to betroth her, not to effect a complete marital bond.]

[P]   Even in accord with the one who said that from the very outset the money is given over to her for the purposes of designation, the usufruct of her labor belongs to her husband. [Why?] [Because] he is in the status of one who says to a woman, "Lo, you are betrothed to me on condition that the usufruct of your labor belongs to me [even while you are merely betrothed to me, not in a fully consummated union]." [Consequently, even in this position one may maintain the same position as is given to one in the contrary view.]

[Q]   If the master was married to her sister [in which case he was not permitted to marry her as well], and the sister died,

[R]   the one who said that only at the end is the money given over to her for the purposes of designation [betrothal] will maintain that she requires the payment of another sum of money [to accomplish the designation as the master's betrothed, since in any event she was not suitable to marry him while the sister was alive, so no funds have been transferred for this purpose].

[S] [But] in the view of the one who said that from the very outset the money is given over to her for the purposes of designation, she does not have to be given another sum of money, [because we deem the money originally paid over to serve retroactively as the betrothal payment].

[T] [No, that proposition is rejected:] Even in accord with the one who said that from the very outset the money is given over to her for the purposes of designation, she still has to be given another sum of money, [because we certainly do not deem the money originally paid over to serve retroactively as the betrothal payment].

[U] Why? Because all parties concur that a betrothal is not valid in the case of a prohibited connection. [That is, if while the sister is yet alive the master should betroth the girl, the betrothal is null, since while the sister is alive there is no possibility of betrothing her; hence there is also no possibility of a retroactive interpretation of the money originally paid as having served for purposes of designation as the master's betrothal payment.]

[V] Does R. Yosé b. R. Judah maintain the view that this act of designation that takes place here [at the end of the six years of labor, in which there is yet enough time for the girl to perform a perutah's worth of labor, as explained above] enjoys the status of a betrothal as authorized by the laws of the Torah?

[W] Said R. Abun, "R. Yosé b. R. Judah is of the same view as R. Simeon b. Eleazar, as we have learned in the following."

[X] He who says to a woman, "Lo, you are betrothed to me through my bailment that you have in your hand,"

[Y] [if] she went off and found that it had been stolen or had gotten lost,

[Z] if there was left in her possession something worth a perutah,

[AA] she is betrothed, and if not, she is not betrothed.

[BB] [But if it concerned] a loan, even though there was something worth a perutah left in her possession, she is not betrothed.

[CC] R. Simeon b. Eleazar says in the name of R. Meir, "A loan is equivalent to a bailment. If there remained in her hand something worth a perutah, she is betrothed. And if not, she is not betrothed" [T. Qid . 3:1].

[DD] Just as R. Simeon b. Eleazar treats a loan as equivalent to a bailment, so R. Yosé b. R. Judah treats funds paid for the girl for purposes of designation as equivalent to a loan.

Once more, the relevant verse of Scripture is amplified:

[XII.A] "If he designates her for his son, [he shall deal with her as a daughter]" (Ex. 21:9).

[B] He designates her for his son, but he does not designate her for his brother.

[C] And let him be free to designate her for his brother, on the basis of the following argument a fortiori:

[D] Now if in the case of the son, who does not stand in his stead for purposes of the rite of removing the shoe or for levirate marriage, lo, he designates her for him,

[E]   his brother, who does stand in his stead for purposes of the rite of removing the shoe and for levirate marriage – is it not logical that he should be free to designate her for him?

[F]   No. If you have stated the rule in regard to the son, who stands in his stead in regard to a field received as an inheritance (M. Arakh. 7:2), will you say the same of his brother, who does not stand in his stead in regard to a field received as an inheritance?

[G]   Since he does not stand in his stead in that regard, it is not logical that he should be free to designate her for him.

[H]   Scripture states, "And if he designates her for his son," meaning, for his son he designates her, and he may not designate her for his brother.

[I]   "And if he designates her for his son" – and he may not designate her for his son's son.

[J]   Samuel bar Abba raised the question before R. Zeira: "In the law dealing with inheritances you treat the son of the son as equivalent to the son. But here you do not treat the son of the son as equivalent to the son."

[K]   R. Zeira said, "To whoever can explain this matter to me, I shall give a glass of spiced wine!"

[L]   R. Nahum answered, "Lo, [59c] in connection with inheritances, you treat the brother as equivalent to the son, and all other relatives as equivalent to the son, and so, likewise, you treat the son of the son as equivalent to the son.

[M]   "But here, in a case in which you have not treated the brother as equivalent to the son, and all other relatives as equivalent to the son, there is hardly much reason to treat the son of the son as equivalent to the son."

[N]   The rabbis of Caesarea objected: "Lo, in the matter of the priest's becoming unclean for a deceased relative, you have treated a brother as equivalent to the son, and all other relatives [listed, for whom the priest may become unclean with corpse uncleanness required in burying the deceased] likewise are treated as equivalent to the son. But you do not treat the son of the son as equivalent to the son."

[O]   They said, "There goes the cup of spiced wine" [since Zeira now did not owe it to Nahum].

[XIII.A]   "If he designates her for his son" (Ex. 21:9) –

[B]   it must be with the son's knowledge and consent.

[C]   Said R. Yohanan, "There is no requirement here for the son's knowledge and consent."

[D]   Said R. Jacob bar Aha, "There is indeed a requirement here for the son's knowledge and consent, along the lines of the position of R. Yosé b. R. Judah. [The money the father got at the outset was for selling the girl, not for purposes of betrothing her. It follows that if there is to be a betrothal it comes later on, hence with the girl's agreement. Likewise, if the father wishes to betroth her to his son, it must be with the son's agreement.]"

[E]   Said R. Samuel b. bar Abedoma, "Even if you say that this is in accord with the view of R. Yosé b. R. Judah, there is no need for advance knowledge and consent, "For cannot the son be a minor [who has no legal right of knowledge and consent, since the verse simply says 'son' with no qualifications (following Pené Moshe)]."

[XIV.A] "If he designates her for his son" (Ex. 21:9) – it must be with the son's knowledge and consent.

[B] R. Yohanan said, "He designates her, whether for his adult son or his minor son, whether with his knowledge and consent or not with his knowledge and consent."

[C] R. Simeon b. Laqish said, "He designates her only for his adult son, for it must be done with the son's knowledge and consent [and a minor legally has neither]."

[D] [Both views will be tested against the following:] A son who is nine years and one day old [who is married to a woman and dies] turns [that woman] into a widow [so far as her being prohibited to marry] a high priest; or [if he divorces his wife or performs the rite of removing the shoe with his sister-in-law], he turns [that woman] into a divorcée or a woman who has removed the shoe [so far as her being prohibited to marry] an ordinary priest [is concerned]. [Consequently, he is deemed for the present purposes to be a husband.]

[E] Now so far as R. Yohanan is concerned, who interprets that statement to apply to a case in which the father has designated a slave girl as the betrothed for his son, there is no problem.

[F] We deal here with an act of designation in which the son has a right of acquisition in the woman. Consequently, under the stated conditions, on his account the woman may be deemed a widow so far as marriage to a high priest is concerned, or a divorcée or a woman who has carried out the rite of removing the shoe so far as being married to an ordinary priest is concerned.

[G] As to the view of R. Simeon b. Laqish, will he interpret the matter to speak of a case in which the son was married [in an ordinary way]? Then the woman should be exempt from the status of a woman who has performed the rite of removing the shoe and from the requirement of levirate marriage, for have we not learned the following: If a nine-year-old married a woman and died [without children], lo, this woman is exempt [from levirate marriage, since the marriage of a nine-year-old is null. So Yohanan can interpret the cited passage, but by Simeon b. Laqish, who maintains that there is no possibility of designating the slave girl as the wife of a minor, how is the passage to be interpreted?].

[H] Said R. Abin, "The view of R. Simeon b. Laqish accords with the position of R. Yosé b. R. Judah [in the following dispute]:

[I] For so it has been taught:

[J] A son nine years and one day old up to twelve years and one day old who produced two pubic hairs or two hairs under the arm, lo, this [set of hairs] is deemed nothing but a mole [and he is not regarded as mature].

[K] R. Yosé b. R. Judah says, "Lo, these are regarded as valid signs of puberty, and he is deemed an adult."

[L] R. Jacob b. R. Bun in the name of R. Yosé b. Haninah [explaining Yosé's position]: "And that applies when the signs appeared at a time appropriate for producing signs of puberty [in the twelfth year]."

[M] R. Yosé raised the question: "If the signs of puberty appeared during such a period, is he deemed an adult retroactively or only from now on?"

[N] R. Abun: "It is obvious that it is retroactively that he is treated as an adult, all the more so from now on."

[O] [The reason this was obvious to Abun is] that he interpreted this statement of R. Simeon b. Laqish in accord with the position of R. Yosé b. R. Judah. [That is, Simeon b. Laqish accords with Yosé b. R. Judah and maintains that a boy nine years and one day old who dies turns his wife into a widow so far as marriage to a high priest is concerned. We have then a case in which the signs of puberty appeared at a later age; retroactively he is deemed to be an adult. Accordingly, it is obvious that Simeon b. Laqish and Yosé will regard the puberty signs as retroactively effective. As to explaining D, Simeon b. Laqish does so in this wise.]

[P] And why does R. Yosé not interpret the matter of R. Simeon b. Laqish in accord with the position of R. Yosé b. R. Judah?

[Q] Said R. Mana, "Because he was troubled by this problem. R. Yosé wanted to know, if the puberty signs appeared at the right time, whether retroactively he is deemed to be an adult, or only from now on. Now in this case, it poses no problem as to his turning his wife into a widow, but how can he turn her into a divorcée [for a minor may not give a writ of divorce]?" One may interpret the case to be one in which he had sexual relations and gave her a writ of divorce, or gave one when he became an adult.

[R] In the case of her becoming a widow who has removed the shoe on his account, interpret the case in which he had sexual relations with his wife, then died, and his brother had performed the rite of · removing the shoe with his widow. So on account of his brother, she entered the status of a woman with whom the rite of removing the shoe had been performed.

[S] "If that is the case, then why not invoke the same rule in the case of a boy less than nine years old [who later had intercourse and divorced his wife]?"

[T] Said R. Samuel b. Abodema, "And that is indeed correct. [It does apply.] But since [the Tannaite authority] wished to phrase the entire set of statements to concern a nine-year-old, he treated this particular case also in terms of a nine-year-old."

[U] R. Judah bar Pazzi in the name of R. Joshua b. Levi, "R. Yosé b. R. Judah derived the facts from Ahaz, for it has been taught: Ahaz fathered a son at the age of nine; Haran at the age of six; Caleb at the age of ten."

[V] And this is in accord with him who maintains that Caleb son of Hesron is the same as Caleb the son of Yefuneh [cf. B. San. 69a].

[XV.A] "If the father of the girl sold her to this one [in line with Ex. 21:7-11] and betrothed her to someone else, the father has ridiculed the master, [for what he has done is valid in both cases,]" the words of R. Yosé b. R. Judah.

[B] And the sages say, "The father has not ridiculed the master [who has every right to designate the girl as his betrothed, despite the father's deed with the other party]. [Sages maintain that by selling the girl he has accepted betrothal money, and consequently his betrothal to another party was null.]"

[C] [The theory of Yosé b. R. Judah is this:] The master is in the position of one who says to a woman, "Lo, you are betrothed to me after thirty days." Now if someone says to a woman, "Lo, you are betrothed to me after thirty days," and someone else came along and betrothed her during the thirty days, is it possible that she is not betrothed to the second party? [Obviously not. She certainly is betrothed to the second party, tor there is no intervening rite of betrothal.]

[D] [The theory of rabbis is this:] If he said to her, "Lo, you are betrothed to me from this point, effective in thirty days," and someone else came along and betrothed her during the period of thirty days, is it possible that she is not betrothed to the two of them [by reason of doubt]? [Obviously not. She is betrothed and yet prohibited to both parties by reason of doubt.]

[E] [Now the betrothal effected by the master's designation of the girl to be his wife] is already [effective] whenever he wishes [to consummate the marriage]. [Accordingly, it is parallel to the case outlined just now, betrothal on condition. For the rabbis maintain that the money originally paid over also serves as betrothal money.]

[F] All concur, to be sure, that if the father actually had married the girl off, he has ridiculed the master, [who can do nothing about it].

[XVI.A] "When a man sells his daughter as a slave" (Ex. 21:7) –

[B] "Solely as a slave. This teaches that he has the right to sell her to the master and to stipulate with him that it is on condition that he not have the right to designate her as his betrothed," the words of R. Meir.

[C] And sages say, "In so stating, he has done nothing whatever, for he has made a stipulation contrary to what is written in the Torah, and whoever stipulates contrary to what is written in the Torah – what he has stipulated is null."

[D] Now does R. Meir not concur that whoever stipulates contrary to what is written in the Torah – what he has stipulated is null?

[E] He maintains that one's stipulation is null if it is not possible for him to carry it out without actually violating the rules of the Torah. But in the present case it is possible for him to carry it out in the end. [For the owner is not obligated by the Torah to designate the girl as his betrothed at all. Meir thus maintains that such a stipulation is valid. So this one has every possibility of carrying out the stipulation in the end without violating the Torah.]

[F] And do rabbis [vis-à-vis Meir] not maintain that a stipulation is valid if it is possible for him to carry it out in the end without violating the Torah?

[G] They concur that a stipulation is valid [if it is contrary to the Torah] so long as it is possible for him to carry it out in the end without violating the Torah. [But that is the case in which the stipulation deals with] a monetary matter, [while the present stipulation deals with] a matter covering the person herself.

[H] Now lo, it is taught: "A man marries a woman and stipulates with her that it is on condition that he not have the obligation to provide for her food, clothing, or marital rights" [Ex. 21:10].

[I] Now that poses no problem as to food or clothing. But marital rights do affect the body [the person herself].

[J] Said R. Hiyya bar Ada, "Interpret the passage to speak of a minor girl."

[K] As to the Tannaite authority who maintains that the stipulation is null, how does he interpret the reference to selling her for a slave girl?

[L] He maintains that the father may sell her if she is a widow to a high priest, and if she is a divorcée or a woman who has undergone the rite of removing the shoe to an ordinary priest, [and the purpose of the specification "for a slave" is to indicate that that is permitted].

[M] And how does the other Tannaite authority interpret the specification "for a slave," [since he holds, as we shall see, that a man may not sell his daughter as a slave girl after he has sold her for marriage, since from that view, one may not interpret the matter to apply to selling the girl as a widow to a high priest, for, in this Tannaite authority's view, once she was married and widowed, the father may not sell her anyway]?

[N] Said R. Yosé b. R. Bun, "Interpret the statement to apply to a case in which the girl was widowed out of the status of merely being betrothed."

[O] But has it not been taught [in a passage that can speak only of the status of betrothal, not of a fully consummated marriage]: "A man may sell his daughter for marriage [and if she became widowed or divorced] he may do so again [provided she is still a minor]." Similarly, he may sell her as a slave girl, [and if she was a minor when receiving her freedom through the end of the six-year period or the Jubilee Year or her master's death] he may do so again. He may sell her for a slave girl, [and if she became free] he may sell her for marriage. However, he may not sell her as a slave girl after he had already sold her for marriage.

[P] Said R. Yohanan, "There are two opinions. The one who holds that the passage refers to the father's selling her only as a slave girl, and that our case refers to a widow sold to a high priest [and consequently she cannot marry the high priest], maintains that the father may sell her as a slave girl after she has been married [and, as we see, widowed after being merely betrothed]."

[Q] "The one who holds that the passage does not speak of a widow's being sold to a high priest also does not concur that the father has the right to sell the girl as a slave girl after she has been married."

[R] Then how does this second party interpret the language of Scripture, "as a slave girl"?

[S] Said R. Mattenaiah, "Interpret the passage to a case in which he was married to her sister. [Scripture thus indicates that the father may sell the girl to a man who already has married the girl's sister, since he sells her as a slave girl and not for the purpose of designation as the master's betrothed.]"

[T]   R. Simeon b. Yohai taught, "Just as the father may not sell the girl as a slave girl after she has been married, so he may not sell her as a slave girl after she already has been sold as a slave girl."

[U]   What is the scriptural basis for the position of R. Simeon b. Yohai?

[V]   "Since he has dealt faithlessly with her" (Ex. 21:8).

[W]   One time he has the opportunity to deal faithlessly with her, and he does not have the opportunity to deal faithlessly with her a second time.

[X]   How do rabbis [who do not concur with Simeon's position] interpret this prooftext as adduced in evidence by Simeon b. Yohai, "since he has dealt faithlessly with her"i

[Y]   Once [the master] has spread his cloak over her [and had sexual relations with her], the father has no further domain over her.

We proceed to a speculative question:

[XVII.A]   R. Simeon b. Laqish raised the question before R. Yohanan: "A Hebrew slave girl should go forth if she is wed [to someone other than the master, going forth at that point from the domain of the master].

[B]   "This position is based upon an argument a fortiori.

[C]   "Now if the appearance of the signs of puberty, which do not remove her from the domain of the father, lo, do remove her from the domain of the master, the fact that she is married, which does remove her from the domain of the father – is it not a matter of logic that it should also remove her from the domain of the master?"

[D]   He said to him, "I know only what the Mishnah states: The Hebrew slave girl has an advantage over him, for she acquires herself through the appearance of tokens of puberty [M. 1:2C-D] – [that and no more]."

[XVIII.A]   Bar Pedaiah said, "A Hebrew slave girl goes forth at the death of her master."

[B]   What is the scriptural basis for that view?

[C]   "And to your bondwoman you shall do likewise" (Deut. 15:17).

[D]   And it is written, "He shall be your bondman forever" (Deut. 15:17).

[E]   Scripture thereby links the rule covering the Hebrew slave girl to the slave whose ear is pierced.

[F]   Just as the slave whose ear is pierced goes free at the death of his master, so the Hebrew slave girl goes free at the death of her master.

[G]   And this teaching of Bar Pedaiah accords with what the following Tannaite authority taught, for it has been taught:

[H]   A Hebrew slave boy serves the son and does not serve the daughter. A Hebrew slave girl serves neither the daughter nor the son (following QE).

[I]   There is a Tannaite authority who teaches, "Whether it is a Hebrew slave girl or a Hebrew slave boy, they do not serve either the son or the daughter [but go free at the death of the master]."

[J] How does that Tannaite authority interpret the language of Scripture, "And to your bondwoman you shall do likewise" (Deut. 15:17)?

[K] He interprets that language to apply to the matter of sending forth the slave well supplied. [("And when you let him go free from you, you shall not let him go empty-handed; you shall furnish him liberally out of your flock, out of your threshing floor, and out of your winepress," Deut. 15:13). That is, when the slave girl goes forth, she, too, should be liberally supplied by the master.]

[L] For it has been taught: These are the ones whom one supplies liberally when they go forth:

[M] He who goes forth at the end of his years of service and at the Jubilee, and the Hebrew slave girl who acquires possession of herself through the appearance of puberty signs.

[N] But he who goes forth by deducting [what is owing] or at the death of the master – they do not supply these liberally.

[XIX.A] It is written, "And his master shall bring him to the judges, and he shall bring him to the door or the doorpost" (Ex. 21:6).

[B] How is this possible?

[C] The slave who was sold by a court is subject to the statement, "And his master will bring him to the judges."

[D] And the one who sells himself is subject to the statement, "And he shall bring him to the door."

[E] R. Ami raised the question: "It is self-evident that, as to the one who is sold by a court, the court writes out [59d] his writ for him.

[F] "But as to the one who sells himself, who writes out the writ for him?" [This question is not answered.]

[XX.A] It is written, "It shall not seem hard to you, when you let him go free from you; for at half the cost of a hired servant he has served you six years" (Deut. 15:18).

[B] A hired hand works by day but does not work by night.

[C] A Hebrew slave works by day and by night.

[D] It is written, "He shall not rule with harshness over him in your sight" (Lev. 15:53), and yet you say this?

[E] R. Ami in the name of R. Yohanan: "His master marries off a Canaanite woman to him, so he turns out to work by day and by night [fathering children for the master by night]."

[F] R. Ba bar Mamel raised the question before R. Ami: "But take note. What if he purchased a priest? [He then could not marry a Canaanite woman.]"

[G] He said to him. "And is an Israelite not released from the general prohibition [against such marriages]? [Likewise a priest in these circumstances is no different.]" When R. Ba bar Mamel heard this, he retracted.

[XXI.A] R. Judah b. R. Bun interpreted this word: "The lobe of the ear is pierced so that, should the slave be a priest, he is not invalidated for service.

[B] R. Meir says, "He was pierced at the gristle [cartilage forming the ear]."

[C] On this basis R. Meir did say, "A priest is not to have his ear pierced [as a slave], lest he thereby be blemished and so be invalidated for the Temple service."

[D] But why should that be a problem? Let the gristle be pierced with a hole less than the size of a yetch, [which will not be a blemish].

[E] Perhaps it may become a hole the size of a yetch [and so blemish the priest].

[F] So let him be pierced with a hole the size of a yetch, [and what difference does that make]?

[G] The Torah has said, "And he shall return to his property ' (Lev. 25:27) – That means, he must return whole [and not blemished].

[H] Now would he have his ear pierced, unless he had a wife and children [and, it follows, that that applies even to a priest, who is also given a Canaanite woman].

[XXII.A] "With an awl" (Ex. 21:6): I know that one may use only an awl. How do I know that it may be done with a wooden prick, thorn, or shard of glass?

[B] Scripture says, "And he will pierce" [by whatever means].

[C] Up to this point [we have answered the question] in accord with R. Aqiba['s mode of exegesis]. How does R. Ishmael answer the same question?

[D] R. Ishmael taught: "In three places the practical law supersedes the biblical text, and in one the legitimate interpretation of the text [ignoring the rules of interpretation].

[E] "The Torah has said, 'in a book' (Deut. 24:1), and the practical law says that on anything that is uprooted from the ground [a writ of divorce may be written].

[F] "The Torah has said, 'with dirt' [the blood is to be covered up] (Lev. 17:13), but the practical law requires that it be done with anything in which seeds will grow.

[G] "The Torah has said, 'with an awl,' but the practical law permits use of a wooden prick, thorn, or shard of glass.

[H] "And in one place the legitimate interpretation of the text:

[I] "[R. Ishmael taught] 'And it shall be on the seventh day he shall shave all his hair (Lev. 14:9)' – a generalization; 'of his head and his beard and his eyebrows' – a particularization; 'even all his hair he shall shave off' – generalization. Where there is a general proposition followed by a particular specification and again followed by a general proposition, only what is like the particulars is included.

[J] "This then tells you, 'Just as the particularization refers explicitly to a place on the body on which hair is gathered together and is visible, so I know only that every place on the body where hair is gathered together and is visible is to be shaved off.'

[K] "But the law rules: 'He should shave him as [smooth as] a gourd.'"

[XXIII.A] "With an awl": Just as an awl is made of metal so anything made of metal [will serve].

[B] Rabbi says, "This refers to a large spit."

[C] R. Yosé b. R. Judah says, "This refers to a chisel."

[D]   "And he shall bring him to the door" (Ex. 21:6). Is it possible to suppose that that is the case even if the door is lying [on the ground]?

[E]   "Scripture says, 'Or to the doorpost' (Ex. 21:6).

[F]   "Just as the doorpost is standing, so the door must be standing.

[G]   "It is a matter of shame to the slave and a matter of shame to a family."

[XXIV.A]   It was taught: R. Eliezer b. Jacob says, "Why is it that he is brought to the door? It is because it is through [blood placed over the lintel on the] door that [the Israelites] went forth from slavery to freedom."

[B]   His disciples asked Rabban Yohanan b. Zakkai, "Why is it that this slave has his ear pierced, rather than any other of his limbs?"

[C]   He said to them, "The ear, which heard from Mount Sinai, 'You will have no other gods before me' (Ex. 20:3), and yet this one broke off the yoke of the kingdom of Heaven and accepted upon itself the yoke of flesh and blood –

[D]   "the ear which heard before Mount Sinai, 'For to me the people of Israel are slaves, they are my slaves whom I brought forth out of the Land of Egypt: I am the Lord your God' (Lev. 25:55), yet this one went and got another master for himself –

[E]   "therefore let the ear come and be pierced, for it has not observed the things it heard."

[XXV.A]   "His ear" [(Ex. 21:6) is stated here, and] "his ear" [is stated elsewhere (Lev. 14:14)] –

[B]   just as "his ear" stated later on refers to the right ear, so "his ear" stated here is the right ear.

[C]   "But if, saying, the slave says..." (Ex. 21:5). Two speeches are under discussion, one at the end of the sixth year of service, the other at the beginning of the Seventh Year –

[D]   one at the end of the sixth year of service, while he is still in his period of service, and one at the beginning of the Seventh Year – [the phrase] "I will not go out free" [supposes that he could if he wishes, and that occurs only at the beginning of the Seventh Year].

[E]   "I love my master, my wife, and my children" (Ex. 21:5). This teaches that he does not have his ear pierced before he has a wife and children, and before his master has a wife and children,

[F]   before he has come to love his master, and his master to love him,

[G]   before the master's possessions are greatly blessed on his account, as it is said, "since he fares well with you" (Deut. 15:16).

[XXVI.A]   And he acquires ownership of himself at the Jubilee [M. 1:2F]: As it is written, "He shall be released in the year of the Jubilee, he and his children with him" (Lev. 25:54),

[B]   or at the death of the master: As it is written, "And he shall be your bondman forever" (Deut. 15:16) – for the "ever" of the master.

On the basis of the passage at hand, it is exceedingly difficult to justify this entire inquiry. All I see is a rather low-level amplification of the Mishnah's and Scripture's treatment of a given topic, with some secondary speculation on details. I cannot identify a premise of an other than exegetical character, on the one side, or practical-logical quality, on the other. On the basis of this passage, we are hardly justified in supposing that a sizable, important corpus of presuppositions of a broad, general character precipitates the formulation of compositions, let alone the construction of composites. Indeed, the notion of "composite" scarcely applies to what is in the aggregate a running commentary devoted to a topic and some propositional allegations on said topic. A brief review shows how these general obervations emerge.

Following the pattern familiar from the discussion of Y. 1:1, we begin with an extensive exercise in proving the Mishnah's propositions on the basis of Scripture. Unit I carries out that exercise. Units II and III then provide a gloss to the Mishnah's language, again out of Scripture. Unit IV proceeds to discuss the language used in a writ. Unit V turns to the exposition of Scripture, relevant to, but not required by, the Mishnah. Unit VI carries forward that same range of interests. Its problem is entirely unrelated to the Mishnah. Units VII-IX proceed to the redemption of the male slave, and unit X to the female one. The main point of unit VII is to take up the matter of setting the purchase price for redemption. This is defined to the slave's maximum advantage. Unit VIII goes on to the matter of the slave's family s redeeming him. The principal issue is whether he must then serve out the original term. Unit IX, finally, provides an exegesis of verses relevant to the entire procedure. Unit X then goes on to the next clause of the Mishnah, now on the freeing of the Hebrew slave girl through her reaching sexual maturity. Units XI-XIV take up the slave girl who is to go free because the master does not designate her for himself (Ex. 28:8). This matter is allowed to follow its own program of inquiry rather than the Mishnah's. The exegesis of the pertinent verses occupies the center of attention.

Unit XI expresses the dispute over the character of the money originally paid by the master to the girl's father. One position is that at the very outset that money has the character of payment for betrothal. The other is that only at the end, once it is so characterized, is that money deemed payment for betrothal. It is not assumed to be such until it is explicitly specified that the money is meant to betroth the girl. The operative language here is "designate," but for all intents and purposes what is meant is betrothal. Unit XII takes up the somewhat simpler issue of whether the master may designate her for someone else besides himself or his son. Units XIII and XIV continue this same inquiry. Unit XV completes the exposition of the views of Yosé b. R. Judah and sages, a construction leaving no obscure points. Unit XVI goes on to the Scripture's specification that the father sells the daughter as a slave girl. The issue is raised about what stipulations the father may make in that regard, and the familiar conundrum about stipulating against the requirements of the Torah is once more addressed. Unit XVII deals with

M. I:2C-D, and unit XVIII adds to the Mishnah another occasion on which the slave girl goes free. Units XIX-XXVI all take up M. 1:2E-F, the slave whose ear is pierced and who serves for life. Once more the principal point of interest is the exegesis of the relevant Scriptures.

II. The Talmud of Babylonia to M. Qiddushin 1:2

1:2

A. A Hebrew slave is acquired through money and a writ.
B. And he acquires himself through the passage of years, by the Jubilee Year, and by deduction from the purchase price [redeeming himself at his outstanding value (Lev. 25:50-51)].
C. The Hebrew slave girl has an advantage over him.
D. For she acquires herself [in addition] through the appearance of tokens [of puberty].
E. The slave whose ear is pierced is acquired through an act of piercing the ear (Ex. 21:5).
F. And he acquires himself by the Jubilee and by the death of the master.

Predictably, we start with the scriptural basis for the Mishnah's rule:

I.1   A. A Hebrew slave is acquired through money and a writ:
      B. *How do we know this?*
      C. Said Scripture, "He shall give back the price of his redemption out of the money that he was bought for" (Lev. 25:51).
      D. So we have found the source of the rule governing a Hebrew slave sold to a gentile, since the only way of acquiring him is by money. How do we know that the same rule applies to one sold to an Israelite?
      E. Said Scripture, "Then he shall let her be redeemed" (Ex. 21:8) – this teaches that she deducts part of her redemption money and goes free.
      F. So we have found the rule governing the Hebrew slave girl, since she is betrothed with a money payment, she is acquired with a money payment. How do we know of it a Hebrew slave boy?
      G. Said Scripture, "If your brother, a Hebrew man or a Hebrew woman, is sold to you and serves you six years" (Deut. 15:12) – Scripture treats as comparable the Hebrew slave boy and the Hebrew slave girl.
      H. So we have found the rule governing those sold by a court, since they are sold willy-nilly. If they have sold themselves, how do we know that that is the case?

The next step is to challenge the logical exegetical premise of the foregoing:

      I. We derive the parallel between the one and the other because of the use of the word "hired hand" [Lev. 25:39: One who sells himself;

one sold by a court, Deut. 15:12ff.; the same word appears in both cases, so the same method of purchase applies to both (Freedman)].

J. *Well, that poses no problems to him who accepts the consequences drawn from the verbal analogy established by the use of the word "hired hand," but for him who denies that analogy and its consequences, what is to be said?*

K. Said Scripture, "And if a stranger or sojourner with you gets rich" (Lev. 25:47) – thus adding to the discussion that is just prior, teaching rules governing what is prior on the basis of rules that govern in what is to follow. [The "and" links Lev. 25:47-55, one who sells himself to a non-Jew, to Lev. 25:39-46, one who sells himself to a Jew; just as the purchase in the one case is carried out by money, so is that of the other (Freedman)].

Then we proceed to investigate the exegetical issue inhering in the foregoing, identifying the authority who stands against the opening exegetical initiative:

I.2

A. *And who is the Tannaite authority who declines to establish a verbal analogy based on the recurrent usage of the word "hired hand" in the several passages?*

B. *It is the Tannaite authority behind the following, which has been taught on Tannaite authority:*

C. He who sells himself may be sold for six years or more than six years; if it is by a court, he may be sold for six years only.

D. He who sells himself may not have his ear bored as a mark of perpetual slavery; if sold by the court, he may have his ear bored.

E. He who sells himself has no severance pay coming to him; if he is sold by a court, he has severance pay coming to him.

F. To him who sells himself, the master cannot assign a Canaanite slave girl; if sold by a court, the master can give him a Canaanite slave girl.

G. R. Eleazar says, "Neither one nor the other may be sold for more than six years; both may have the ear bored; to both severance pay is given; to both the master may assign a Canaanite slave girl."

H. *Isn't this what is at stake: The initial Tannaite authority does not establish a verbal analogy based on the appearance of "hired hand" in both passages, while R. Eleazar does establish a verbal analogy based on the occurrence of "hired hand" in both passages?*

I. *Said R. Tabyumi in the name of Abbayye, "All parties concur that we do establish a verbal analogy based on the appearance in both passages of 'hired hand.' And here, this is what is the operative consideration behind the position of the initial Tannaite authority, who has said, He who sells himself may be sold for six years or more than six years? Scripture has stated a limitation in the context of one sold by a court: 'And he shall serve you six years' (Deut. 15:12), meaning, he but not one who sells himself."*

J. *And the other party?*

K. "And he shall serve you" – not your heir.

L. *And the other party?*

M. *There is another "serve you" in context [at Deut. 15:18].*

N.   *And the other party?*

O.   *That is written to tell you that* the master must be prepared to give severance pay.

I.3   A.   *And what is the scriptural foundation for the position of the initial Tannaite authority, who has said,* He who sells himself may not have his ear bored as a mark of perpetual slavery; if sold by the court, he may have his ear bored?

B.   *Because the All-Merciful has already imposed a limitation in the context of one sold by a court, namely:* "And his master shall bore his ear through with an awl" (Ex. 21:6) – his ear, but not the ear of the one who has sold himself.

C.   **[15A]** *And the other party?*

D.   *That comes for the purpose of establishing a verbal analogy, for it has been taught on Tannaite authority:*

E.   R. Eliezer says, "How on the basis of Scripture do we know that the boring of the ear of the Hebrew slave (Ex. 21:5) must be the right ear?   Here we find a reference to 'ear,' and elsewhere, the same word is used [at Lev. 14:14]. Just as in the latter case, the right ear is meant, so here, too, the right ear is meant."

F.   *And the other party?*

G.   *If so, Scripture should have said merely,* "ear." *Why* "his ear"?

H.   *And the other party?*

I.   *That is required to make the point,* "his ear" not "her ear."

J.   *And the other party?*

K.   *That point derives from the statement,* "But if the slave shall plainly say..." (Ex. 21:5) – the slave boy, not the slave girl.

L.   *And the other party?*

M.   *That verse is required to make the point,* he must make the statement while he is still a slave.

N.   *And the other party?*

O.   *That fact derives from the use of the language* "the slave," *rather than simply,* "slave."

P.   *And the other party?*

Q.   *He draws no such conclusion from the use of the language* "the slave," *rather than simply,* "slave."

I.4   A.   *And what is the scriptural basis for the position of the initial Tannaite authority, who has said,* He who sells himself has no severance pay coming to him; if he is sold by a court, he has severance pay coming to him?

B.   *The All-Merciful expressed an exclusionary clause in regard to one sold by a court, namely,* "You shall furnish him liberally": (Deut. 15:14) – him, but not one who sells himself.

C.   *And the other party?*

D.   *That verse is required to make the point,* "You shall furnish him liberally": (Deut. 15:14) – him, but not his heir.

E.   *But why not provide for his heirs? For Scripture has classified him as a hired hand:* Just as the wages of a hired hand belong to his heirs, so here, too, his wages belong to his heirs?

F.   *Rather: Him – and not his creditor. [And it is necessary to make that point, for] since we concur in general with R. Nathan, as it has been taught on Tannaite authority: R. Nathan says, "How on the basis of*

Scripture do we know that if someone claims a maneh from someone else, and the other party claims the same amount of money from a third party, the money is collected from the third party and paid out directly to the original claimant? 'And give it to him against whom he has trespassed' (Num. 5:7)," *the word "him" in the present case serves to exclude that rule here.*

G. *And the other party?*

H. *Otherwise, too, we do in point of fact differ from R. Nathan.*

I.5   A. *And what is the scriptural basis for the position of the initial Tannaite authority, who has said,* To him who sells himself, the master cannot assign a Canaanite slave girl; if sold by a court, the master can give him a Canaanite slave girl?

B. *The All-Merciful expressed an exclusionary clause in regard to one sold by a court, namely,* "If his master give him a wife" (Ex. 21:4) – him, but not one who sells himself.

C. *And the other party?*

D. "Him" – even against his will.

E. *And the other party?*

F. *He derives that rule from the phrase,* "for to the double of the hire of a hired servant has he served you" (Deut. 15:18), *for it has been taught on Tannaite authority:* "For to the double of the hire of a hired servant has he served you" (Deut. 15:18) – a hired hand works only by day, but a Hebrew slave works by day and night.

G. Well, now can you really imagine that a Hebrew slave works day and night? But has not Scripture stated, "Because he is well off with you" (Deut. 15:16), meaning, he has to be right there with you in food and drink [eating what you eat and living like you], and said R. Isaac, "On this basis it is the rule that his master gives him a Canaanite slave girl."

H. *And the other party?*

I. *If I had to derive the rule from that passage, I might have supposed that that is the case only with his full knowledge and consent, but if it is against his will, I might have thought that that is not so. So we are informed that that is not the case.*

It is scarcely necessary at this point to underscore that the premises of argument are two: scriptural basis for the law of the Mishnah, logical rules for the exegesis of Scripture in relationship to the Mishnah. The interest in the authorities behind the conflicting exegetical-logical principles, of course, responds to a concern to extend the range of analysis; by finding a named authority, we can introduce a variety of topics at which the issue is one and the same, that of exegetics:

I.6   A. *And who is the Tannaite authority who declines to establish a verbal analogy based on the recurrent usage of the word "hired hand" in the several passages?*

B. *It is the Tannaite authority behind the following, which has been taught on Tannaite authority:*

C. "And go back to his own family, and return to the possession of his fathers":

D. Said R. Eliezer b. R. Jacob, "Concerning what classification of slave does Scripture speak?

E. "If it concerns a slave who has had his ear pierced to the doorjamb with an awl, lo, that classification has already been covered.

F. "If it concerns the one who has sold himself, lo, that one has already been covered.

G. "Lo, Scripture speaks only of one who has sold himself for one or two years prior to the Jubilee.

H. "The Jubilee in his case frees him" [Sifra CCLVI:I.12 Parashat Behar Pereq 7].

I. *Now if it should enter your mind that R. Eliezer b. Jacob accepts the verbal analogy based on the recurrent usage of the word "hired hand" in the several passages, what need do I have for this verse and its exegesis? Let him derive the point from the verbal analogy.*

J. *Said R. Nahman bar Isaac, "In point of fact he does accept the verbal analogy involving the hired hand. But nonetheless, the proof we required is given here. For it might have entered your mind to suppose that it is one who sells himself alone who is subject to the law, for he has done no prohibited deed, but if the court has sold the man, in which case it is because he has done a prohibited deed, I might have supposed that we impose an extrajudicial penalty on him and deny him the present advantage. So we are informed that that is not so."*

I.7 A. The master has said: "If it concerns a slave who has had his ear pierced to the doorjamb with an awl, lo, that classification has already been covered": *Where?*

B. *It is as has been taught on Tannaite authority:*

C. "When each of you shall return to his property and each of you shall return to his family":

D. Said R. Eliezer b. Jacob, "Concerning what classification of slave does Scripture speak here?

E. "If it concerns a [Hebrew slave] sold for six years, that of course has already been dealt with. And if it concerns a person sold for a year or two, that of course has already been dealt with.

F. "The passage therefore addresses only the case of the slave who before the Jubilee has had his ear pierced to the doorjamb so as to serve in perpetuity.

G. "The Jubilee serves to release him" [Sifra CCXLVIII:I.1 Parashat Behar Pereq 2].

H. *How so?*

I. Said Raba bar Shila, "Said Scripture, 'And you shall return, every man' (Lev. 25:10) – now what is the rule that applies to a man but not to a woman? You have to say, it is the boring of the ear."

J. *Now it was necessary for Scripture to deal with the case of the court's selling him, and it was necessary for Scripture to deal with the one whose ear has been bored. For had we been informed of the case of the one whom the court has sold, that might have been because his term had not yet expired, but as for him whose ear was bored, since his term had expired, I might have said that we impose an extrajudicial penalty on him. And if we had been informed of the case of the one whose ear was pierced, that might have been because he had already worked for six years, but as to the one* who was sold by the court, who has not yet served for six years, I might have maintained that he is not set free. So it was necessary for Scripture to make both points explicit.

K. And it was further necessary for Scripture to state both "and you shall return" and also "and he shall serve forever." For if the All-Merciful had said only "and he shall serve forever," I might have supposed that that is meant literally. So the All-Merciful found it necessary to state also "and you shall return." And if the All-Merciful had said only "and you shall return," I might have supposed that that is the case when he has not served for six years, but in a case in which he has served for six years, then his latter phase of service should not be subject to a more stringent rule than his former: Just as the first phase of service, when he was sold, was for six years, so his last phase of service should be for only six years; so "forever" informs us, forever to the end of the Jubilee.

I.8 A. And who is the Tannaite authority who declines to establish a verbal analogy based on the recurrent usage of the word "hired hand" in the several passages?

B. It is Rabbi, for it has been taught on Tannaite authority:

C. [15B] "And if he be not redeemed by these" (Lev. 25:54) –

D. Rabbi says, "Through these he is redeemed, but not by the passage of six years. For is not the contrary not plausible, namely, if he who cannot be redeemed by these [a Hebrew slave sold to a Jew, who cannot be redeemed by relatives], can be redeemed through the passage of six years, then this one, who can be redeemed by these, surely should be redeemed through working for six years! So it was necessary to say, 'And if he be not redeemed by these' – through these he is redeemed, but not by the passage of six years."

E. Now if it should enter your mind that Rabbi agrees to establish a verbal analogy based on the recurrent usage of the word 'hired hand' in the several passages, then why does he say, if he who cannot be redeemed by these? Why not deduce the comparable law from the verbal analogy established by the repeated use of "hired hand"?

F. Said R. Nahman bar Isaac, "In point of fact, he does agree to establish a verbal analogy based on the recurrent usage of the word "hired hand" in the several passages. But the case at hand is exceptional, since Scripture has said, 'one of his brothers shall redeem him' (Lev. 25:48) – but not another" [a slave sold to a Jew (Freedman)].

I.9 A. And who is the Tannaite authority who differs from Rabbi?

B. It is R. Yosé the Galilean and R. Aqiba, for it has been taught on Tannaite authority:

C. "And if he be not redeemed by these" (Lev. 25:54) –

D. R. Yosé the Galilean says, "'By these' persons for emancipation, but by anybody else for further subjugation [until the Jubilee]. [If anyone other than the listed relatives redeems him, it is for continued slavery.]"

E. R. Aqiba says, "'By these persons' for further subjugation [until the Jubilee], but by anybody else for emancipation" [Sifra CCLXIX:I.1 Parashat Behar Pereq 9].

F. What is the scriptural basis for the position of R. Yosé the Galilean?

G. Said Scripture, "And if he be not redeemed by these" – but by a stranger – "then he shall go out in the year of Jubilee."

H.   And R. Aqiba?

I.   "And if he be not redeemed by these" – by any but these – "then he shall go out in the year of Jubilee."

J.   And R. Yosé the Galilean?

K.   *Is the language, "by any but these"?*

L.   *Rather, they differ on the following verse:* "Or his uncle, or his uncle's son, may redeem him" (Lev. 25:59) – this speaks of redemption by a relative. "Or if he gets rich" (Lev. 25:39) – this speaks of redeeming oneself. "And he shall be redeemed" (Lev. 25:49) – this speaks of redemption by strangers.

M.   *R. Yosé the Galilean takes the view that the verse is read in the context of what precedes, which join redemption by relatives with redemption of oneself:* Just as when one redeems oneself, it is for freedom, so if relatives do so, it has the same result.

N.   *And R. Aqiba maintains that* a verse of Scripture is read in the context of what follows, *which joins the act of redemption by others to the redemption of oneself:* Just as redemption of himself leads to liberation, so redemption by outsiders yields freedom.

O.   *Well, then, why say* "by these"?

P.   *If the phrase,* "by these," *were not set forth, I might have supposed,* a verse of Scripture is read in the context of either what precedes or what follows, with the result that redemption of any kind yields freedom.

Q.   *If so, our problem comes home again. Rather, it must be that at issue between them is a matter of logic. R. Yosé the Galilean takes the view that it is logic that redemption carried out by others should yield slavery, for if you say it would yield liberation, people would refrain and not redeem him. But R. Aqiba finds more reasonable the view that redemption by relatives yields slavery. For if you say it yields freedom, then every day the man is going to go out and sell himself.*

I.10   A.   Said R. Hiyya bar Abba said R. Yohanan, "Well, then, that represents the view of R. Yosé the Galilean and R. Aqiba. But sages say, 'Redemption by any party at all yields liberation.'"

B.   *Who are* "sages"?

C.   *It is Rabbi, who utilizes* "by these" *for a different interpretation, while the verse indeed is read in the context of either what precedes or what follows, with the result that redemption of any kind yields freedom.]*

D.   *Then how does Rabbi read the verse,* "Then he shall go out in the year of jubilee"?

E.   *He requires it in line with that which has been taught on Tannaite authority:*

F.   "Then he shall go forth in the Jubilee Year": **[16A]** Scripture speaks of a gentile who is subject to your authority.

G.   Well, maybe it speaks of a gentile who is not subject to your authority?

H.   How can you say so, for, if so, what can be done to him [Freedman: how can he be forced to provide facilities for redemption]?

I.   You must say, therefore, Scripture speaks of a gentile who is subject to your authority.

The established program generates yet another familiar inquiry:

II.1 A. [A Hebrew slave is acquired through money] or a writ:
B. *How on the basis of Scripture do we know that fact?*
C. Said Ulla, "Said Scripture, 'If he take him another wife' (Ex. 21:10) [in addition to the Hebrew slave girl] – Scripture thus treats the Hebrew slave girl as another wife: Just as another wife would be acquired by a writ, so a Hebrew slave girl is acquired through a writ."
D. *Well, that proof would clearly pose no problem to him who says, "The writ of a Hebrew slave girl – the master writes it," but from the perspective of him who says, "The father writes it," what is to be said? For it has been stated:*
E. The writ of a Hebrew slave girl – who writes it?
F. R. Huna said, "The master writes it."
G. R. Hisda said, "The father writes it."
H. *So the proposed derivation from Scripture poses no problems, but from the perspective of R. Hisda, what is to be said?*
I. Said R. Aha bar Jacob, "Said Scripture, 'She shall not go forth as slave boys do' (Ex. 21:7) [if the master blinds them or knocks out their teeth] – but she may be purchased in the manner in which slave boys are purchased. *And what might that way be? A writ.*"
J. *Well, why not say:* But she may be purchased in the manner in which slave boys are purchased. *And what might that way be?* Usucaption?
K. Said Scripture, "And you shall make [gentile slaves] an inheritance for your children after you" (Lev. 25:46) – they are acquired by usucaption, and slaves of no other classification are acquired by usucaption.
L. *Well, why not say:* They are acquired by a writ, and slaves of no other classification are acquired by a writ?
M. But isn't it written, "She shall not go forth as slave boys do" (Lev. 21:7)?
N. Well, then, how come you prefer the one reading rather than the other?
O. *It stands to reason that a writ is encompassed as a medium of acquiring title,* since a writ serves to divorce an Israelite woman [Freedman: just as it is effective in one instance, so in another].
P. *To the contrary, usucaption should have been encompassed as a medium of acquiring title,* since it serves to effect acquisition of the property of an heirless proselyte.
Q. *But we don't find such a medium of acquisition relevant when it comes to matters of marital relationship. Or, if you prefer, I shall say that the language, "if he takes another" serves to make that very point* [Freedman: "she shall not go out" teaches that she may be acquired by deed, as is implied by the analogy of "another"].
R. *Now how does R. Huna deal with the clause, "She shall not go forth as slave boys do" (Ex. 21:7) [if the master blinds them or knocks out their teeth]?*
S. *He requires that verse to indicate that* she does not go forth at the loss of the major limbs, as does a slave boy.
T. And R. Hisda?

U. *If so, Scripture should have said,* "She shall not go forth like slave boys." *Why say,* "She shall not go forth as slave boys do" (Ex. 21:7) [if the master blinds them or knocks out their teeth]? *That yields two points.*

III.1   A. **And he acquires himself through the passage of years:**
        B. For it is written, "Six years he shall serve, and in the seventh he shall go free for nothing" (Ex. 21:2).

IV.1   A. **By the Jubilee Year:**
        B. *For it is written,* "He shall serve with you into the year of Jubilee" (Lev. 25:40).

V.1   A. **And by deduction from the purchase price [redeeming himself at this outstanding value]:**
        B. Said Hezekiah, "For said Scripture, 'Then shall he let her be redeemed' (Ex. 21:8) – this teaches that she makes a deduction from her redemption money and goes out free."

V.2   A. *A Tannaite statement:* And he acquires title to himself through money or a cash equivalent or through a writ.
        B. *Now with respect to money, there is no difficulty, for it is written in so many words,* "He shall give back the price of his redemption out of the money he was bought for" (Lev. 25:51). *And as to a cash equivalent, too:* "He shall give back the price of his redemption," *the All-Merciful has said,* extended the law covering cash to a cash equivalent. *But as to this writ, how is it to be imagined? Should we say that the slave writes a bond for the redemption money? Then it is tantamount to money. But if it is a writ of manumission, then why a deed? Let the master say to the slave in the presence of two witnesses of a court:* "Go"?
        C. Said Raba, "That is to say, a Hebrew slave is owned by his master as to his very body, so a master who remitted the deduction – the deduction is not remitted."

VI.1   A. **The Hebrew slave girl has an advantage over him. For she acquires herself [in addition] through the appearance of tokens [of puberty].**
        B. Said R. Simeon b. Laqish, "A Hebrew slave girl has acquired from the domain of her master possession of herself [as a free woman] upon the death of her father. That is the result of an argument a fortiori: If the appearance of puberty signs, which do not free her from her father's authority, free her from the authority of her master, then death, which does free her from her father's authority [the father's heirs have no claim on her], surely should free her from her master's authority [whose heirs should not inherit her]!"
        C. *Objected R. Oshayya,* "**The Hebrew slave girl has an advantage over him. For she acquires herself [in addition] through the appearance of tokens [of puberty].** *But if what he has said were so, then the list should include reference to her father's death as well!*"
        D. *The Tannaite authority has listed some items and left out others.*
        E. *Well, then, what else has he left out, if he has left out this item?*
        F. *He leaves out reference to her master's death.*
        G. *Well, if that is all he has left out, then he has left out nothing, since that would pertain also to a male slave as well, it is omitted anyhow.*
        H. *But why not include it?*

I.   *The Tannaite framer of the passage has encompassed what is subject to a fixed limit [the six years, the proportionate repayment of the purchase price, the Jubilee], but what is not subject to a fixed limit he does not include in his Tannaite rule.*

J.   *But lo, there is the matter of puberty signs, which are not subject to a fixed limit, but the Tannaite framer of the passage has covered them, too.*

K.   Said R. Safra, "They have no fixed limit above, but they are subject to a fixed limit **[16B]** below. *For it has been taught on Tannaite authority:* A boy aged nine who produced two pubic hairs – these are classified as a mere mole; from the age of nine years to twelve years and one day, they are classified as a mere mole. R. Yosé b. R. Judah says, 'They are classified as a mark of puberty.' From thirteen years and one day onward, all parties concur that they are classified as a mark of puberty."

L.   *Objected R. Sheshet,* "R. Simeon says, 'Four are given severance pay, three in the case of males, three in the case of females. And you cannot say there are four in the case of the male, because puberty signs are not effective in the case of a male, and you cannot say there is boring of the ear in the case of the female.' *Now if what R. Simeon b. Laqish has said were valid* ['A Hebrew slave girl has acquired from the domain of her master possession of herself as a free woman upon the death of her father'], *then the death of the father also should be included here. And should you say, the Tannaite authority has listed some items and left out others, lo, he has said matters explicitly in terms of four items! And if you should say, the Tannaite framer of the passage has encompassed what is subject to a fixed limit [the six years, the proportionate repayment of the purchase price, the Jubilee], but he has left off what is not subject to a fixed limit, lo, there is the matter of puberty signs, which are not subject to a fixed limit, and he has encompassed them in the Tannaite statement. And should you say, here as a matter of fact he, too, accords with R. Safra, well, then, there is the matter of the death of the master, which is not subject to a fixed definition as to time, and yet the Tannaite framer has included it. So what are the four items to which reference is made?"*

M.   [1] Years, [2] Jubilee, [3] Jubilee for the one whose ear was bored, and [4] the Hebrew slave girl freed by puberty signs. *And that stands to reason, since the concluding clause goes on to say,* and you cannot say there are four in the case of the male, because puberty signs are not effective in the case of a male, and you cannot say there is boring of the ear in the case of the female. *But if it were the case [that the master's death is covered], then you would have four items for the woman. So that's decisive proof.*

N.   *Objected R. Amram,* "And these are the ones that get severance pay: Slaves freed by the passage of six years of service, the Jubilee, the master's death, and the Hebrew slave girl freed by the advent of puberty signs. *And if the stated proposition were valid, the father's death also should be on the list. And should you say, the Tannaite authority has listed some items and left out others, lo, he has said,* and these are the ones [which is exclusionary, these – no others]. *And if you should say, the Tannaite framer of the passage has encompassed what is subject to a fixed limit [the six years, the proportionate repayment of the purchase price, the Jubilee], but he has left off what is not subject to a fixed limit, lo, there is the matter of puberty signs, which are not subject to a fixed limit, and he has encompassed them in the Tannaite statement. And should you say, here as a matter of fact he, too, accords with R. Safra, well, then, there is the matter of the death of the master. So isn't this a refutation of R. Simeon b. Laqish's position?"*

O. *Sure is.*

P. *But lo, R. Simeon b. Laqish has set forth an argument a fortiori!*

Q. *It's a flawed argument a fortiori, along these lines:* The distinguishing trait of puberty signs is that they mark a change in the body of the girl, but will you say the same of the death of the father, by which the body of the girl is left unaffected?

VI.2 A. *One Tannaite version states,* The severance pay [the gifts given at the end of six years] of a Hebrew slave boy belongs to himself and that of a Hebrew slave girl belongs to herself. *Another Tannaite version states,* The severance pay [the gifts given at the end of six years] of a Hebrew slave girl and things that she finds belong to her father, and her master has a claim only to a fee for loss of time [taken up by finding the lost object]. *Is it not the case that the one speaks of a girl who goes forth by reason of the advent of puberty signs [in which case the severance pay goes to the father], the other liberated at the death of the father?*

B. *Not at all, both speak of freedom by reason of puberty signs, but there is still no conflict, in the one case, the father is alive, in the other, not.*

C. *There is no problem with the statement,* The severance pay [the gifts given at the end of six years] of a Hebrew slave girl belongs to herself, *for it serves to exclude any assignment to her brothers, as has been taught on Tannaite authority:* "And you make them an inheritance for your children after you" (Lev. 25:46, speaking of Canaanite slaves] – them you leave to your sons, and your daughters you do not leave to your sons. This states that a man does not leave title to his daughter as an inheritance to his son. *But as to the statement,* The severance pay [the gifts given at the end of six years] of a Hebrew slave boy belongs to himself, *surely that is obvious! Who else should get it?*

D. *Said R. Joseph, "I see hear a molehill made into a mountain. [This is all redundant.]"*

E. Abbayye said, "This is what R. Sheshet said: 'Who is the authority behind this unattributed statement? It is Totai. For it has been taught on Tannaite authority: Totai says, "'You shall furnish him' (Deut. 15:14) – him, not his creditor"' [and that is the point of the statement at hand]."

VI.3 A. *Reverting to the body of the foregoing:* And these are the ones that get severance pay: Slaves freed by the passage of six years of service, the Jubilee, the master's death, and the Hebrew slave girl freed by the advent of puberty signs. But one who runs away or who is freed by deduction from the purchase price don't get severance pay.

B. R. Meir says, "A runaway doesn't get severance pay, but he who is freed by deduction from the purchase price does get severance pay."

C. R. Simeon says, "Four are given severance pay, three in the case of males, three in the case of females. And you cannot say there are four in the case of the male, because puberty signs are not effective in the case of a male, and you cannot say there is boring of the ear in the case of the female."

D. *What is the source of these rulings?*

E. *It is in line with that which our rabbis have taught on Tannaite authority:*

F. **Is it possible to suppose that a gift is provided only to those who go forth after six years of work? How on the basis of Scripture do we know that one who goes forth on the occasion of the jubilee, or on the death of the owner, or a female slave who goes forth on the appearance of puberty signs [also gets a liberal gift]?**

G. **Scripture says, "When you set him free," "When you do set him free."**

H. **Is it possible to suppose that a runaway and one who goes out through a deduction get it? Scripture states, "When you do set him free," meaning, to him whom you set free you give a gift, and you do not give a gift to him who is set free on his own account [Sifré Deut. CXIX:I.1].**

I. R. Meir says, "A runaway doesn't get severance pay, since his liberation is not on your account, but he who is freed by deduction from the purchase price does get severance pay, for his liberation is on your account."

VI.4 A. *A runaway?! But he has to serve out his term of service. For it has been taught on Tannaite authority:* How on the basis of Scripture do we know that a runaway has to complete his term of service? Scripture states, "Six years he shall serve" (Ex. 21:2).

B. [17A] Might one suppose that that is so even if he got sick?

C. Scripture says, "And in the Seventh Year he shall go out free."

D. *Said R. Sheshet, "Here with what situation do we deal? With a slave that ran away and the Jubilee Year came into force for him. What might you have thought? Since the Jubilee Year is what has sent him forth, we classify the case as one in which you are the one who has sent him forth, and we do not impose a judicial penalty on him but rather we give him severance pay? So we are informed that that is not the case."*

VI.5 A. A master has said: "Might one suppose that that is so even if he got sick? Scripture says, 'And in the Seventh Year he shall go out free – even if he were sick all six years'":

B. *But has it not been taught on Tannaite authority:* If he was sick for three years and worked for three years, he doesn't have to make up the lost time. If he was sick all six years, he is obligated to make up the time?

C. Said R. Sheshet, "It is a case in which he could still do needlework."

D. *Lo, there is an internal contradiction. You have said,* If he was sick for three years and worked for three years, he doesn't have to make up the lost time. *Lo, if it were four, he would have to make up the time. Then note the concluding clause:* If he was sick all six years, he is obligated to make up the time. *Lo, if it were four, he would not have to make up the time!*

E. *This is the sense of the matter:* If he was sick for four years, he is treated as though he were sick all six, and he does have to make up the time.

VI.6 A. *Our rabbis have taught on Tannaite authority:*

B. How much do they give in severance pay?

C. "Five selas worth of each kind mentioned in Scripture [Deut. 15:14: 'Out of your flock and out of your threshing floor and out of your wine press'], that is, fifteen in all," the words of R. Meir.

D. R. Judah says, "Thirty, as in the thirty paid for a gentile slave" [Ex. 21:32].

E. R. Simeon says, "Fifty, as in the fifty for valuations" [Lev. 27:3].

VI.7 A. The master has said, "'Five selas worth of each kind mentioned in Scripture [Deut. 15:14: "out of your flock and out of your threshing floor and out of your wine press"], that is, fifteen in all,' the words of R. Meir."

B. [With reference to "that is, fifteen in all," we ask:] *Well, then, is it R. Meir's intention to inform us how to count?*

C. *What he proposes to tell us is that he may not diminish the total, but if he gives less of one classification and more of another, we have no objection.*

D. *What is the scriptural basis for R. Meir's conclusion?*

E. *He forms a verbal analogy on the basis of the occurrence of the word "empty-handed" here and with reference to the firstborn [Deut. 15:13: "You shall not let him go empty-handed"; Ex. 34:20: "All the first born of your sons you shall redeem, none shall appear before me empty-handed"]. Just as in that case, five selas is the fixed sum, so here, too, five selas is the fixed sum.*

F. *Might one say then, there must be five selas worth of each item?*

G. *If the word "empty-handed" had been written at the end of the verse, it might be as you say; but since the word "empty-handed" is written at the outset, the word "empty-handed" pertains to "flock," "threshing floor," and "wine press," item by item.*

H. *Why not derive the meaning of the word "empty-handed" from the verbal analogy deriving from the burnt-offering brought at one's appearance on the pilgrim festival [and much less than five selas is required there]?*

I. Said Scripture, "As the Lord your God has blessed you you shall give to him" (Deut. 15:14).

VI.8 A. R. Judah says, "Thirty, as in the 'thirty' paid for a gentile slave" [Ex. 21:32]:

B. *What is the scriptural basis for the position of R. Judah?*

C. *He establishes a verbal authority on the basis of the occurrence of the word "giving" here and in the case of the slave. Just as in that case, thirty selas is involved, so here, too, thirty selas is involved.*

D. *Why not establish the verbal analogy with the common use of the word "giving" with reference to severance pay and valuations, with the result:* Just as in that case, fifty selas is involved, so here, too, fifty selas is involved.

E. *First of all, if you hold onto a great deal, you hold nothing, but if you hold onto a little, you will hold onto it, and, furthermore, you should establish the verbal analogy on the basis of passages that speak in particular of slaves.*

VI.9 A. R. Simeon says, "Fifty, as in the fifty for valuations" [Lev. 27:3].

B. *What is the scriptural basis for the position of R. Simeon?*

C. *He establishes a verbal authority on the basis of the occurrence of the word "giving" here and in the case of valuations.* Just as in that case, fifty selas is involved, so here, too, fifty selas is involved.

D. *Might one say it may be the least sum that will serve for a valuation [which is five sheqels, Lev. 27:6]?*

E. *"...As the Lord your God has blessed you"* (Deut. 15:14).

F. *And why not establish a verbal authority on the basis of the occurrence of the word "giving" here and in the case of the slave.* Just as in that case, thirty selas is involved, so here, too, thirty selas is involved, *for, after all, first,* if you hold onto a great deal, you hold nothing, but if you hold onto a little, you will hold onto it, *and, furthermore, you should establish the verbal analogy on the basis of passages that speak in particular of slaves?*

G. *R. Simeon draws his verbal analogy on the basis of the recurrent word "poverty"* [Lev. 25:39 for the slave, Lev. 27:8 for the valuation].

VI.10 A. *Well, now, from R. Meir's perspective, we can understand why Scripture states, "out of your flock and out of your threshing floor and out of your wine press"* (Deut. 15:14). *But from R. Judah's and R. Simeon's viewpoint, why are these items –* flock and threshing floor and wine press *– required?*

B. *These are required in line with that which has been taught on Tannaite authority:*

C. *"...Of the flock, threshing floor, and vat":*

D. Might one suppose that one furnishes a gift solely from the flock, threshing floor, and vat in particular? How on the basis of Scripture do I know to encompass every sort of thing?

E. Scripture says, "Furnish him...with whatever the Lord your God has blessed you, you shall give to him," which serves to encompass every sort of thing.

F. If so, why is it said, "...of the flock, threshing floor, and vat"?

G. "Just as the flock, threshing floor, and vat are characterized by being worthy of blessing, so is excluded a payment of cash, which is not the occasion for a blessing": The words of R. Simeon.

H. R. Eliezer b. Jacob says, "What is excluded are mules, which do not produce offspring" [Sifré Deut. CXIX:II.3].

VI.11 A. And R. Simeon?

B. *Mules themselves can increase in value.*

C. And R. Eliezer b. Jacob?

D. *One can do business with ready cash.*

Here we come to a familiar initiative of the Bavli, showing why a variety of items must be specified, by identifying differences between one and the next:

VI.12 A. *And it was necessary for all of these items to be made articulate. For if the All-Merciful had made reference to the flock, I might have thought that the law applies to animate creatures but not to what grows from the soil. So the All-Merciful has written, "threshing floor." And if the Scripture had made reference only to threshing floor, I might have thought that the gift* *may be what grows from the soil but not animate creatures. So Scripture wrote, "flock."*

B.   *What need do I have for a reference to the vat?*
C.   [17B] *In the view of one master, it serves to exclude ready cash, of the other, mules.*

VI.13   A.   *Our rabbis have taught on Tannaite authority:*
B.   "Furnishing him, you shall furnish him liberally" (Deut.15:14):
C.   I know only that if the household of the master has been blessed on account of the slave, that one must give a present. How do I know that even if the household of the master was not blessed on account of the slave, a gift must be given?
D.   Scripture says, "Furnishing him, you shall furnish him liberally" (Deut.15:14) – under all circumstances.
E.   R. Eleazar b. Azariah says, "If the household has been blessed for the sake of the slave, a present must be given, but if not, then the present need not be made" [Sifré Deut. CXIX:III.1].
F.   *Then what is the sense of "Furnishing him"?*
G.   In this case Scripture used language in an ordinary way.

VI.14   A.   *Our rabbis have taught on Tannaite authority:*
B.   The Hebrew slave boy serves the son but doesn't serve the daughter. The Hebrew slave girl serves neither the son nor the daughter. The slave whose ear has been bored and the slave that is sold to a gentile serves neither the son nor the daughter.

VI.15   A.   The master has said, "The Hebrew slave boy serves the son but doesn't serve the daughter":
B.   *What is the source for that ruling?*
C.   *It is in line with that which has been taught on Tannaite authority:*
D.   "[If a fellow Hebrew, man or woman, is sold to you,] he shall serve you six years":
E.   ["You,"] and also your son. [The Hebrew slave remains the possession of the son, if the father dies within the six-year spell.]
F.   Might one think that the same rule applies to the heir [other than the son]?
G.   Scripture says, "Six years he shall serve you."
H.   What is it that moved you to include the son but to exclude any other heir?
I.   I include the son because the son takes the father's place in [Hammer:] designating [the Hebrew bondwoman as his wife], and in recovering for his family an ancestral field that has been alienated.
J.   But I exclude any other heir, because any other heir does not take the father's place in [Hammer:] designating [the Hebrew bondwoman as his wife], and in recovering for his family an ancestral field that has been alienated [CXVIII:IV.1] [given in Sifré Deut.'s wording].
K.   But to the contrary: I should encompass the brother, who takes the place of the deceased childless brother for a levirate marriage! Is there a levirate marriage except where there is no offspring? If there is an offspring, there is no levirate marriage.
L.   *Then the operative consideration is that there is this refutation, but otherwise, would the brother be preferable?*

M. *Why not infer the opposite: Here where there is a son, there are two points in his favor, there, only one?*

N. *The consideration of the son in regard to the field of inheritance is also inferred from this same refutation, namely: Is there a levirate marriage except where there is no son?*

VI.16 A. The Hebrew slave girl serves neither the son nor the daughter.

B. *What is the source for that ruling?*

C. Said R. Peda, "Said Scripture, 'And if he say to you, I will not go out from you...then you shall take an awl and thrust it through his ear...and also to your slave girl you shall do likewise' (Deut. 15:16-17). In this way Scripture has treated her as comparable to him whose ear is bored: Just as the latter serves neither the son nor the daughter, so the former serves neither the son nor the daughter."

D. *Well, is that the purpose that is served by this verse? It surely is required in line with that which have been taught on Tannaite authority:*

E. **"Do the same with your female slave":**

F. **That refers to providing a generous gift when she leaves.**

G. **What about piercing her ear to the door?**

H. **Scripture says, "But should he say to you...," the slave, not the slave girl [Sifré Deut. CXXI.V.3].**

I. How then do I deal with the clause, "and also to your female slave do the same"?

J. It is in regard to the severance pay.

K. *If so, Scripture should have said, "and also to your slave girl likewise," why add, "you shall do"? It makes both points.*

VI.17 A. The slave whose ear has been bored and the slave that is sold to a gentile serves neither the son nor the daughter.

B. The slave whose ear has been bored: "And his master shall bore his ear through with an awl, and he shall serve him forever" (Ex. 21:6) – him but not his son or daughter.

C. And the slave that is sold to a gentile serves neither the son nor the daughter: *What is the source for that ruling?*

D. Said Hezekiah, "Said Scripture, 'And he shall reckon with his purchaser' (Lev. 25:50) – but not with his purchaser's heirs."

VI.18 A. Said Raba, "By the law of the Torah, a gentile may inherit his father's estate, as it is said, 'And he shall reckon with his purchaser,' but not with his purchaser's heirs, *which proves that he has heirs.* A proselyte's inheriting from a gentile is not based on the law of the Torah but only on the rulings of scribes. *For we have learned in the Mishnah:* **A proselyte and a gentile who inherited [the property of] their father, [who was] a gentile – he [the proselyte brother] may say to him [the gentile brother], "You take the idols and I [will take] the coins; you [take] the libation wine and I [will take] the produce." And if [he said this] after it [the property] came into his possession, this [arrangement] is forbidden [M. Dem. 6:9A-E].** *Now if it should enter your mind that it is by the law of the Torah that the proselyte inherits his gentile father's estate, then even if the goods have not yet come into his possession, when he takes the money or produce, he is taking something in exchange for an idol* [which would be forbidden, since the inheritance is automatically of a half-share of everything, whether he has taken possession or not (Freedman)]. *So* *it follows that it is by rabbinical law, a preventive measure enacted by rabbis to take account of the threat that he may return to his wickedness."*

B. So, too, it has been taught on Tannaite authority: Under what circumstances? In a case of inheritance. But in a case of mere partnership, such an arrangement is forbidden [and the proselyte may not derive benefit from an idol or libation wine].

C. [Raba continues,] "A gentile inherits the estate of a proselyte, or a proselyte inherits the estate of a proselyte, neither by the law of the Torah nor by the law of the scribes. *For it has been taught on Tannaite authority:* A man who borrows money from a proselyte whose children converted with him must not return the money to the children [who are not his heirs], and if he does, sages are not pleased with him."

D. *But it also has been taught on Tannaite authority,* and if he does, sages are pleased with him!

E. *No problem,* the former refers to a case in which his conception and birth were not in a circumstance of sanctification, **[18A]** the latter, a case in which his conception was not in conditions of sanctification, but his birth was in conditions of sanctification.

F. R. Hiyya bar Abin said R. Yohanan said, "A gentile inherits his father's estate by the law of the Torah, as it is written, 'Because I have given Mount Seir to Esau for an inheritance' (Deut. 2:5)."

G. *But perhaps the case of an Israelite apostate is exceptional?*

H. *Rather, proof derives from the following:* "Because I have given to the children of Lot Ar as an inheritance" (Deut. 2:9).

I. *And how come R. Hiyya bar Abin does not rule as does Raba?*

J. *Is it written, "and he shall reckon with his purchaser but not his purchaser's heirs"?*

K. *And how come Raba does not rule as does R. Hiyya bar Abin?*

L. *Because the honor owing to Abraham makes the situation exceptional.*

VI.19 A. *Our rabbis have taught on Tannaite authority:*

B. "...A fellow Hebrew, man or woman":

C. Rules pertain to the Hebrew male that do not pertain to the Hebrew female,

D. and rules pertain to the Hebrew female that do not pertain to the Hebrew male:

E. Rules pertain to the Hebrew male: For a Hebrew male goes forth through the passage of years and at the Jubilee and through the deduction of the years yet to be served by the payment of money and through the death of the master, none of which applies to the Hebrew female slave.

F. A Hebrew female slave goes forth when she produces puberty signs, she may not be sold to third parties, she may be redeemed even against her wishes, none of which applies to the Hebrew male slave.

G. Lo, since it is the fact, therefore, that rules pertain to the Hebrew male that do not pertain to the Hebrew female, and rules pertain to the Hebrew female that do not pertain to the Hebrew male, it is necessary to make explicit both the Hebrew man and the Hebrew woman [Sifré Deut. CXVIII:III.2].

VI.20   A.   The master has said: **"Rules pertain to the Hebrew male that do not pertain to the Hebrew female":**

       B.   *By way of contradiction:* **The Hebrew slave girl has an advantage over him. For she acquires herself [in addition] through the appearance of tokens [of puberty]***!*

       C.   Said R. Sheshet, "For instance, if he designated her as his wife" [in which case these signs would not apply].

       D.   *If he designated her as his wife? Obviously! She would require a writ of divorce in that case!*

       E.   *What might you imagine? In her instance the rules pertaining to a Hebrew slave girl are not suspended? So we are informed that that is not the case.*

       F.   *If so, then how come she goes forth through the advent of the tokens of puberty?*

       G.   *This is the sense of the matter:* If he did not designate her for marriage, then she would go forth by the advent of the tokens of puberty as well.

VI.21   A.   **She may not be sold to third parties:** *So does that imply that a slave boy may be sold to third parties? But has it not been taught on Tannaite authority:*

       B.   "If he have nothing, then he shall be sold for his theft" (Ex. 22:2) – but not for paying the double indemnity [that is owing by a thief, Ex. 22:3].

       C.   "If he have nothing, then he shall be sold for his theft" (Ex. 22:2) – but not for paying the indemnity brought on him by testimony of his that has been shown part of a conspiracy of perjury.

       D.   "If he have nothing, then he shall be sold for his theft" (Ex. 22:2) – once he has been sold one time, you are not again permitted to sell him. [There can be no sale to third parties.]

       E.   *Said Raba, "No problem, the one speaks of a single act of theft, the other of multiple acts of theft."*

       F.   *Said to him Abbayye, "'...for his theft...' bears the sense of any number of thefts."*

       G.   *Rather, said Abbayye, "No problem, the one speaks of a single individual, the other of two or more."*

VI.22   A.   *Our rabbis have taught on Tannaite authority:*

       B.   If the theft was worth a thousand zuz and the thief is worth only five hundred, he is sold and resold. If his theft was worth five hundred zuz and he was worth a thousand, he is not sold at all.

       C.   R. Eliezer says, "If his theft was worth his sale price, he is sold, and if not, he is not sold."

VI.23   A.   *Said Raba, "In this matter R. Eliezer got the better of rabbis, for what difference does it make whether what he stole is worth five hundred and he is worth a thousand, in which case he is not sold? It is because Scripture says, 'then he shall be sold,' meaning, all of him, not half. Well, here, too, Scripture says, 'he shall be sold for his theft,' but not for half of his theft."*

VI.24   A.   **She may be redeemed even against her wishes, none of which applies to the Hebrew male slave:**

       B.   *Raba considered interpreting, "...against the wishes of the master."*

C. Said to him Abbayye, "What would be the case? That a bond is written for the master covering her value? But then why does he have to accept the bond? The guy's holding a pearl in his hand, shall we give him a sherd?"

D. Rather, said Abbayye, "The meaning can only be, against the father's will, because of the embarrassment of the family."

E. If so, then the same should apply to the Hebrew slave – let the members of his family be forced to redeem him because of the embarrassment of his family.

F. But he may just go and sell himself again, and here, too, the father will just go and sell her again!

G. But hasn't it been taught as part of the Tannaite statement at hand: **She may not be sold to third parties?** [So that can't happen]. And who is the authority? It is R. Simeon, for it has been taught on Tannaite authority: A man may sell his daughter into marriage, then do the same for bondage, then do the same for marriage after bondage, but he may not sell her into bondage after she has been married. R. Simeon says, "Just as he may not sell his daughter into bondage after marriage, so a man may not sell his daughter into bondage after he has sold her into bondage."

H. This involves the dispute of the following Tannaite statements, as has been taught on Tannaite authority:

I. "To sell her unto a strange people he shall have no power, since he has dealt deceitfully with her" (Ex. 21:8):

J. [18B] "Since he spread his cloth over her [reading the letters that yield 'dealt deceitfully' as though they bore the vowels to yield 'his cloth'], he may not again sell her," the words of R. Aqiba.

K. R. Eliezer says, "'...since he has dealt deceitfully with her' (Ex. 21:8) – he may not again sell her."

L. What is at issue here?   R. Eliezer rejects the view that the reading supplied by the vowels dictates the sense of Scripture, R. Aqiba affirms the view that the reading supplied by the vowels dictates the sense of Scripture, R. Simeon both maintains and denies the view that the reading supplied by the vowels dictates the sense of Scripture.

VI.25   A. Rabbah bar Abbuha raised this question: "Does designating the slave girl for marriage effect the status of a fully consummated marriage or does it bring about the status of betrothal? The upshot is the familiar issue of whether or not he inherits her estate, contracts uncleanness to bury her if he is a priest and she dies, and abrogates her vows. What is the law?"

B. Come and take note: "since he spread his cloth over her [reading the letters that yield 'dealt deceitfully' as though they bore the vowels to yield 'his cloth], he may not again sell her" – so what he can't do is sell her, but lo, he may designate her for marriage. Now, if you maintain that the designation effects a consummated marriage, then, once she has married, her father has no more power over her. So must it not follow that the designation effects only a betrothal?

C. Said R. Nahman bar Isaac, "Here the issue concerns a betrothal in general [not only the slave girl's being designated by her master for marriage to himself or his son], and this is the sense of the statement: Since the father has handed her over to one who accepts liability to provide for 'her food, clothing, and conjugal rights' (Ex. 21:10) [and so betrothed her], he may not sell her again."

D. *Come and take note:* The father may not sell her to relatives [who because of consanguinity cannot designate her as a wife]. In the name of R. Eliezer, they have said, "He may sell her to relatives." But both sides concur that, if she is a widow, he may nonetheless sell her to a high priest, and, if she is a divorcée or a woman who has executed the rite of removing the shoe, he may sell her to an ordinary priest." *Now as to the widow, what sort of a situation confronts us? Shall we say that she accepted a betrothal in her own behalf? Then can she be classified as a widow?* [Freedman: Not at all, her actions are null, as would be the case of any other minor.] *So it must mean that her father has betrothed her. But can he have sold his daughter for bondage after she was married? And lo,* a man may not sell his daughter into bondage after she has been married, *and in that connection said R. Amram said R. Isaac, "Here we deal with a case of designation, within the theory of R. Yosé b. R. Judah, who has said, 'The original money for her was not given for betrothal.'"* [The money paid for the slave girl is not for betrothal; when the girl is designated for marriage, it is via the work she owes him, not the money he has given; therefore the father can resell her after the master's death, and it is not regarded as bondage after betrothal, since he didn't accept the original money as betrothal money (Freedman).] *Now, if you take the position that the designation has effected a consummated marriage, then, once she is married, her father has no longer got any authority over her?*

E. *Yes, but, what's the sense of* "it effects a betrothal" or of "and both agree"? *For lo,* a man may not sell his daughter into bondage after she has been married! *Rather, what do you have to say? An act of betrothal done by her is different from one done by her father?* [Freedman: When her father receives a token of betrothal on her behalf, he loses his authority to sell her later on; but when she gets it, for example, through her labor, meaning, renunciation of the work she owes, her father still has the right to sell her.] *But then, even if you maintain that designation effects a fully consummated marriage, her own arrangement of the fully consummated marriage still will differ in effect from her father's.*

F. *But how are the matters parallel? True enough, the act of betrothal that she undertakes will produce a different result from the act of betrothal that her father undertakes, but will there be any difference between an act of consummated marriage done by her and one done by her father?*

G. **[19A]** *And from the perspective of R. Nahman bar Isaac, who said even from the viewpoint of R. Yosé b. R. Judah, "The original money for her was not given for betrothal," how are you going to explain the matter?*

H. *It will be in accord with R. Eliezer, who has said, "It is for a condition of subjugation after another condition of subjugation that he cannot sell her, but he can sell her for subjugation after marriage."*

VI.26   A. *R. Simeon b. Laqish raised this question: "What is the law on designating the slave girl for his minor son? 'His son' [Ex. 21:9] is what Scripture has said, meaning, his son of any classification? Or perhaps, 'his son' comparable to him, meaning,* just as he is an adult, so his son must be an adult?"

B. *Said R. Zira, "Come and take note:* ['And the man who commits adultery with another man's wife, even he who commits adultery with his neighbor's wife, the adulterer and the adulteress shall surely be put to death' (Lev. 20:10)]. 'A man' – excluding a minor. '...who commits adultery with another man's wife' – excluding the wife of a minor. Now if you say that he can designate [her for a minor], then you find the possibility of a matrimonial bond in the case of a minor."

C. *So what's the upshot? That he can't designate her for a minor son? Then why should Scripture exclude that possibility? Rather, on this basis, solve the problem to indicate that he can designate her for a minor [since that's the only way a minor male can be legally married]!*

D. *Said R. Ashi, "In this case we deal with a levir who is nine years and a day old who has sexual relations with his levirate bride, in which case, on the basis of the law of the Torah, she is a suitable wife for him. Now what might you have said? Since on the strength of the law of the Torah, she is a suitable wife for him, and his act of sexual relations is valid, then he who has sexual relations with her is liable on the count of doing so with a married woman? So we are informed to the contrary."*

E. *So what's the upshot of the matter?*

F. *Come and take note:* Said R. Yannai, "The designation of the slave girl for a wife can take place only with an adult male; the designation of a slave girl for a wife may take place only with full knowledge and consent of the man," [which solves Simeon b. Laqish's problem].

G. *Two items?*

H. *The sense of the matter is what is set forth, that is, how come* the designation of the slave girl for a wife can take place only with an adult male? *It is because* the designation of a slave girl for a wife may take place only with full knowledge and consent of the man.

I. *But why not say, what is the meaning of* full knowledge and consent? It must be full knowledge and consent of the woman!

J. *For Abbayye b. R. Abbahu repeated as a Tannaite statement:* "'If she does not please her master, who has not espoused her' – this teaches that he has to inform her that he plans to designate her." He is the one who repeated it, and he is the one who explained it: "It refers to the betrothal effected by designation, *and accords with the position of R. Yosé b. R. Judah,* who said, 'The original money for her was not given for betrothal.'"

K. *R. Nahman bar Isaac said, "You may even maintain that the money was given for betrothal, but this case is exceptional, for the All-Merciful has said, 'designate' [meaning, designate with full knowledge and consent]."*

VI.27 A. *What is the source for the position of R. Yosé b. R. Judah?*

B. *It is in line with that which has been taught on Tannaite authority:*

C. "If she does not please her master, who has espoused her to himself, then he shall let her be redeemed" – there must be enough time in the day to allow redeeming her [Freedman: if her master wishes to designate her on the very last day of her servitude, her labor still owing must be worth at least a penny, so that she could be redeemed from the work; otherwise he cannot designate her]. On the strength of that fact, said R. Yosé b. R. Judah, "If there is enough time left on that last day for her to work for him to the value of a penny, she is betrothed, and if not, she is not betrothed." *Therefore he takes the position that* the original money for her was not given for betrothal.

D. R. *Nahman bar Isaac said, "You may even maintain that* the original money for her was given for betrothal, *but this case is different, for said the All-Merciful, 'then he shall let her be redeemed.'"*

VI.28 A. Said Raba said R. Nahman, "*A man may say to his minor daughter, 'Go, accept your own token of betrothal.' This is on the basis of what R. Yosé b. R. Judah has said. For didn't he say that* the original money for her was not given for betrothal? *But when the master leaves her only a penny's worth of her labor, that serves for a token of betrothal, so here, too, it is no different.*"

VI.29 A. And said Raba said R. Nahman, "He who betroths a woman through transfer of a debt on which there is a pledge – she is betrothed. *This is on the basis of what R. Yosé b. R. Judah has said. For didn't he say that* the original money for her was not given for betrothal? [19B] *But this work represents a loan, for which she herself is pledge, when the master leaves her only a penny's worth of her labor, that serves for a token of betrothal, so here, too, it is no different.*"

VI.30 A. *Our rabbis have taught on Tannaite authority:*
       B. How is the religious duty of designating the slave girl carried out?
       C. The master says to her in the presence of two valid witnesses, "Lo, you are consecrated to me," "Lo, you are betrothed to me,"
       D. – even at the end of six years, even near sunset at the end of that time.
       E. And he then deals with her in the custom of a matrimonial bond and he does not deal with her in the custom of servitude.
       F. R. Yosé b. R. Judah says, "If there is enough time left on that last day for her to work for him to the value of a penny, she is betrothed, and if not, she is not betrothed."
       G. This matter may be compared to one who says to a woman, "Be betrothed to me as from now, after thirty days have gone by," and someone else comes along and betroths her within the thirty days. So far as the law of designation is concerned, she is betrothed to the first party.

VI.31 A. *Now whose position is served by this parable? Should we say the parable pertains to the position of R. Yosé b. R. Judah? Lo, if there is enough* time left on that last day for her to work for him to the value of a penny, she is betrothed, and if not, she is not betrothed! [Freedman: This proves that the betrothal commences not at the beginning of her servitude but only at the last moment; here, too, the betrothal commences at the end of thirty days, and therefore if another man betroths her in the meantime, she is betrothed to the second.]
       B. *Said R. Aha b. Raba, "The parable serves to illustrate the position of rabbis."*
       C. *Yeah, so what else is new?*
       D. *What might you otherwise have supposed? The master didn't say, "As from now"?* [Freedman: Therefore in the analogous case, even if he says, "You are betrothed after...," and another does so within the

thirty days, she is betrothed to the first.] *So we are informed that that consideration does not come into play.*

VI.32   A.   *It has further been taught on Tannaite authority:*

B.   "He who sells his daughter and went and accepted betrothal for her with a second party has treated the master shabbily, and she is betrothed to the second party," the words of R. Yosé b. R. Judah.

C.   But sages say, "If he wants to designate her as a wife for himself or for a son, he may do so."

D.   This matter may be compared to one who says to a woman, "Be betrothed to me after thirty days have gone by," and someone else comes along and betroths her within the thirty days. So far as the law of designation is concerned, she is betrothed to the second party.

VI.33   A.   *Now whose position is served by this parable? Should we say the parable serves the position of rabbis? Lo, rabbis maintain, "If he wants to designate her as a wife for himself or for a daughter, he may do so." Said R. Aha b. Raba, "The parable serves to illustrate the position of rabbis."*

B.   *Yeah, so what else is new?*

C.   *What might you otherwise have supposed? Lo, he did not say to her, "After thirty days"? So we are informed that that is not the operative consideration.* [Freedman: Her master did not say he would designate her after a certain period, therefore the second man's betrothal is valid; but if he said, "Be betrothed after...," I might have thought she is betrothed to him, and the second man's betrothal is null. Now, since Scripture empowered him to designate her through purchase, it is as though he had said he would subsequently designate her; the cases are analogous.]

VI.34   A.   *It has further been taught on Tannaite authority:*

B.   "He who sells his daughter and agreed that it was on condition that her master not designate her a wife for himself or his son, the stipulation is valid," the words of R. Meir.

C.   And sages say, "If he wanted to designate her as a wife for himself or his son, he may do so, since he has made a stipulation contrary to what is written in the Torah, and any stipulation in violation of what is written in the Torah is null."

VI.35   A.   *Well, then, from R. Meir's perspective, is his stipulation valid? And hasn't it been taught on Tannaite authority:*

B.   "He who says to a woman, 'Lo, you are betrothed to me on the stipulation that you have no claim upon me for provision of food, clothing, and sex' – lo, she is betrothed, and his stipulation is null," the words of R. Meir.

C.   And R. Judah says, "With respect to property matters [food, clothing], his stipulation is valid."

D.   *Said Hezekiah, "This case is exceptional, for Scripture has said, '...and if a man sell his daughter to be a slave girl' (Ex. 21:7) – there are occasions on which he may sell her only to be a slave girl alone."*

E.   *And as to rabbis, how do they deal with this statement, "and if a man sell his daughter to be a slave girl" (Ex. 21:7)?*

F.   *They require it in line with that which has been taught on Tannaite authority:*

G. "And if a man sell his daughter to be a slave girl" (Ex. 21:7) – this teaches that he may sell her to those who are invalid to marry her [for example, a mamzer].

H. But does that fact not follow merely from a logical argument, namely, if he can betroth her to unfit persons, can't he sell her to unfit persons?

I. But what makes it possible for him to betroth her to unfit persons is that a man may betroth his daughter when she is in the status of pubescent, but can he sell her to unfit persons, since he cannot sell his daughter when she is pubescent? Therefore it is required to prove that point from Scripture's explicit statement, "he may sell her to those who are invalid to marry her [for example, a mamzer]," which teaches that he may sell her to those who are invalid to marry her [for example, a mamzer].

J. R. Eliezer says, "If the purpose is to indicate that he may sell her to those who are invalid to marry her [for example, a mamzer], lo, that is already indicated by the verse, 'if she displease her master so that he has not espoused her,' meaning, she was displeasing in regard to an entirely valid matrimonial bond. So what is the point of the verse, 'and if a man sell his daughter to be a slave girl' (Ex. 21:7)? This teaches that he may sell her [20A] to relatives."

K. But does that fact not follow merely from a logical argument, namely, if he can betroth her to unfit persons, can't he sell her to relatives?

L. What makes it possible for him to sell her to unfit persons is that, if he wanted to designate her as a wife, he may do so, but can he sell her to relatives, who, if one of them wished to designate her as a wife, may not do so? So it was necessary for Scripture to say, "he may sell her to those who are invalid to marry her [for example, a mamzer]," which teaches that he may sell her to relatives.

M. And R. Meir?

N. *That he may sell her to unfit persons is a proposition he derives from the same verse used by R. Eliezer for that proposition, and as to selling her to relatives, he concurs with rabbis, who take the position that* he may not sell her to relatives.

VI.36 A. *One Tannaite statement holds:* He may not sell her to relatives, *and another Tannaite statement,* he may sell her to his father, but he may not sell her to his son, *and yet another Tannaite statement,* he may not sell her either to his father or to his son.

B. *Now there is no problem understanding the position,* he may not sell her either to his father or to his son, *since this would accord with rabbis. But in accord with what authority is the position,* he may sell her to his father, but he may not sell her to his son? *This is neither in accord with rabbis nor with R. Eliezer?*

C. *In point of fact is is in accord with rabbis, for rabbis concede in a case in which there is a possibility of designating her as a wife* [the father for the son, who may be her uncle; but the son cannot betroth her for himself nor designate her for his son (Freedman)].

VI.37 A. *Our rabbis have taught on Tannaite authority:*

B. "If he came in by himself, he shall go out by himself" (Ex. 21:3) – he comes in with his body whole and undamaged, and he goes out in the same condition.

C. R. Eliezer b. Jacob says, "He comes in single, he goes out single."

VI.38　A. *What is the meaning of the phrase, he comes in with his body whole and undamaged, and he goes out in the same condition?*

B. Said Raba, "This is to say that he is not freed through loss of his major limbs, as a gentile slave is."

C. *Said to him Abbayye, "That proposition derives from the language, 'She shall not go out as slave boys do' (Ex. 21:7)."*

D. *"If I had to rely on that verse, I should have thought that he has to pay him, at least, the value of his eye, at which point he also frees him. So we are informed that that is not the case."*

VI.39　A. *What is the meaning of the phrase, he comes in single, he goes out single?*

B. *Said R. Nahman bar Isaac, "This is the sense of the statement: If a Hebrew slave does not have a wife and children, his master cannot give him a Canaanite slave girl. If he does have a wife and children, his master may give him a Canaanite slave girl."*

VI.40　A. *Our rabbis have taught on Tannaite authority:*

B. If a person was sold as a slave for a maneh and increased in value so that he was then worth two hundred zuz, how do we know that they reckon with his value only at the rate of a maneh?

C. As it is said, "He shall give back the price of his redemption out of the money that he was bought for" (Lev. 25:51).

D. If he was sold for two hundred zuz and lost value and was priced at a maneh, how do we know that we reckon his worth only at a maneh?

E. As it is said, "According to his years shall he give back the price of his redemption" (Lev. 25:52).

F. Now I know thus far that that is the rule for a Hebrew slave who is sold to an idolator, and who is redeemed [by his family], for his hand is on the top. How do I know that the same rule applies to an Israelite [who owns a Hebrew slave who is up for redemption]?

G. Scripture states, "A hired servant" in two different contexts [Lev. 25:40, a slave sold to an Israelite, and Lev. 25:50, a slave sold to an idolator], serving therefore to establish an analogy between them [and to invoke for the one the rules that govern the case of the other. The lenient ruling for the slave governs the redemption of the field].

VI.41　A. Said Abbayye, "Lo, I am equivalent to Ben Azzai in the marketplaces of Tiberias [who challenged all comers to ask him hard questions]." [Abbayye is challenged, B, G-V, and replies at C-F, then W + Y-BB.]

B. *One of the rabbis [taking up the challenge] said to Abbayye, "There is the possibility of interpreting [the verses referring to the redemption of the Hebrew slave] in a lenient way [favoring the redemption and making it easy] and in a strict way. Why do you choose to do so in a lenient way? I might propose that they should be interpreted in a strict way."*

C. *"Let not the thought enter your mind, for the All-Merciful was lenient to [the Hebrew slave]. "For it has been taught on Tannaite authority:*

D. "'Because he fares well with you' (Deut. 15:16). He must be with you [and at your status] in food and in drink, so that you may not eat a piece of fine bread while he eats a piece of coarse bread, you may not drink vintage wine while he drinks new wine, you may not sleep on a soft bed while he sleeps on the ground.

E. "On this basis it is said that he who buys a Hebrew slave is like one who buys a master for himself."

F. *"But might one not say, that pertains to what has to do with eating and drinking, so as not to distress him, but, so far as redemption, we should impose a strict rule on him, along the lines of what R. Yosé b. R. Hanina said?"*

G. For it has been taught on Tannaite authority: R. Yosé bar Hanina says, "Come and see how harsh is the dust kicked up in connection with the laws of the Seventh Year. [Even if one violates only derivative rules, the result is severe.] If a person trades in produce grown in the Seventh Year, in the end he will have to sell his movables, as it is said, 'In this year of Jubilee you shall return, every man to his possession' (Lev. 25:13), and it is said, 'If you sell anything to your neighbor or buy anything from your neighbor's hand' (Lev. 25:14). [The two verses are juxtaposed to indicate that if a person does the one, he will be punished by the other, so for selling or buying produce of the Seventh Year, he will have to sell his property, in this case], movables, something acquired from hand to hand.

H. "If the person does not perceive [what he has done], in the end he will have to sell his fields, as it is said, 'If your brother becomes poor and has to sell some of his possessions' (Lev. 25:25).

I. "It is not brought home to him, so in the end he will have to sell his house, as it is said, 'And if a man sells a dwelling house in a walled city' (Lev. 25:29)" [T. Arakhin 5:9].

J. *What is the difference between the two cases, in that, in the former instance, it says, "If the person does not perceive," and in the latter, "It is not brought home to him"?*

K. *The answer accords with what R. Huna said.*

L. *For R. Huna said, "Once a person has committed a transgression and done it again, it is permitted to him."*

M. "It is permitted to him" *do you say?*

N. *Rather, I should say,* "It is transformed for him so that it appears to be permitted."

O. [Continuing I:] "It is not brought home to him so in the end he will sell his daughter, as it is said, 'And if a man sells his daughter to be a maidservant' (Ex. 21:7).

P. *[Abbayye continues:] "And even though the matter of one's selling his daughter is not mentioned in the present context, it would be better for a person to sell his daughter and not to borrow on usurious rates, for in the case of his daughter, what is owing gradually diminishes [as she works off the debt], while in the present instance, the debt grows and grows.*

Q. "Then it is not brought home to him, so in the end he will sell himself into slavery, as it is said, 'And if your brother becomes poor with you and sells himself to you' (Lev. 25:39).

R. "And not to you, but to a proselyte, as it is said, 'To the proselyte' (Lev. 25:47).

S. "And not to a sincere proselyte but to a resident alien, as it is said, 'To a resident alien' (Lev. 25:47).

T. "'A proselyte's family' refers to an idolator.

U. "When Scripture further states, 'Or to the stock,' [20B] it refers to one who sells himself to become a servant of the idol itself.'

V. *He [Abbayye, A] replied,* "But Scripture restores him [to his status]."

W. *And a member of the household of R. Ishmael repeated as a Tannaite statement,* "Since this one has gone and sold himself to an idol, [one might have thought], 'Let us throw a stone after the fallen.' Scripture therefore has said, 'After he is sold, he shall be redeemed, one of his brothers shall redeem him' (Lev. 25:48)."

X. *Might I maintain that* "He shall be redeemed" *means that, while he is not to be permitted to be absorbed among the idolators, as to the matter of redeeming him, we should impose a strict ruling?*

Y. *Said R. Nahman bar Isaac,* "It is written, 'If there be yet increases in the years' (Lev. 25:51) and 'If there remain but little in the years' (Lev. 25:51). Now are there years that are prolonged and years that are shortened? [Surely not.] Rather, if his value should be increased, then 'out of the money that he was bought for' he shall be redeemed, and if his value diminishes, then 'in accord with the remaining years.'"

Z. *And might I propose a different reading, namely, where he has worked two years and four remain, let him pay the four years at the rate of* "the money that he was bought for," *and if he had worked for four years, with two remaining, then let him repay two years* "according to his year"?

AA. "If that were the case, then Scripture should have stated, 'If there be yet many years.' *Why does it say,* 'in years'? *It means, as stated above,* if his value should be increased, [then his redemption shall be paid] 'out of the money that he was bought for,' and if his value decreased, then the basis of the fee for redemption will be] 'according to his remaining years.'"

BB. *Said R. Joseph,* "R. Nahman has interpreted these verses as if from Sinai."

VI.42 A. *R. Huna bar Hinena asked R. Sheshet,* "A Hebrew slave sold to a gentile – may he be redeemed by halves, or may he not redeemed by halves? Do we derive the meaning of 'his redemption' by analogy to the rule governing redeeming a field of possession, namely, just as a field of possession cannot be redeemed by halves, so he cannot be redeemed by halves? *Or maybe we invoke that analogy to produce a lenient rule but not to produce a strict rule?"*

B. *He said to him,* "Didn't you say in that context, he is sold whole but not by halves? *So here, too, he is redeemed whole but not by halves."*

C. *Said Abbayye,* "If you find grounds for maintaining, he may redeemed by halves, then you turn out to produce a ruling that is lenient for him and also strict for him. The leniency is, if the gentile bought him for a hundred zuz and then the slave paid back fifty, which is half his value, and then he went up in value and was worth two hundred, if you say, he can be half-redeemed, he pays him another hundred and goes out a free man; but if you say, he cannot be half-redeemed, then he has to pay him a hundred and fifty."

D.   But you said, "if he increased in value, he is redeemed out of the money that he was bought for"!

E.   *That would refer to a case in which he was valuable when he was bought then lost value then gained value.*

F.   *"And also strict for him: If he bought him for two hundred, and the slave paid back a hundred, which was half his value, and then went down in value to a hundred — if you say he can be half-redeemed, he has to pay him fifty and go free; but if you say he cannot be redeemed by halves, then the hundred was merely a bailment held by the master, and the slave gives that to him and goes free."*

VI.43 A.   R. Huna bar Hinena asked R. Sheshet, "He who sells a house in a walled city – is the house redeemed by halves or is it not redeemed by halves? Do we derive the meaning of 'his redemption' by analogy to the rule governing redeeming a field of possession, namely, just as a field of possession cannot be redeemed by halves, so he cannot be redeemed by halves? *Or maybe where Scripture made that point explicit, it stands, but where not, it is not made explicit and so is null?"*

B.   He said to him, "We derive the answer from the exegesis of R. Simeon that one may borrow and redeem and redeem by halves. *For it has been taught on Tannaite authority:* '"And if a man shall sanctify to the Lord part of the field of his possession, and if he that sanctified the field will indeed redeem it" (Lev. 25:52) – this teaches that one may borrow and redeem and redeem by halves. Said R. Simeon, "What is the reason? The reason is that we find in the case of one who sells a field of possession that he enjoys certain advantages. That is, if the Jubilee Year comes and the field has not been redeemed, it automatically reverts to the owner at the Jubilee Year. On the other hand, for that very reason, he suffers the disadvantages that he may not borrow to redeem the field and he may not redeem the field in halves. But [the opposite considerations apply to] one who sanctifies a field of possession. For, on the one side, he suffers a disadvantage in that, if the Jubilee Year comes and the field has not been redeemed, it automatically goes forth to the ownership of the priests. So, by contrast, he is given an advantage, in that he may borrow in order to redeem the field and he may redeem it in halves."' *Lo, one who sells a house in a walled city, too* – since he suffers the disadvantage in that, if a complete year goes by and the field is not redeemed, it is permanently alienated; but he gains the advantage that he can borrow and redeem and redeem by halves."

C.   *An objection was raised:* "And if he will indeed redeem it" – this teaches that he can borrow and redeem and redeem by halves. For one might have supposed that logic dictates the opposite conclusion, namely: If one who sells a field of possession, who enjoys the advantage that, if the Jubilee comes and the field has not been redeemed, it reverts to its original owner in the Jubilee, but who suffers the disadvantage that he may not borrow money and redeem it and redeem it by halves, then he who sanctifies a field, who suffers the disadvantage that, if the Jubilee comes and he has not redeemed the field, the field goes out to the ownership of the priests at the Jubilee, surely it follows that he does not enjoy the advantage such that he can borrow and redeem or redeem by halves [but has not got that right].

D. But as for the one who sells a field of possession, the reason is that the advantage he enjoys is not so strong, for he cannot redeem the field forthwith. But will you say the same of one who sanctifies a field, who enjoys a considerable advantage, in that he can redeem the field forthwith?

E. Let the one who sells a house in a walled city prove the contrary, since his advantage is sufficiently puissant that he can redeem the field forthwith – and yet he can't borrow and redeem the field or redeem the field by halves.

F. *There is no problem,* **[21A]** *the one represents the view of rabbis, the other, R. Simeon.* [Freedman: Sheshet's answer having been deduced from Simeon's statement; Simeon holds that the reason of a scriptural law must be sought, and when found it may modify the rule and provide a basis for other laws; rabbis disagree; Simeon argues that the disabilities require compensating privileges and finds this embodied in the laws of sanctification of a field of possession, from which the same principles are applied to analogous cases; rabbis argue that when Scripture impairs one's privileges in one direction, they are weakened in all a fortiori, the sanctification of an inherited field being explicitly excepted by Scripture.]

G. *One Tannaite statement holds:* He who sells a house in a walled city may borrow and redeem and redeem by halves. *One Tannaite statement holds:* He who sells a house in a walled city may not borrow and redeem and redeem by halves.

H. *There is no problem, the latter represents the view of rabbis, the former, R. Simeon.*

VI.44 A. *Said R. Aha b. Raba to R. Ashi, "One may raise the following objection:* What characterizes the one who sells a house in a walled city is that he is at a disadvantage since he can never redeem it again [after the first year has passed, Lev. 25:30]. But can you say the same of one who consecrates a field, who has the power to redeem the field at any time?"

B. *Said R. Aha the Elder to R. Ashi, "Because one can say, let the argument run full circle, and invoke a proof on the basis of shared traits among otherwise different classes, namely:* One who sells a field of possession will prove the contrary, for his power is such that he can redeem the field at any time in the future, but he may not borrow and redeem the field or redeem the field by halves. But what characterizes the one who sells a field of possession is that he is at a disadvantage in regard to redeeming the field immediately. Then one who sells a house in the walled cities will prove the contrary – and so we go around in a circle. The definitive trait of the one is not the same as the definitive trait of the other, but what characterizes them all in common is that they may be redeemed, one may not borrow and redeem, and one may redeem them all by halves. So I introduce the case of one who sanctifies a field, which may be redeemed, but one may now borrow and redeem or redeem by halves."

C. *Said Mar Zutra b. R. Mari to Rabina, "One may raise the following objection:* What they have in common is that the owner is at a disadvantage, in that they cannot be redeemed in the second year [after the act; one who sells an inherited field can redeem it only from the third year, the seller of a house in a walled city can't redeem it after the first year has passed]. But then will you say the same of one who sanctifies a field, who has the power, after all, to redeem the field in the second year?"

D. *Said to him Rabina, "It is because one may say:* A Hebrew slave sold to a gentile will prove the contrary, for he has the advantage of being redeemed in the second year, but he may not borrow and redeem himself, nor may he be redeemed by halves."

VI.45 A. *R. Huna bar Hinena asked this question of R. Sheshet:* "He who sells a house in a walled city – may the house by redeemed by relatives or may the house not be redeemed by relatives? Do we draw a verbal analogy based on the appearance of 'his redemption' both here and with regard to a field of possession: Just as a field of possession may not be redeemed by halves but may be redeemed by relatives, *so the same would apply here, namely,* this, too, may not be redeemed by halves but may be redeemed by relatives. *Or maybe, when the word 'redemption' is stated by Scripture, it serves to establish an analogy with respect to redeeming the field by halves, but it is not stated by Scripture with regard to redemption by relatives?"*

B. He said to him, "It may not be redeemed by relatives."

C. *An objection was raised: "'And in all the land of your possession you shall effect a redemption for the land' (Lev. 25:24) – that serves to encompass houses and Hebrew slaves [relatives may redeem these]. Doesn't this refer to houses in walled cities?"*

D. *No, it refers to houses in villages.*

E. *But Scripture explicitly refers to houses in villages:* "They shall be reckoned with the fields of the country" (Lev. 25:31).

F. *That verse serves to impose as an obligation the duty of redemption by relatives, in line with the position of R. Eliezer, for it has been stated on Tannaite authority: "'If your brother become poor and sell some of his possessions, then shall his kinsman that is next to him come and redeem that which his brother has sold' (Lev. 25:25) – that is an option."*

G. "You say it is an option, but maybe it's an obligation? Scripture states, 'And if a man has no kinsman' (Lev. 25:26). Now is it conceivable that there can be an Israelite who has no [kinsmen to serve as] redeemers? Rather, this refers to one who has such but whose kinsman doesn't want to repurchase it, showing he has the option to do so," the words of R. Joshua.

H. R. Eliezer says, "'If your brother become poor and sell some of his possessions, then shall his kinsman that is next to him come and shall redeem that which his brother has sold' (Lev. 25:25) – that is an obligation.

I. "You say it is an obligation, but maybe it's only an option? Scripture states, 'and in all...you shall effect a redemption' (Lev. 25:26) – thus Scripture establishes it as an obligation."

J. *Rabbis said to R. Ashi, and some say, Rabina to R. Ashi, "There is no problem for one who maintains that it serves to encompass houses in walled cities, that is in line with Scripture's statement, 'in all.' But from the perspective of the one who says that it encompasses houses in villages, what is the meaning of 'in all'?"*

K. *That's a problem.*

L. *Objected Abbayye,* "Why does the clause, 'he shall redeem him' occur three times [at Lev. 25:48, 49, 52]? It serves to encompass all instances of redemption, indicating that they are to be redeemed in this manner [encompassing redemption by relatives]. *Doesn't this mean houses in walled cities and Hebrew slaves?"*

M. No, it refers to houses in villages and fields of possession.

N. *But Scripture explicitly covers the matter of* houses in villages and fields of possession, in the language, "They shall be reckoned with the fields of the country"!

O. *It is in line with what R. Nahman bar Isaac said,* "It is to indicate that the closer the relation, the greater his priority." *Here, too, it is to indicate,* the closer the relation, the greater his priority. [Freedman: It is in the same order of priority as the kinsmen enumerated at Lev. 25:48, 49.]

VI.46   A. *In what connection is this statement of R. Nahman bar Isaac made?*

B. *It is in connection with the question that was raised:* "A Hebrew slave sold to an Israelite – is he redeemed by relatives or is he not redeemed by relatives? *With respect to Rabbi that is not an issue, for he has said,* 'Through these he is redeemed, but not by the passage of six years.' *Therefore he cannot be redeemed. Our question addresses the view of rabbis. What is the law? Do we establish a verbal analogy on the strength of the recurrent use of the word 'hired hand,' and we do not derive a lesson from the language,* 'one of his brothers may redeem him' (Lev. 25:38)? *Or perhaps,* 'he may redeem him,' *means, him but no one else* [a Hebrew slave sold to an Israelite]*?"*

C. *Come and take note:* "'In all...you shall effect a redemption' – this encompasses houses and Hebrew slaves." *Doesn't that mean houses in a walled city and Hebrew slaves sold to Israelites?*

D. No, it means a Hebrew slave sold to a gentile.

E. *A Hebrew slave sold to a gentile is covered by an explicit statement of Scripture,* "or his uncle or his uncle's son may redeem him" (Lev. 25:49) – **[21B]** that serves to make doing so obligatory, and even from the perspective of R. Joshua.

F. *Come and take note:* "Why does the clause, 'he shall redeem him' occur three times [at Lev. 25:48, 49, 52]? It serves to encompass all instances of redemption, indicating that they are to be redeemed in this manner [encompassing redemption by relatives]. *Doesn't this mean houses in walled cities and Hebrew slaves sold to Israelites?"*

G. No, it refers to houses in villages and fields of possession.

H. *But Scripture makes explicit reference to the matter of the field of possession:* "They shall be reckoned with the fields of the country"!

I. Said R. Nahman bar Isaac, "It is to indicate that the closer the relation, the greater his priority."

VII.1 A. **The slave whose ear is pierced is acquired through an act of piercing the ear [Ex. 21:5]:**

B. *For it is written,* "Then his master shall bore his ear through with an awl" (Ex. 21:6).

VIII.1 A. **And he acquires himself by the Jubilee or by the death of the master:**

B. *For it is written,* "and he shall serve him" but not his son or daughter;

C. "forever" – until the "forever" of the Jubilee.

VIII.2 A. *Our rabbis have taught on Tannaite authority:*

B. "'An awl' (Deut. 15:17):

C. "I know only that an awl is sufficient for boring the ear of the slave. How do I know that sufficient also would be a prick, thorn, borer, or stylus?

D. "Scripture states, 'Then you shall take' (Deut. 15:12) – including everything that can be taken in hand," the words of R. Yosé b. R. Judah.

E. Rabbi says, "Since the verse says, 'an awl,' we draw the conclusion that the awl is made only of metal, and so anything that is used must be metal.

F. "Another matter: 'You shall take an awl' – teaches that a big awl is meant."

G. Said R. Eleazar, "R. Yudan b. Rabbi would expound as follows: 'when they pierce the ear, they do it only through the earlobe.'

H. "Sages say, 'A Hebrew slave of the priestly caste is not subjected to the boring of the ear, because that thereby blemishes him.'"

I. *Now if you hold that the boring is done only through the earlobe, then the Hebrew slave of the priestly caste cannot be blemished thereby, since we bore only through the top part of the ear [and in any event, boring makes a blemish, and Yosé takes the view that even a needle's point, a smaller hole than a lentil's size, constitutes maiming]!*

VIII.3 A. *What is at issue here?*

B. *Rabbi invokes the categories of an encompassing rule followed by an exclusionary particularization:*

C. "You shall take" is an encompassing rule; "an awl" is an exclusionary particularization; "through his ear into the door" reverts and gives an encompassing rule. So where you have an encompassing rule, an exclusionary particularization, and another encompassing rule, you cover under the encompassing rule only what bears the traits of the exclusionary particularization; just as the exclusionary particularization states explicitly that the object must be of metal, so must anything used for the purpose be of metal.

D. *R. Yosé b. R. Judah interprets the categories of scriptural evidences of inclusionary and exclusionary usages:*

E. "You shall take" is inclusionary; "an awl" is exclusionary; "through his ear into the door" reverts and forms an inclusionary statement. Where you have an inclusionary, an exclusionary, and an inclusionary statement, the upshot is to encompass all things.

F. *So what is excluded? An ointment.*

VIII.4   A.   The master has said: "'You shall take an awl' – teaches that a big awl is meant":
         B.   *On what basis?*
         C.   It is in line with what Raba said, "'Therefore the children of Israel don't eat the sinew of the hip that is on the hollow of the thigh' (Gen. 32:33) – the right thigh; here, too, 'the awl,' means, the most special of awls."

VIII.5   A.   Said R. Eleazar, "R. Yudan b. Rabbi would expound as follows: 'When they pierce the ear, they do it only through the earlobe.' Sages say, 'A Hebrew slave of the priestly caste is not subjected to the boring of the ear, because that thereby blemishes him'":
         B.   So let him be blemished!
         C.   Said Rabbah b. R. Shila, "Said Scripture, 'And he shall return to his own family' (Lev. 25:41) – to his family's presumptive rights."

VIII.6   A.   *The question was raised: "A Hebrew slave who is a priest – what is the law as to his master's giving him a Canaanite slave girl? Is this an anomaly, in which case there is no distinguishing priests from Israelites? Or perhaps priests are exceptional, since Scripture imposes additional religious duties on them?"*
         B.   Rab said, "It is permitted."
         C.   And Samuel said, "It is forbidden."
         D.   *Said R. Nahman to R. Anan, "When you were at the household of Master Samuel, you wasted your time playing chess. Why didn't you reply to him on the basis of the following: Sages say, 'A Hebrew slave of the priestly caste is not subjected to the boring of the ear, because that thereby blemishes him'? Now if you say his master can't give him a gentile slave girl, the law that a Hebrew slave who is a priest is not bored simply follows that we require that the slave be able to say, 'I love my master, my wife, and my children' and that is not possible here [cf. Ex. 21:5]."*
         E.   *Nothing more is to be said.*

VIII.7   A.   *The question was raised: "A priest – what is the law as to his taking 'a woman of goodly form' (Deut. 21:11)? Is this an anomaly, in which case there is no distinguishing priests from Israelites? Or perhaps priests are exceptional, since Scripture imposes additional religious duties on them?"*
         B.   Rab said, "It is permitted."
         C.   And Samuel said, "It is forbidden."
         D.   *With respect to the first act of sexual relations, all parties concur that it is permitted, for* the Torah spoke only with reference to the human desire to do evil. *There there is a disagreement, it concerns* a second and later act of sexual relations.
         E.   Rab said, "It is permitted."
         F.   And Samuel said, "It is forbidden."
         G.   Rab said, "It is permitted, *for once it is permitted, it remains so.*"
         H.   And Samuel said, "It is forbidden, *for she is a proselyte, and a proselyte is not a worthy bride of a priest.*"
         I.   There are those who say that with respect to the second act of sexual relations all parties concur that it is permitted, since she is a proselyte. Where there is a disagreement, it concerns the first act of sexual relations.

J.   Rab said, "It is permitted, *for* the Torah spoke only with reference to the human desire to do evil. "

K.   And Samuel said, "It is forbidden, *for in any case in which one can invoke the verse,* 'then you shall bring her home to your house' (Deut. 21:12), *we also invoke the verse,* 'and see among the captives' (Deut. 21:11), *but in any case in which one cannot invoke the verse,* 'then you shall bring her home to your house' (Deut. 21:12), *we also do not invoke the verse,* 'and see among the captives' (Deut. 21:11)."

VIII.8   A.   *Our rabbis have taught on Tannaite authority:*

B.   ["When you take the field against your enemies, and the Lord your God delivers them into your power, and you take some of them captive, and you see among the captives a beautiful woman and you desire her and would take her to wife, you shall bring her into your house, and she shall trim her hair, pare her nails, and discard her captive's garb. She shall spend a month's time in your house lamenting her father and mother. After that you may come to her and possess her, and she shall be your wife. Then, should you no longer want her, you must release her outright. You must not sell her for money; since you had your will of her, you must not enslave her" (Deut. 21:10-14)].

C.   "...And you see among the captives":

D.   At the time of the taking of the captives.

E.   "...A [beautiful] woman":

F.   Even a married woman [Sifré Deut. CCXI:II.1-2].

G.   "...A [beautiful] woman":

H.   .The Torah spoke only with reference to the human desire to do evil. It is better for the Israelites to eat meat of [22A] beasts about to die but properly slaughtered than the meat of dying animals that have perished on their own without slaughter.

I.   "And you desire" – even if she's not pretty.

J.   "Her" – but not her and her girlfriend [the soldiers get one each].

K.   "...And would take her to wife": – you have marriage rights over her.

L.   "...For yourself to wife": – that is so that you may not say, "Lo, this one is for father," "Lo, this one is for my brother" [Sifré Deut. CCXI:II.4].

M.   "And you shall bring her home" – this teaches that he must not molest her in battle.

VIII.9   A.   *Our rabbis have taught on Tannaite authority:*

B.   "But should he say to you, 'I do not want to leave you,' [for he loves you and your household and is happy with you, you shall take an awl and put it through his ear into the door, and he shall become your slave in perpetuity. Do the same with your female slave. When you do set him free, do not feel aggrieved, for in the six years he has given you double the service of a hired man. Moreover, the Lord your God will bless you in all you do]" (Deut. 15:12-17):

C.   Is it possible to suppose that this may take place one time only?

D.   Scripture says, "But should he say to you, 'I do not want to leave you,'" – unless he says so and repeats it.

E. If he said so during the six years, but did not say so at the end of the six years, lo, this one does not have his ear pierced to the doorpost,

F. for it is said, "I do not want to leave you" – which applies only if said at the time of his leaving.

G. If he said so at the end of the six years, but did not say so during the six years, lo, this one does not have his ear pierced to the doorpost,

H. for it is said, "But if the slave should say to you...,"

I. that is, while he is yet a slave [Sifré Deut. CXXI.I.1-3].

VIII.10 A. The master has said, "If he made the statement at the beginning of the sixth year but not at the end, he is not bored, for it is said, 'I will not go out free'" [so he has to make the statement when he is about to leave].

B. *But we derive the law from the passage,* "I will not go out free," *why not derive the rule from the fact that he has to say,* "I love my master, my wife, and my children," *which condition is not met? Furthermore,* "If he says it at the end of the sixth year but not at the beginning, he is not bored, for it is said, 'the slave...'": *isn't he then a slave at the end of the sixth year?*

C. Said Raba, "The meaning is, 'at the beginning of the last penny's worth of service, and at the end of the same.'"

VIII.11 A. *Our rabbis have taught on Tannaite authority:*

B. If he has a wife and children, and his master does not have a wife and children, lo, this one does not have his ear pieced to the doorpost,

C. as it is said, "...for he loves you and your household and is happy with you." [Sifré Deut. CXXI:II.2].

D. If his master has a wife and children and he doesn't have a wife and children, he is not bored, as it is said, "I love my master, my wife, and my children."

E. "...For he loves you and your household and is happy with you":

F. Since it is said, "I have loved my master" (Ex. 21:5), do I not know that "he loves you and your household and is happy with you"?

G. On this basis, you may rule:

H. If the slave loved the master, but the master did not love the slave,

I. if he was beloved of his master, but he did not love his master –

J. lo, this one does not have his ear pieced to the doorpost, as it is said, "...for he loves you and your household and is happy with you" [Sifré Deut. CXXI:II.1].

K. "...Is happy with you":

L. Lo, if he was sick, or his master was, lo, this one does not have his ear pieced to the doorpost [Sifré Deut. CXXI:III].

VIII.12 A. *R. Bibi bar Abbayye raised this question:* "If both of them are sick, what is the law? *We require 'with thee' which pertains, or maybe we require 'because he is well with thee,' which doesn't pertain?"*

B. *The question stands.*

VIII.13 A. *Our rabbis have taught on Tannaite authority:*

B. "Because he fares well with you" (Deut. 15:16). He must be with you [and at your status] in food and in drink, so that you may not eat a piece of fine bread while he eats a piece of coarse bread, you may not drink vintage wine while he drinks new wine, you may not sleep on a soft bed while he sleeps on the ground.

C. On this basis it is said that he who buys a Hebrew slave is like one who buys a master for himself.

VIII.14 A. *Our rabbis have taught on Tannaite authority:*

B. "Then he shall go out from you, he and his children with him" (Lev. 25:41):

C. Said R. Simeon, "If he was sold, were his sons and daughters sold? But on the basis of this verse, it is the fact that his master is obligated for food for his children."

D. Along these same lines:

E. "If he is married, then his wife shall go out with him" (Ex. 21:3):

F. Said R. Simeon, "If he was sold, was his wife sold? But on the basis of this verse, it is the fact that his master is obligated for food for his wife."

VIII.15 A. *And both items were required. For had we been told the fact concerning his children, it is because they are not able to work for a living, but as to a wife, who can work for her living, I might say, "Well, then, let her earn her keep." If we had the rule only concerning the wife, that might be because it is inappropriate for her to go begging, but as for the children, who may appropriately go begging, I might have thought that that is not the case. So both items were necessary.*

VIII.16 A. *Our rabbis have taught on Tannaite authority:*

B. [22B] If Scripture had said, "...his ear on the door," I might have thought, then let a hole be bored against his ear through the door. So it is only the door, but not his ear.

C. "Not his ear"?! But it's written, "and his master shall bore his ear through with an awl" (Ex. 21:6).

D. Rather, I might have said, the ear is bored outside and then placed on the door, and a hole bored through the door opposite his ear. Therefore it is said, "and you shall thrust it through his ear into the door." How? The boring goes on until the door is reached.

VIII.17 A. "The door":

B. May I then infer that that is so whether it is removed from the hinges or not?

C. Scripture states, "unto the door or unto the doorpost" (Ex. 21:6): Just as the doorpost must be standing in place, so the door must be standing in place.

VIII.18 A. Rabban Yohanan ben Zakkai would expound this verse in the manner of a homer exegesis: "How come the ear was singled out of all the limbs of the body? Said the Holy One, blessed be He, 'The ear, which heard my voice at Mount Sinai at the moment that I said, "For to me the children of Israel are slaves, they are my slaves" (Lev. 25:55), nonetheless went and acquired a master for itself. So let it be pierced.'"

B. R. Simeon b. Rabbi would expound this verse of Scripture in the manner of a homer exegesis: "How come the door and doorpost were singled out from all other parts of the house? Said the Holy One, blessed be He, 'The door and the doorpost, which were witnesses in Egypt when I passed over the lintel and the doorposts and proclaimed, "For to me the children of Israel are slaves, they are my slaves" (Lev. 25:55), not servants of servants, now I brought them forth from slavery to freedom; yet this man has gone and acquired a master for himself – let him be bored before them in particular.'"

Once again, a protracted inquiry yields only disappointment. The notion that, at the foundations of the Talmud of Babylonia, we may discover a deep layer of principles, whether philosphical or theological, that carry us outward to other documents, proves chimerical. Neither of the Talmuds yields a single proposition that can be taken out of its particular context and introduced into many other contexts as a means of explaining what is at stake throughout. To the contrary, this Talmud, like the other, may be described in a few, simple words: it concerns its particular issues, no others; there are no premises that carry us far beyond the limits of its cases or problems. The sole broad, encompassing premises, which serve as media of generalization, prove those of logic and exegesis – and not proposition or premise in any consequential way.

A review of what we have seen leaves no meaningful doubt that the search for the Judaism behind the two Talmuds yields nothing of substance. I.1+2-6+7-10 commence with attention to the scriptural source for the Mishnah's law. II.1, III.1, IV.1, V.1-2 all do the same, but with less elaboration. The sustained composite at VI.1-2, with a long thematic appendix at Nos. 3-5, 6+7-13, 14+15-18 utilizes a clause of our Mishnah paragraph to work out a problem of its own. None of this is put together as Mishnah commentary; the whole is worked out in its own terms and parachuted down for the reason given. Only at VI.19, with its talmud at Nos. 20-21, and a Tannaite complement at No. 22, with its talmud at No. 23, and further talmud at Nos. 24-25, do we regain the Mishnah sentence that is under discussion, there complemented with a Tannaite formulation. The string of theoretical problems that extend from the original tangential discussion of the designation of a slave girl for marriage continues at No. 26, with a footnote at Nos. 27+28-29. No. 30+31, 32+33, 34+35-36, 37+38-39, 40+41, continue with a Tannaite formulation this sizable appendix on a tangential topic. Nos. 42-43+44, 45 with its footnote at 46, pursue the same general theme, though the strung out character of the composite is entirely self-evident. Clearly, a rather formidable talmud had taken shape around the themes expounded here, and the whole was then preserved as a huge appendix to a rather modest discussion of a Mishnah statement. VII.1, VIII.1 find a source for the Mishnah's rule. VIII.2, with a talmud at Nos. 3+4-5, with what is now the usual thematic appendix at Nos. 6-8, then addresses the topic of the Mishnah's rule. Another well composed set, Nos. 9-18, forms an appropriate, and sizable, composite on the theme of our Mishnah topic. So the rather considerable corpus of materials for VIII.1 really does amplify the theme at hand in a relevant manner.

II. The Exegetical Programs of Yerushalmi and of the Bavli Compared

Our task is now to compare the two Talmuds' fundamental programs, not merely in form as we did for M. Qid. 1:1, but for the basic intellectual program that each Talmud brings to its reading of the Mishnah paragraph. Here we shall begin the search for those premises of discourse that pertain to exegesis, since, as we have noted in two successive exercises, considerations of logic and exegetical principle, not proposition or presupposition or premise, alone underpin the whole.

What we are going to discover concerns a different type of premise from the one that has engaged us to this point. Specifically, we shall now see that we can scarcely treat the two Talmuds as comparable in their the heuristic morphology: they have nothing in common. The Bavli is different simply because it is different: it draws upon a corpus of compositions and composites that differs beginning to end from the Yerushalmi's corpus of compositions and composites. Where for our pericope the two Talmuds intersect, it is at the Mishnah's topic; but that topic does not then tell the Bavli's framers to study the issues that engaged the Yerushalmi's framers. They have their own interests, which they pursue in their own way: a different Talmud, produced in a different place by different people. The profound differences that separate one Talmud from the other will in due course come to expression in the premises operative in each. For the moment, we have to identify how the documents differ:

1:2 I: How on the basis of Scripture do we know that the Hebrew male slave is acquired as the Mishnah maintains? Underlying issue: correct hermeneutics. Does what derives from one proposition serve to teach the rule for another?
1:2 II: **Through money**: money, not goods.
1:2 III: **Through a writ**: writ covering money that has been paid over, not writ of gift.
1:2 IV: Language of sale, of betrothal.
1:2 V: When in the seven-year cycle does the Hebrew slave go forth, end of sixth or end of Seventh Year?

1:2 I.1: How do we know this + verse of Scripture.
1:2 I.2: Who is the Tannaite authority behind one of the foregoing demonstrations.
1:2 I.3: What is the scriptural foundation for the position of the initial Tannaite authority, who has said....
1:2 I.4: What is the scriptural foundation for the position of the initial Tannaite authority, who has said..
1:2 I.5: What is the scriptural foundation for the position of the initial Tannaite authority, who has said....

1:2 VI: How do I know that one is freed in the Seventh Year even though he has not worked all six years?

1:2 VII A-D: **And he acquires himself through the passage of years etc.**: he may be sold for less than six years but not for more than six vs. not.

1:2 VII E: Prooftext for Mishnah detail.

1:2 VII F: Prooftext for Mishnah detail.

1:2 VIII: Exegesis of prooftext.

1:2 IX: Exegesis of prooftexts & harmonization thereof.

1:2 X: **Hebrew slave girl has an advantage** + prooftext, exegesis of prooftext.

1:2 XI: Exegesis of prooftext.

1:2 XII: Exegesis of prooftext.

1:2 XIII: Exegesis of prooftext.

1:2 XIV: Exegesis of prooftext.

1:2 XV: Exegesis of prooftext.

1:2 XVI: Exegesis of prooftext.

1:2 XVII: Simeon b. Laqish raised the question to Yohanan: A Hebrew slave girl should go forth if she marries someone other than the master, on an argument a fortiori.

1:2 XVIII: Hebrew slave girl goes forth at death of master + prooftext.

1:2 XIX: Prooftext and clarification.

1:2 XX: As above.

1:2 XXI: Piercing lobe of ear, where, and exceptions to rule (priests).

1:2 XXII: Exegesis of prooftext on ear piercing.

1:2 XXIII: As above.

1:2 XXIV: Why the door?

1:2 XXV: Right ear; other exegeses of operative verses.

1:2 I.6: Who is the Tannaite authority who declines to establish....

1:2 I.7: Footnote to the foregoing.

1:2 I.8: Who is the Tannaite authority who declines to establish....

1:2 I.9: Who is the Tannaite authority who differs from...

1:2 I.10: That represents...but who are....

1:2 II.1: How on the basis of Scripture do we know that fact?

1:2 III.1: For it is written....

1:2 IV.1: For it is written....

1:2 V.1: For said Scripture....

1:2 V.2: Tannaite statement plus its talmud.

1:2 VI.1: Said X + theoretical statement: Hebrew slave girl acquires possession of herself as a free woman on death of her father; theoretical inquiry into that proposition, which adds to the Mishnah an additional advantage of the Hebrew slave girl. Contrast to Y. 1:2 X.

1:2 VI.2: Contrast and harmonization of Tannaite statements.

1:2 VI.3: Footnote to the foregoing.

1:2 VI.4: Continuation of footnote.

1:2 VI.5: Citation and gloss of a sentence in the footnote.

1:2 VI.6: Tannaite statement on how much is severance pay.

1:2 VI.7: Gloss of sentence in foregoing.

1:2 VI.8-12: Continuation of gloss. Ending with "and it was necessary."

1:2 VI.13: Tannaite statement on Deut. 15:14.

1:2 VI.14: Tannaite statement.

1:2 VI.15: Talmud to foregoing, source of ruling.

1:2 VI.16: Hebrew slave girl doesn't serve son or daughter of master + Scriptural source for that proposition.

1:2 VI.17: Slave whose ear has been bored, etc. serves neither son nor daughter + prooftexts.

1:2 VI.18: Said Raba, by the law of the Torah, a gentile may inherit his father's estate.

1:2 VI.19: Tannaite rule: rules pertain to Hebrew male slave that don't pertain to female and vice verse.

1:2 VI.20-24: Talmud to foregoing.

1:2 VI.25: Rabbah bar Abbuha raised this question: does designating the slave girl for marriage effect the status of a fully consummated marriage or does it bring about the status of betrothal?

1:2 VI.26: Simeon b. Laqish raised this question: what is the law on designating the slave girl for his minor son?

1:2 VI.27: Footnote to foregoing.

1:2 VI.28-29: Two theoretical proposals based on foregoing.

1:2 VI.30+31: Tannaite rule: how is duty of designating the slave girl as a bride carried out? + talmud.

1:2 VI.32+33: Tannaite rule: he who slaves his daughter and went and accepted betrothal for her with another party has treated the first party poorly and she is betrothed to the second + gloss as to authority behind a detail of the foregoing.

1:2 VI.34-5: Tannaite rule contiguous to foregoing + secondary talmud.

1:2 V.36: Contrast and harmonization of two Tannaite statements on the topic now under discussion, sale of slave girl.

1:2 VI.37-39: Tannaite rule + talmuds, interpreting Ex. 21:3.

1:2 VI.40: Tannaite rule: if a person was sold as a slave for a maneh and went up in value, how do we know he is valued only at a maneh?

1:2 VI.41: Various possibilities of interpreting verses on redemption of Hebrew slave – topic contiguous to foregoing, but treated autonomously.

1:2 VI.42: Huna asked Sheshet: a Hebrew slave sold to a gentile – may he be redeemed by halves?

1:2 VI.43-44: Huna asked Sheshet: he who sells a house in a walled city – is the house redeemed by halves or not?

1:2 VI.45+46: Huna asked Sheshet: he who sells a house in a walled city – may the house be redeemed by relatives? + footnote.

1:2 VII.1: **Slave whose ear is pierced** + for it is written.

1:2 VIII.1: **And he acquires** + for it is written.

1:2 VIII.2+3, 4, 5: Tannaite statement on awl (Deut. 15:17) + Yosé b. R. Judah + what is at issue here? That is, generalization on conflict of exegetical principles; footnote glosses.

1:2 VIII.6: Question was raised: Hebrew slave who is a priest – what is law on master's giving him a Canaanite slave girl? Is this an anomaly or are priests excepted from the law + Rab, Samuel dispute.

1:2 VIII.7: Question was raised: priest – what is the law as to his taking a woman of goodly form, Deut. 21:11 – formulated as before.

1:2 VIII.8: Tannaite statement on woman of goodly form, tacked on to foregoing.

1:2 VIII.9-11+12: Sif. Deut. on Deut. 15:12-17 + secondary theoretical question.

1:2 VIII.13: Tannaite statement on Deut. 15:15.

1:2 VIII.14+15: Complementary Tannaite statement on Lev. 25:41 + "both items necessary."

1:2:VIII.16: Tannaite statement on verses of Scripture on boring the ear to the door.

1:2 VIII.17: Continuation of foregoing.

1:2 VIII.18: Free-standing exegesis: how was ear singled out of all the limbs of the body.

If I had to characterize the Yerushalmi's interest in the Mishnah paragraph before us, I should say that it is principally in the prooftexts that undergird the Mishnah's rule – that, and the secondary exegesis of those same texts. True, at some points there is analysis of the Mishnah rule and its language, secondary problems being generated in those connections as well. But if we eliminated the treatment of relevant Scripture, we should have no sustained commentary to the Mishnah paragraph, and, in sheer volume, very little talmud. The premises of the Yerushalmi concern what Mishnah exegesis requires, and the presupposition of the Yerushalmi's reading of the Mishnah is that Scripture must be shown to form the foundation of the Mishnah's rules. That, sum and substance, defines the exegetical given of the first Talmud.

The Bavli has a different conception altogether, and in due course we shall find it possible to spell out what, at the foundations, distinguishes the Yerushalmi's from the Bavli's corpus of presuppositions of an exegetical character. Bavli 1:2 I:1-10 form a completely unitary composition, which to be sure draws upon available materials, as indicated, and which systematically investigates the theories as to Scripture exegesis and Mishnah exegesis of diverse authorities. (We did not ask about the premises of the Bavli's compositions, focusing as we did on the character of the composite; it suffices to note, in passing, that we observed nothing remarkable at the basis of the compositions, nearly all of which rested on a common foundation of inquiries.) While in general covering the same Mishnah paragraph, the composition is simply incomparable to the Yerushalmi's treatment. Its topical program is dictated by the Mishnah and what is clearly the exegetical sine qua non of Mishnah reading: the scriptural basis. From that point on, such considerations as governing principles of hermeneutics, recourse to various authorities who take various positions on said principles, consistency of position of said authorities, balanced proofs afforded to all cited authorities, indications of how each authority deals with the proofs of the other – these enormous issues are sorted out and worked out in such a way as to create the massive and sustained discourse before us. The Bavli is spun out of premises of an exegetical logical character that are utterly its own; a detailed examination of how the two Talmuds treat the same problem makes that point:

Yerushalmi 1:2		Bavli 1:2	
[X.A]	[The Hebrew slave girl has an advantage over him. For she acquires herself in	VI.1	A. The Hebrew slave girl has an advantage over him. For she acquires herself [in

addition through the appearance of tokens of puberty (M. 1:1C-D):] "She shall go out for nothing, without payment of money" (Ex. 21:11).

[B] "For nothing" – refers to the time of pubescence.

[C] "Without payment of money" – refers to the tokens of maturity.

[D] And why should the law not refer to only one of them?

[E] If it had referred to only one of them, I might have maintained, "If she goes forth through the appearance of the signs of puberty, all the more so will she go forth at the time of pubescence."

[F] If so, I would have maintained, the time of pubescence is the only time at which she goes forth, and not the time at which she produces signs of puberty.

[G] Now logic would suggest as follows: Since she leaves the domain of the father and leaves the domain of the master, just as from the domain of the father she goes forth only when she has produced the signs of puberty, also from the domain of the master she should go forth only when she produces signs of puberty.

addition] through the appearance of tokens [of puberty].

B. Said R. Simeon b. Laqish, "A Hebrew slave girl has acquired from the domain of her master possession of herself [as a free woman] upon the death of her father. That is the result of an argument a fortiori: If the appearance of puberty signs, which do not free her from her father's authority, free her from the authority of her master, then death, which does free her from her father's authority [the father's heirs have no claim on her], surely should free her from her master's authority [whose heirs should not inherit her]!"

C. Objected R. Oshayya, "The Hebrew slave girl has an advantage over him. For she acquires herself [in addition] through the appearance of tokens [of puberty]. But if what he has said were so, then the list should include reference to her father's death as well!"

D. The Tannaite authority has listed some items and left out others.

E. Well, then, what else has he left out, if he has left out this item?

F. He leaves out reference to her master's death.

G. Well, if that is all he has

[H] On that account it was necessary to state:

[I] "For nothing" – refers to the time of pubescence.

[J] "Without a payment of money" – refers to the signs of puberty.

[K] And perhaps matters are just the opposite [so that "she will go forth for nothing" refers to the period of twelve and a bit more in which she is a girl, and "without a payment" refers to the time at which she has reached puberty]?

[L] R. Tanhuma in the name of R. Huna: "'Without money' – in any context in which the father receives money, the master does not receive money."

left out, then he has left out nothing, since that would pertain also to a male slave as well, it is omitted anyhow.

H. But why not include it?

I. The Tannaite framer of the passage has encompassed what is subject to a fixed limit [the six years, the proportionate repayment of the purchase price, the Jubilee], but what is not subject to a fixed limit he does not include in his Tannaite rule.

J. But lo, there is the matter of puberty signs, which are not subject to a fixed limit, but the Tannaite framer of the passage has covered them, too.

K. Said R. Safra, "They have no fixed limit above, but they are subject to a fixed limit [16B] below. For it has been taught on Tannaite authority: A boy aged nine who produced two pubic hairs – these are classified as a mere mole; from the age of nine years to twelve years and one day, they are classified as a mere mole. R. Yosé b. R. Judah says, 'They are classified as a mark of puberty.' From thirteen years and one day onward, all parties concur that they are classified as a mark of puberty."

L. Objected R. Sheshet, "R. Simeon says, 'Four are given severance pay, three in the case of males, three in the case of females. And you cannot say there are four in the case of the male, because puberty signs are not effective in the case of a male, and you cannot say there is boring of the ear in the case of the female.' *Now if what R. Simeon b. Laqish has said were valid* ['A Hebrew slave girl has acquired from the domain of her master possession of herself as a free woman upon the death of her father'], *then the death of the father also should be included here. And should you say, the Tannaite authority has listed some items and left out others, lo, he has said matters explicitly in terms of four items! And if you should say, the Tannaite framer of the passage has encompassed what is subject to a fixed limit [the six years, the proportionate repayment of the purchase price, the Jubilee], but he has left off what is not subject to a fixed limit, lo, there is the matter of puberty signs, which are not subject to a fixed limit, and he has encompassed them in the Tannaite statement. And should you say, here as a matter of fact he, too, accords with R. Safra, well, then, there is the matter of the death of the master, which is not subject to a fixed definition as to time, and yet the Tannaite framer has included it. So what are the four items to which reference is made?"*

M. [1] Years, [2] Jubilee, [3] Jubilee for the one whose ear was bored, and [4] the Hebrew slave girl freed by puberty signs. *And that stands to reason, since the concluding clause goes on to say,* and you cannot say there are four in the case of the male, because puberty signs are not effective in the case of a male, and you cannot say there is boring of the ear in the case of the female. *But if it were the case [that the master's death is covered], then you would have four items for the woman. So that's decisive proof.*

N. *Objected R. Amram,* "And these are the ones that get severance pay: Slaves freed by the passage of six years of service, the Jubilee, the master's death, and the Hebrew slave girl freed by the advent of puberty signs. *And if the stated proposition were valid, the father's death also should be on the list. And should you say, the Tannaite authority has listed some items and left out others, lo, he has said,* and these are the

ones [which is exclu-
sionary, these – no
others]. *And if you
should say, the Tannaite
framer of the passage has
encompassed what is
subject to a fixed limit
[the six years, the pro-
portionate repayment of
the purchase price, the
Jubilee], but he has left
off what is not subject to
a fixed limit, lo, there is
the matter of puberty
signs, which are not
subject to a fixed limit,
and he has encompassed
them in the Tannaite
statement. And should
you say, here as a matter
of fact he, too, accords
with R. Safra, well, then,
there is the matter of the
death of the master. So
isn't this a refutation of
R. Simeon b. Laqish's
position?"*

O.   *Sure is.*

P.   *But lo, R. Simeon b.
Laqish has set forth an
argument a fortiori!*

Q.   *It's a flawed argument a
fortiori, along these
lines:* The distinguish-
ing trait of puberty
signs is that they mark
a change in the body
of the girl, but will
you say the same of
the death of the father,
by which the body of
the girl is left unaf-
fected?

The two Talmuds have in common most matters of form, but no
matters of intellectual substance. Once the Yerushalmi cites our Mishnah
sentence, it proceeds to its prooftext, Ex. 21:11; spells out its implications,
asks whether a prooftext is required when the logic of hierarchical
classification yielding an argument a fortiori can have produced the same
result [G], and shows that that is not the case. So much for the problem

at hand. The Bavli's interest is in a theoretical problem, Simeon b. Laqish's, which utilizes the Mishnah's fact for its own purposes. We note, of course, that this Simeon belongs to the Land of Israel; the Bavli's framers drew as they liked on sayings formulated in the other country's schools. But what they did with those sayings accorded with their own modes of thought about their own interests. These sayings are treated as a sentence of the Mishnah is treated, that is to say, for whatever purpose the Bavli's framers had in mind in general. For it is the simple fact that the Mishnah sentence shared by both Talmuds in no way permits us to predict the shape and program of the Bavli's composition's authors.

If I had to specify the point at which the Talmuds part company, it is in the role of the Mishnah in each. For the Yerushalmi, the Mishnah is the only thing; for the Bavli, it is not even the main thing. The fact of the Mishnah is inert, not an active ingredient in a dialectical inquiry. This produces a sustained reading of the Mishnah text as evidence for or against the proposition at hand, C-F. The Mishnah's rule now is a passive ingredient, rather than the active and determinative force behind the talmud composition at hand. It is hardly necessary to spell out the enormous differences from that point to the end.

The penultimate and ultimate framers of the two Talmuds utilized what they had in hand, and each document's framers drew upon a corpus of materials utterly different from that available to the other. Where sayings are shared by the two Talmuds, they are episodic, ad hoc, singular; rarely do entire compositions make their way from the former to the latter document, and whole composites, never. Referring in common with the authors of the Yerushalmi's composites and even compositions to the same Scripture, Mishnah, Tosefta, Sifra, and the two Sifrés, the Bavli's authorship drew upon composites and compositions that differed, beginning to end and top to bottom, from the Yerushalmi's counterparts.

The question remains: Do the two Talmuds not share – at least – a single exegetical heritage, one that would permit us to ask about shared premises at least of one order? To answer that question, let us review what each has to say about Deut. 15:17ff.

I.1 A. A Hebrew slave is acquired through money and a writ:
     B. *How do we know this?*
     C. Said Scripture, "He shall give back the price of his redemption out of the money

that he was bought
for" (Lev. 25:51).

D. So we have found the
source of the rule
governing a Hebrew
slave sold to a gentile,
since the only way of
acquiring him is by
money. How do we
know that the same
rule applies to one
sold to an Israelite?

E. Said Scripture, "Then
he shall let her be
redeemed" (Ex. 21:8) –
this teaches that she
deducts part of her
redemption money
and goes free.

F. So we have found the
rule governing the
Hebrew slave girl,
since she is betrothed
with a money pay-
ment, she is acquired
with a money pay-
ment. How do we
know of it a Hebrew
slave boy?

[I.A] It is written. "If your
brother, a Hebrew
man, or a Hebrew
woman, is sold to you,
he shall serve you six
years, and in the
Seventh Year you shall
let him go free from
you" (Deut. 15:12).

[B] Scripture treats in the
same context a
Hebrew man and
woman.

[C] Just as the Hebrew
woman is acquired
through money or a
writ, so a Hebrew man
is acquired through
money or a writ....

[I] But as to R. Ishmael,
who does not concur
that what derives from

G. Said Scripture, "If
your brother, a He-
brew man or a He-
brew woman, is sold
to you and serves you
six years" (Deut.
15:12) – Scripture
treats as comparable
the Hebrew slave boy
and the Hebrew slave
girl.

H. So we have found the
rule governing those
sold by a court, since
they are sold willy-
nilly. If they have sold
themselves, how do
we know that that is
the case?

I. We derive the parallel
between the one and
the other because of

one proposition may then serve to teach the rule for another, [how do we prove that a Hebrew manservant is acquired through a writ]?

[J] The following Tannaite teaching is available: R. Ishmael teaches in regard to this statement, "freedom has not been given to her" (Lev. 19:20), "You shall let him go free from you" (Deut. 15:12). [The latter is interpreted in the light of the former.]

[K] Now in all [other] contexts R. Ishmael does not concur that what derives from one proposition may then serve to teach the rule for another, and yet here [at J] he does indeed hold that view.

[L] It [that is. the teaching at J] was taught in the name of a sage. "How does R. Ishmael prove [that a writ is applicable to the Hebrew manservant]?

[M] "'Sending forth' is stated at Deut. 15:12, and also 'sending' is stated at Deut. 24:1.

[N] Just as 'sending forth' stated in regard to a divorce means that it is done through a writ, so the 'sending forth' stated in regard to the slave means that it is done through a writ."

[O] [But the issue is not the same.] The two

the use of the word "hired hand" [Lev. 25:39: One who sells himself; one sold by a court, Deut. 15:12ff.; the same word appears in both cases, so the same method of purchase applies to both (Freedman)].

J. *Well, that poses no problems to him who accepts the consequences drawn from the verbal analogy established by the use of the word "hired hand," but for him who denies that analogy and its consequences, what is to be said?*

K. Said Scripture, "And if a stranger or sojourner with you gets rich" (Lev. 25:47) – thus adding to the discussion that is just prior, teaching rules governing what is prior on the basis of rules that govern in what is to follow. [The "and" links Lev. 25:47-55, one who sells himself to a nonJew, to Lev. 25:39-46, one who sells himself to a Jew; just as the purchase in the one case is carried out by money, so is that of the other (Freedman)].

I.2 A. *And who is the Tannaite authority who declines to establish a verbal analogy based on the recurrent usage of the word "hired hand" in the several passages?*

B. *It is the Tannaite authority behind the following, which has*

cases are dissimilar.
For in the case of the
divorce of the woman,
the writ serves to give
her full possession of
herself. But here the
writ serves to give
possession of the He-
brew slave to others.
[The proposition is to
prove that a Hebrew
man is acquired
through a writ, and
that has not been
proved.]

[P] Said R. Mattenaiah,
"The use of the lan-
guage of sale will
prove the case. ['If
your brother...is sold
to you' (Deut. 15:12);
'If your brother be-
comes poor and sells
part of his property'
(Lev. 25:25).] Just as
'sale' stated in the lat-
ter case involves use
of a writ, so the lan-
guage of 'sale' used
here involves use of a
writ."

*been taught on Tannaite
authority:*

C. He who sells himself
may be sold for six
years or more than six
years; if it is by a
court, he may be sold
for six years only.

D. He who sells himself
may not have his ear
bored as a mark of
perpetual slavery; if
sold by the court, he
may have his ear
bored.

E. He who sells himself
has no severance pay
coming to him; if he is
sold by a court, he has
severance pay coming
to him.

F. To him who sells
himself, the master
cannot assign a
Canaanite slave girl; if
sold by a court, the
master can give him a
Canaanite slave girl.

G. R. Eleazar says,
"Neither one nor the
other may be sold for
more than six years;
both may have the ear
bored; to both sever-
ance pay is given; to
both the master may
assign a Canaanite
slave girl."

H. *Isn't this what is at
stake: The initial Tan-
naite authority does not
establish a verbal anal-
ogy based on the appear-
ance of "hired hand" in
both passages, while R.
Eleazar does establish a
verbal analogy based on
the occurrence of "hired
hand" in both passages?*

I. *Said R. Tabyumi in the name of Abbayye,* "All parties concur that we do establish a verbal analogy based on the appearance in both passages of 'hired hand.' *And here, this is what is the operative consideration behind the position of the initial Tannaite authority, who has said,* He who sells himself may be sold for six years or more than six years? *Scripture has stated a limitation in the context of one sold by a court:* 'And he shall serve you six years' (Deut. 15:12), meaning, he but not one who sells himself."

J. *And the other party?*

K. "And he shall serve you" – not your heir.

L. *And the other party?*

M. *There is another* "serve you" *in context [at Deut. 15:18].*

N. *And the other party?*

O. *That is written to tell you that* the master must be prepared to give severance pay.

VIII.2 A. *Our rabbis have taught on Tannaite authority:*

B. "'An awl' (Deut. 15:17):

C. "I know only that an awl is sufficient for boring the ear of the slave. How do I know that sufficient also would be a prick, thorn, borer, or stylus?

D. "Scripture states, 'Then you shall take' (Deut. 15:12) – including everything

that can be taken in
hand," the words of R.
Yosé b. R. Judah.

E. Rabbi says, "Since the
verse says, 'an awl,'
we draw the conclu-
sion that the awl is
made only of metal,
and so anything that is
used must be metal.

F. "Another matter: 'You
shall take an awl' –
teaches that a big awl
is meant."

G. Said R. Eleazar, "R.
Yudan b. Rabbi would
expound as follows:
'when they pierce the
ear, they do it only
through the earlobe.'

H. "Sages say, 'A Hebrew
slave of the priestly
caste is not subjected
to the boring of the
ear, because that
thereby blemishes
him.'"

I. *Now if you hold that the*
boring is done only
through the earlobe, then
the Hebrew slave of the
priestly caste cannot be
blemished thereby, since
we bore only through the
top part of the ear [and
in any event, boring
makes a blemish, and
Yosé takes the view that
even a needle's point, a
smaller hole than a
lentil's size, constitutes
maiming]!

VIII.3 A. *What is at issue here?*

B. *Rabbi invokes the cate-*
gories of an encompass-
ing rule followed by an
exclusionary particular-
ization:

C. "You shall take" is an
encompassing rule;

"an awl" is an exclusionary particularization; "through his ear into the door" reverts and gives an encompassing rule. So where you have an encompassing rule, an exclusionary particularization, and another encompassing rule, you cover under the encompassing rule only what bears the traits of the exclusionary particularization; just as the exclusionary particularization states explicitly that the object must be of metal, so must anything used for the purpose be of metal.

D. *R. Yosé b. R. Judah interprets the categories of scriptural evidences of inclusionary and exclusionary usages:*

E. "You shall take" is inclusionary; "an awl" is exclusionary; "through his ear into the door" reverts and forms an inclusionary statement. Where you have an inclusionary, an exclusionary, and an inclusionary statement, the upshot is to encompass all things.

F. *So what is excluded? An ointment.*

VIII.4 A. The master has said: "'You shall take an awl' — teaches that a big awl is meant":

B. *On what basis?*

C. It is in line with what Raba said, "'Therefore the children of Israel don't eat the sinew of

the hip that is on the
hollow of the thigh'
(Gen. 32:33) – the right
thigh; here, too, 'the
awl,' means, the most
special of awls."

VIII.5   A.   Said R. Eleazar, "R.
Yudan b. Rabbi would
expound as follows:
'When they pierce the
ear, they do it only
through the earlobe.'
Sages say, 'A Hebrew
slave of the priestly
caste is not subjected
to the boring of the
ear, because that
thereby blemishes
him'":

B.   So   let   him   be
blemished!

C.   Said Rabbah b. R.
Shila, "Said Scripture,
'And he shall return to
his own family' (Lev.
25:41) – to his family's
presumptive rights."

VIII.9   A.   *Our rabbis have taught
on Tannaite authority:*

B.   **"But should he say to
you, 'I do not want to
leave you,' [for he
loves you and your
household and is
happy with you, you
shall take an awl and
put it through his ear
into the door, and he
shall become your
slave in perpetuity.
Do the same with
your female slave.
When you do set him
free, do not feel
aggrieved, for in the
six years he has given
you double the
service of a hired
man. Moreover, the
Lord your God will**

bless you in all you do]" (Deut. 15:12-17):

C. Is it possible to suppose that this may take place one time only?

D. Scripture says, "But should he say to you, 'I do not want to leave you'" – unless he says so and repeats it.

E. If he said so during the six years, but did not say so at the end of the six years, lo, this one does not have his ear pierced to the doorpost,

F. for it is said, "I do not want to leave you" – which applies only if said at the time of his leaving.

G. If he said so at the end of the six years, but did not say so during the six years, lo, this one does not have his ear pierced to the doorpost,

H. for it is said, "But if the slave should say to you...,"

I. that is, while he is yet a slave [Sifré Deut. CXXI.I.1-3].

VIII.10 A. The master has said, "If he made the statement at the beginning of the sixth year but not at the end, he is not bored, for it is said, 'I will not go out free'" [so he has to make the statement when he is about to leave].

B. *But we derive the law from the passage,* "I will

not go out free," *why
not derive the rule from
the fact that he has to
say,* "I love my master,
my wife, and my chil-
dren," *which condition
is not met?* Further-
more, **"If he says it at
the end of the sixth
year but not at the
beginning, he is not
bored, for it is said,
'the slave...'":** *isn't he
then a slave at the end of
the sixth year?*

C. Said Raba, "The
meaning is, 'at the
beginning of the last
penny's worthy of
service, and at the end
of the same.'"

While Deut. 15:12 serves both Talmuds in the same way – proving
that the Hebrew male slave is subject to the same law as the Hebrew
female slave – that fact, critical to the Yerushalmi's composition, is
secondary to the focus of interest of the Bavli's. The Bavli's inquiry
concerns a problem not dealt with in the Mishnah at all, namely, how we
know that a Hebrew slave sold to an Israelite is subject to the same law
as one sold to a gentile. With that problem in hand, we invoke the
prooftext at hand. The point for our inquiry is not to be missed: where
the Talmuds share the same prooftext and read it in the same way and
with the same propositional consequence, still, the Bavli's interest in the
matter is defined by its larger program, and that program differs
radically and persistently from the Yerushalmi's. That the Bavli has its
own hermeneutic is shown at I.2 in our sample, which asks a question
that simply does not occur in the Yerushalmi, even when the same
prooftext plays a role in both Talmuds. A second reading of Deut. 15:12
occurs at VIII.2, and that Tannaite reading plays no role in the
Yerushalmi's presentation of the Mishnah pericope under discussion.
No reasonable person would insist that the framers of the Yerushalmi
never knew Rabbi's and Yosé b. R. Judah's dispute about the meaning of
the reference to "an awl." After all, both are principal late Tannaite
authorities in the Land of Israel itself!

But, when we consider the continuation of the matter, at VIII.3 – the
dispute on the classification of the components of the verse:
encompassing rule, exclusionary particularization, then encompassing

rule, vs. inclusionary and exclusionary usages – we realize that, whatever they inherited from the corpus of sayings of the Land of Israel's Tannaite masters, the Bavli's composition authors did whatever they liked; and what they liked was not to the taste of the Yerushalmi's composition authors. That is clear because the latter do not do what the former do. The provision then of a footnote, VIII.4, and a secondary expansion, at VIII.5, characterize the Bavli but never the Yerushalmi. So what is shared in common proves inert, and what is done with received facts by the Bavli's composition writers and composite makers is unique: the Bavli's voice is unique. That VIII.9-10 stand on their own simply underlines that conclusion.

5

The Premises of the Authors of Compositions: Qiddushin 1:3 in Yerushalmi and Bavli

No purpose is served by a detailed reproduction of the remainder of this chapter in the two Talmuds. Instead, I give only a severely abbreviated reprise, sufficient to show the uniform traits of the two treatments of the Mishnah, respectively. That will suffice to validate the concluding chapter's discussion of the premises of thought that emerge from the two writings, and that is the purpose of the work as a whole.

1:3

A. A Canaanite slave is acquired through money, through a writ, or through usucaption.

B. "And he acquires himself through money paid by others or through a writ [of indebtedness] taken on by himself," the words of R. Meir.

C. And sages say, "By money paid by himself or by a writ taken on by others,

D. "on condition that the money belongs to others."

I. M. Qiddushin 1:3 in the Talmud of the Land of Israel

[I.A] It is written, "[As to Canaanite slaves] you may bequeath them to your sons after you, to inherit as a possession forever; you may make slaves of them" (Lev. 25:46).

[B] Acquisition of slaves thereby is treated under the same rubric as inherited real estate.

[C] Just as inherited real estate is acquired through money, writ, or usucaption so a Canaanite slave is acquired through money, writ, or usucaption.

[D] How do we know that inherited real estate itself is acquired through money, writ, or usucaption?

[E]   It is written, "Fields will be bought for money, deeds will be signed and sealed and witnessed" (Jer. 32:44)....

[II.A]   [The statement that land is acquired only through usucaption] is not in accord with the view of R. Eliezer.

[B]   For R. Eliezer said, "If one merely traversed the field, he has acquired it [without usucaption]."

[C]   For it has been taught: "If one traversed a field lengthwise and breadthwise, he has acquired it up to the place in which he has walked," the words of R. Eliezer.

[D]   And sages say, "He acquires it only once he effects possession through usucaption."

[E]   All concur in the case of one who sells a path to his fellow, that once he has walked in it, he has acquired it.

[F]   What is the scriptural basis for that position [of Eliezer]?

[G]   "Arise, walk through the length and the breadth of the land, for I will give it to you" (Gen. 13:17).

The next exercise is of more than routine interest, since it shows an inquiry into the theory of the Mishnah on an interstitial category, showing that the Mishnah treats the same category in an inconsistent manner. The premise, the perfection of the Mishnah, of course is not new, but the type of inquiry is of special concern here. A further point of interest will be the systematic indentation of secondary materials, footnotes and appendices. This will permit us to assess whether or not the compositions on their own bear data of interest in an inquiry into premises of such compositions.

[III.A] There are Mishnah rules that maintain slaves are equivalent to real estate; there are Mishnah passages that maintain they are equivalent to movables; and there are Mishnah passages that maintain they are neither like real estate nor like movables.

[B]   A Mishnah passage that treats slaves as equivalent to real estate is what we have learned there:

[C]   **Title by usucaption to houses, cisterns, trenches, vaults, dovecotes, bathhouses, olive presses, irrigated field, and slaves, [and whatever brings a regular return, is gained by usucaption during three complete years] [M. B.B. 3:1].**

[D]   A Mishnah passage that treats slaves as not equivalent to real estate is in line with what we have learned there (following QE):

[E]   **How is usucaption [established in the case of] slaves?**

[F]   **[If] he [the slave] tied on his [the master's] sandal, or loosened his sandal, or carried clothes after him to the bathhouse, lo, this is usucaption.**

[G]   **[If] he lifted him up [the slave lifted the master up] –**

[H]   **R. Simeon says, 'You have no act of usucaption more effective than that!" [T. Qid. 1:5].**

[I]   What rabbis have stated implies that slaves are equivalent to movables.

[J]   For R. Yosé said in the name of rabbis, "No lien applies to one who makes a gift [unless it is made explicit]. They do not exact payment from a debtor's slaves as they do from his real estate. [That is, slaves cannot be treated as mortgaged for payment of a debt.]

[K]   Said R. Mana to R. Shimi, "Who are these rabbis?"

[L]   He said to him, "They are R. Isaac and R. Imi."

[M]   A widow seized a slave girl as payment for her marriage settlement. R. Isaac ruled, "Since she has seized her, she is properly seized, [and the action is valid]. [But that is not the case at the outset, and hence, in general, the slave is not equivalent to real estate.]"

[N]   R. Imi took the slave away from her, for she thought that the slave belonged to her, and she was not hers [for the collection of her outstanding marriage settlement]. [The slave is in the status of movables, not real estate.]

The foregoing free-standing composition bears no interesting premises that I can identify. We proceed with another proposition in the unfolding of the composition at hand:

[O]   Slaves are not equivalent to real estate, for it has been taught: [If one sold] real estate and slaves to someone, when he has taken possession of the real estate, [he has not taken possession of the slaves].

[P]   Now if you maintain that slaves are in the status of real estate, once the purchaser has taken possession of the real estate, he should be deemed to have taken possession of the slaves.

[Q]   For R. Yosa in the name of R. Yohanan has said, "If someone had two fields, one in Judah and one in Galilee, and the purchaser took possession of this one in Judah, intending also to acquire ownership of that one in Galilee,

[R]   "or if he took possession of that one in Galilee, [60a] intending to take possession of this one in Judah,

[S]   "he has acquired possession thereof. [Consequently, by taking possession of one piece of real estate, one may take possession of all the real estate. But in the cited case, taking possession of real estate has no effect upon ownership of the slaves, which therefore are not equivalent to real estate.]"

[T]   They are not equivalent to movables:

[U]   If you say that slaves are equivalent to movables, once the purchaser has acquired possession of real estate, he should have acquired possession of the slaves [at O].

[V]   For we have learned there: **If one has to take an oath in regard to movables, the oath may be extended to real estate as well, [and movables are acquired along with real estate].**

[IV.A]   **Through money [paid by others] [M. 1:3B]:** R. Jeremiah said, "[It is money paid] by another party to his master."

[B]   Lo, if it is money paid by his master to someone else, there is no [freedom for the slave]. [Meir's view is that it is a disadvantage to the slave to go out to freedom. If a third party gives money to the master, then by accepting the money the master makes the slave accept his freedom. The third party thus does not impose an unwanted disadvantage on the slave. But if the master should give money to others, he cannot on that account force the slave to leave his service.]

[C] [Differing from this view,] said R. Zeira, "Even if it is payment from his master to another party. For what this third party takes from the master is for the slave himself."...

The following shows us Mishnah exegesis of a routine order; we seek the authority behind the anonymous rule of the Mishnah:

[V.A] **[One who is half-slave and half-free works for his master one day and for himself the next (M. Git. 4:5A).]** Said R. Abun, "This accords with Rabbi.

[B] "For Rabbi has said, 'A man emancipates half of his slave.'"

[C] And do rabbis not hold that a man emancipates half of his slave?

[D] They agree that that is the case when it is a slave owned by partners, but in the case of a slave wholly owned by one man, it is different. For it is as if he has passed a writ of emancipation from the right hand [of the slave] to the left [and that means nothing].

[E] In Rabbi's view is it not as if he has passed a writ of emancipation from his right hand to his left hand?

[F] He concurs in that principle. But here he effects acquisition through another's intervention.

[G] And do rabbis not concur that he acquires ownership of himself by means of another party?

[H] Rabbis maintain that he who is suitable to acquire for himself, [that is, a writ of emancipation,] is suitable for others to acquire in his behalf, and he who is not suitable to acquire in his own behalf is not suitable for others to acquire in his behalf.

[I] Rabbi says, "Even though it is not suitable for him to acquire in his own behalf, it is suitable for others to acquire in his behalf."

Yet another analytical problem follows; we raise a theoretical question, spell out the theories that can pertain, and choose between them:

[VI.A] [If a slave] picked up a lost object and said, "It is with the stipulation that I acquire ownership of it, and not my master," [what is the law]?

[B] [Do we say,] despite his wishes, he and his master [hence, his master] acquire ownership of the object, or is it that he has acquired ownership and not his master?

[C] Let us derive the answer from the following case:

[D] **He who was prohibited by vow from imparting any benefit to his son-in-law, but who wants to give his daughter some money says to her, "Lo, this money is given to you as a gift, on condition that your husband has no right to it, but you dispose of it for your own personal use"** [M. Ned. 11:8].

[E] In this regard it was taught, "[He must say,] 'It is not yours [except for your personal use]. [You do not acquire ownership of this money, except what you actually use.]'"

[F] Said R. Zeira, "Who taught, [He must add,] 'And it is not yours'? It is R. Meir. For R. Meir treats the hand of the slave as the hand of the master."

[G] In the case of a gift [the law] is in accord with the view of R. Meir, that the hand of the wife is tantamount to the hand of the husband.

[H] But as regards a lost object, will the law accord with rabbis? [All the more so should the law accord with Meir, as at M. Ned. 11:8].

[I] Said R. Zeira before R. Mana, "The case [of M. Ned. 11:8] is different [from the present one], for it is a case in which she has made acquisition with the knowledge and consent of another party [namely, the father]."

[J] He said to him, "Is it not an argument a fortiori: Now if, in the cited case in which she has made acquisition with the knowledge and consent of another party, namely, her father, you maintain that when the woman makes acquisition her husband makes acquisition, here, in a case in which he makes acquisition in his own behalf [without third-party intervention], is it not all the more so the case that when the slave makes acquisition, his master should acquire the object? [That is, in the case of the slave, there is no question of the intervention of a donor. that is. the father. All the more so should the master enjoy ownership of whatever the slave finds.]"

Another dispute concerning Mishnah exegesis follows:

[VII.A] [In listing the means by which a slave goes free], why do we not learn that he also goes free at the loss of limbs that do not grow back?

[B] Said R. Yohanan b. Mareh, "It is because there is a dispute about the matter.

[C] "Specifically, there is a Tannaite authority who teaches that [if he loses his limbs] he still requires a writ of emancipation from the master, and there is a Tannaite authority who teaches that, in that circumstance, he does not require a writ of emancipation from his master."

[VIII.A] It is self-evident that a slave receives a gift from someone else for someone else, from someone else for his master [who acquires the object as soon as it hits the hand of the slave], but not from his master for himself, [for whatever the master gives him remains the property of the master].

[B] But as to what comes from another party to the slave himself there is a dispute between R. Meir and sages.

[C] "If someone says to him, 'Here is some money for you, on condition that your master has no right to it,' once the slave has acquired possession of the money, the owner has acquired possession of it," the words of R. Meir.

[D] And sages say, "The slave acquires ownership of the money, and the master does not acquire the ownership of it."

[E] What is a problem is this: What about a gift from the master to a third party?

[F]   Just as the slave acquires possession of an object from a third party in behalf of his master, so does the slave acquire ownership of the object from his master for a third party?...

Here comes a sequence of theoretical questions provoked by the rules at hand:

[IX.A] R. Zeira and R. Hiyya in the name of R. Yohanan: "It appears that the slave should acquire ownership of a writ of emancipation [for his fellow slave], for he does have a right to a writ of emancipation.

[B]   "But he should not acquire a writ of divorce of a woman [to deliver for her husband], for he is not subject to the laws of a writ of divorce of a woman."

[C]   "If you say that the Tannaite teaching [that follows disputes this point at E, I shall answer that objection]:

[D]   "'Lo, you are a slave, but your offspring is free' –

[E]   "if she was pregnant, she makes acquisition of the writ of emancipation for the fetus' – [so how can she acquire the writ for the fetus?] –

[F]   "they have treated the fetus as one of her limbs, [and she may receive such a writ for herself, A]."

[G]   R. Ba bar Hiyya in the name of R. Yohanan, "It appears that a slave may receive a writ of emancipation [for his fellow slave],

[H]   "but not [if they belong to] the same [master] –

[I]   "if you say that the Tannaite teaching has already made the same point –

[J]   "'Lo, you are a slave, but your offspring is free,' if she was pregnant she acquires the writ of emancipation for her fetus –

[K]   "they have treated the fetus as one of her limbs."

[X.A]   "As to Madame So-and-so, my slave girl, I issue a writ to her, so that she could not be subjugated as a slave [after I die]"– [are the heirs bound by that statement]?

[B]   R. Eleazar and S. Simeon b. Yaqim brought a case to R. Yohanan.

[C]   He said, "He has not got the power to encumber his heirs."

[D]   What is her children's status? They are slaves.

[E]   What did he then allow her [in so stating]?

[F]   The right to retain the usufruct of her own labor.

[XI.A] R. Abba and R. Yosé both maintain that [IX.J-K] is the view of Rabbi.

[B]   For Rabbi said, "A man may free half of his slave."

[C]   If one wrote over all of his property to two of his slaves simultaneously, both of them go forth to freedom,

[D]   and each of them has to free the other.

[E]   R. Judah in the name of Samuel, R. Abbahu in the name of R. Yohanan, "That statement follows the view of Rabbi, for Rabbi has said, 'A man frees half of his slave.' [Each slave owns half of himself and half of the other.]"

[F]   Said R. Zeira to R. Ba, "Does that not imply that a slave may acquire ownership of an object in behalf of a third party?"

[G]   He said to him, "What are you thinking? It is that after they have acquired ownership of the property [including half of each other], they go forth to freedom?

[H]   "But that is not so. It is simultaneously that the slaves and the property go forth to freedom."

[XII.A]   "Lo, you are free, but your offspring is a slave"–

[B]   "Her offspring is in the same status as she is," the words of R. Yosé the Galilean.

[C]   And sages say, "He has not done a thing."

[D]   Said R. Eleazar, "So did R. Hoshaiah, father of the Mishnah explain the matter [of C]: "Both of them are deemed to be free." [The language of A frees mother and child.]

[E]   R. Imi in the name of R. Yohanan: "Both of them are regarded as slaves."

[F]   In the opinion of R. Yohanan, it is understandable that there is a dispute [of Yosé and sages].

[G]   But in the opinion of R. Eleazar, why should there be a dispute?

[H]   But thus is the law to be taught:

[I]   "his statement is valid," the words of R. Yosé the Galilean.

[J]   And sages say, "He has accomplished nothing at all."

[K]   What is the meaning of "He has accomplished nothing at all"?

[L]   Said R. Eleazar, "Thus did R. Hoshaiah, father of the Mishnah, explain the matter: 'Both of them are free.'"

[M]   R. Ami in the name of R. Yohanan: "Both of them are slaves."

[N]   And it accords with Rabbi, for Rabbi has said, "A man frees half of his slave."

Once more, the search for operative premises produces little more than some a priori conceptions taken for granted in the formation of theoretical inquires into applied law. The entire focus is the Mishnah, its topics, its rules, and secondary issues that emerge therefore. Unit I introduces the paramount theme of the discussion, the ambiguous status of the Canaanite slave: like real estate, like movables, like neither, like both. But the point is that the slave is in the status of real estate, for the stated reason. Unit II completes the clarification of the opening proposition. Unit III takes up the analogies applicable to the slave once more. Unit IV returns to the modes by which the Canaanite slave acquires himself, M. 1:3B, beginning with money. The main interest of unit IV is in whether a slave can acquire a writ or money so as to secure his own emancipation. The secondary issue is Meir's view that it is no advantage to a slave to go free. So the tertiary issue is, may this be done not in the presence of the slave, for example, by third parties, when in general people may secure advantages, but may not accept disadvantages, for a third party? The solution is at IV.O-R. Unit V takes up the possibility of acquiring half a slave, the other half remaining free, and the issue is the same as at unit IV, namely, how a slave may be freed in part. The problem is to describe the way ownership or acquisition is effected, and this Rabbi does. Unit VI carries forward the same problem, namely, how and whether a slave effects acquisition of anything, since whatever comes into his domain belongs forthwith to his master. Unit VII raises and answers a simple question. Unit VIII returns to the matter of whether, and how, a slave effects acquisition of an object, seeing that, in Meir's view, whatever falls into his hand belongs to his master anyway. Unit IX pursues a different side to the same problem, namely, a slave's acting in behalf of a third party. Since he may receive a writ of emancipation for himself, he also may receive one for someone else, but not a writ of divorce. IX.A-F gives us one version, IX.G-K a second. Unit X is distinct from the rest, a separate problem. Unit XI returns us to unit IX. How can the slave acquire the writ for the fetus? The answer is that a man may free half of his slave, and the fetus is half of the slave girl. Unit XII takes up the question of freeing a slave, again giving us two versions of a simple dispute. I see nothing whatsoever that justifies the inquiry of this volume, but much that calls into question the premises of the present study that premises or presuppositions operate not within, but between and among documents, even of the same canonical venue.

II. M. Qiddushin 1:3 in the Talmud of Babylonia

1:3

A.   A Canaanite slave is acquired through money, through a writ, or through usucaption.

B.   "And he acquires himself through money paid by others or through a writ [of indebtedness] taken on by himself," the words of R. Meir.

C.   And sages say, "By money paid by himself or by a writ taken on by others,

D.   "on condition that the money belongs to others."

I.1 A.   *How on the basis of Scripture do we know this fact?*

B.   As it is written, "And you shall make them [gentile slaves] an inheritance for your children after you, to possess as an inheritance" (Lev. 25:46) – Scripture thus has treated them as comparable to a field of inheritance. Just as a field of inheritance is acquired through money, writ, or usucaption, so **a Canaanite slave is acquired through money, through a writ, or through usucaption**....

A further point of interest is in the corpus of Tannaite formulations of rules pertinent to the Mishnah's topic but omitted by the Mishnah. These, too, will be analyzed, in precisely the way in which the Mishnah is examined; what we will want to know here is why a given detail or clause has been omitted by the Mishnah:

I.2 A.   *A Tannaite statement:* Also through barter.

B.   *What about the Tannaite statement before us [which omits that medium of acquisition]?*

C.   *He has specified those modes of acquisition that do not apply to movables; but what applies to movables [and also to slaves, in that same category] he does not specify in his Tannaite formulation.*

I.3   A.   Said Samuel, "A Canaanite slave is acquired also through drawing. How so? If the purchaser grabs the slave and he goes with him, he acquires title to him; if he calls him and he goes to him, he does not acquire title to him."

B.   *What about the Tannaite statement before us [which omits that medium of acquisition]?*

C.   *There is no problem in explaining the omission of drawing, for he has specified those modes of acquisition that do not apply to movables; but what applies to movables [and also to slaves, in that same category] he does not specify in his Tannaite formulation. But as to that other Tannaite authority [the one cited at No. 2], should his formulation not encompass drawing?*

D.   *What he has encompassed in his Tannaite statement are modes of acquisitions that pertain to both real estate and movables, but drawing, which pertains to movables but not to real estate, he has not encompassed in his Tannaite formulation.*

I.4   A.   "How so? If the purchaser grabs the slave and he goes with him, he acquires title to him; if he calls him and he goes to him, he does not acquire title to him":

B.   *Well, now, he doesn't, does he? Then what about that which has been taught on Tannaite authority:*

C.   How is an animal acquired through the mode of handing over [delivery] [Slotki: harnessing, like drawing, is one of the modes of acquiring right of ownership; the buyer takes possession of the animal by performing some act that resembles harnessing, or, in the case of other objects, obtaining full delivery]? If the buyer takes hold of the hoof, hair, saddle, saddle bag that is upon it, bit in the mouth, or bell on the neck, he has acquired title. How is it done through drawing the object? If he calls the beast and it comes, or if he strikes it with a stick and it runs before him, he acquires title as soon as it has moved a foreleg and a hind leg.

D.   R. Ahi, and some say, R. Aha, says, "That takes place only if it has moved the full length of its body." [The four legs must be moved from their original position.]

E.   *Say: A beast moves on its master's will, a slave on his own.*

F.   Said R. Ashi, "A minor slave is classified as a beast."

I.5   A.   *Our rabbis have taught on Tannaite authority:*

B.   How is a slave acquired through an act of usucaption? If the slave fastened the shoe of the man or undid it, or if he carried his clothing after him to the bathhouse, or if he undressed him or washed him or anointed him or scraped him or dressed him or put on his shoes or lifted him up, the man acquires title to the slave.

C.   Said R. Simeon, "An act of usucaption of this kind should not be greater than an act of raising up, since raising up an object confers title under all circumstances."

Let us consider the next passages within the theory that the framers of the Talmud include in their text statements we should now relegate to the position of footnotes or appendices:

I.6   A.   *What is the meaning of this statement?*

        B.   Said R. Ashi, "[*This is the sense of his statement:*] If the slave lifted up his master, the master acquires title, but if the master lifts up the slave, the master does not acquire ownership of the slave. Said R. Simeon, 'An act of usucaption of this kind should not be greater than an act of raising up, since raising up an object confers title under all circumstances.'" [Simon: If the master lifts up the slave, this action also confers ownership.]

I.7   A.   *Now that you have said,* if the slave lifted up his master, the master acquires title, *then what about the following:* A Canaanite slave girl should be acquired through an act of sexual relations [since in that situation she lifts up the master]?

        B.   *When we invoke the stated rule, it is in a case in which* the one party derives pleasure, but the other party suffers anguish. *But here,* this one enjoys it and so does that one.

        C.   *Well, then, what about anal intercourse?*

        D.   Said R. Ahai bar Ada of Aha, "Who's going to tell us that both of them don't get a kick out of it? And, furthermore, the language that Scripture uses is, 'you shall not lie with mankind with the lyings of a woman' (Lev. 18:22), in which case Scripture has treated as comparable anal and vaginal sexual relations."

I.8   A.   R. Judah the Hindu was a proselyte, so he had no heirs. *He fell ill. Mar Zutra came to inquire after his health. He saw that he was dying, so he said to his slave, "Take off my shoes and take them to my house for me" [so that when the proselyte died, the slave would be engaged in a service to him, and he would thereby acquire title through usucaption].*

        B.   *There are those who say, the slave was an adult.*

        C.   [23A] *This one left for death and the other one [the slave] left to life.*

        D.   *Others say, he was a minor, and this did not accord with what Abba Saul said, for it has been taught on Tannaite authority:*

        E.   A proselyte who died, and Israelites grabbed his property, and among them were slaves, whether adult or minor, the slaves have acquired title to themselves as free persons.

        F.   Abba Saul says, "The adults have acquired title to themselves as free persons, but the minors – whoever takes hold of them has acquired title to them."

Here we have an independent composition; I see no premises of interest.

II.1   A.   **"And he acquires himself through money paid by others or through a writ [of indebtedness] taken on by himself," the words of R. Meir:**

       B.   **Through money paid by others** – but not by money paid by the slave himself? *With what situation do we deal? Should we say,* without his knowledge and consent? *Then note: We have heard that R.* Meir holds, it is a disadvantage for the slave to go forth from the possession of his master to freedom, *and we have learned as a Tannaite statement in the Mishnah,* **For they act to the advantage of another person not in his presence, but they act to his disadvantage only in his presence [M. Git. 1:6F].** *So it is obvious that it is with the slave's knowledge and consent, and so we are informed that* it may be done through money paid by others – but not by money paid by the slave himself. *Then it follows that* there is no possibility for a slave to acquire title to anything without his owner's participation. *But then note what follows:* **Through a writ [of indebtedness] taken on by himself!** So if it is taken on by himself, it is a valid medium of emancipation, but if it is taken on by others, it is not! *Now if it is with his own knowledge and consent, then why cannot it be validly done by third parties? And should you say, what is the meaning of,* **through a writ [of indebtedness] taken on by himself?** *It means,* even through a writ [of indebtedness] taken on by himself, *and so we are informed that* the advent of his writ of emancipation and his right to form a domain unto himself come about simultaneously, *lo, that is not how it has been taught as a Tannaite statement, for lo, it has been taught on Tannaite authority:* **"...By a writ undertaken on his own account, but not one undertaken by others," the words of R. Meir [T. Qid. 1:6F].**

       C.   *Said Abbayye, "In point of fact, it is not with his knowledge and consent. But a slave acquired by reason of a monetary obligation [that he is unable to meet, on account of which he is sold into slavery] is exceptional, for, since the master acquires title to him willy-nilly, the master also transfers title back to him willy-nilly."*

       D.   *If so, the same rule should pertain to a writ!*

       E.   *This sort of deed stands by itself [with its own wording] and that kind of writ stands by itself.*

       F.   *Well, then, here, too, this money stands by itself and that money stands by itself [since each is paid for its own purpose]!*

       G.   *They have the same mint mark.*

       H.   Raba said, "As to money, when the master receives it, it effects his liberation, but as for a deed, when others receive it, it effects his liberation."

III.1   A.   **And sages say, "By money paid by himself or by a writ taken on by others":**

       B.   If the money is paid by himself, it liberates him, but if it is paid by others, it doesn't? *Now why should this be the case? Granting that this is without his knowledge and consent, in any event notice: We know that rabbis take the position that* it is to the slave's advantage to leave the master's domain for freedom, *and we have learned in the Mishnah,* **For they act to the advantage of another person not in his presence, but they act to his disadvantage only in his presence [M.**

Git. 1:6F]. *And should you say, what is the meaning of* **paid by himself?** Also money paid by himself, *and so we are informed that* here is every possibility for a slave to acquire title to anything without his owner's participation, *if so, note what follows:* **By a writ taken on by others** – not undertaken by him himself! *And yet it is an established fact for us that* the advent of his writ of emancipation and his right to form a domain unto himself come about simultaneously. *And should you say, what is the meaning of* **by a writ taken on by others?** Also by a writ taken on by others, *and so we are informed that* it is to the slave's advantage to leave the master's domain for freedom, *if so, then why not blend the whole and repeat the entire matter in a single statement, namely:* With money and with a writ, whether taken on by others or taken on by himself?

C. *Rather, the sense must be:* With money, whether taken on by others or taken on by himself, or with a writ, if it is taken on by others, but not if it is taken on by the slave himself, *and the whole represents the position of R. Simeon b. Eleazar, for it has been taught on Tannaite authority:*

D. **R. Simeon b. Eleazar says, "Also by a writ when taken on by others, but not when taken on by himself"** [T. Qid. 1:6F].

E. There are three different opinions on the matter [Meir, money through others, without his knowledge, but not through his own agency, and by deed through his own agency but not that of others; Simeon b. Eleazar, both by money and deed, through the agency of others but not through his own; rabbis, both by money and by deed, through the agency of others and his own (Freedman)].

F. Said Rabbah, "What is the scriptural foundation for the position of R. Simeon b. Eleazar? He derives a verbal analogy on the basis of the same word, to her, that occurs with reference to a slave and a wife, namely, just as a woman is divorced only when the writ of divorce will be taken into a domain that does not belong to the husband, so a slave, too, is liberated only when the writ reaches a domain that is not his master's."

None of the foregoing qualifies as more than standard Mishnah exegesis. We now move on to a theoretical question, which provides a secondary expansion to the foregoing and therefore belongs as an indented unit; what follows depends upon the foregoing, and its presuppositions are all limited to the givens of the case at hand:

III.2 A. *Rabbah asked,* [23B] "From the perspective of R. Simeon b. Eleazar, what is the law on a Canaanite slave's appointing a messenger to receive his writ of emancipation from the hand of his master? *Since we derive a verbal analogy on the basis of the word 'to her' that appears both in this context and in that of a woman, he is in the status of a woman, or perhaps, as to a woman, since she has the power to receive her writ of divorce, an agent also can do so, but a slave, who has not got the power to receive his writ of emancipation, also has not got the power to appoint an agent?"*

B.   *After he raised the question, he solved it:* "We do deduce the verbal analogy on the basis of the common word that joins the slave to the married woman, so he is in the status of a married women."

C.   *Then what about that which R. Huna b. R. Joshua said, namely:* "The priests serve as the agents of the All-Merciful," *for if it should enter your mind that they are our slaves, is there something that we could not do, but they have the power to do in our behalf? Well, isn't there anything? Then what about the case of a slave, for he can't accept his writ of emancipation in his own behalf, but he can appoint someone as an agent to do so!*

D.   *But the analogy is null.* For an Israelite has no relevance to the rules governing offerings at all, but a slave most certainly bears a relevance to writs of severance, *for it has been taught on Tannaite authority:* It is quite appropriate that a slave may accept a writ of emancipation in behalf of his fellow from the hand of the other's master, but not from his own.

The following analysis of the Mishnah rule explicitly identifies the operative premises of the rule at hand, as the Bavli does many times. In no aspect are these premises going to yield something more than an ad hoc generalization, relevant to the case at hand.

IV.1   A.   **On condition that the money belongs to others:**

B.   *May we then say that this is what is at issue between sages and R. Meir: R. Meir takes the position that* the slave has no right of effecting title without his master's participation, and a woman has no right of effecting title without her husband's participation, *while rabbis maintain that* the slave has the right of effecting title without his master's participation, and a woman has the right of effecting title without her husband's participation?

C.   *Said Rabbah said R. Sheshet,* "All parties concur that the slave has no right of effecting title without his master's participation, and a woman has no right of effecting title without her husband's participation. And here with what case do we deal? It is one in which a stranger gave the slave a title to a maneh, with the stipulation, 'this is on the stipulation that your master has no right to it.' R. Meir maintains that, when the donor said to him, 'Acquire title,' the slave acquired title and so did the master, and the statement, 'this is on the stipulation that your master has no right to it,' is null. And rabbis maintain that once he said to him, 'this is on the stipulation that your master has no right to it,' the stipulation takes effect."

D.   *And R. Eleazar said,* "In any case such as this, all parties concur that what the slave acquires the master acquires. Here with what situation do we deal? With a case in which a third party gave him title to a maneh and said to him, 'It is on the stipulation that with this money you go forth to freedom.' R. Meir maintains that, when the donor said to him, 'Acquire title,' the slave acquired title and so did the master, and the statement, 'this is on the stipulation that your master has no right to it,' is null. And rabbis maintain that he did not accord title of it even to the slave, for he said to him, 'It is on the stipulation that with this money you go forth to freedom.'"

E.   *Now there is a contrast between what R. Meir has said with another statement of R. Meir, and likewise between what rabbis have said and another statement of rabbis, for it has been taught on Tannaite authority:*

F.   [24A] **A woman may not redeem second tithe without adding a fifth to its value.**

G.   **R. Simeon b. Eleazar says in the name of R. Meir, "A woman does redeem second tithe without adding a fifth to its value" [T. M.S. 4:7D-E].** [Freedman: When one redeems second tithe produce of his own and turns its value into ready cash, he adds a fifth to its value, but if he does the same for produce belonging to another, he does not have to do so unless the owner made him his agent to do so.]

H.   *Now with what situation do we deal here? If we say that the money belongs to the husband and the produce in the status of second tithe likewise belongs to the husband, then the wife is just carrying out the commission of her husband [so she surely should have to pay the added fifth]! So it must be a case in which the money belongs to her and the produce in the status of second tithe belongs to her husband. But what Scripture has said, is, "And if a man will redeem any of his tithe, then he shall add thereto the fifth party" (Lev. 27:31) – he but not his wife. So it must be a case in which a third party has given the wife title to a maneh and said to her, "It is on the stipulation that with it you redeem the produce in the status of second tithe." So we infer that they hold contrary opinions [to the ones they announce with respect to the slave's freedom.]* [Freedman: The rights of a slave and a woman are similar: Either they can both acquire independently or they both cannot.]

I.   *Said Abbayye, "Big deal – so reverse the attributions."*

J.   *Raba said, "Under no circumstances reverse the attributions. Here we deal with produce in the status of second tithe that comes to the woman from her father's household as his heir. R. Meir is consistent with views expressed elsewhere, for he has said, 'Tithe is property belonging to what has been sanctified,' so that her husband does not acquire title to it. And rabbis are consistent with views expressed elsewhere, for they maintain, 'Tithe is property belonging to the ordinary person,' so that her husband does acquire title to it. Therefore she does indeed carry out the commission of her husband."*

We proceed to another Tannaite statement, not found in the Mishnah but pertinent to its theme and therefore subject to analysis in this topically ordered composite:

IV.2 A.   *A Tannaite statement:* A gentile slave goes free through the loss of his eye, tooth, or major limbs that do not grow back [in line with Ex. 21:26-27].

     B.   *Now there is no problem understanding why that is so for the eye and tooth, since they are made explicit in Scripture, but on what basis do we know that that is the fact for the loss of the major limbs?*

     C.   *These are comparable to the tooth and eye:* Just as the loss of the tooth or eye represent blemishes that are exposed to sight and these do not grow back, so any blemishes that are exposed to sight and that are not going to grow back are covered by the same loss.

D. *But why not say:* The reference to "tooth" and "eye" constitute two rules that are redundant [Freedman: for the analogy could not be drawn if only one of them were mentioned], and whenever you have two verses that are redundant, they cannot be used to illuminate other cases.

E. *But both are required and they are not redundant, for if the All-Merciful had made reference only to the matter of the tooth, I might have supposed that even* **[24B]** *a milk tooth's loss would suffice; so the All-Merciful made reference to "eye" as well. And if the All-Merciful had made reference only to "eye," I would have supposed:* Just as the eye was created with the person himself, so that would apply to any such limb, *but the law would not cover the tooth, which grew in later on.*

F. *Well, why not say,* "and if a man smite" (Ex. 21:26-27) forms an encompassing generalization; "the tooth...the eye" form a particularization; in any case in which you have an encompassing generalization followed by a particularization, covered by the generalization is only what is contained in the particularization, with the result that the slave goes free for the loss of the tooth or the eye, *but nothing else.*

G. "He shall go free" forms another encompassing generalization, and wherever you have a sequence made up of an encompassing generalization, a particularization, and another encompassing generalization, you include under the rule what is similar to the particularization: Just as the particularization makes explicit that the slave goes free by reason of blemishes that are exposed to sight and these do not grow back, so any blemishes that are exposed to sight and that are not going to grow back are covered by the same loss and with the same outcome.

H. *Well, how about this:* Just as the particularization makes clear that a blemish that is exposed to sight, which causes the body part to cease to work, and which body part does not grow back, serves to liberate the slave, so any sort of blemish that is exposed to sight, which causes the body part to cease to work, and which body part does not grow back, serves to liberate the slave? *Then how come it has been taught on Tannaite authority:* If the owner pulled out the slave's beard and loosened his jaw, the slave is freed on that account?

I. "He shall let him go free" forms an extension of the law.

J. Well, if it's an extension of the law, then even if he hit him on his hand and it withered but is going to get better, he also should go free. *Then how come it has been taught on Tannaite authority:* If he hit him on his hand and it withered but is going to get better, he does not go free?

K. *If he did go free, then what's the point of tooth and eye?*

IV.3 A. *Our rabbis have taught on Tannaite authority:*

B. "In all these cases, a slave goes forth to freedom, but he requires a writ of emancipation from his master," the words of R. Simeon.

C. R. Meir says, "He doesn't require one."

D. R. Eliezer says, "He requires one."   '

E. R. Tarfon says, "He doesn't require one."

F. R. Aqiba says, "He requires one."

G. Those who settle matters in the presence of sages say, "The position of R. Tarfon makes more sense in the case of a tooth or eye, since the Torah has itself assigned him freedom on these counts, but the position of R. Aqiba is more sensible in the case of other parts of the body, because the freedom that is assigned in those cases represents an extrajudicial penalty imposed by sages on the master."

H. *It is an extrajudicial penalty? But there are verses of Scripture that are interpreted here!*

I. Rather, "Since it is an exposition of sages."

IV.4 A. *What is the scriptural basis for the position of R. Simeon?*

B. *He derives the sense of "sending her" from the use of the same word in the case of a woman: Just as the woman is sent forth by a writ, so a slave is sent forth by a writ.*

C. *And R. Meir?*

D. *If the words "to freedom" were included at the end of the verse in question, it would be as you say, but since it is written at the outset, "to freedom shall he send him away," the sense is, to begin with he is free.*

IV.5 A. *Our rabbis have taught on Tannaite authority:*

B. If the master hit the slave on his eye and blinded him, on his ear and deafened him, the slave goes forth by that reason to freedom. If he hit an object that was opposite the slave's eye, and the slave cannot see, or opposite his ear, so that he cannot hear, the slave does not go forth on that account to freedom.

IV.6 A. *Said R. Shemen to R. Ashi, "Does that bear the implication that noise is nothing? But didn't R. Ammi bar Ezekiel teach as a Tannaite statement: A chicken that put its head into an empty glass jar and crowed and broke the jar – the owner pays full damages? And said R. Joseph, 'They say in the household of the master: A horse that neighed or an ass that brayed and broke utensils – the owner pays half-damages'!"*

B. *He said to him, "Man is exceptional, for, since he is self-aware, he frightens himself [and is responsible if he is frightened by noise], for it has been taught on Tannaite authority:* **He who frightens his fellow to death is exempt under the laws of humanity but liable under the laws of heaven. How so? If he blew on the ear and deafened him, he is exempt. If he seized him and tore him on the ear and deafened him, he is liable.** [In the latter case he did a deed of consequence.] [cf. T. B.Q. 9:26]*."*

IV.7 A. *Our rabbis have taught on Tannaite authority:*

B. If he hit his eye and impaired his eyesight, his tooth and loosened it, but he still can use them at this time, the slave does not go forth on their account to freedom, but if not, the slave does go forth on their account to freedom.

C. *It has further been taught on Tannaite authority:*

D. If the slave had poor eyesight but the master totally blinded him, or if his tooth was loose and the master knocked it out, then, if he could use them before times, the slave goes free on their account, but if not, the slave does not go free on their account.

IV.8   A.   *And it was necessary to state both rules, for had we been informed of only the first rule, it might have been because to begin with the man had healthy vision and now he has weak vision, but in this case, since to begin with he had weak vision, I might have said that that is not the rule. And if we had been informed only of the second case, then it might have been because now he has totally blinded him, but in that case, in which he did not totally blind him, I might have said that the slave does not go free. So both were needed.*

IV.9   A.   *Our rabbis have taught on Tannaite authority:*

B.   Lo, if his master was a physician, and the slave told him to paint his eye with an ointment, and the master blinded him, or to drill his tooth and he knocked it out, the slave just grins at his master and walks out free.

C.   Rabban Simeon b. Gamaliel says, "'...and he destroy it' (Ex. 21:26) – only if he intends to destroy it."

IV.10   A.   *So how do rabbis deal with the clause, "...and he destroy it" (Ex. 21:26)?*

B.   *They require it in line with that which has been taught on Tannaite authority:*

C.   *R. Eleazar says, "Lo, if the master stuck his hand into his slave girl's womb and blinded the foetus that was in her belly, he is exempt from punishment. How come? Scripture said, '...and he destroy it' (Ex. 21:26) – only if he intends to destroy it."*

D.   *And the other party?*

E.   *That rule he derives from the language, "and he destroy it" instead of the language, "and he destroy."*

F.   *And the other party?*

G.   *He derives no lesson from the language, "and he destroy it" instead of the language, "and he destroy."*

IV.11   A.   Said R. Sheshet, "If the slave's eye was blind and the master removed it, the slave goes forth to freedom on that account. How come? Because he now lacks a limb."

B.   *And a Tannaite statement is repeated along these same lines:* Freedom from blemish and male gender are required in the case of animals for sacrifice, but not for fowl. Might one then suppose that if the wing was dried up, the foot cut off, the eye plucked out, the bird remains fit? Scripture said, "And if the burnt-offering be of fowl" (Lev. 1:14), but not all fowl.

IV.12   A.   Said R. Hiyya bar Ashi said Rab, "If the slave had [25A] an extra finger and the master cut it off, the slave goes out free."

B.   Said R. Huna, "But that is on condition that the extra finger counts along with the hand."

Next comes a free-standing composition, inserted for obvious reasons but not generated by the discussion before us:

IV.13   A.   *The elders of Nezonayya didn't come to the public sessions of R. Hisda. He said to R. Hamnuna, "Go, excommunicate them."*

B.   *He went and said to him, "How come rabbis have not come to the session?"*

C.	*They said to him, "Why should we come? For when we ask him a question, he can't answer it for us."*
D.	*He said to them, "Well, have you ever asked me a question that I couldn't answer for you?"*
E.	*They asked him the following:* "A slave whose master castrated him, what is the law on classifying this blemish? *Is it tantamount to one that is visible to the eye or is it not?"*
F.	*He didn't know the answer.*
G.	*They said to him, "So what's your name?"*
H.	*He said to them, "Hamnuna."*
I.	*They said to him, "It's not Hamnuna but Qarnuna."*
J.	*He came before R. Hisda. He said to him "Well, they asked you a question that can be answered from the Mishnah, for we have learned in the Mishnah:* **Twenty-four tips of limbs in man which are not susceptible to uncleanness because of quick flesh: The tips of the joints of hands and feet, and the tips of the ears, and the tip of the nose, and the tip of the penis. And the tips of the breasts which are in the woman. R. Judah says, 'Also of the man.' R. Eliezer says, 'Also the warts and the wens are not susceptible to uncleanness because of quick flesh'** [M. Neg. 6:7]. *And a Tannaite statement in that connection:* And on account of the loss of all of these, a slave goes forth to freedom. Rabbi says, 'Also on account of castration.' Ben Azzai says, 'Also on account of the tongue.'"

IV.14 A.	The master has said: "Rabbi says, 'Also on account of castration'":
B.	*Castration of what? Should I said castration of the penis? But that is the same as loss of the penis [to which reference is explicitly made]. So it must mean, castration of the testicles.*
IV.15 A.	Rabbi says, "Also on account of castration":
B.	*And doesn't Rabbi include in the last removal of the tongue? And by way of contrast:* If a priest was sprinkling a man made unclean by corpse uncleanness with purification water, and a sprinkle hit his mouth – Rabbi says, "This constitutes a valid act of sprinkling." And sages say, "This does not constitute a valid act of sprinkling." *Now isn't this sprinkling on his tongue* [Freedman: so Rabbi regards the tongue as an exposed limb, contradicting his exclusion of the tongue in the case of a slave]?
C.	*No, it means on his lips.*
D.	*Well, if it means on his lips, then that is self-evidently the rule and it hardly needs to be spelled out!*
E.	*What might you otherwise have supposed, sometimes the lips are tightly pressed together? So we are informed that, one way or the other [they are regarded as exposed].*
F.	*But it has been taught on Tannaite authority:* "On his tongue," *and it further has been taught on Tannaite authority:* And that, the greater part of the tongue has been removed. R. Judah says, "The greater part of the fore-tongue"!
G.	*Rather, Rabbi says, "castration, and it is not necessary to say, the tongue, too."*

H.   Ben Azzai says, "The tongue but not castration."

I.   *And what is the point of saying "also"?*

J.   *It refers to the first clause.*

K.   *If so, then Ben Azzai's statement should have come first.*

L.   *The Tannaite framer of the passage heard Rabbi's statement and set it in place, then he heard Ben Azzai's statement and repeated it,* but the initial Tannaite formulation of the Mishnah paragraph did not move from the place assigned to it.

M.   Said Ulla, "All concur in regard to the tongue that, so far as issues of uncleanness are concerned, it is held to be exposed with respect to dead creeping things. *How come? The All-Merciful has said, 'and whomsoever he who has a flux touches,'* (Lev. 15:11), *and this, too, can be touched.* With respect to immersion, however, it is tantamount to a concealed part of the body. *What is the scriptural basis? The All-Merciful has said, 'And he shall bathe his flesh in water'* (Lev. 15:13) – *just as the flesh is exposed, so everything that has to be touched by the water must be exposed.* They differ only with respect to sprinkling in particular. *Rabbi compares it to the matter of uncleanness, and sages invoke the analogy of immersion, and both parties differ with respect to this one verse of Scripture:* 'And the clean shall sprinkle upon the unclean' (Num. 19:19) – Rabbi interprets the matter, 'And the clean shall sprinkle upon the unclean on the third day and on the seventh day and purify him,' *and rabbis read,* 'and on the seventh day he shall purify him and he shall wash his clothes and bathe himself in water' [Freedman: hence sprinkling must be on the same part that needs immersion, excluding the tongue, which doesn't]."

N.   *So why don't rabbis make the comparison to the matter of uncleanness?*

O.   *We seek governing analogies for matters of cleanness from matters of cleanness.*

P.   And why shouldn't Rabbi invoke the analogy of immersion?

Q.   "And he shall wash his clothes" *closes the subject* [Freedman: therefore "shall purify" cannot be linked with "bathe himself"].

R.   *But does Rabbi really take the view that, with respect to immersion, the tongue is regarded as concealed?* But didn't Rabin bar R. Ada say R. Isaac said, "There is the case of the slave girl of Rabbi, who immersed, and when she came up out of the water, a bone that constitutes interposition between her body and the water was found between her teeth, so Rabbi required her to immerse a second time"?

S.   *To be sure, we don't require that the water enter the spot, but we do require that there be the possibility of its entering, and that accords with what R. Zira said, for* said R. Zira, "In the case of whatever is suitable for mingling, actual mingling is not essential, and in the case of whatever is not suitable for mingling, actual mingling is indispensable." [Cashdan,

Menahot 18B: In Zira's view the law before us is that mingling can be omitted so long as it is possible to do so if one wants, and the Mishnah's rule would mean that no water at all was poured in.]

T. *There is a conflict of Tannaite statements on the same matter:*

U. "'That which has its stones bruised, crushed, torn, or cut' (Lev. 22:24) – all of them affect the testicles," the words of R. Judah.

V. "In the stones" but not in the penis? Rather: "Also in the stones," the words of R. Judah.

W. R. Eliezer b. Jacob says, "All of them refer to defects in the penis."

X. R. Yosé says, "'Bruised, crushed' also can refer to the testicles, but 'torn, or cut' can refer to the penis, but in the testicles do not constitute a blemish."

Once more the search for premises of broad consequence yields only disappointment. The Talmud is formed for the purpose of the exegesis of the Mishnah and of the law that the Mishnah treats, in that order. Where independent compositions are inserted, these, too, stand well within the topical program at hand, and the presuppositions that they take for granted also bear minimal implications for law beyond themselves, and none for theology. The bulk of the sizable composite performs familiar functions. Specifically, I.1 finds a scriptural basis for the Mishnah's rule. Nos. 2-3+4 address a further Tannaite statement on the same topic. Then we have a Tannaite complement, tacked on to the foregoing for obvious reasons, at No. 5, with its talmud at Nos. 6, 7. No. 8 illustrates the foregoing. II.1 analyzes the language of the Mishnah sentence. III.1+2 follow suit. IV.1 Nos. 2-3+4, 5-6, 7-8, 9-10, 11-12, 13 then move on to a tangential theme, relevant to our topic but not to the particular rule at hand. Nos. 13+14-15 are added because of its general congruence to the foregoing, but, of course, we have moved from a supplement to an appendix.

III. The Exegetical Programs of Yerushalmi and of the Bavli Compared

In preparation for the concluding chapter, we once more take up the comparison of the heuristic morphology of the two Talmuds, with the Yerushalmi at the left, the Bavli at the right, as before.

1:3 I Comparison of the acquisition of slaves and the acquisition of real estate, based on a verse of Scripture, Lev. 25:46, yielding the rule that the Mishnah has presented. How do we know that inherited real estate is acquired through money, writ or usucaption?	1:3 I.1 How on the basis of Scripture do we know this fact? Lev. 25:46 treats acquisition of slaves as equivalent to acquisition of a field of inheritance. Might one suppose that just as a field of inheritance reverts to the original owner at the Jubilee, so does the Canaanite slave?

1:3 II Statement that land is acquired only through usucaption does not accord with Eliezer [footnote to the foregoing].

1:3 III There are Mishnah rules that maintain slaves are equivalent to real estate, others that maintain slaves are equivalent to movables, others that compare them neither to real estate nor to movables.

1:3 IV Gloss on M. 1:3B: money paid to the master. Issue of how the transfer takes place, secondary question of whether one may transfer a benefit to someone in the beneficiary's absence.

1:3 V Analysis of M. Git. 4:5A: one who is half-slave and half-free.

1:3 VI If a slave picked up a lost object, can he avoid giving it to the master? Intersects with M. Ned. 11:8. Basic point: hand of slave is equivalent to hand of master.

1:3 VII Why doesn't the Mishnah list also make the point that the slave goes free at loss of limbs?

1:3 VIII Meir and sages on status of a gift from a third party to the slave.

1:3 IX Slave should acquire ownership of writ of emancipation for a fellow slave, since he has right to a writ of emancipation, but he should not acquire a writ of divorce of a woman, since he is not subject to that law.

1:3 X Are heirs bound by a writ of emancipation issued to take effect upon the master's death?

1:3 XI Continuation of foregoing.

1:3 XII You are free but your offspring is a slave.

Scripture closes off that possibility. While the prooftext is the same as the Yerushalmi's, the issue that is raised – maybe the slave reverts – is different.

1:3 I.2 Slave may be acquired also through barter. This point is not raised in the Yerushalmi.

1:3 I.3 Slave may be acquired through drawing. This point is not raised in the Yerushalmi.

1:3 I.4 Continues foregoing.

1:3 I.5 Tannaite rule: how a slave is acquired through an act of usucaption. Clarifies the Mishnah rule. This point is not raised in the Yerushalmi.

1:3 I.6 Continues foregoing.

1:3 I.7 Continues foregoing.

1:3 I.8 Case. No counterpart in the Yerushalmi to the problem addressed here.

1:3 II.1 Gloss of Meir's statement: can someone act in behalf of a third party not in his presence? Intersects with M. Git. 1:6. The problem is the same as the Yerushalmi's, but the treatment is different, since Abbayye insists the case is not one in which it is not with his knowledge and consent. So the issue intersects, but it is treated entirely differently in the Bavli.

1:3 III.1 Clarification of Mishnah statement: with money – whether taken on by others or by himself; with a writ, if taken on by others but not by himself; this represents the position of Simeon b. Eleazar. In fact, there are three positions on this issue, Meir's, Simeon's, and rabbis'. This analysis does not have a counterpart in the Yerushalmi.

1:3 III.2 Continues the foregoing.

1:3 III.3 What is at issue in the Mishnah dispute? Meir – slave has no right to acquire title without master's participation and woman has no right without her husband's; rabbis – slave may do so, wife may do so.

1:3 IV.2 Tannaite complement: slave goes free through loss of major limbs. Why is that so in case of major limbs, since Scripture refers only to tooth and eye? The Yerushalmi does not know this problem.

1:3 IV.3 Tannaite statement: does slave require a writ of emancipation if he goes forth because of loss of major limb? The Yerushalmi does not know this problem.

1:3 IV.4 Continuation of foregoing.

1:3 IV.5 If the master fitfully hit the slave etc., the slave is freed; if the injury was indirect, the slave doesn't go free. The Yerushalmi knows nothing of this problem.

1:3 IV.6 Continuation of foregoing.

1:3 IV.7 If the slave can still use his eyes, etc., he is not freed.

1:3 IV.8 It was necessary to talk about the several possibilities just now listed.

1:3 IV.9 If the master was a physician and the slave told him to paint the eye and the master blinded him, the slave goes free.

1:3 IV.10 Continuation of foregoing.

1:3 IV.11 Secondary development of foregoing.

1:3 IV.12 Supplementary rule added to foregoing.

1:3 IV.13 Story that contains a supplementary rule for the foregoing.

1:3 IV.14 Footnote to the foregoing.

1:3 IV.15. Continuation of the footnote.

The two Talmuds intersect at a few points, as noted. Where they intersect, it is because of the contents of the Mishnah. It is on the issue of how the slave acquires ownership of himself, since what the slave acquires belongs automatically to the master, that the two Talmuds come closest together. But, as we see, while the issue is shared, the Bavli goes its own way. The question is the same, but the treatment of the question in the later Talmud is not continuous with the treatment of the same matter in the earlier one. And, still more interesting, the Bavli asks about matters that the Yerushalmi treats superficially or simply ignores, for instance, other modes of acquisition, on the one side, and the freeing of the slave through the loss of major limbs, on the other.

Not only so, but even where the same verse of Scripture figures, as at Y 1:3Y = B. 1:3 I.1, the discussions of the two Talmuds exhibit strikingly distinctive characters:

[I.A]	It is written, "[As to Canaanite slaves] you may bequeath them to your sons after you, to inherit as a possession forever; you may make slaves of them" (Lev. 25:46).	
[B]	Acquisition of slaves thereby is treated under the same rubric as inherited real estate.	
[C]	Just as inherited real estate is acquired through money, writ, or usucaption so a Canaanite slave is acquired through money, writ, or usucaption.	
[D]	How do we know that inherited real estate itself is acquired through money, writ, or usucaption?	
[E]	It is written, "Fields will be bought for money, deeds will be signed and sealed and witnessed" (Jer. 32:44).	
[F]	"And signed and sealed and witnessed" – "signed and sealed" refers to witnesses to a writ; "witnessed" refers to witnesses to usucaption.	
[G]	Or perhaps these latter serve as witnesses to the writ?	
[H]	Since it already is written, "And signed and sealed," [which	

I.1

A. *How on the basis of Scripture do we know this fact?*

B. As it is written, "And you shall make them [gentile slaves] an inheritance for your children after you, to possess as an inheritance" (Lev. 25:46) – Scripture thus has treated them as comparable to a field of inheritance. Just as a field of inheritance is acquired through money, writ, or usucaption, so **a Canaanite slave is acquired through money, through a writ, or through usucaption.**

C. Might one then propose: Just as a field of inheritance reverts to its original owner at the Jubilee, so a Canaanite slave reverts to the original owner at the Jubilee?

D. Scripture states, "Of them shall you take your slaves forever" (Lev. 25:46).

must mean a writ, the other witnesses are to usucaption].

[I]   R. Yosa in the name of R. Mana, R. Tanhum, R. Abbahu in the name of R. Yohanan: "Real estate is not acquired for less than a perutah."

[J]   What is the scriptural basis for that statement?

[K]   "Fields will be bought for money" [and less than a perutah is not deemed money].

[L]   Now [Yohanan] disputes what R. Haninah said: "All references to shekels in the Torah are to selas; in the Prophets, to litras, and in the Writings to qintin." [Thus Jeremiah refers to twenty-five selas = a litra.]

[M]   Said R. Judah bar Pazzi, "That is except for the shekels of Ephron, which are qintin [a hundred selas]."

[N]   What is the scriptural basis for this statement?

[O]   "For the full price let him give it to me" (Gen. 23:9) [and "full price" implies the larger coin].

[P]   But the cases are not similar. There [Jer. 32:14] it is written "money," but here it is written "shekels."

[Q]   They objected, "Lo, there is the case of the rapist [Deut. 22:28], and lo, in that case

> what is written is only
> 'money,' and do you
> say it refers to
> shekels? [So there is a
> dispute even when
> 'money' stands by
> itself.]"

Here is a fine instance in which, dealing with the same problem and the same prooftext, the Bavli's framers go their own way. We noted that the Yerushalmi asks about the omission of the loss of major limbs from the Mishnah's list. A glance back at the Bavli shows that that Talmud has taken over a huge exposition of that topic, with a broad range of secondary issues, fully exposed and carefully analyzed. So even when the framers of both Talmuds are puzzled by the Mishnah's omission, the later Talmud goes its own way, pursuing its own method, and its method is self-evidently different from that of the earlier Talmud.

This question of the difference in heuristic morphology may now be addressed head-on. Here is what the Yerushalmi and Bavli have to say about the loss of major limbs:

[VIII.A] [In listing the means by which a slave goes free], why do we not learn that he also goes free at the loss of limbs that do not grow back?	IV.7 A. *Our rabbis have taught on Tannaite authority:*
	B. If he hit his eye and impaired his eyesight, his tooth and loosened it, but he still can use them at this time, the slave does not go forth on their account to freedom, but if not, the slave does go forth on their account to freedom.
[B] Said R. Yohanan b. Mareh, "It is because there is a dispute about the matter.	
[C] "Specifically, there is a Tannaite authority who teaches that [if he loses his limbs] he still requires a writ of emancipation from the master, and there is a Tannaite authority who teaches that, in that circumstance, he does not require a writ of emancipation from his master."	C. *It has further been taught on Tannaite authority:*
	D. If the slave had poor eyesight but the master totally blinded him, or if his tooth was loose and the master knocked it out, then, if he could use them beforetimes, the slave goes free on their account, but if not, the slave does not

go free on their ac-
count.

IV.8   A.   *And it was necessary to state both rules, for had we been informed of only the first rule, it might have been because to begin with the man had healthy vision and now he has weak vision, but in this case, since to begin with he had weak vision, I might have said that that is not the rule. And if we had been informed only of the second case, then it might have been because now he has totally blinded him, but in that case, in which he did not totally blind him, I might have said that the slave does not go free. So both were needed.*

IV.9   A.   *Our rabbis have taught on Tannaite authority:*

      B.   Lo, if his master was a physician, and the slave told him to paint his eye with an ointment, and the master blinded him, or to drill his tooth and he knocked it out, the slave just grins at his master and walks out free.

      C.   Rabban Simeon b. Gamaliel says, "'...and he destroy it' (Ex. 21:26) – only if he intends to destroy it."

IV.10 A.   *So how do rabbis deal with the clause, "...and he destroy it" (Ex. 21:26)?*

      B.   *They require it in line with that which has been taught on Tannaite authority:*

C.   R. Eleazar says, "Lo, if the master stuck his hand into his slave girl's womb and blinded the foetus that was in her belly, he is exempt from punishment. How come? Scripture said, '...and he destroy it' (Ex. 21:26) – only if he intends to destroy it."

D.   *And the other party?*

E.   *That rule he derives from the language,* "and he destroy it" *instead of the language,* "and he destroy."

F.   *And the other party?*

G.   *He derives no lesson from the language,* "and he destroy it" *instead of the language,* "and he destroy."

IV.11 A.   Said R. Sheshet, "If the slave's eye was blind and the master removed it, the slave goes forth to freedom on that account. How come? Because he now lacks a limb."

B.   *And a Tannaite statement is repeated along these same lines:* Freedom from blemish and male gender are required in the case of animals for sacrifice, but not for fowl. Might one then suppose that if the wing was dried up, the foot cut off, the eye plucked out, the bird remains fit? Scripture said, "And if the burnt-offering be of fowl" (Lev. 1:14), but not all fowl.

IV.12 A. Said R. Hiyya bar Ashi said Rab, "If the slave had [25A] an extra finger and the master cut it off, the slave goes out free."

B. Said R. Huna, "But that is on condition that the extra finger counts along with the hand."

IV.13 A. *The elders of Nezonayya didn't come to the public sessions of R. Hisda. He said to R. Hamnuna, "Go, excommunicate them."*

B. *He went and said to him, "How come rabbis have not come to the session?"*

C. *They said to him, "Why should we come? For when we ask him a question, he can't answer it for us."*

D. *He said to them, "Well, have you ever asked me a question that I couldn't answer for you?"*

E. *They asked him the following:* "A slave whose master castrated him, what is the law on classifying this blemish? *Is it tantamount to one that is visible to the eye or is it not?"*

F. *He didn't know the answer.*

G. *They said to him, "So what's your name?"*

H. *He said to them, "Hamnuna."*

I. *They said to him, "It's not Hamnuna but Qarnuna."*

J. *He came before R. Hisda. He said to him, "Well, they asked you a* question that can be answered from the Mishnah, for we have learned in the Mishnah: Twenty-four tips of limbs in man which are not susceptible to uncleanness because of quick flesh: The tips of the joints of hands and feet, and the tips of the ears, and the tip of the nose, and the tip of the penis. And the tips of the breasts which are in the woman. R. Judah says, 'Also of the man.' R. Eliezer says, 'Also the warts and the wens are not susceptible to uncleanness because of quick flesh' [M. Neg. 6:7]. *And a Tannaite statement in that connection:* And on account of the loss of all of these, a slave goes forth to freedom. Rabbi says, 'Also on account of castration.' Ben Azzai says, 'Also on account of the tongue.'"

IV.14 A.   The master has said: "Rabbi says, 'Also on account of castration'":

B.   *Castration of what? Should I have said castration of the penis? But that is the same as loss of the penis [to which reference is explicitly made]. So it must mean, castration of the testicles.*

IV.15 A.   Rabbi says, "Also on account of castration":

B. *And doesn't Rabbi in-
    clude in the last removal
    of the tongue? And by
    way of contrast:* If a
    priest was sprinkling a
    man made unclean by
    corpse uncleanness
    with purification wa-
    ter, and a sprinkle hit
    his mouth – Rabbi
    says, "This constitutes
    a valid act of sprin-
    kling." And sages say,
    "This does not consti-
    tute a valid act of
    sprinkling." *Now isn't
    this sprinkling on his
    tongue* [Freedman: so
    Rabbi regards the
    tongue as an exposed
    limb, contradicting his
    exclusion of the
    tongue in the case of a
    slave]?

C. *No, it means on his lips.*

D. *Well, if it means on his
    lips, then that is self-
    evidently the rule and it
    hardly needs to be
    spelled out!*

E. *What might you other-
    wise have supposed,
    sometimes the lips are
    tightly pressed together?
    So we are informed that,
    one way or the other
    [they are regarded as ex-
    posed].*

F. *But it has been taught
    on Tannaite authority:*
    "On his tongue," *and it
    further has been taught
    on Tannaite authority:*
    And that, the greater
    part of the tongue has
    been removed. R. Ju-
    dah says, "The greater
    part of the fore-
    tongue"!

G. Rather, Rabbi says, "castration, *and it is not necessary to say,* the tongue, too."

H. Ben Azzai says, "The tongue but not castration."

I. *And what is the point of saying* "also"?

J. *It refers to the first clause.*

K. *If so, then Ben Azzai's statement should have come first.*

L. *The Tannaite framer of the passage heard Rabbi's statement and set it in place, then he heard Ben Azzai's statement and repeated it,* but the initial Tannaite formulation of the Mishnah paragraph did not move from the place assigned to it.

M. Said Ulla, "All concur in regard to the tongue that, so far as issues of uncleanness are concerned, it is held to be exposed with respect to dead creeping things. *How come? The All-Merciful has said, '*and whomsoever he who has a flux touches,' (Lev. 15:11), *and this, too, can be touched.* With respect to immersion, however, it is tantamount to a concealed part of the body. *What is the scriptural basis? The All-Merciful has said, '*And he shall bathe his flesh in water' (Lev. 15:13) – just as the flesh is exposed, so everything that has to be touched by the water must be exposed. They differ only with respect to sprinkling in particular. *Rabbi compares it to the matter of uncleanness, and sages invoke the analogy of immersion, and both parties differ with respect to this one verse of Scripture:* 'And the clean shall sprinkle upon the unclean' (Num. 19:19) – Rabbi interprets the matter, 'And the clean shall sprinkle upon the unclean on the third day and on the seventh day and purify him,' *and rabbis read,* 'and on the seventh day he shall purify him and he shall wash his clothes and bathe himself in water' [Freedman: hence sprinkling must be on the same part that needs immersion, excluding the tongue, which doesn't]."

N.　*So why don't rabbis make the comparison to the matter of uncleanness?*

O.　*We seek governing analogies for matters of cleanness from matters of cleanness.*

P.　And why shouldn't Rabbi invoke the analogy of immersion?

Q.　"And he shall wash his clothes" *closes the subject* [Freedman: therefore "shall purify" cannot be linked with "bathe himself"].

R.   *But does Rabbi really take the view that, with respect to immersion, the tongue is regarded as concealed?* But didn't Rabin bar R. Ada say R. Isaac said, "There is the case of the slave girl of Rabbi, who immersed, and when she came up out of the water, a bone that constitutes interposition between her body and the water was found between her teeth, so Rabbi required her to immerse a second time"?

S.   *To be sure, we don't require that the water enter the spot, but we do require that there be the possibility of its entering, and that accords with what R. Zira said,* for said R. Zira, "In the case of whatever is suitable for mingling, actual mingling is not essential, and in the case of whatever is not suitable for mingling, actual mingling is indispensable."

[Cashdan, *Menahot* 18B: In Zira's view the law before us is that mingling can be omitted so long as it is possible to do so if one wants, and the Mishnah's rule would mean that no water at all was poured in.]

T.   *There is a conflict of Tannaite statements on the same matter:*

U.   "'That which has its stones bruised, crushed, torn, or cut'

(Lev. 22:24) – all of
them affect the testi-
cles," the words of R.
Judah.

V.   "In the stones" but not
in the penis? Rather:
"Also in the stones,"
the words of R. Judah.

W.   R. Eliezer b. Jacob
says, "All of them
refers to defects in the
penis."

X.   R. Yosé says,
"'Bruised, crushed'
also can refer to the
testicles, but 'torn, or
cut' can refer to the
penis, but in the testi-
cles do not constitute a
blemish."

As is clear, the Bavli has its own program, the shape and structure of
which are replicated at every point. And the Yerushalmi has a program,
too, a different one, and one that, clearly, the Bavli's framers did not find
to be a suitable model for their work. It is time to raise the question, do
the two Talmuds' framers share premises on what Mishnah commentary
requires? We have seen a sufficient sample of the two documents to
close off all other questions of premise and presupposition and to turn to
the final one: Do the documents at least take for granted the same rules
of reading when they open the same document, the Mishnah?

6

Documentary Presuppositions of Composites: Do the Two Talmuds' Framers' Premises as to the Character of Talmud Compilation Coincide?

Apart from premises particular to the task of Mishnah commentary, that the Mishnah rests on Scripture, and that the Mishnah is a flawless document, can we find in the two Talmuds points of concurrence that account for the character and program of those documents? The answer to that question completes our inquiry into the givens of the Rabbinic documents. It will either show us that premises transcend the writings that they animate, or prove for us that the entire question of premises and presuppositions proves monumentally misplaced. So the stakes prove formidable.

If we can show that the two Talmuds rest upon shared presuppositions as to the character of the work at hand, then, it follows, the search for the givens of the Rabbinic writings – the "what else do we know, if we know this?" – may go forward. The reason is that we shall have found firm reason to suppose documents appeal to prior and common convictions – the Judaism behind the texts we seek to define. Then, it will be clear, the presuppositions of individual documents transcend those documents. Premises common to a number of texts will attest to a Judaism behind a variety of writings and generative of them all.

But if it turns out that the two Talmuds take distinct and separate paths toward the accomplishment of their common task, Mishnah exegesis, it will follow that even the Talmuds, addressing a common, prior document and answering to a single task, that of exegesis, therefore constituting writings most like one another, in fact rest on disparate and essentially unrelated foundations. If no "Judaism behind the texts" can be defined for the two Talmuds, it is difficult to identify two or more other documents that may fairly be asked to yield evidence of such a prior, and a priori set of convictions. Then any claim that documents share common premises or bring to concrete expression shared presuppositions will prove chimerical. The search for a specific "Judaism behind the texts" that one may define will have yielded nothing we did not know when we undertook the quest: banalities, platitudes, truisms, none of them of generative consequence whatsoever.

We come, then, to a systematic comparison of the two Talmuds, with the stated problem defining the questions we must address. Obviously, points in common define the search; comparison and contrast, the method. What we shall now see is that the Bavli and the Yerushalmi in the end simply do not sustain comparison, because the Bavli is in quality and character different from the Yerushalmi, so different that the two Talmuds are incomparable. The reason is that, in intellectual morphology, the two documents share no prior or a priori convictions, neither of logic nor, all the more so, of program. The one talks in details, the other in large truths; the Yerushalmi tells us what the Mishnah says, the Bavli, what it means, which is to say, how its laws form law, the way in which its rules attest to the ontological unity of truth, a term that will presently become clear in the context of the reading of the Bavli against the backdrop of the Mishnah. The Bavli thinks more deeply about deep things, and, in the end, its authors think about different things from those that occupy the writers of the Yerushalmi. The Judaism behind the texts that animates the two Talmuds is not an inchoate body of ideas, still less a corpus of intellectual methods or attitudes. It is only the Mishnah (with its associated Tannaite corpera, the Tosefta and such Tannaite formulations as both Talmuds acknowledge and cite). But that is not that Judaism behind the texts that we sought to define.

How do the Talmuds compare? The first Talmud analyzes evidence, the second investigates premises; the first remains wholly within the limits of its case, the second vastly transcends them; and the first wants to know the rule, the second asks about the principle and its implications for other cases. The one Talmud provides an exegesis and amplification of the Mishnah, the other, a theoretical study of the law in all its magnificent abstraction – transforming the Mishnah into testimony to a deeper reality altogether: to the law behind the laws. Each Talmud has its own definition of the work of Talmud making; no "Judaism" has defined for the distinct authorships the character of their common task.

Let me give a concrete example of what it means for each of the documents to take its own way, indifferent not only to the other but also to a received program of how thought is to unfold. At their reading of

M. Gittin 1:1, where the Talmuds intersect but diverge in the reading of the Mishnah paragraph, we are able to identify what is at issue. Here is an occasion on which we can see the differences between the Yerushalmi's and the Bavli's representation of a conflict of principles contained within a Mishnah ruling. The Yerushalmi maintains that at issue is the inexpertness of overseas courts vs. a lenient ruling to avoid the situation of the abandoned wife; the Bavli, inexpertness of overseas courts vs. paucity of witnesses. How these diverse accounts differ in intellectual character and also program is hardly revealed by that brief precis.

What differentiates the two Talmuds can emerge by allowing the Bavli its full voice. Only then will my insistence on the real difference, the Talmuds' fundamental difference in the intellectual morphology and structure that form the substrate of each writing, emerge in all its clarity. Despite commonalities of form, which validate comparison, the two Talmuds in fact are utterly unlike pieces of writing. The second of the two Talmuds makes its own statement not merely because it very often says different things from the Bavli, or because it says different things in different ways (though both are the case). It stands on its own not only because its framers think differently; nor merely because their modes of thought and analysis in no way correspond to those of the Yerushalmi. The governing reason is that, for the framers of the Bavli, what is at stake in thought is different from the upshot of thought as conceived by the authors of the Yerushalmi's compositions and compilers of its composites.

Specifically, for the sages who produced the Bavli, the ultimate compilers and redactors of the document, what is at issue is not laws but law: how things hold together at the level of high abstraction. The Judaism behind the Bavli maintains that laws stand for unitary principles of being; the unity of God carries the principle of the ontological unity of even the rules that govern social existence; a single principle governs multiple cases – and we can discover that principle and show its coherence with other such governing principles. It suffices to say that the Judaism behind the Yerushalmi contains no such instructions, defines no such tasks of speculative thought. So that Judaism does not extend to the quest for the unity of being that the Bavli's framers – writers of compositions, compilers of composites alike – time and again propose to discover. I can think of no more profound point of comparison and contrast than that, and no more vivid evidence of the essential autonomy, at their deepest layers of premise and presupposition, of these two so very comparable documents. Let us now compare the Talmuds at this crucial point, examining how each explains M. Git. 1:1:

[I.A] Now here is a problem. In the case of one who brings a deed of gift from overseas, does he have to state, "Before me it was written and before me it was signed"? [Why is the rule more strict for writs of divorce?]

[B] R. Joshua b. Levi said, "The case [of writs of divorce] is different, for [overseas] they are not expert in the details of preparing writs of divorce [properly]."

[C] Said R. Yohanan, "It is a lenient ruling which [sages] have provided for her, that she should not sit an abandoned wife [unable to remarry]."

[D] And is this a lenient ruling? It is only a stringent one, for if the messenger did not testify, "In my presence it was written, and in my presence it was signed," you are not indeed going to permit the woman to remarry [at all], [so what sort of a lenient ruling do we have here]?

[E] Said R. Yosé, "The strict requirement which you have imposed on the matter at the outset, requiring the messenger to testify, 'Before me it was written and before me

I.1 A. What is the operative consideration here?

B. Said Rabbah, [2B] "Because [Israelites overseas] are inexpert in the requirement that the writ be prepared for the particular person for whom it is intended."

C. Raba said, "Because valid witnesses are not readily found to confirm the signatures [and the declaration of the agent serves to authenticate the signatures of the witnesses]."

D. *So what is at issue between these two explanations?*

E. *At issue between them is a case in which two persons brought the writ of divorce [in which case Raba's consideration is null], or a case in which a writ of divorce was brought from one province to another in the Land of Israel [in which case the consideration of Rabbah is null], or from one place to another in the same overseas province.*

I.2 A. *And from the perspective of Rabbah, who has said,*

it was signed,' turns out to be a lenient ruling which you have set for the case at the end. For if the husband later on should come and call into question the validity of the document, his cavil will be null."

[F] [As to the denial of credibility to the husband's challenge to the validity of the writ of divorce,] R. Mana contemplated ruling, "That applies to a complaint dealing with matters external to the body of the document itself."

[G] But as to a complaint as to the body of the document itself [do we believe him]? [Surely we take seriously his claim that the document is a forgery.]

[H] And as to a complaint [against the writ] which has no substance [one may not take the husband's cavil seriously].

[I] And even in the case of a cavil which has substance [should he not be believed]? [Surely he should be believed.]

[J] Said R. Yosé b. R. Bun, "[No, the original statement stands in all these cases]. [That is to say,] since you have said that the reason you have applied in the case a more stringent requirement at the outset, that the

"Because [Israelites overseas] are inexpert in the requirement that the writ be prepared for the particular person for whom it is intended," *there should still be a requirement that the writ of divorce is brought by two persons, such as is the requirement in respect to all acts of testimony that are spelled out in the Torah [in line with Deut. 19:15]!*

B. An individual witness is believed where the question has to do with a prohibition [for example, as to personal status, but not monetary matters].

C. *Well, I might well concede that we do hold, an individual witness is believed where the question has to do with a prohibition, for example, in the case of a piece of fat, which may be forbidden fat or may be permitted fat, in which instance the status of a prohibition has not yet been assumed. But here, with regard to the case at hand, where the presence of a prohibition is assumed, namely, that the woman is married, it amounts to a matter involving prohibited sexual relations, and a matter involving sexual relations is settled by no fewer than two witnesses.*

D. Most overseas Israelites are expert in the rule that the doc-

messenger must declare, 'Before me it was [written, and before me it was] signed,' you have imposed a lenient ruling at the end, for if the husband later on should come and call into question the validity of the document, his cavil will be null, and we must conclude that there is no difference at all whether the complaint against the validity of the document pertains to matters external to the body of the document or to matters internal to the body of the document, nor is there any difference whether the complaint deals with matters of no substance or matters of substance. [Once the necessary formula is recited by the messenger, the document has been validated against all future doubts.]"

[K] And yet should one not take account that invalid witnesses may have signed the document?

[L] Said R. Abun, "The husband is not suspect of disrupting [the wife's future marriage] in a matter which is in the hands of Heaven, [but is suspect of doing so only in a matter which lies before a court]. [Hence we do not take

ument has to be written for the expressed purpose of divorcing this particular woman.

E. *And even R. Meir, who takes account of not only the condition of the majority but even that of the minority [in this case, people not expert in that rule], concedes the ordinary scribe of a court knows the law full well, and it was rabbis who imposed the requirement. But here* [3A] *so as to prevent the woman from entering the status of a deserted wife [unable to remarry], they made the rule lenient.*

F. *Is this really a lenient ruling? It is in fact a strict ruling, since, if you require that the writ of divorce be brought by two messengers, there is no possibility of the husband's coming and challenging its validity and having it invalidated, but if only one person brings the document, he can still do so!*

G. Since the master has said, "As to how many persons must be present when the messenger hands over the writ of divorce to the wife, there is a dispute between R. Yohanan and R. Hanina. One party maintains it must be at least two, the other three." *Now, since that is the fact, the messenger will clarify the husband's intentions to begin with, and the* account of the husband's issuing such a complaint as is entered at G.]

[M] "In a court proceeding he is suspect of disrupting the wife's [future marriage]. For since he knows full well that if he should come and register a complaint against the validity of the document, his complaint will be deemed null, even he sees to it [when he prepares the writ] that it is signed by valid witnesses."

husband under such circumstances is not going to come and try to invalidate the writ and so get himself into trouble later on.

I.3 A. *Now from the perspective of Raba, who said that the operative consideration is, "Because valid witnesses are not readily found to confirm the signatures [and the declaration of the agent serves to authenticate the signatures of the witnesses]," there should still be a requirement that the writ of divorce is brought by two persons, such as is the requirement in respect to all acts of confirming the validity of documents in general!*

B. An individual witness is believed where the question has to do with a prohibition [for example, as to personal status, but not monetary matters].

C. *Well, I might well concede that we do hold,* an individual witness is believed where the question has to do with a prohibition, *for example, in the case of a piece of fat, which may be forbidden fat or may be permitted fat, in which instance the status of a prohibition has not yet been assumed. But here, with regard to the case at hand, where the presence of a prohibition is assumed, namely, that the woman is married, it amounts to a matter involving prohibited sexual relations,* and a matter involving sexual relations is settled by no fewer than two witnesses.

D. *Well, in strict law, there should be no requirement that witnesses confirm the signature on other documents either, in line with what R. Simeon b. Laqish said, for* said R. Simeon b. Laqish, "Witnesses who have signed a document are treated as equivalent to those who have been cross-examined in court." *It was rabbis who imposed the requirement. But here so as to prevent the woman from entering the status of a deserted wife [unable to remarry], they made the rule lenient.*

E. *Is this really a lenient ruling? It is in fact a strict ruling, since, if you require that the writ of divorce be brought by two messengers, there is no possibility of the husband's coming and challenging its validity and having it invalidated, but if only one person brings the document, he can still do so!*

F. Since the master has said, "As to how many persons must be present when the messenger hands over the writ of divorce to the wife, there is a dispute between R. Yohanan and R. Hanina. One party maintains it must be at least two, the other three." *Now, since that is the fact, the messenger will clarify the husband's intentions to begin with, and the husband under such circumstances is not going to come and try to invalidate the writ and so get himself into trouble later on.*

I.4   A.   *So how come Raba didn't give the operative consideration that Rabbah did?*

B.   *He will say to you,* "Does the Tannaite rule state, **In my presence it was written** for the purpose of divorcing this woman in particular, **and in my presence it was signed** for the purpose of divorcing this woman in particular?"

C.   And Rabbah?

D.   *Strictly speaking, it should have been formulated for Tannaite purposes in that way. But if you get verbose, the bearer may omit something that is required.*

E.   *Yeah, well, even as it is, the bearer may omit something that is required!*

F.   *One out of three phrases he may leave out, but one out of two phrases he's not going to leave out.*

G.   *So how come Rabbah didn't give the operative consideration that Raba did?*

H.   *He will say to you, "If so, the Tannaite formu-*

late should be, **In my presence it was signed** – *and nothing more! What need do I have for the language,* **In my presence it was written?** *That is to indicate that we require that the writ be prepared for the sole purpose of divorcing this particular woman.*

I. And Raba?

J. *Strictly speaking, it should have been formulated for Tannaite purposes in that way. But if it were done that way, people might come to confuse the matter of the confirmation of documents in general and hold that only a single witness is required for that purpose.*

K. And Rabbah?

L. *But is the parallel all that close? There the required language is, "We know that this is Mr. So-and-so's signature," while here it is, "In my presence...." In that case, a woman is not believed to testify, in this case, a woman is believed to testify. In that case, an interested party cannot testify, here an interested party can testify.*

M. And Raba?

N. *He will say to you, "Here, too, if the agent says, 'I know...,' he is believed, and since that is the fact, there really is the consideration [if he says only, 'In my presence it was signed' (Simon)], peo-*

ple might come to confuse the matter of the confirmation of documents in general and hold that only a single witness is required for that purpose."

I.5 A. *From the perspective of Rabbah, who has said,* "Because [Israelites overseas] are inexpert in the requirement that the writ be prepared for the particular person for whom it is intended," *who is the authority that requires that* the writ of divorce be both written for the particular person for whom it is intended *and also requires* [3B] that it be signed for the particular person for whom it is intended? *It obviously isn't R. Meir, for he requires the correct declaration as to the signing of the document, but not as to the writing of the document, for we have learned in the Mishnah:* **They do not write [a writ of divorce] on something which is attached to the ground. [If] one wrote it on something attached to the ground, then plucked it up, signed it, and gave it to her, it is valid [M. 2:4A-B].** [The anonymous rule, assumed to stand for Meir, holds that what matters is the signing, not the writing, of the document.] *It also cannot be R. Eleazar,* *who maintains that the writing be done properly* [with correct intentionality as to the preparation of the document for the particular woman to whom it is to be given as a writ of divorce], *but as to the signing, he imposes no such requirement. And, further, should you say that, in point of fact, it really is R. Eleazar, and as to his not requiring correct procedure as to the signing of the document with proper specificity* [with correct intentionality as to the preparation of the document for the particular woman to whom it is to be given as a writ of divorce], *that is on the strength of the authority of the Torah, but as to the position of rabbis, he would concur that that requirement must be met — if that is your claim, lo, there are three kinds of writs of divorce that rabbis have declared invalid [but the Torah has not invalidated], and among them, R. Eleazar does not include one that has not been signed with appropriate intentionality for that particular woman, as we see in the following Mishnah:* **There are three writs of divorce which are invalid, but if the wife [subsequently] remarried [on the strength of those** documents], the off-spring [nonetheless] is valid: [If] he wrote it in his own hand-writing, but there are no witnesses on it; there are witnesses on it, but it is not dated; it is dated, but there is only a single wit-ness – lo, these are three kinds of invalid writs of divorce, but if the wife [sub-sequently] remarried, the offspring is valid. R. Eleazar says, "Even though there are no witnesses on it [the document itself], but he handed it over to her in the presence of witnesses, it is valid. And she collects [her marriage contract] from mortgaged property. For wit-nesses sign the writ of divorce only for the good order of the world" [M. Git. 9:4].

B. *Well, then, it must be R. Meir, and so far as he is concerned, as to his not requiring correct proce-dure as to the signing of the document with proper specificity* [with correct intentionality as to the preparation of the document for the particular woman to whom it is to be given as a writ of di-vorce], *that is on the strength of the authority of the Torah, but as to the position of rabbis, he would concur that that requirement must be met.*

C.   Yes, but said R. Nah-
      man, "R. Meir would
      rule, 'Even if one
      found it in the garbage
      [4A] and had it prop-
      erly signed and
      handed it over to her,
      it is a valid writ of di-
      vorce'"! *And, as a mat-*
      ter of fact, this ruling is
      to say, "valid so far as
      the Torah is concerned,"
      then the language that
      R. Nahman should have
      used is not, R. Meir
      would rule, *but rather,*
      The rule of the Torah
      is....

D.   *Rather, the position be-*
      fore us represents the
      view of R. Eleazar, and
      the case in which R.
      Eleazar does not require
      a signature incised for
      the sake of the particular
      woman for whom the
      document is prepared,
      that is a case in which
      there are no witnesses at
      all. But in a case in
      which there are wit-
      nesses, he does impose
      that requirement. For
      said R. Abba, "R.
      Eleazar concurs in the
      case of a writ disqual-
      ified on the base of its
      own character that it is
      invalid [and here we
      have invalid wit-
      nesses]."

E.   *R. Ashi said, "Lo, who is*
      the authority at hand?
      It is R. Judah, for we
      have learned in the
      Mishnah: **R. Judah**
      declares it invalid, so
      long as writing it and
      signing it are [not] on
      something which is

plucked up from the ground."

F. *So to begin with why didn't we assign the passage to R. Judah?*

G. *We first of all reverted to R. Meir, for an otherwise unattributed statement in the Mishnah belongs to R. Meir. We reverted to R. Eleazar, because it is an established fact for us that in matters of writs of divorce, the decided law is in accord with his position.*

I.6 A. **We have learned in the Mishnah: Rabban Gamaliel says, "Also: He who delivers [a writ of divorce] from Reqem or from Heger [must make a similar declaration]." R. Eliezer says, "Even from Kefar Ludim to Lud":**

B. *And said Abbayye, "We deal with* towns that are near the Land of Israel and those that are entirely surrounded by the Land of Israel."

C. *And said Rabbah bar bar Hannah, "I myself have seen that place, and the distance is the same as that between Be Kube and Pumbedita."*

I.7 A. *Does it then follow that the initial Tannaite authority before us takes the view that when bringing a writ of divorce from the places named here, one need not make the stated declaration? Then is not this what is under dis-*

pute between the two au-
thorities: The one au-
thority takes the view
that the operative con-
sideration is, because
[Israelites overseas]
are inexpert in the re-
quirement that the
writ be prepared for
the particular person
for whom it is in-
tended, *and the resi-*
dents of these areas have
learned what to do; and
the other authority holds
that the operative con-
sideration is, because
valid witnesses are not
readily found to con-
firm the signatures
[and the declaration of
the agent serves to au-
thenticate the signa-
tures of the witnesses],
and in these places, too,
witnesses are not readily
found.

B.   *Not at all. Rabbah can*
work matters out in
accord with his theory,
and Raba   can work
matters out in accord
with his theory.

C.   *Rabbah can work mat-*
ters out in accord with
his theory: All parties
concur that the reason
for the required declara-
tion is that [Israelites
overseas] are inexpert
in the requirement
that the writ be pre-
pared for the particu-
lar person for whom it
is intended, *and here,*
what is at issue is, the
initial authority holds
that since these are lo-
cated near the Land of
Israel, they learn what is
required; then Rabban

Gamaliel comes along to say that those located in areas surrounded by the Land of Israel have learned the rules, while those nearby have not, then R. Eliezer comes along to indicate that those located in areas surrounded by the Land of Israel also are not exempt, so as not to make a distinction among territories all assigned to the category of "overseas."

D. *Raba can work matters out in accord with his theory: All parties concur that the reason for the required declaration is that* valid witnesses are not readily found to confirm the signatures. *The initial Tannaite authority takes the view that these locales, since they are located near the border, will produce witnesses; Rabban Gamaliel comes along to say that in the areas surrounded by the Land of Israel, witnesses are going to be readily turned up, while in the areas near the Land, that is not the case; then R. Eliezer comes along to say that also in the areas surrounded by the Land of Israel, that is not the case,* so as not to make a distinction among territories all assigned to the category of "overseas."

I.8 A. *We have learned in the Mishnah:* **And sages say, "He must state, 'In my presence it** was written, and in my presence it was signed,' only in the case of him who delivers a writ of divorce from overseas, and him who takes [one abroad]":

B. *Does it then follow that the initial Tannaite authority before us takes the view that one who takes a writ of divorce overseas is not required to make the stated declaration? Then is not this what is at issue? The one authority maintains that the operative consideration is,* because [Israelites overseas] are inexpert in the requirement that the writ be prepared for the particular person for whom it is intended, [4B] *and the residents of these areas have learned what to do; and the other authority holds that the operative consideration is,* because valid witnesses are not readily found to confirm the signatures [and the declaration of the agent serves to authenticate the signatures of the witnesses], *and in these places, too, witnesses are not readily found.*

C. *Rabbah can work matters out in accord with his theory, and Raba can work matters out in accord with his theory.*

D. *Rabbah can work matters out in accord with his theory: All parties concur that the reason for the required declaration is that* [Israelites overseas] are inexpert in the requirement that the writ be prepared for the particular person for whom it is intended, *and here, what is at issue is, whether we make a decree extending the obligation that applies to one who brings a writ from overseas to the Land of Israel to the person who takes a writ from the Land of Israel overseas, and the rabbis cited below maintain that we do make a decree covering one who takes such a writ overseas on account of the decree covering bringing such a decree to the Land of Israel.*

E.   *Raba can work matters out in accord with his theory: All parties concur that the reason for the required declaration is that* valid witnesses are not readily found to confirm the signatures. *The rabbis cited later on propose to explain the reasoning behind the position of the initial authority.*

I.9   A.   *We have learned in the Mishnah:* And he who delivers [a writ of divorce] from one overseas province to another must state, "In my presence it was written, and in my presence it was signed."

B.   Lo, if he takes it from one place to another in the same overseas province, he does not have to make the required declaration. *Now that poses no problem to Raba [who can explain why], but it does present a conflict with the position of Rabbah!*

C. *Do not draw the conclusion that* if he takes it from one place to another in the same overseas province, he does not have to make the required declaration. *Rather, draw the conclusion that* if he brings it from one province to another in the Land of Israel, he does not have to make that declaration.

D. *But that position is spelled out explicitly in the Mishnah paragraph itself:* **He who delivers a writ of divorce in the Land of Israel does not have to state, "In my presence it was written, and in my presence it was signed"!**

E. *If I had only that statement to go by, I should have concluded that that is the case only after the fact, but to begin with, that is not the rule. So we are informed to the contrary.*

F. *There are those who set up the objection in the following language:* **[And he who delivers [a writ of divorce] from one overseas province to another must state, "In my** presence it was written, and in my presence it was signed":] Lo, if he takes it from one place to another in the same overseas province, he does not have to make the required declaration. *Now that poses no problem to Rabbah [who can explain why], but it does present a conflict with the position of Raba!*

G. Do not draw the conclusion *that* if he takes it from one province to another in the Land of Israel he does not have to make the declaration, *but say:* Lo, if it is within the same province overseas, he does not have to make that declaration, but if it is from one province to another in the Land of Israel, *what is the law?* He has to make the declaration.

H. *Then the Tannaite formulation ought to be:* And he who delivers [a writ of divorce] without further articulation.

I. In point of fact, even if one brings a writ of divorce from one province to another in the Land of Israel, *he also does not have to make the declaration, for, since there are pilgrims, witnesses will always be available.*

J. *That poses no problem for the period at which the house of the sanctuary is standing, but for* the period in which the house of the sanctuary is not standing, what is to be said?

K. *Since courts are well established, there still will be plenty of witnesses.*

I.10 A. *We have learned in the Mishnah:* **Rabban Simeon b. Gamaliel says, "Even [if he brings one] from one jurisdiction to another [in the same town]":**

B. And said R. Isaac, "There was a town in the Land of Israel called Assassiot, in which were two governors, jealous of one another. Therefore it was necessary to refer also to the case of bringing a writ **from one jurisdiction to another [in the same town]."**

C. *Now to Raba that poses no problems, but to Rabbah it presents a question!*

D. *Not at all, Rabbah for his part also accepts the consideration important to Raba.*

E. *Then what is at stake between them?*

F. *At stake between them is a case in which two persons brought the writ, or if it was brought from one locale to another in the same province overseas.*

I.11 A. *We have learned in the Mishnah:* **He who delivers a writ of divorce from overseas and cannot say, "In** my presence it was written, and in my presence it was signed," if there are witnesses [inscribed] on it – it is to be confirmed by its signatures [M. 1:3C-E]. *Now in reflecting on that matter, [we said], what is the meaning of the language,* and cannot say? *[5A] If we say, it refers to a deaf-mute, can a deaf-mute come along and raise an objection and invalidate the decree? And lo, we have learned in the Mishnah:* All are valid for delivering a writ of divorce, except for a deaf-mute, an idiot, and a minor, a blind man, and a gentile [M. 2:5E-G]. *And said R. Joseph, "Here with what case do we deal? A case in which* he gave it to her when he was of sound senses, but he did not have time to say, 'Before me it was written and before me it was signed,' before he was struck dumb." *To Raba that poses no problems, but to Rabbah it is a challenge!*

B. *Here with what situation do we deal? It was after the requirement of intentionality had been widely learned.*

C. *If so, then one may indeed invoke the conception,* we have to take precaution lest the matter revert to its former chaos.

D.   *If so, then the same rule
      should pertain even if
      the bearer cannot make
      such a statement?*

E.   *A case in which one had
      sound senses but then
      was struck dumb is not
      commonplace, and for
      matters that are not
      commonplace rabbis did
      not make precautionary
      decrees.*

F.   *Well, the matter of a
      woman's bringing the
      writ of divorce is
      uncommon, and yet we
      have learned in the
      Mishnah:* **A woman
      herself delivers her
      writ of divorce [from
      abroad], on condition
      that she must state,
      "In my presence it
      was written, and in
      my presence it was
      signed" [M. 2:7E-F].**

G.   It is to avoid making
      distinctions among
      classifications of
      bearers.

H.   *If that is the case, then
      the husband, too, should
      be subject to the law of
      declaration, so how come
      it has been taught on
      Tannaite authority:* He
      himself who brought
      his own writ of
      divorce does not have
      to say, "Before me it
      has been written, and
      before me it has been
      signed"?

I.   *Well, exactly why did
      rabbis say,* "It is
      necessary to declare,
      'Before me it was
      written and before me
      it was signed'"? *It is
      because the husband
      may come along and*

challenge the writ of divorce and invalidate it. But in this case, the man is holding it in his own hands, so is he going to raise questions about its validity?

I.12   A. Come and take note of what Samuel asked R. Huna: "As to two persons who brought a writ of divorce from overseas, do they have to say, 'Before us it was written and before us it was signed,' or do they not have to say that?"

B. He said to him, "They do not have to say that. *For if they had said in our presence, 'He has divorced her,' would they not be believed?"*

C. *That poses no problem to Raba, but it is a problem for Rabbah!*

D. *Here with what situation do we deal? It was after the requirement of intentionality had been widely learned.*

E. *If so, then one may indeed invoke the conception,* we have to take precaution lest the matter revert to its former chaos.

F. *If so, then the same rule should pertain even if two persons brought the writ.*

G. *Two persons bringing a writ of divorce is uncommon, and for matters that are not commonplace rabbis did not make precautionary decrees.*

H. *Well, the matter of a woman's bringing the writ of divorce is uncommon, and yet we have learned in the Mishnah:* **A woman herself delivers her writ of divorce [from abroad], on condition that she must state, "In my presence it was written, and in my presence it was signed" [M. 2:7E-F].**

I. It is to avoid making distinctions among classifications of bearers.

J. *If that is the case, then the husband, too, should be subject to the law of declaration, so how come it has been taught on Tannaite authority:* He himself who brought his own writ of divorce does not have to say, "Before me it has been written, and before me it has been signed"?

K. *Well, exactly why did rabbis say,* "It is necessary to declare, 'Before me it was written and before me it was signed'"? *It is because the husband may come along and challenge the writ of divorce and invalidate it. But in this case, the man is holding it in his own hands, so is he going to raise questions about its validity?*

I.13 A. *Come and take note:* He who brings a writ of divorce from overseas and gave it to the woman but did not say to her, "Before me it was written and before me it was signed," if the writ can be confirmed through its signatures, it is valid, and if not, it is invalid. It must follow that the requirement of saying, "Before me it was written and before me it was signed," has been imposed not to treat the wife's situation in accord with a strict rule but rather in accord with a lenient rule.

B. *That poses no problem to Raba, but it is a problem for Rabbah!*

C. *Here with what situation do we deal? It was after the requirement of intentionality had been widely learned.*

D. *If so, then one may indeed invoke the conception,* we have to take precaution lest the matter revert to its former chaos.

E. Here it is a case in which the woman has remarried.

F. *If so, then how can you say,* the requirement of saying, "Before me it was written and before me it was signed," has been imposed not to treat the wife's situation in accord with a strict rule but rather in accord with a lenient rule! *Is the reason that we allow the writ to be confirmed through the*

*signatures because she
has remarried?*

G.   *This is the sense of the
statement:* [The writ
can be confirmed
through its signa-
tures], *and should you
say, we should impose a
strict rule on her and
force [the husband] to
divorce her, lo, it is the
intent in* requiring the
statement, "Before us
it was written and be-
fore us it was signed,"
not to treat the wife's
situation in accord
with a strict rule but
rather in accord with a
lenient rule! *Now* [5B]
*what is the operative
consideration? Perhaps
the husband may come
and challenge the writ of
divorce and invalidate
it? Since here the origi-
nal husband is not rais-
ing any objection, are we
going to go and raise
problems?*

Readers will stipulate that Bavli at I.14 proceeds in the same fair and
balanced manner to expose the dispute of Yohanan and Joshua b. Levi.
But enough has been given to provide a full grasp of the Bavli's
intellectual morphology. Here the Yerushalmi, as much as the Bavli,
presents a sustained argument, not just a snippet of self-evidently
informative information, as at its reading of M. B.M. 1:1. So we now
examine a fully exposed argument in the Yerushalmi as against its
counterpart in the Bavli.

The Yerushalmi presents two theses, A-C, then challenges the second
of the two, D-E. This produces a secondary inspection of the facts of the
matter, F-I, and a resolution of the issues raised, J; then another
secondary issue, K-M. Is there an *Auseinandersetzung* between the two
conflicting parties, Joshua b. Levi and Yohanan? Not at all. There is, in
fact, no exchange at all. Instead of a dialogue, formed into an ongoing set
of challenges, we have the voice of the Talmud intervening, "and is this a
lenient ruling at all?" There is no pretense that Joshua asks a question to
Yohanan, or Yohanan to Joshua. The controlling voice is that of the

Talmud itself, which sets up pieces of information and manipulates them. B. I.5, by contrast, presents us with one of the Bavli's many superb representations of issues, and we see that the goal of contention is not argument for its own sake, nor is the medium the message, as some have imagined.

We now see a concrete case of what it means for the Bavli's writers and compilers to undertake the search for the unitary foundations of the diverse laws. This they do through an inquiry into the premises of discrete rules, the comparison and contrast of those premises, the statement of the emergent principles, and the comparison and contrast of those principles with the ones that derive from other cases and their premises – a process, an inquiry, without end, into the law behind the laws. What the Bavli wants, beyond its presentation of the positions at hand, is to draw attention to the premises of those positions, the reasoning behind them, the evidence that supports them, the argument that transforms evidence into demonstration, and even the authority, among those who settle questions by expressing opinions, who can hold the combination of principles or premises that underpin a given position.

B. at I.1 states the contrary explanations and identifies the issues between them. Then one position is examined, challenged, defended – fully exposed. The second position is given equal attention, also challenged, also defended, in all, fully exposed. The two positions having been fairly stated and amply argued, we proceed to the nub of the matter: if X is so right, then why has Y not adopted his position? And if Y, then why not X? This second level of exchange allows each position to be re-defended, re-explained, re-exposed – all on fresh grounds. Now at this point, we have identified two or more principles that have been combined to yield a position before us, so the question arises, what authority, among those who stand behind the law, holds these positions, which, while not contradictory, also are not commonly combined in a single theory of the law? I.5 then exposes the several possibilities – three major authorities, each with his several positions to be spelled out and tested against the allegations at hand.

Now, when we observe that one Talmud is longer than the other, or one Talmud gives a fuller account than the other, we realize that such an observation is trivial. The real difference between the Talmuds emerges from this – and I state with emphasis: *the Bavli's completely different theory of what it wishes to investigate*. And that difference derives not from intellectual morphology, but generative purpose: why the framers of the Bavli's compositions and composites did the work to begin with. The outlines of the intellectual character of the work flow from the purpose of the project, not the reverse; and thence, the modes of thought, the specifics of analytical initiative – all these are secondary to intellectual morphology. So first comes the motivation for thought, then the morphology of thought, then the media of thought, in that order.

Let me spell out what I conceive to be at stake. The difference between the Yerushalmi and the Bavli is the difference between jurisprudence and philosophy; the one is a work of exegesis in search of jurisprudential system, the other, of analysis in quest of philosophical truth. To state matters simply, the Yerushalmi presents the laws, the rule for this, the rule for that – pure and simple; "law" bears its conventional meaning of jurisprudence. The Bavli presents the law, now in the philosophical sense of, the abstract issues of theory, the principles at play far beneath the surface of detailed discussion, the law behind the laws. And that, we see, is not really "law," in any ordinary sense of jurisprudence; it is law in a deeply philosophical sense: the rules that govern the way things are, that define what is proportionate and orderly and properly composed.

The reason that the Bavli does commonly what the Yerushalmi does seldom and then rather clumsily – the balancing of arguments, the careful formation of a counterpoint of reasons, the excessively fair representation of contradictory positions (why doesn't X take the position of Y? why doesn't Y take the position of X? Indeed!) – is not that the Bavli's framers are uninterested in conclusions and outcome. It is that for them, the deep structure of reason is the goal, and the only way to penetrate into how things are at their foundations is to investigate how conflicting positions rest on principles to be exposed and juxtaposed, balanced, and, if possible, negotiated, if necessary, left in the balance.

If I am correct that, at the foundation, the Talmuds differ in not only the epiphenomenon of fundamental intellectual morphology, but in generative purpose, then even when they say pretty much the same thing, or go over the same problem, we should observe these same fixed differences. In my view that is the case in the following, where both Talmuds consider the same facts concerning the same issue, dealing with another Mishnah paragraph of Mishnah-tractate Gittin, 1:4:

[I.A] As regards monetary matters [Samaritans] are suspect, and, [consequently,] as regards their testimony in monetary matters they are deemed invalid [witnesses].	I.1 A. *Who is the Tannaite authority behind the unassigned Mishnah paragraph before us? It cannot be either the initial authority or R. Eleazar or Rabban Simeon b. Gamaliel in the following, which has been*
[B] They are not deemed	

suspect in regard to observing the laws of forbidden connections.

[C] And testimony in capital cases is equivalent to testimony in cases involving prohibited connections. [Samaritan testimony is accepted in capital cases.]

[D] [Now M. 1:3A refers to only a single Samaritan witness.] But if what has just been said is so, then even if both witnesses are Samaritans, [the writ of divorce should be deemed valid].

[E] It is different [when both are Samaritans], since they are not experts in the details of preparing writs of divorce.

[F] If that is the case, then even a single Samaritan witness should be invalid?

[G] Said R. Abin, "Interpret the Mishnah to speak of a document in which the Israelite [witness] signed at the end [certifying that this particular Samaritan is knowledgeable]."

[H] Said R. Yosé, "That statement accords with the view of him who said that witnesses sign on the document not in one another's presence. [That is why we want the Israelite signature at the end, certifying that the Samaritan is

taught on Tannaite authority:

B. Unleavened bread prepared by Samaritans is permitted for use on Passover, and a person carries out the obligation for eating such unleavened bread on Passover by eating Samaritan unleavened bread. But R. Eleazar prohibits doing so, for they are by no means expert in the details of the laws of unleavened bread. Rabban Simeon b. Gamaliel says, "Any religious duty that the Samaritans preserved they observe with far great punctiliousness than Israelites" [T. Pes. 2:3].

C. *Now this cannot be the initial Tannaite authority, for from his perspective, even other documents should be valid if bearing a Samaritan witness's signature; and it cannot be R. Eleazar, for from his perspective, even other documents should not be valid if bearing a Samaritan witness's signature; and it cannot stand for the position of Rabban Simeon b. Gamaliel, for, from his perspective, if the Samaritans continued to hold fast to a given procedure, then even other documents attested by them should be valid, and if they didn't, then even a writ of divorce for a woman should not be valid. And*

knowledgeable. Then there is no possibility that the Samaritan has signed at the end, after the Israelite, such that the Israelite has no knowledge of the suitability of the Samaritan.]

[I] "But in the view of him who said, 'Witnesses sign only in the presence of one another,' even if the Samaritan had signed at the end, it would be a valid document, [since the Israelite in any event will know about the character of the Samaritan signatory]."

[J] R. Ila in the name of R. Yosé: "It accords with the view of him who said, 'The witnesses sign only in the presence of one another.'

[K] "But in the view of him who said, 'The witnesses sign not in one another's presence,' even if the Israelite had signed at the end, it is nonetheless invalid. [The Israelite might leave space for the earlier signature without knowing the character of the signatory.]"

[L] A writ bearing four signatures of witnesses, the first two of which turn out to be relatives or otherwise invalid – the writ is valid, and is to be confirmed by the remainder of the signatures [the valid ones]

should you maintain that it is Rabban Simeon b. Gamaliel, and from his viewpoint, our Mishnah maintains that the Samaritans keep the regulations concerning writs of divorce and emancipation of slaves, but they don't keep the rules on other documents, then in that case, why in the passage before us do we speak of only a single Samaritan witness? It should be valid even if there were two. And if that were the case, why would R. Eleazar maintain that a writ of divorce of the present classification has been validated only if there is a single Samaritan signature on it but not two?

D. *In point of fact, it is R. Eleazar, and at hand is a case in which an Israelite signed the document at the end* **[10B]**, *for if it were not that the Samaritan were in the status of an associate [reliable in matters of details of the law], the Israelite would never have allowed him to sign his name prior to the Israelite's own signature.*

E. *But if so, how come other documents would not be equally valid?*

F. *We maintain that he left space for someone senior to [= of greater authority than] himself.*

G. *Well, then, here, too, we maintain that he left space for someone senior to himself.*

[cf. T. Git. 7:15].

[M] But should this not be treated as a document on which the witnesses' signatures are distant from the body of the text itself, [so that it is possible that the testimony was signed before, or separate from, the writing of the document which the witnesses attest, in which case] the document is invalid?

[N] You cannot invalidate it on such a basis, for in accord with R. Yosé in the name of R. Jeremiah: "Invalid witnesses do not cause the testimony on the document to be treated as if we have the signatures of the witnesses distant from the body of the text itself, for the invalid witnesses are included only to validate the writ [by filling up space, so that there can be no further doubt as to the validity of the document, on the foundation of the signatures of the valid witnesses]."

H. Said R. Pappa, "That is to say, witnesses to a writ of divorce do not sign except in the presence of one another."

I. *How come?*

J. Said R. Ashi, "It is a precautionary decree on account of the consideration of the rule, 'all of you.'" [**If he said, "All of you write it," one of them writes it, and all of them sign it. Therefore if one of them died, lo, this is an invalid writ of divorce (M. 6:7H-I)].**

I.2 A. *Reverting to the body of the prior discussion:* Said R. Eleazar, "They validated a writ of divorce of the present classification only if there is a single Samaritan signature on it but not two."

B. *So what does he tell us that we don't know? For we have learned in the Mishnah:* **Any sort of writ on which there is a Samaritan witness is invalid, except for writs of divorce for women and writs of emancipation for slaves!**

C. *If I had to rely on our Mishnah paragraph, I might have supposed that the same rule applies even if there are two witnesses, in which case the writ would be valid, and the reason that the Tannaite formulation made reference to a single witness is on account of other documents, indicating that even such other documents with a single Samaritan signature are invalid. R. Eleazar's statement consequently was required.*

D. *Well then, is it the fact that a document with two Samaritan signatures is invalid? Doesn't the Mishnah paragraph say in so many words:* There was this precedent: They brought before Rabban Gamaliel in Kepar Otenai the writ of divorce of a woman, and the witnesses thereon were Samaritan witnesses, and he did declare it valid?

E. *Said Abbayye, "Repeat as the Tannaite formulation:* Its witness was...."

F. *And Raba said, "In point of fact they really were two, and Rabban Gamaliel differs, and the passage is flawed, so this is the correct Tannaite formulation:* And Rabban Gamaliel validates one bearing two witnesses. There was this precedent: They brought before Rabban Gamaliel in Kepar Otenai the writ of divorce of a woman, and the witnesses thereon were Samaritan witnesses, and he did declare it valid."

What troubles the Yerushalmi's author, Y. 1:4 I, is not the fact that Samaritans' testimony is accepted in one matter, not in another. It is the Mishnah's claim that in the matter at hand, a single Samaritan witness is invalid, and that presents us with an excluded middle. If the prevailing rule – Samaritans observe the laws governing forbidden family connections – is valid, then two such witnesses should be acceptable. We resolve the issue by saying that they are inexpert in the matter. But then, why should one such witness not invalidate the writ? We solve the problem by placing an Israelite signature underneath, certifying that this Samaritan is knowledgeable, and that solves the problem. We then introduce the intersecting consideration: Do the witnesses sign in one another's presence? This, too, has to be sorted out.

Now, on the surface, the Bavli does not appear to address the issue before us. It wants to know who is the authority behind the Mishnah paragraph. That hardly conforms to my allegations about the character of the Bavli, or even about the difference between the Talmuds. But once we enter into the facts adduced in evidence, we discover, at B. 1:5A-C I.1C, that precisely the same considerations are in play. That is, if Samaritans are valid witnesses, then two should be acceptable; if not, then none. And we solve the problem in the same way: an Israelite certifies that the Samaritan is valid in this case. Then how distinguish this document from others? And the problem unfolds. Now, we recall, Y. introduces the Mishnah's evidence; indeed, it focuses upon the interpretation of the issue in its repertoire of issues and arguments; it is framed as Mishnah exegesis in the simplest form. B., by contrast, treats the same evidence and arguments, but only in the form of a footnote to I.1. I.2 introduces exactly the same evidence as played exactly the same role in the Yerushalmi, but it does so as a challenge: What does he tell us that we don't know! Then, if I had to rely on the Mishnah paragraph alone, I might have supposed that a proposition is valid that in fact is invalid. And this plays itself out.

What I find interesting therefore is that even when the facts are the same, the issues identical, and the arguments matched, the Bavli's author manages to lay matters out in a very distinctive way. And that way yields as a sustained, somewhat intricate argument (requiring us to keep in the balance both names and positions of authorities and also the objective issues and facts) what the Yerushalmi's method of representation gives us as a rather simple sequence of arguments. If we say that the Bavli is "dialectical," presenting a moving argument, from point to point, and the Yerushalmi is static, through such a reductive understatement we should vastly misrepresent the difference. The Yerushalmi's argument unfolds; the Bavli's argument assumes a formally static position at I.2. Rather, the Bavli's presentation is one – as we have seen before – of thrust and parry, challenge and response, assertion and counterassertion; theoretical possibility and its exposure to practical facts ("if I had to rely...I might have supposed..."); and, of course, the authorities of the Bavli (not only the framers) in the person of Abbayye are even prepared to rewrite the received Tannaite formulation. That initiative can come, I should think, only from someone totally in command of the abstractions and able to say, the details have to be this way; so the rule of mind requires; and so it shall be.

The Yerushalmi's message is that the Mishnah yields clear and present rules; its medium is the patient exegesis of Mishnah passages, the provision and analysis of facts required in the understanding of the Mishnah. That medium conveys its message about not the Mishnah alone, but – through its silences, which I think are intellectual failures of millenial dimensions – about the laws. The Bavli, for its part, conveys its message in a coherent and persistent manner through its ever-recurring medium of analysis and thought. We miss the point of the message if we misconstrue the medium: it is not the dialectical argument, and a mere reportage of questions and answers, thrust and parry, proposal and counterproposal – that does not accurately convey the medium of the Bavli, not at all. The dialectical argument bears the message but itself is not the message (nor can a mode of thought constitute a proposition, though it may give expression to one). Where we ask for authority behind an unstated rule and find out whether the same authority is consistent as to principle in other cases altogether, where we show that authorities are consistent with positions taken elsewhere – here above all we stand in the very heart of the Bavli's message – but only if we know what is at stake in the medium of inquiry. Happily, our sages of blessed memory leave no doubts about what is at stake.

It has become easy to state the prior, a priori "Judaism" that the Bavli proposes to realize in literary form, instantiate in analytical method, and embody in implicit message throughout – the Bavli, but not the Yerushalmi. Demonstrating in conclusion and in message that the truth is one, whole, comprehensive, cogent, coherent, harmonious, showing that fact of intellect – these sustained points of insistence on the character of mind and the result of thought form the goal of the Bavli's framers. It is by comparison to the Yerushalmi that we have come to recognize the salient intellectual traits of the Bavli. Where we identified initiatives characteristic of the Bavli and unusual in the Yerushalmi, there we were able to describe the Bavli in particular. On that basis, we have identified as indicative the paramount trait, emerging from a variety of episodic distinctions, of the Bavli, its quest through abstraction for the unity of the law, the integrity of truth. Whatever animated the framers of the Yerushalmi – and we hardly need affirm that they, too, were monotheists, a fine example of a trivial banality indeed – it was not the conviction that monotheism came to expression in intellect; that profound proposition of a Judaism behind this text emerges only in this text.

Specifically, in the comparison with the Yerushalmi we came to appreciate that the Bavli's quest for unity leads to the inquiry into the named authorities behind an unassigned rule, showing that a variety of figures can concur, meaning, names that stand for a variety of distinct principles can form a single proposition of integrity. That same quest insists on the fair and balanced representation of conflicting principles behind discrete laws, not to serve the cause of academic harmony (surely a lost cause in any age!), but to set forth how, at their foundations, the complicated and diverse laws may be explained by appeal to simple and few principles; the conflict of principles then is less consequential than the demonstration that diverse cases may be reduced to only a few principles.

Take for example the single stylistically indicative trait of the Bavli, its dialectical, or moving, argument. The dialectical argument opens the possibility of reaching out from one thing to something else, not because people have lost sight of their starting point or their goal in the end, but because they want to encompass, in the analytical argument underway, as broad and comprehensive a range of cases and rules as they possibly can. The movement from point to point in reference to a single point that accurately describes the dialectical argument reaches a goal of abstraction, leaving behind the specificities of not only cases but laws, carrying us upward to the law that governs many cases, the premises that undergird many rules, and still higher to the principles that infuse diverse premises; then the principles that generate other, unrelated premises, which, in turn, come to expression in other, still-less intersecting cases. The meandering course of argument comes to an end when we have shown how things cohere. That is what we have learned about the Bavli in this comparison of the two Talmuds.

May we then say that the Bavli stands alone, without links of a profound order to any prior document? The answer is both yes and no. In the terms just now set forth, the Judaism that lies behind the Bavli proves unique to the Bavli. But the motif of monotheism – one God, behind all creation – not only must be attributed to all writers of all documents – therefore a banal Judaism indeed. It also forms a specific, but then distinct and distinctive, premise of the Mishnah. And when we have compared the Mishnah's and the Bavli's intellectual realizations of monotheism, we shall see what the claim of a Judaism behind the texts must actually demand for its demonstration.

The single metaproposition that encompasses the multitude of the Mishnah's proposition is, all classes of things stand in a hierarchical relationship to one another, and, in that encompassing hierarchy, there is place for everything. The theological proposition that is implicit but never spelled out, of course, is that one God occupies the pinnacle of the hierarchy of all being; to that one God, all things turn upward, from complexity to simplicity; from that one God, all things flow downward, from singularity to multiplicity.

Specifically, the Mishnah's authority repeatedly demonstrates that all things are not only orderly, but are ordered in such wise that many things fall into one classification. So one thing may hold together many things of diverse classifications. These two matched and complementary propositions – [1] many things are one, [2] one thing encompasses many – complement each other. In forming matched opposites, the two provide a single, complete and final judgment of the whole of being, social, natural, supernatural alike. Nearly the whole of the document's tractates in one way or another repeat that simple point. The metaproposition is never expressed but it is everywhere demonstrated by showing, in whatever subject is treated, the possibility always of effecting the hierarchical classification of all things: each thing in its taxon, all taxa in correct sequence, from least to greatest.

Showing that all things can be ordered, and that all orders can be set into relationship with one another, we of course transform method into message. The message of hierarchical classification is that many things really form a single thing, the many species a single genus, the many genera an encompassing and well-crafted, cogent whole. Every time we speciate, we affirm that position. Each successful labor of forming relationships among species, for example, making them into a genus, or identifying the hierarchy of the species, proves it again. Not only so, but when we can show that many things are really one, or that one thing yields many (the reverse and confirmation of the former), we say in a fresh way a single immutable truth, the one of this philosophy concerning the unity of all being in an orderly composition of all things within a single taxon. Exegesis always is repetitive – and a sound exegesis of the systemic exegesis must then be equally so, everywhere explaining the same thing in the same way.

To state with emphasis what I conceive to be that one large argument – the metaproposition – that the Mishnah's authorship sets forth in countless small ways: *the very artifacts that* appear *multiple in fact form classes of things, and, moreover, these classes themselves are subject to a reasoned ordering, by appeal to this-worldly characteristics signified by properties and indicative traits.* Monotheism hence is to be demonstrated by appeal to those very same data that for paganism prove the opposite.

The way to one God, ground of being and ontological unity of the world, lies through "rational reflection on themselves and on the world," this world, which yields a living unity encompassing the whole. That claim, conducted in an argument covering overwhelming detail in the Mishnah, directly faces the issue as framed by paganism. Immanent in its medium, it is transcendent in its message.

To show how the metaproposition is stated through the treatment of a wide range of subjects, concrete recapitulations of this abstract statement are now required. So I turn to a very brief reprise of my demonstration, concerning the Mishnah, of the sustained effort to demonstrate how many classes of things – actions, relationships, circumstances, persons, places – are shown really to form one class.

The evidence in behalf of this reading of the Mishnah covers nearly the entirety of the document. It is not episodic but structural, in that entire tractates can be demonstrated to take shape around issues of hierarchical classification and the principles that guide correct classification. It does not seem to me plausible that it is merely by accident that these sustained efforts, covering the vast surface of the writing – sixty-one usable tractates (omitting reference to tractates Eduyyot and Abot) and more than five hundred and fifty chapters – go through the same process time and again. Hierarchization defines the problematic throughout, as I have shown in *Judaism as Philosophy. The Method and Message of the Mishnah* (Columbia, 1991: University of South Carolina Press). It is certainly possible to propose a variety of recurrent concerns that animate the document, for example, the inquiry into the power of human intentionality. But these can be shown to find a subordinated position within the overriding interest, since the purpose of intentionality is taxonomic, and the goal of taxonomy of course, hierarchical classification. To this point no one has met the challenge of suggesting some other metaproposition that circulates throughout a piece of writing, different from one that I might have proposed. Whether or not others may perceive no metaproposition at all is not equivalently obvious; for a sustained effort at showing that what I see is simply not there has yet to be undertaken. So to review my opening questions: What about the possibility that another metaproposition may be shown to inhere, different from the one that as a matter of hypothesis is set forth at the outset? Or what if a proposed metaproposition is shown not to be present at all? My detailed demonstration that the proposed metaproposition is not only the best, but the only possible one is in hand. More than that I cannot contribute.

It is therefore the incontrovertible fact that the framers of the Mishnah set forth not only cases, examples, propositions as to fact, but also, through the particulars, a set of generalizations about classification and the relationships of the classes of things that yield a metaproposition. The whole composition of thought is set forth, in the correct intellectual manner, through the patient classification of things by appeal to the traits that they share, with comparison and contrast among points of difference then yielding the governing rule for a given classification. And the goal was through proper classification of things to demonstrate the hierarchical order of being, culminating in the proposition that all things derive from, and join within, (in secular language) one thing or (in the language of philosophy of religion) the One, or (in the language of Judaism) God.

The Judaism behind the Mishnah then lays down the principle of the integrity of truth. Inheriting this philosophical given, the Bavli's framers' articulation of that "Judaism," that is, the principle of the integrity of truth required them to demonstrate the cogency of (jurisprudential) laws in (philosophical) law. This Judaism they bring to articulation by showing that cases rest on premises, which point toward principles; principles carry us to other premises, that yield other cases; and diverse cases, their premises and their principles, then can be shown to coalesce in, if not harmonious statements, then statements of fixed and few differences at the level of high abstraction. We then reduce the range of diversity to a few differences; demonstrate the harmony of discrete rules; show the operation of some few laws, so moving jurisprudence upward to the level of philosophy. In the context defined by the Mishnah, the proposition of the Mishnah about the ontological unity of being is matched by the persistent results of the process of thought instantiated throughout the Bavli, demonstrating the intellectual unity of thought.

To show how the Bavli has received but carried forward and developed the Mishnah's prior, and a priori "Judaism," I forthwith turn to a case in point, at M. Erub. 2:2H:

| [II.A] | R. Simeon says, "If he deceived her to her advantage, she is betrothed" [M. 2:2H]. | II.1 | A. | R. Simeon says, "If he deceived her to [her] advantage, she is betrothed": |
| | | | B. | *But doesn't R. Simeon accept the following:* wine, and it turned out to be vinegar, vinegar, and it turned out to be wine, – both parties have the power to retract [M. B.B. 5:6K-L]*? Therefore, there are people who are perfectly happy* |

with wine, others with vinegar; so here, too, some are happy with silver and not with gold at all.

C. *Said R. Shimi bar Ashi, "I bumped into Abbayye, who was in session and explaining this matter to his son: here with what case do we deal?* It is one in which a man said to his agent, 'Go, lend me a silver denar, and with it betroth Miss So-and-so in my behalf,' and the agent went and lent him a gold denar. *One authority maintains that the man was meticulous about the instructions, and the other, that* all he was doing was giving him good advice on how to proceed ['showing him the place']."

D. *If it is true that the Mishnah speaks of an agent, then the language should be not,* **B e betrothed to me,** *but rather,* **Be betrothed to him!** *And so, too, not* **If he deceived her to [her] advantage,** *but rather,* **If he deceived him to [his] advantage!**

E. *But to begin with it was of gold* [Freedman: the agent knew full well that he was giving a gold denar].

F. *Rather, said Raba, "I am the lion of the group and I explain it – and who might that be? It is R. Hiyya bar Abin: here with what case do we* deal? *One in which* she said to her agent, 'go and receive for my token of betrothal from Mr. So-and-so, who said to me, "be betrothed to me with a denar of silver,"' and he went and the other gave him a denar of gold. *One authority maintains that the woman was meticulous about the instructions, and the other, that* all she was doing was giving him good advice on how to proceed ['showing him the place']. "

G.   *And what is the meaning of the language,* **and it turns out to be?**

H.   *It was wrapped up in a cloth [and only when the women got it did she know what it was].*

II.2   A.   *Said Abbayye, "R. Simeon, Rabban Simeon b. Gamaliel, and R. Eleazar, all take the view that, in a case such as this, in giving these instructions, all he was doing was giving him good advice on how to proceed ['showing him the place']. "*

B.   *R. Simeon: as we have just now said.*

C.   *R. Simeon, Rabban Simeon b. Gamaliel: as we have learned in the Mishnah:* **[49A] An unfolded document [has] the signatures within [at the bottom of a single page of writing]. And one which is folded has the signatures behind** [each fold]. An unfolded document, on which its witnesses signed at the back, or a folded document, on which its witnesses signed on the inside – both of them are invalid. R. Hananiah b. Gamaliel says, "One which is folded, on the inside of which its witnesses signed their names, is valid, because one can unfold it." Rabban Simeon b. Gamaliel says, "Everything is in accord with local custom" [M. B.B. 10:1]. *Now in reflecting on this matter [we said], well, doesn't the first authority concur,* **Everything is in accord with local custom?** *And said R. Ashi, "This refers to a place in which a plain one was customary, and a folded one was made, or a place in which a folded one was customary, and a plain one was made. All parties concur that the one who gave instructions was meticulous about the matter. Where is the point of dispute? Where both forms are acceptable, and the husband said to the scribe, 'Make a plain one,' but the scribe went and made a folded one. One authority maintains that the husband was meticulous about the instructions, and the other, that* all he was doing was giving him good

advice on how to pro-
ceed ['showing him
the place']."

D.   R. *Eleazar: as we have
learned in the Mishnah:*

E.   **The woman who said,
"Receive my writ of
divorce for me in
such-and-such   a
place," and he [the
messenger] received
it for her in some
other place –**

F.   **it is invalid.**

G.   **R. Eliezer declares it
valid [M. Git. 6:3K-
M].**

H.   *Therefore* all he was
doing was giving him
good advice on how to
proceed ['showing
him the place']."

[B]   R. Yohanan said, "R.
Simeon concurs that if
he deceived her about
an advantage as to
genealogy, she is not
betrothed."

[C]   Said R. Yosé, "The
Mishnah itself has
made the same point:
'**On condition that I
am a priest,**' and he
**turns out to be a
Levite** [etc.]"[M. 2:21].

[D]   Now there is no
problem in the case in
which he claimed to
be **a priest and turns
out to be a Levite,
[that she is not
betrothed].**

[E]   [But if he claimed to
be] a Levite and he
turned out to be a
priest, [there, too, she
is not betrothed, for]
she has the right to
say, "I do not want his
superior airs to lord it
over me."

II.3   A.   Said Ulla, "The Mishnah's controversy
concerns only a mone-
tary advantage, but as
to a genealogical ad-
vantage, all parties
concur that she is not
betrothed. *How come?
'I really don't want a
shoe that is bigger than
my foot.'*"

B.   *So, too, it has been
taught on Tannaite au-
thority:* **R. Simeon
concedes that if he
deceived her to her
advantage in a matter
of genealogy, she is
not betrothed [T. Qid.
2:5I].**

C.   *Said R. Ashi, "A close
reading of our Mishnah
paragraph yields the
same conclusion, for the
Tannaite formulation is
as follows:*

D.   **"'...on condition that I
am a priest,' and he
turns out to be a**

Levite,

E. "'...on condition that I am a Levite,' and he turns out to be a priest,

F. "'...a Netin,' and he turns out to be a mamzer,

G. "'...a mamzer,' and he turns out to be a Netin [M. 2:3A-D].

H. *"And in these matters, R. Simeon does not take issue."*

I. *Objected Mar bar R. Ashi, "Well, note the further Tannaite formulation:*

J. "'...on condition that I have a daughter or a slave girl who is an adult [alt.: a hairdresser],' and he has none,

K. "'...on condition that I have none,' and he has one –

L. *"and these represent monetary advantages, and yet here, too, R. Simeon does not take issue! Rather, he differs in the first clause, and likewise in the second, and here, too, he differs in the first clause, and here, too!'*

M. *But how are the matters comparable? In that case, both items represent a monetary advantage, so he differs in the first clause, and the same in the second. But here, where it is a matter of a genealogical advantages, if he did differ, it should have been made explicit in the Tannaite formulation.*

N.   *And if you prefer, I shall
say, here, too, genealogical advantage is what is
at issue. Do you imag-
ine that* **an adult** *is
meant literally? It
means, of superior
standing, for the
betrothed woman can
say, "It is not acceptable
to me that she should
take my words from me
and go and tell them
around the neighbor-
hood."*

The Yerushalmi's composition wants to make the point that Simeon will
go along with an advantageous claim as to genealogy, a point that the
Mishnah rule itself is shown to register. And that concludes the
Yerushalmi's message. The comparison with the Yerushalmi once more
permits us to define the Bavli's givens and so identify that "Judaism"
that the Bavli takes for granted.

This we see in a blatant way. The Bavli covers the same ground, but
much more, and in a more complex manner. First, we address the
generalization, not a particular detail. And we frame the issue in another
context altogether, that of a transaction in wine. So the Bavli
accomplishes its principal purpose of moving always toward the general,
transcending the details of a case in favor of its principle, moving
beneath the surface of a particular toward its abstract premise. And that
is accomplished not in so many words but implicitly, in the simple
statement before us. Not only so, but, if this did not accomplish the
purpose, II.2 states matters in general terms all over again – but the terms
now shift to another matter altogether. How do we interpret instructions
that a person gives an agent? Now, it is clear, that issue inheres in a
variety of cases, which we review; it can be shown to inhere in ours as
well. But Abbayye's statement, II.2.B does not go back into our case in
detail; it suffices to allude to II.1.F. Then we go into another matter
altogether, Simeon b. Gamaliel's ruling on the rules covering the
preparation of documents; then yet another item, the receipt of a writ of
divorce. Now all these cases have in common is the premise that we
have articulated, and it is the glory of the Bavli to demonstrate that fact,
time and again.

Does that mean the Bavli's Mishnah exegesis falls below the standard
of clarity attained in the Yerushalmi? Not at all, for at II.3 we state
explicitly the exegetical proposition that the Yerushalmi has established.

But here, too, we present that proposition in a remarkably fresh way. Ashi sustains the proposed proposition (on which Y. concurs), but then his son, Mar, takes issue with that reading; once more, a proposition is transformed into a point of contention, a thesis is offered that requires us to read the Mishnah paragraph in a contrary way, and that thesis is grounded on a close and careful reading of the formulation of the language of the Mishnah itself. And in these ways, and in others that will become clear when we consider the Talmuds' reading of Mishnah tractate Hagigah Chapter Three, the Bavli's voice is unique.

What follows carries us once more to the same broad level of generalization about the Talmuds' differences, and the Bavli's distinctive traits and unique voice. In the contrast of the two Talmuds' reading of M. Hag. 3:1 we see how the Bavli's composites' authors aim at showing the integrity of truth, by which I mean, the cogency, indeed, the harmony, of laws in a comprehensive and unifying law. For the two Talmuds' treatment of M. Hag. 3:1B, I give only the principal part of Bavli's reading; its secondary expansion, through I.8, should be noted as well, but the abstract here suffices to make the point.

[II.A]	[As to M. 3: 1B, not immersing one utensil inside another,] R. La [=B.'s Illa] in the name of R. Yohanan: "If the unclean object was as heavy as a liter, they do not immerse it [inside of another one, since it will weigh down on the container and so interpose between the container and the immersion pool's water]."	I.1	A.	[**They immerse utensils inside of other utensils for purification for use with food in the status of heave-offering, but not for purification for use with food in the status of Holy Things:**] *why not* **for use with [food in the status of] Holy Things?**
[B]	Abba Saul says, "Also in the case of utensils used for the preparation of food in the status of heave-offering, they immerse [one such vessel inside of another] only in the case of a wicker basket [in which other utensils may be placed]. [But other utensils may not serve as con-		B.	Said R. Ila, "Because the weight of the inner utensil interposes [between the outer utensil and the water itself]." [Abraham: It prevents the water from reaching every part of the utensils, thus invalidating the immersion of both the outer and the inner utensils.]

tainers for immersion.]"

[C] Said R. Yohanan, "Abba Saul and R. Simeon have both said the same thing.

[D] "For we have learned there: He who kept hold on a man or on utensils and immersed them – they are unclean [since the water has not touched the place by which he holds on to them]. If he rinsed his hand in the water, they are clean. R. Simeon says, 'He should loose his hold on them so that the water may come into them'"[M. Miq. 8:5D-F].

[E] Said R. Yohanan, "It is reasonable to suppose that R. Simeon will concur with the view of Abba Saul. But Abba Saul will not concur with R. Simeon. [Simeon will be concerned with the weight of the utensil. Abba Saul will not concur with Simeon that rinsing off prior to immersion will not suffice. Abba Saul will accept rinsing off prior to immersion.]"

[F] Rabbis of Caesarea in the name of R. Yohanan: "The decided law follows the view of Abba Saul."

[G] And so it has been taught: "The law accords with his view."

C. But since the concluding clause of the Mishnah invokes the consideration of interposition, it would follow that the opening clause is not based on the consideration of interposition, for the Tannaite formulation states: The rule for Holy Things is not like the rule for heave-offering. For in the case of [immersion for use of] Holy Things one unties a knot and dries it off, immerses and afterwards ties it up again. And in the case of heave-offering one ties it and then one immerses.

D. Both the opening and the closing rules invoke the consideration of interposition, but it was necessary to underline that that consideration operates throughout. For had we been informed of that consideration only for the opening clause, I might have supposed that the operative consideration that it is not permitted to immerse utensils within utensils for food in the status of Holy Things is the weight of the utensils, which causes interposition, but in the latter case, where there is no such consideration of the weight of a utensil, I might have thought it would not be a matter of interposition even for Holy Things. Moreover, if the Mishnah had informed us of the latter clause alone, I might have imagined that the reason that one may not immerse utensils within utensils for food in the status of Holy Things is because of the consideration of **[21B]** *a knot tightens in the water,* while in the first of the two clauses, where the water makes the utensil float, that would be no matter of interposition; accordingly, it was necessary to make the point in both instances.

I.2 A. *R. Ila is consistent with opinions stated elsewhere [when he invokes the consideration of interposition], for* said R. Ila said R. Hanina bar Pappa, "There are ten points at which Holy Things exceed in strictness food in the status of heave-offering that are set forth in our Mishnah; the first five apply to both Holy Things and unconsecrated food prepared according to the rules governing the cleanness of Holy Things, the latter five apply to Holy Things but not to unconsecrated food prepared according to the rules governing the cleanness of Holy Things.

[H] Said R. Jonah, "The Mishnah [which regards M. 3:1B, immersion of one utensil inside another as valid for heave-offering but not Holy Things as a gradation that treats

B. *"How come? In connection with the first five, there is the possibility of uncleanness such as is decreed by the Torah, so, in these cases, rabbis made a precautionary decree covering both*

Holy Things as supe-
rior to heave-offering]
follows the view of R.
Meir.

[I]   "But in the view of
sages they may do so
·   [in the case of a large
wicker basket] even
for food in the status
of Holy Things."

Holy Things and uncon-
secrated food prepared in
accord with the rules
governing the cleanness
of Holy Things. In con-
nection with the latter
five, in which there is no
risk of uncleanness such
as is decreed by the
Torah, rabbis made pre-
cautionary decrees with
respect to Holy Things
but not with respect to
the governance of un-
consecrated food pre-
pared in accord with the
rules of uncleanness
governing   Holy
Things."

C.   *Raba said, "Since the*
second five are governed
by the consideration of
interposition, the former
five cannot be governed
by the consideration of
interposition; and as to
the clause discussed at
the outset, the operative
consideration is this: it
is a precautionary de-
cree, against immers-
ing needles and hooks
in a utensil the mouth
of which is not the size
of the spout of a skin
bottle [such as would
permit free entry of
water], *as we have*
learned in the Mishnah:
The intermingling of
immersion pools is
through a hole the
size of the spout of a
water-skin, in the
thickness and capac-
ity – [22A] **two fingers**
turned around in full.
[If there is doubt
whether it is the size
of the spout of a wa-
ter-skin or not the

size of the spout of a water-skin, it is unfit, because it derives from the Torah [M. Miq. 6:5A-D]. "

D. *[Raba] accords with that which* R. Nahman said Rabbah bar Abbuha said, "There are eleven points at which Holy Things exceed in strictness food in the status of heave-offering that are set forth in our Mishnah; the first six apply to both Holy Things and unconsecrated food prepared according to the rules governing the cleanness of Holy Things, the latter five apply to Holy Things but not to unconsecrated food prepared according to the rules governing the cleanness of Holy Things."

E. *So what's at issue between Raba's and R. Ila's statements?*

F. *At issue between them is the case of* a basket or net that was filled with utensils and immersed. *In the opinion of him who has said that the operative consideration is interposition, that consideration applies here, too; according to him who maintains that* it is a precautionary decree, against immersing needles and hooks in a utensil the mouth of which is not the size of the spout of a skin bottle [such as would permit free entry of water], *well, that consideration would not come into play here.*

I.3   A.   *Raba is consistent with views expressed elsewhere, for* said Raba, "A basket or net that was filled with utensils and immersed – the utensils are clean. But an immersion pool that one divided by using a basket or a net – he who immerses therein has gained nothing from the immersion. *For lo, while the earth is wholly perforated* [in that water flows through hollows of the earth, and water appearing anywhere is bound to be connected to a large aquifer elsewhere, the connection is not valid (Abraham)], *nonetheless, we require that the forty seahs of valid water be collected in a single place. And that is the rule in reference to a utensil that is clean, but in respect to a utensil that is unclean, since the immersion serves quite well for the entire utensil, it serves also for the utensils that are in it. For we have learned in the Mishnah:* A bucket which is full of utensils, which one dunked – lo, they [the utensils] are clean. And if it did not immerse, the water is not mingled [with that of the immersion pool], until it [the water in the bucket] is

                                              mingled [with the
                                              water of the pool] by
                                              [a stream] the size of
                                              the spout of a water-
                                              skin [M. Miq. 6:2]."

Now we note that precisely the same consideration operates in both
answers to the question, the consideration of interposition. Not only so,
but the same authority, Ila, stands behind the matter. What Y. does with
that statement is simple. The fact is extended by Abba Saul to another
circumstance, then two authorities are shown to have concurred, with
some secondary analysis of that allegation. So the main point is allowed
to stand without significant challenge. So much for the Yerushalmi.

What the Yerushalmi treats as a settled fact, the Bavli handles as a
challenge to discerning intellect. Ila's statement is tested against the
evidence of the wording of the rule itself, something the Yerushalmi's
compositions' framers rarely do. This challenge from the wording is
resolved at D, in a familiar initiative: had matters not been spelled out
time and again, I might have read the language of the Mishnah to yield a
point that is in fact not true. A second step follows, which is to test the
consistency of the authorities at hand: they invoke here the same
principle that they invoke elsewhere. The payoff of such an inquiry is to
link discrete cases into a common law – again, the quest for the law
behind the laws in the guise of a testing of the consistency of authorities'
positions, and I.2, 3 accomplish that goal. But this leads to a secondary
issue, since Raba is cited in connection with the evidence concerning Ila,
and the issues between their positions are spelled out. Then, I.3, Raba is
himself shown to be consistent. What follows at I.4 is a mere footnote,
but I.5 takes up the quest for the law behind the laws, now proposing
that the difference of opinion between Raba and Ila links to a difference
of opinion among Tannaite authorities as well, and that difference turns
out to pertain to the same problem as the one at our Mishnah, so is not
farfetched at all. When we reach the law behind the laws, we stand at
the goal of the Bavli's labors: to add to the Mishnah yet another singular
truth about the truth, which is to say, the Torah.

May we now define the Judaism behind the Mishnah and the Bavli?
Indeed so. Stated in the mythic language of revelation, the Torah
through many things says one thing, through many commandments, sets
forth one commandment, through diversity in detail makes a single,
main point. And we know what that point is. By "the integrity of truth,"
in secular language, we say the same thing that we express when, in
mythic language, we speak of "the one whole Torah of Moses, our
rabbi." But now, by "one" and by "whole," very specific statements are
made: jurisprudence reaches upward toward philosophy, on the one

side, and the teachings and rules of the Torah are wholly harmonious and cogent, on the other. In the language that I have used here, the upshot is very simple: mind is one, whole, coherent; thought properly conducted yields simple truth about complex things. The way that the law behind the laws emerges is, first, generalization of a case into a principle, then, the recasting of the principle into an abstraction encompassing a variety of otherwise free-standing principles.

But the positive results of this part of our inquiry contain only a negative judgment upon the hypothesis that a single Judaism lies behind the texts and awaits articulation and definition: the Judaism behind the texts forming that Judaism everywhere taken for granted but no where given more than tacit representation. For the Judaism behind the Bavli proves unique to the Bavli, a particular development out of the Mishnah's modes of thought, not a general characteristic of a variety of writings at all. The Bavli makes a statement that is distinctive and particular to those who framed the whole, and, also, in very great measure, to those who wrote up the principal parts of the document: nearly all of the composites, and the vast majority of the compositions. It stands for different people, talking to different people about different things, from the Yerushalmi's authors, their address, their audience, their intent. It lays before us the opposite of a Judaism behind the texts.

The Bavli shows us a Judaism behind this text in particular, one that, to be sure, permeates all texts in general, but only one prior document in a concrete and consequential way. The only Judaism to which we have access in the Rabbinic literature is the Judaism that each text sets forth, and if these several documents define for us details of a single Judaism, that fact remains to be demonstrated and explained. The conception of a single Judaism behind the texts at the end of this research report proves null; the contrary view, of a single Judaism emerging from them all, awaits systematic analysis.

Index

Aaron, 132

Abba, 25, 64, 84, 145, 150, 228, 270

Abba bar Kahana, 25

Abba bar Mammel, 117

Abba Meri, 84, 145, 150

Abba Saul, 43, 232, 304, 309

Abbahu, 25, 78, 117, 145

Abbayye, 97, 100, 102, 104, 107, 117, 122, 124, 126, 165, 174, 181-182, 188-190, 194, 215, 233, 236, 243, 271, 290, 292, 297-298, 302

Abin, 75, 155, 287

Abiram, 32

Abodah Zarah, 6, 9

abomination, 43

Abot, 23, 295

Abraham, 19, 26, 91, 180, 303, 308

Abun, 153, 156, 226, 262

Adam, 31

adultery, 45, 92, 117, 128-129, 131, 184

agglutination, 36

Aha, 21, 79, 231-232

Aha b. Raba, 185-186, 192

Aha bar Huna, 126

Aha bar Jacob, 171

Aha the Elder, 192

Ahai, 127

Ahai bar Ada, 232

Ahaz, 156

Alexandri, 24

All-Merciful, 95-96, 101, 115, 124, 130, 166-167, 169, 172, 177, 184-185, 188, 235, 237, 241, 253

altar, 109

Amemar, 27, 119

Ammi, 113, 160, 229

Ammi bar Ezekiel, 238

Amos, 25

Amram, 173, 183, 209

analogy, 75, 78, 80, 91, 123, 147, 165-169, 171, 176-177, 185-186, 188, 190-194, 213-215, 234-235, 237, 241, 254

Anan, 196

angel of death, 32

anoint, 231

anonymity, 226, 267

appendix, 13-15, 21, 26, 30, 32, 34-35, 37, 134, 200, 224, 232, 242

Aqiba, 31, 37-38, 43, 89-90, 123, 143, 149, 161, 169-170, 182, 237-238

Aqilas, 89

Arakhin, 189

Aramaic, 14, 41, 106, 142

argument a fortiori, 76-77, 94, 97-98, 101, 103, 118, 120-121, 131-133, 136, 153, 159, 172, 174, 202, 206, 210, 227

Aristotle, 51-54, 56-57, 59-62

Ashi, 64, 69, 98-99, 106-108, 110, 112, 130, 132, 184, 192, 194, 231-232, 238, 270, 289, 299-300, 303

Assi, 122-123, 128-129

atonement, 46, 132

authorship, 3, 12, 49, 211, 294

autonomy, 6, 259

Azariah, 19

Ba bar Hiyya, 228

Ba bar Mamel, 160

Baba Qamma, 57, 63

Babylonia, 1, 12, 25, 45, 50-51, 66, 91, 164, 200, 230

Balaam, 26-27, 35, 96

Bar Pedaiah, 159

barter, 94, 107, 111, 128, 230, 243

Bavli, 6, 9, 12, 51, 63, 73, 134, 136-138, 141-142, 143, 177, 201, 205, 211, 220-221, 223, 235, 242-244, 247, 256, 258-259, 284-286, 291-293, 296, 302-303, 309-310

Ben Azzai, 188, 240-241, 251, 253

Ben Bag Bag, 67, 121-122

Benaah, 33

Beor, 27

Beruriah, 45

betrothal, 74, 77-83, 85, 87-91, 93-96, 98, 100-110, 112-128, 145, 147, 151-159, 163-164, 182-187, 201, 203, 212, 296-298, 300, 302

Bibi, 85, 114

Bibi bar Abbayye, 198

Bible, 161

Bildad the Shuhite, 19

blame, 51, 53-57, 62, 67, 70-71

blemish, 161, 195, 216, 237, 239-240, 242, 249-250, 256

blood, 78, 128, 161-162

Bun bar Hiyya, 147

burnt-offering, 109, 129, 176, 239, 249

buyer, 231

Caesar, 42

Caleb, 156

Canaan, 245

Canaanites, 68, 76-77, 90, 106-108, 120-121, 160-161, 165, 167, 174, 188, 196, 204, 214, 223, 229-232, 234, 242, 245

canon, 2, 7-8, 230

Cashdan, 241, 255

catalogue, 48

category formation, 51, 53, 56, 61-63, 65, 70-71

causation, 16, 19, 24, 35, 47, 51-57, 59-67, 69-72, 75-76, 92-93, 121, 274, 289, 293

childbirth, 126

childless, 31, 73, 75, 87-89, 98-99, 131-132, 147, 178

children of Israel, 17, 196, 199-200, 217

Chr., 41

Christianity, 8, 25, 37-38, 46, 48

cleanness, 84, 241, 254, 304-308

cogency, 1, 7, 13-14, 36, 46, 68, 134, 292, 294, 296, 303, 310

commandment, 29, 31-33, 130-131, 309

comparison, 52, 81, 87, 100, 136, 138, 140, 241-242, 254, 258-259, 285, 292-293, 296, 302

compilation, 1, 6-8, 10-12, 36, 49, 72, 138, 257

composite, 6, 10, 12-15, 21, 26, 35-37, 46-48, 49-50, 65-66, 71, 142, 143, 163, 200, 205, 221, 236, 242

composite, free-standing, 70, 72

composition, 1, 4, 6-7, 9-10, 12-15, 21-22, 26, 34-37, 46-48, 49-50, 63, 66, 70-72, 73, 75, 134-135, 137-138, 141-142, 143, 163, 201, 205, 211, 220-221, 223-225, 232, 239, 242, 259, 285, 294, 296, 302, 309-310

congruence, 35, 242

consecration, 76, 79, 91, 99, 102-105, 109, 115-116, 123, 130, 132, 150, 185, 192, 305-306

continuity, 52

contrast, 13, 24, 26, 34, 70, 97, 129, 136, 138-139, 191, 202-203, 236, 240, 252, 258-259, 285, 291, 296, 303

convert, 20

corpse uncleanness, 154, 240, 252

covenant, 19

creation, 19, 31, 293

culpability, 52-58, 60-61, 65-66

Dan., 17

Daniel, 19

Dathan, 32

David, 20, 29-31, 35

Day of Atonement, 132

deaf-mute, 279

death, 30-32, 35, 39, 42-44, 67, 73-74, 77-78, 86-87, 89-92, 117-118, 120, 128-132, 136, 143, 152, 155-156, 158-160, 162, 164, 172-175, 180, 183-184, 195, 202, 206, 208-210, 232, 238, 243, 289

death penalty, 74, 85, 117-118, 130

debt, 82, 107-108, 129, 185, 189, 225

Deuteronomy, 15, 17, 20, 29, 31-33, 38, 43, 56, 68-69, 74-76, 79, 86-87, 91-94, 96-100, 104, 106, 108, 113, 115-118, 124, 130-133, 143, 159-162, 164-167, 174-180, 189, 195-198, 202, 204, 211-215, 219-220, 246, 261

dialectic, 49, 64-65, 67-69, 135-136, 211, 291-293

dialogue, 284

Dimi, 124-125

Dimi bar Hama, 18

disciple, 37, 41, 44-45, 162

Divine Name, 42-43

divorce, 73, 75-76, 79-80, 83, 86-87, 89-91, 93-94, 99-100, 104-106, 116, 119, 126, 128, 130-133, 143, 155-156, 158, 161, 171, 181, 213-214, 228, 230, 234, 243, 260-264, 267-269, 271, 274-277, 279-282, 284, 287-290, 300, 302

divorcée, 87, 155-156, 158, 183

doctrine, 52

domain, public, 60-63, 68

Dosetai b. R. Yannai, 125

Dual Torah, 1-2, 4, 7-8

East, 5

economics, 51

Edel, Abraham, 52

Eduyyot, 295

Egypt, 162, 199

Egyptian, 43

Eleazar, 27, 77-78, 106, 112, 115, 165, 195-196, 214, 216, 218, 229, 235, 239, 249, 267-271, 286-290, 298, 300

Eleazar b. Arakh, 88

Eleazar b. Azariah, 178

Eleazar b. Dordia, 39-40

Eleazar b. Parta, 41-42

Eleazar b. R. Simeon, 89

Eliezer, 30, 37, 46, 48, 58, 80, 93, 166, 181-183, 187, 193, 224, 237, 240, 243, 251, 271, 273, 300

Eliezer b. Jacob, 41, 162, 168, 177, 188, 242, 256

Elihu son of Barachel the Buzite, 19

Elijah, 34, 42, 45

Eliphaz the Temanite, 19

encompassing rule, 195, 216-217, 220

Epicurean, 43

Esau, 180

estate, 107-108, 110-111, 119, 128, 130, 179-180, 182, 203, 223-225, 229, 231, 242-243, 245-246

ethics, 57

exclusionary particularization, 195, 220

execution, 37, 44-45, 78, 183

exegesis, 1, 3-5, 7, 15, 50, 75, 77, 79, 87-88, 90-91, 96, 102-103, 115, 117, 124, 131, 133, 139, 141, 161-165, 167-168, 191, 199-202, 204-205, 211, 226-227, 234, 242, 257-258, 286, 291-292, 294, 302

Exodus, 17-19, 24, 30, 32, 43, 57, 75, 82, 90, 92, 94-95, 118, 123-124, 143, 145-146, 150-151, 153-164, 166-167, 171-172, 175-176, 179, 181-183, 186-189, 195-196, 198-199, 203, 206, 210, 212, 236-237, 239, 248-249, 252, 254, 273, 275, 289

Ezek., 24, 26, 38

festival, 14-15, 20, 176

fire, 44, 57, 60, 113

flame, 24

flog, 89, 126-127

flux, 92-93, 241, 253

foetus, 228, 230, 239, 249

footnote, 13-15, 21, 34-37, 45-46, 134, 139-140, 200, 202-204, 221, 224, 232, 243-244, 291, 309

forbidden, 14, 37-38, 79, 81, 91, 97, 104, 120-121, 126, 130-132, 179-180, 196-197, 261, 263, 287, 291

forgiveness, 26, 35

fraud, 86

Freedman, H., 91, 95, 97, 108, 111-113, 115, 117, 121-122, 125, 127, 129-130, 132, 165, 169-171, 179, 183-187, 192, 194, 213, 234, 236-237, 240-241, 252, 254, 297

Galilee, 225

Gamaliel, 271, 273, 290

Gehenna, 23, 39, 46

generation of the flood, 128-129

Genesis, 16, 19, 25-26, 30-33, 77-78, 91, 97-98, 129, 196, 218, 224, 246

gentile, 13-16, 18-20, 24, 29, 33-34, 37, 45-46, 48, 77-79, 90, 106, 121, 149, 164, 170-171, 176, 178-180, 188, 190, 193-194, 196, 203-204, 212, 220, 230, 236, 245, 279

Giddal, 116

Gittin, 259, 286

gloss, 13, 29-30, 32, 35, 46, 134-136, 138-139, 141, 163, 202-204, 243

God, 1, 4-5, 13, 17, 21-22, 24, 26-28, 31, 34-35, 38, 41-43, 45, 48, 78-79, 85, 129, 162, 176-177, 197, 218, 259, 293-296

Gog and Magog, 20

Gospels, 11

grace, 22, 33-34

Greco-Roman, 52

guilt, 39, 74, 78, 82

guilt-offering, 89

Hab., 17-18, 23

Haggai, 145

Hagigah, 303

halakhah, 3, 5

Hama, 114-115

Hama bar R. Hanina, 24

Hammer, 178

Hamnuna, 239-240, 250

Hananiah, 19, 79

Hananiah, Prefect of the Priests, 23

Hanin, 79, 106

Hanina, 18, 23, 40-41, 43, 126, 262, 264

Hanina b. Teradion, 41-46

Hanina bar Pappa, 16, 305

harmonization, 37, 91, 135, 139, 141, 202-203

heave-offering, 120, 303-306

Heaven, 19-20, 23, 37, 40, 43-44, 48, 92, 129, 162, 238, 262

Hebrew, 26, 75-76, 81, 90, 94, 96-99, 101, 117-118, 124, 143-145, 150-151, 159-160, 163-164, 166-169, 171-174, 178-182, 188-190, 193-196, 199, 201-206, 208-209, 211-214, 216, 218, 220 hermeneutics, 64-65, 90, 201, 205, 220

Hezekiah, 75, 124, 179, 186

hierarchy, 135-136, 141, 210, 294-296

high priest, 18, 38, 87, 119, 130, 155-156, 158, 183

Hinduism, 232

Hinena, 79, 83, 147

Hinena bar Pappa, 24

Hisda, 16, 38-39, 66, 126, 171, 239-240, 250

history, 1, 57

Hiyya, 74, 79, 85-86, 89-90, 126, 147, 228

Hiyya bar Abba, 145, 170

Hiyya bar Abin, 180, 297

Hiyya bar Ashi, 239, 250

Hiyya the Elder, 79

Holy One, 16-29, 31, 33, 79, 199

Holy Things, 96-97, 99, 303-307

Hos., 25, 34, 128-129

Hoshaiah, 147, 152, 229

House of Hillel, 73, 81-85, 123-125

House of Shammai, 73, 81-84, 122-124

householder, 69

Houses (of Shammai and Hillel), 83, 90

Huna, 41, 79, 87, 94-95, 101-103, 105-106, 112, 146, 151, 171, 189, 204, 207, 239, 250, 281

Huna b. R. Joshua, 15, 127, 235

Huna bar Abin, 113

Huna bar Hinena, 190-191, 193

husband, 68-69, 73-74, 76-77, 79, 86-89, 91-92, 95-96, 98, 100-101, 104, 115-119, 122, 130-132, 147, 152, 155, 226-228, 234-236, 243, 261-263, 265, 280, 282, 284, 299

hypothesis, 12, 117, 295, 310

idiom, 61

idol, 19, 40, 179-180, 190

idolatry, 13-15, 33, 46, 188, 190

ignorance, 54-55, 60

Ila, 288, 303, 305, 307, 309

immersion, 84, 241, 253-255, 303-306, 308

inheritance, 31, 42, 77, 88, 119, 121, 129, 150, 154, 171-172, 174, 179-180, 182, 192-193, 203, 206, 221, 223, 230, 242, 245, 296

injury, 44, 54, 58, 60-64, 68, 244

injustice, 54

intentionality, 269, 279, 281, 283, 295

interpretation, 105, 153, 161, 170, 291

intertextuality, 21

involuntary, 53-55, 62

Isa., 15-16, 18-19, 21-22, 24, 28, 30-31, 33-34, 40-42

Isaac, 20-21, 88-89, 113, 167, 183, 225, 241, 255, 278

Ishmael, 90, 143, 161, 190, 212-213

Israel, 4-5, 8, 14-19, 24, 27, 29, 32-35, 41, 48, 73, 75, 77-79, 90-91, 131, 143, 162, 196, 199-200, 211, 217, 220-221, 223, 260, 271-273, 275-278

Israelites, 13, 15, 18, 20, 24, 29, 31-33, 37, 42, 48, 77-81, 101-102, 120-121, 124, 131, 149, 160, 162, 164, 171, 180, 188, 193-194, 196-197, 212, 220, 232, 235, 260-261, 267, 272, 274-275, 287-288, 291

Jacob, 38, 128

Jacob bar Aha, 80-81, 83, 149, 154

Jacob of Kefar Sakhnayya, 38

jealousy, 278

Jer., 19, 43, 91, 115, 129, 224, 245-246

Jeremiah, 115, 148, 225, 246

Jerusalem, 21, 84, 86, 123

Jesse, 30

Jesus, 38

Jew, 165, 169, 213

Job, 22, 24, 30

Jonah, 77, 305

Jonathan, 30, 40, 118

Joseph, 17-18, 26, 28, 110-111, 125-126, 174, 190, 238, 279

Joshua, 193-194, 284

Joshua b. Levi, 15, 20, 28-29, 156, 260, 284

Josiah, 118

Jubilee, 68, 86, 143, 146, 148-150, 158, 160, 162, 164, 168-170, 172-175, 180, 189, 191-192, 195, 207-210, 242, 245

Judah, 14, 21, 23, 66-67, 69, 94, 105-106, 122-123, 128-129, 131, 176-177, 186, 225, 240, 251, 270-271

Judah b. Betera, 84, 120, 122

Judah bar Pazzi, 78-79, 82, 156, 246

Judah the Hindu, 232

Judaism, 1-5, 7-8, 10-12, 51-52, 79, 91, 141, 200, 257-259, 292-293, 295-296, 302, 309-310

Judea, 105

judgment, 2, 12, 14, 16, 21, 23-24, 26, 28, 30, 35, 37, 43, 47-48, 61, 72, 78, 81-82, 90, 123, 160, 294, 310

justice, 21, 24, 28-29, 43, 64

Kahana, 67, 111-112

Kgs., 16, 27

Khuzistan, 106

kings, 28, 37

Kirzner, E.W., 67-68

Laban, 19

Lam., 32

Land of Israel, 5, 73, 75, 90-91, 143, 211, 220-221, 223, 260, 271-273, 275-278

law, 1, 4-5, 38, 51, 55-57, 63, 65-72, 75, 77-82, 84-85, 87, 89-91, 98-99, 101, 103, 105-109, 114-116, 119, 121, 126-127, 129-130, 135, 138-139, 141-142, 144-145, 150, 153-155, 161, 167-169, 172, 177, 179-180, 182-186, 189, 192, 194, 196, 198, 200, 203-204, 206, 219-220, 226-229, 234, 237-238, 240, 242-243, 250, 255, 258-259, 262, 264, 271, 277, 280, 282, 285-288, 291-293, 296, 303-304, 309-310

laws of sacrilege, 130

leavening, 80, 287

Levi, 22

Leviathan, 21-22

levirate marriage, 87, 131, 153-155, 178-179

Levite, 18, 300-301

Leviticus, 3, 18, 32, 38, 77, 82, 89, 96, 99, 101, 105, 110-111, 115, 121, 132, 143, 145, 148-150, 160-162, 164-166, 168-172, 174, 176-177, 179, 184, 188-194, 196, 199-200, 204, 212-214, 218, 223, 230, 232, 236, 239, 241-242, 245, 249, 253, 256

liability, 56, 59, 65-66, 69, 130, 182

libation, 179-180

literature, 4, 51, 310

Lloyd, G.E.R., 51-52

loan, 107, 130, 153, 185

logic, 49, 56, 76-77, 87, 90, 99, 132-133, 135-138, 141-142, 143, 151, 159, 170, 191, 200-201, 206, 210, 258

Lord, 16-24, 26-27, 33, 37-38, 42-44, 79, 89, 92, 132, 162, 176-177, 191, 197, 218, 300

Lot Ar, 180

M. Abot, 23

M. Ar., 86, 150, 154

M. B.B., 69, 116, 224, 296, 299

M. B.M., 86, 284

M. B.Q., 124

M. Bekh., 124

M. Bik., 93

M. Dem., 179

M. Erub., 296

M. Git., 93, 106, 226, 233, 243, 259, 269, 300

M. Hag., 303

M. Ket., 94, 119, 147

M. M.S., 86, 105, 123

M. Miq., 84, 304, 307, 309

M. Naz., 104

M. Ned., 95, 226-227, 243

M. Neg., 240, 251

M. Nid., 120

M. Qid., 73, 81, 86, 91, 143, 164, 201, 223, 230

M. Qin., 129

M. San., 43, 74

M. Shebu., 81, 90, 123

M. Yeb., 83

M. Zab., 92-93

Makkot, 57

Mal., 23, 79

mamzer, 187, 301

Mana, 79, 85-86, 156, 225, 227, 246, 261

Mani, 128

manslaughter, 55, 57

Mar b. R. Ashi, 97, 112, 301

Mar b. Rabina, 18

Mar Uqba, 39

Mar Zutra, 108, 232

Mar Zutra b. R. Mari, 109, 193

Mari, 114

marriage, 74-77, 83, 87-88, 90, 94-95, 98-103, 106, 109, 116, 119-121, 123-124, 126, 128, 130-132, 143, 147, 152-160, 178-179, 181-184, 187, 197, 199-200, 202-203, 225, 235, 261, 263, 269 marriage contract, 99, 147, 269

Mattenaiah, 143, 145, 158, 214

meat, 197

Media, 125-126

Meir, 18, 28, 45, 80, 86, 153, 157, 161, 175-177, 186-187, 223, 225, 227, 229-230, 233-238, 243, 262, 267, 269-271, 306

Menahot, 242, 255

menstruation, 45, 78, 119, 147

Mesharshayya, 69

Messiah, 17, 20

metaphor, 4

metaproposition, 294-296

method, 34, 57, 165, 213, 247, 258, 291-292, 294-295

mezuzah, 20

Mic., 27

midrash, 6-8, 10, 56

Mishael, 19

Mishcon, 16, 22, 24, 29, 31-32

Mishnah, 1-8, 9-15, 23, 34, 36-37, 42, 50-58, 60-65, 70-72, 73, 75-76, 79, 81, 83, 85-86, 88-95, 102-106, 108, 115, 117, 122-125, 129, 131, 133-142, 145, 148, 150, 159, 162-164, 167, 179, 200-202, 205, 210-211, 220, 223-224, 226-227, 229-230, 233-236, 240-244, 247, 251, 253, 256, 257-259, 267-268, 270-271, 273, 275-276, 278-280, 282, 286, 288-298, 300, 302-310

Moab, 27

money, 14, 25, 32, 41-42, 44, 73-77, 79, 81-83, 86, 88, 90-91, 94-105, 107-115, 117-124, 127-129, 131, 143, 145, 148-154, 157, 163-165, 167, 171-172, 179-180, 183-185, 188, 190-191, 197, 201, 206-207, 211-213, 223-227, 229-230, 233-236, 242-243, 245-247

monotheism, 293-294

Moses, 17, 33, 124, 309

Moshe, Pené, 155

Most High, 26-27, 30, 32

Mount Paran, 17

Mount Seir, 180

Mount Sinai, 31, 162, 199

Nah., 24, 26, 139, 246, 251, 255, 270, 287, 300

Nahman, 66-68, 106, 113, 115-116, 127, 185, 190, 196, 270, 307

Nahman bar Isaac, 21, 68, 117, 120, 168-169, 182-185, 188, 190, 194-195

Nahum, 154

Nathan, 82, 166-167

Nazirites, 38, 104

Nebuchadnezzar, 19

necessity, 51, 53, 67

negative commandment, 130-131

negligence, 54-56

Nehardea, 65

Nehardeans, 127

Netin, 301

New Year, 28

Noah, 18

Num., 26-27, 32-33, 68, 95-96, 167, 241, 254

oath, 24, 44, 81-82, 90, 108, 123, 225

Omnipresent, 84

Oral Torah, 8, 70

Oshayya, 106, 125, 172, 206

owner, 57, 59-64, 67-68, 82, 89, 93, 145, 147-148, 151-152, 157, 175, 191, 193, 227, 233-234, 236-238, 242, 245

ownership, 89-90, 92, 107, 110, 117, 120-121, 123, 149, 152, 162, 191-192, 225-229, 231-232, 243-244

paganism, 294-295

Pappa, 26, 64-65, 103-104, 108, 110, 113, 116, 130, 289

Pappi, 25

parables, 25, 185-186, 245

Paran, 17

Passover, 287

Peah, 69

Peda, 179

Pedat, 38

pericope, 12, 63, 79, 89, 201, 220

perjury, 181

Persia, 17

philosophy, 50-53, 55-57, 60, 62-63, 65, 70-71, 286, 294-296, 309

phylactery, 20

Platonism, 52

politics, 51

positive commandment, 130

Potiphar, 19

prayer, 3, 19, 28, 35

preventable, 54-56, 59-63, 65, 70

preventable, not, 55, 60, 62

priest, 18, 23, 38, 87, 96, 101, 107, 111, 119-121, 130, 132, 150, 154-156, 158, 160-161, 182-183, 191-192, 196, 202, 204, 235, 240, 252, 300-301

prohibition, 45, 77-80, 87, 126, 130, 153, 155, 157, 160, 168, 226, 261, 263, 287

prooftext, 35, 159, 202, 205, 210, 220, 243, 247

property, 25, 59-60, 67, 69, 73, 88, 106, 108, 110, 119, 124, 127-130, 143, 161, 168, 171, 179, 186, 189, 214, 227-229, 232, 236, 269

prophet, 27, 45, 246

proposition, 1, 10, 13, 30, 34, 46, 50, 87, 95, 97, 110, 118, 133-136, 138-142, 143-144, 146, 148, 153, 161, 163, 173, 187-188, 200-202, 209, 211, 213-214, 220, 225, 229, 291-296, 302-303

proselyte, 20, 89, 131, 171, 179-180, 190, 196, 232

Prov., 23, 28, 38-39, 41, 92

Ps., 19-24, 26, 28-33, 37, 43, 92

Pum Nahara, 127

Pumbedita, 65, 271

punishment, 13, 22, 24-25, 28, 30, 34, 43-44, 189, 239, 249

purification, 84, 252, 303

purification water, 240

Qiddushin, 7, 73, 91, 143, 164, 223, 230

Qoh., 84

Rab, 14, 21, 80, 84, 94-95, 112, 116, 125-127, 129, 196-197, 204, 239, 250, 253, 273, 290, 299

Raba, 20, 24, 41, 69, 100, 107-110, 115-116, 119, 124, 126-127, 172, 179-181, 185, 196, 198, 203, 217, 220, 233, 236, 260, 265-266, 272-276, 278-279, 281, 283, 290, 297, 306-309

Rabbah, 65, 96, 102, 110, 112, 116, 234-235, 260, 265-267, 272, 274, 276-279, 281, 283

Rabbah b. Abbuha, 182, 203, 307

Rabbah b. Shila, 168, 196, 218

Rabbah bar bar Hannah, 37, 271

Rabbah bar R. Nahman, 307

Rabbi, 33, 40, 42-43, 45, 79, 106, 117-118, 149, 169-170, 194-195, 216, 220, 226, 228-230, 240-241, 251-255, 309

rabbinic, 4, 7, 10, 51, 91, 121, 126, 180, 257, 310

rabbis, 2, 7, 26, 32-33, 37-38, 41, 43, 46, 67, 80, 85, 91, 100-101, 103-104, 113-115, 117-118, 122-124, 126, 128, 146, 151-152, 154, 157, 159, 175-176, 178, 180-181, 185-188, 192, 194-195, 197-199, 215, 218, 224-227, 231, 233-239, 241, 243, 247-248, 250, 254, 262, 264, 268-269, 275, 280-282, 304-306

Rabin, 125

Rabin bar R. Ada, 241, 255

Rabina, 27, 96, 106, 109, 116, 121, 127, 193-194

Randall, Jr., John Herman, 52-53

rape, 123, 246

redaction, 10-11, 49, 66

rejoicing, 31

religion, 2-3, 7, 15, 18-20, 23-24, 29-30, 35, 185, 196, 287, 296

religious system, 7

remarriage, 79, 87, 130, 133, 260, 262, 264, 268-269, 283-284

resident alien, 190

responsibility, 9-10, 33, 51, 53-62, 64-66, 70-72, 113, 120, 132, 238

resurrection, 43

revelation, 309

rite of removing the shoe, 73, 87-88, 94, 131-132, 153-156, 158, 183

Romans, 46

Rome, 16-17, 43, 45, 48

Sabbath, 19

sacrifice, 129-130, 239, 249

sacrilege, 130

Safra, 25, 173-174, 207-208, 210

sage, 2, 4, 7, 11, 31, 37, 41, 46, 49, 51, 62, 89, 120-121, 123, 125, 143, 149, 151, 157, 163, 170, 180, 186, 195-196, 213, 215-216, 218, 223-224, 227, 229-230, 233, 235, 238, 240-241, 243, 252, 254, 259-260, 273, 292, 306

Sam., 30, 89

Samaritan, 286-291

Samuel, 14, 23, 63-65, 77-78, 82, 84, 103-106, 123, 125-126, 128-129, 196-197, 204, 228, 231, 281

Samuel b. Abodema, 156

Samuel b. bar Abedoma, 154

Samuel bar Abba, 150, 154

Samuel bar Judah, 131

Samuel bar Nahman, 79

Samuel bar Nahmani, 30

sanctification, 5, 46, 48, 73, 76, 86-88, 99, 104, 109, 117-118, 123, 180, 191-193, 236

sanctuary, 17, 21, 26, 124, 278

Sanders, E.P., 2, 5-6, 8

scribe, 16, 42, 80, 179-180, 262, 299

Scripture, 1, 3-4, 7, 9-11, 16-21, 23-31, 33, 41, 56-57, 68, 74-78, 81-82, 84, 86-88, 90-92, 94-103, 105, 108-109, 111, 113, 115-119, 122-124, 129-136, 138-142, 143-151, 153-154, 158-172, 175-179, 181-184, 186-188, 190-197, 199-202, 204-205, 211-213, 215, 217-219, 224, 230, 232, 234, 236, 238-239, 241-246, 249, 253-254, 257

sea, 23, 113, 129

seduction, 123

Seir, 17

seller, 61, 115, 193

sexual relations, 39, 73-78, 87-89, 92-93, 97-99, 101-102, 117-121, 126-127, 131, 147, 156, 159, 184, 196, 232, 261, 264

Shammai, 123

Shema, 3

Sherabayya, 116

Sheshet, 107, 126, 173-175, 181, 190-193, 204, 207, 235, 239, 249

Shimi, 225

Shimi bar Ashi, 297

Shimi bar Hiyya, 125

Shisha b. R. Idi, 130

Shittim, 27

Sier, 17

Sifra, 168-169, 211

Sifré to Deuteronomy, 56

Sifrés, 211

Simai, 85, 124-125

Simeon, 35, 88, 93, 159, 173, 175-177, 182, 191-192, 199, 207, 211, 224, 231-232, 237, 243, 296, 298, 300-302, 304

Simeon b. Eleazar, 153, 234, 236, 243

Simeon b. Gamaliel, 85, 106, 125, 239, 248, 278, 286-288, 298-299, 302

Simeon b. Halputa, 246

Simeon b. Laqish, 19, 22-23, 30-32, 43, 108, 116-117, 124, 129, 155-156, 159, 172-174, 183-184, 202-203, 206, 208, 210-211, 264

Simeon b. Rabbi, 199

Simeon b. Yaqim, 228

Simeon b. Yohai, 29, 159

Simlai, 16

Simon, 232, 266

sin, 13, 18-19, 29-31, 35, 39-40, 43, 46, 129

sin-offering, 129, 132

Sinai, 8, 17, 30, 190

slaughter, 26, 197

slave, 42, 68, 75-77, 81, 89-90, 94-99, 101, 106-108, 111, 113, 117-118, 120-124, 143, 145-151, 155, 157-191, 193-209, 211-216, 218-220, 223-245, 247-252, 255, 288-289, 301

Slotki, 95, 231

Sorabji, Richard, 53-54, 56-57, 61-62, 71

status, 9, 74, 76, 78, 83-84, 86, 88, 90, 96, 99, 101, 104, 109, 121, 146, 152-153, 155-156, 158, 182, 187, 189-190, 198, 203, 225, 228-229, 234-236, 243, 261-264, 288, 303-307

Suk., 84

syllogism, 1

T. A.Z., 106

T. B.B., 85, 125

T. B.Q., 67, 238

T. Bekh., 111

T. Git., 289

T. M.S., 236

T. Pes., 287

T. Qid., 79, 103, 106, 113-114, 127-128, 153, 224, 233-234, 300

T. San., 117-118

T. Suk., 84

T. Yeb., 83, 88

Tabernacle, 19-20

Tabyumi, 165, 215

Talmud, 4, 6-8, 9-10, 12-13, 36, 48, 49-51, 56, 62-63, 65-67, 69-72, 75-76, 90, 133-142, 200-203, 205, 210-211, 220, 223, 242, 244-245, 247, 256, 257-259, 285-286, 291, 293, 303

Talmud of Babylonia, 1, 12, 50-51, 91, 164, 200, 230

Talmud of the Land of Israel, 73, 75, 90-91, 143, 223

Tanhum, 246

Tanhuma, 151, 207

Tannaite, 11, 17-18, 20, 25-26, 28, 32-34, 37, 39, 41-43, 46, 69, 91-93, 95-97, 100, 102-106, 109-115, 117-120, 123-125, 127-128, 131-142, 143, 148, 156, 158-160, 165-170, 172-182, 184-193, 195, 197-204, 206-210, 213-215, 218, 220-221, 227-228, 230-244, 247-249, 251-253, 255, 258, 265-266, 271, 274, 277, 280, 282, 286-287, 289-290, 292, 300-301, 309

Tarfon, 123, 131, 237-238

tax, 25

taxa, 36, 93, 294

taxonomy, 11, 57, 138-139, 295

teleology, 72

Teman, 17

Temple, 22, 40, 42-43, 48, 91, 161

text criticism, 13

theology, 1, 3, 7, 50, 61, 63-64, 70-71, 200, 242, 294

tithe, 69, 86, 93, 99, 102, 123, 236

tithe, second, 86, 99, 102, 123, 236

topic, 12, 63, 67, 81, 106, 134, 140, 162-163, 167, 200-201, 203, 205, 229-230, 236, 242, 247

Torah, 1-2, 4-5, 7-8, 9, 16-19, 21-
    23, 26, 28, 31-35, 38, 41-44, 48,
    55, 58, 65, 70-71, 74, 80, 90-93,
    101, 111, 114, 120-123, 127,
    129-130, 147, 150, 153, 157,
    161, 163, 179-180, 184, 186,
    196-197, 203, 238, 246, 261,
    268-270, 305-307, 309-310

Torah study, 22, 34

Tosefta, 6-7, 85-86, 90, 103, 125,
    137, 141, 211, 258

tradition, 65

transgression, 30, 189

translation, 41, 128

Ulla, 38, 64, 101, 121-122, 171,
    241, 253, 300

uncleanness, 84, 92, 119, 154,
    182, 240-241, 251-254, 303-306,
    308

unconsecration, 307

unit of thought, 9-10, 12

unleavened, 287

usucaption, 76-77, 108, 110, 143,
    171, 223-224, 230-232, 242-243,
    245-246

usufruct, 152, 228

Valuation, 110, 150, 177

verbal analogy, 91, 165-169,
    176-177, 193-194, 213-215, 234-
    235

village, 193-194

violation, 28, 38, 46, 85, 157,
    186, 189

violence, 127-128

virgin, 117-119

voice, 39, 199, 221, 259, 284,
    303

voluntary, 53-56, 61-62, 65-66,
    70

vow, 24, 95, 104, 119, 182, 226

water, 34, 44, 61, 66, 84, 93,
    240-242, 254-255, 303-309

West, 62, 64

wickedness, 23, 25-26, 41, 180

widow, 31, 73, 75, 87-89, 98-99,
    102, 108, 130-133, 147, 155-
    156, 158, 183, 225

wife, 19, 42-43, 45, 68, 73-79,
    83, 86-91, 93-94, 97-106, 108-
    109, 115-118, 123, 126, 131-
    132, 155-157, 161-162, 167,
    171, 178, 181, 183-184, 186-
    188, 196-199, 220, 227, 234,
    236, 243, 259-260, 262-264,
    268-269, 283-284

witness, 15-16, 19-20, 29, 78,
    126, 152, 172, 185, 199, 224,
    245-246, 259-264, 266-267, 269-
    270, 272-275, 277-279, 286-291,
    299

woman, 33, 39, 45, 68, 73-81, 83,
    85, 87-94, 97-102, 104-110,
    112, 114-133, 143-144, 147,
    152-153, 155-158, 160-161, 164,
    168, 171-173, 178, 180, 183-
    186, 196-197, 202, 204, 206,
    208-209, 212, 214, 227-228,
    232, 234-236, 238, 240, 243,
    251, 260-266, 268-270, 280,
    282-283, 287, 289-290, 298,
    300, 302

worldview, 4

wrath, 26-28, 35

writ of divorce, 73, 79-80, 83,
    86, 89, 91, 94, 99-100, 104-106,
    116, 119, 126, 130-133, 156,
    161, 181, 228, 230, 234, 243,
    260-264, 267-269, 271, 274-277,
    279-282, 284, 287-290, 300, 302

Written Torah, 8, 9, 55, 58

Yannai, 67, 84, 122, 125, 184

Yavneh, 85

Yemar, 106

Yerushalmi, 73, 134, 136, 138, 141-142, 143, 201, 205, 210-211, 220-221, 223, 242-244, 247, 256, 258-259, 284, 286, 291-293, 302, 309-310

Yohanan, 16-17, 29, 33, 37, 43, 63-64, 74, 79, 83-85, 89, 109, 117, 119, 128-129, 149-150, 154-155, 158-160, 170, 180, 202, 225, 228-229, 246, 260, 262, 264, 284, 303-304

Yohanan b. Bag Bag, 120

Yohanan bar Mareh, 87, 146, 227, 247

Yohanan ben Zakkai, 162, 199

Yoma, 3

Yosa, 149-150, 225, 246

Yosé, 20, 31-32, 78, 80, 89, 101, 105, 145, 155-156, 195, 216, 224, 228-229, 242, 256, 260, 287-289, 300

Yosé b. Qisma, 42-44

Yosé b. R. Bun, 84, 87, 158, 261

Yosé b. R. Judah, 151-157, 161, 163, 173, 183-186, 195, 204, 207, 216-217, 220

Yosé bar Hanina, 155, 189

Yosé the Galilean, 100, 149, 169-170, 229

Yudan, 76, 145

Yudan b. Rabbi, 195-196, 216, 218

Zab, 92-93

Zebid, 64, 68-69, 115

Zech., 24, 83

Zeira, 80, 85, 146, 152, 154, 226-228

zekhut, 30

Zira, 115, 117-118, 122, 184, 241-242, 255

Zophar the Naamatite, 19

South Florida Studies in the History of Judaism

240001	Lectures on Judaism in the Academy and in the Humanities	Neusner
240002	Lectures on Judaism in the History of Religion	Neusner
240003	Self-Fulfilling Prophecy: Exile and Return in the History of Judaism	Neusner
240004	The Canonical History of Ideas: The Place of the So-called Tannaite Midrashim, Mekhilta Attributed to R. Ishmael, Sifra, Sifré to Numbers, and Sifré to Deuteronomy	Neusner
240005	Ancient Judaism: Debates and Disputes, Second Series	Neusner
240006	The Hasmoneans and Their Supporters: From Mattathias to the Death of John Hyrcanus I	Sievers
240007	Approaches to Ancient Judaism: New Series, Volume One	Neusner
240008	Judaism in the Matrix of Christianity	Neusner
240009	Tradition as Selectivity: Scripture, Mishnah, Tosefta, and Midrash in the Talmud of Babylonia	Neusner
240010	The Tosefta: Translated from the Hebrew: Sixth Division Tohorot	Neusner
240011	In the Margins of the Midrash: Sifre Ha'azinu Texts, Commentaries and Reflections	Basser
240012	Language as Taxonomy: The Rules for Using Hebrew and Aramaic in the Babylonia Talmud	Neusner
240013	The Rules of Composition of the Talmud of Babylonia: The Cogency of the Bavli's Composite	Neusner
240014	Understanding the Rabbinic Mind: Essays on the Hermeneutic of Max Kadushin	Ochs
240015	Essays in Jewish Historiography	Rapoport-Albert
240016	The Golden Calf and the Origins of the Jewish Controversy	Bori/Ward
240017	Approaches to Ancient Judaism: New Series, Volume Two	Neusner
240018	The Bavli That Might Have Been: The Tosefta's Theory of Mishnah Commentary Compared With the Bavli's	Neusner
240019	The Formation of Judaism: In Retrospect and Prospect	Neusner
240020	Judaism in Society: The Evidence of the Yerushalmi,Toward the Natural History of a Religion	Neusner
240021	The Enchantments of Judaism: Rites of Transformation from Birth Through Death	Neusner
240022	Åbo Addresses	Neusner
240023	The City of God in Judaism and Other Comparative and Methodological Studies	Neusner
240024	The Bavli's One Voice: Types and Forms of Analytical Discourse and their Fixed Order of Appearance	Neusner
240025	The Dura-Europos Synagogue: A Re-evaluation (1932-1992)	Gutmann
240026	Precedent and Judicial Discretion: The Case of Joseph ibn Lev	Morell
240027	Max Weinreich Geschichte der jiddischen Sprachforschung	Frakes
240028	Israel: Its Life and Culture, Volume I	Pedersen
240029	Israel: Its Life and Culture, Volume II	Pedersen
240030	The Bavli's One Statement: The Metapropositional Program of Babylonian Talmud Tractate Zebahim Chapters One and Five	Neusner

240031	The Oral Torah: The Sacred Books of Judaism: An Introduction: Second Printing	Neusne
240032	The Twentieth Century Construction of "Judaism:" Essays on the Religion of Torah in the History of Religion	Neusne
240033	How the Talmud Shaped Rabbinic Discourse	Neusne
240034	The Discourse of the Bavli: Language, Literature, and Symbolism: Five Recent Findings	Neusne
240035	The Law Behind the Laws: The Bavli's Essential Discourse	Neusne
240036	Sources and Traditions: Types of Compositions in the Talmud of Babylonia	Neusne
240037	How to Study the Bavli: The Languages, Literatures, and Lessons of the Talmud of Babylonia	Neusne
240038	The Bavli's Primary Discourse: Mishnah Commentary: Its Rhetorical Paradigms and their Theological Implications	Neusne
240039	Midrash Aleph Beth	Sawye
240040	Jewish Thought in the 20th Century: An Introduction	Schwei
	in the Talmud of Babylonia Tractate Moed Qatan	Neusne
240041	Diaspora Jews and Judaism: Essays in Honor of, and in Dialogue with, A. Thomas Kraabel	Overman/MacLennar
240042	The Bavli: An Introduction	Neusne
240043	The Bavli's Massive Miscellanies: The Problem of Agglutinative Discourse in the Talmud of Babylonia	Neusne
240044	The Foundations of the Theology of Judaism: An Anthology Part II: Torah	Neusne
240045	Form-Analytical Comparison in Rabbinic Judaism: Structure and Form in *The Fathers* and *The Fathers According to Rabbi Nathan*	Neusne
240046	Essays on Hebrew	Weinber
240047	The Tosefta: An Introduction	Neusne
240048	The Foundations of the Theology of Judaism: An Anthology Part III: Israel	Neusne
240049	The Study of Ancient Judaism, Volume I: Mishnah, Midrash, Siddur	Neusne
240050	The Study of Ancient Judaism, Volume II: The Palestinian and Babylonian Talmuds	Neusne
240051	Take Judaism, for Example: Studies toward the Comparison of Religions	Neusne
240052	From Eden to Golgotha: Essays in Biblical Theology	Moberl
240053	The Principal Parts of the Bavli's Discourse: A Preliminary Taxonomy: Mishnah Commentary, Sources, Traditions and Agglutinative Miscellanies	Neusne
240054	Barabbas and Esther and Other Studies in the Judaic Illumination of Earliest Christianity	Aus
240055	Targum Studies, Volume I: Textual and Contextual Studies in the Pentateuchal Targums	Flesher
240056	Approaches to Ancient Judaism: New Series, Volume Three, Historical and Literary Studies	Neusner
240057	The Motherhood of God and Other Studies	Gruber
240058	The Analytic Movement: Hayyim Soloveitchik and his Circle	Solomon

240059   Recovering the Role of Women: Power and Authority
in Rabbinic Jewish Society   Haas

240060   The Relation between Herodotus' *History*
and Primary History   Mandell/Freedman

240061   The First Seven Days: A Philosophical Commentary on the
Creation of Genesis   Samuelson

240062   The Bavli's Intellectual Character: The Generative Problematic:
In Bavli Baba Qamma Chapter One And Bavli Shabbat
Chapter One   Neusner

240063   The Incarnation of God: The Character of Divinity in Formative
Judaism: Second Printing   Neusner

240064   Moses Kimhi: Commentary on the Book of Job   Basser/Walfish

240066   Death and Birth of Judaism: Second Printing   Neusner

240067   Decoding the Talmud's Exegetical Program   Neusner

240068   Sources of the Transformation of Judaism   Neusner

240069   The Torah in the Talmud: A Taxonomy of the Uses
of Scripture in the Talmud, Volume I   Neusner

240070   The Torah in the Talmud: A Taxonomy of the Uses
of Scripture in the Talmud, Volume II   Neusner

240071   The Bavli's Unique Voice: A Systematic Comparison
of the Talmud of Babylonia and the Talmud of the
Land of Israel, Volume One   Neusner

240072   The Bavli's Unique Voice: A Systematic Comparison
of the Talmud of Babylonia and the Talmud of the
Land of Israel, Volume Two   Neusner

240073   The Bavli's Unique Voice: A Systematic Comparison
of the Talmud of Babylonia and the Talmud of the
Land of Israel, Volume Three   Neusner

240074   Bits of Honey: Essays for Samson H. Levey   Chyet/Ellenson

240075   The Mystical Study of Ruth: *Midrash HaNe'elam*
of the Zohar to the Book of Ruth   Englander

240076   The Bavli's Unique Voice: A Systematic Comparison
of the Talmud of Babylonia and the Talmud of the
Land of Israel, Volume Four   Neusner

240077   The Bavli's Unique Voice: A Systematic Comparison
of the Talmud of Babylonia and the Talmud of the
Land of Israel, Volume Five   Neusner

240078   The Bavli's Unique Voice: A Systematic Comparison
of the Talmud of Babylonia and the Talmud of the
Land of Israel, Volume Six   Neusner

240079   The Bavli's Unique Voice: A Systematic Comparison
of the Talmud of Babylonia and the Talmud of the
Land of Israel, Volume Seven   Neusner

240080   Are There Really Tannaitic Parallels to the Gospels?   Neusner

240081   Approaches to Ancient Judaism: New Series, Volume Four,
Religious and Theological Studies   Neusner

240082   Approaches to Ancient Judaism: New Series, Volume Five,
Historical, Literary, and Religious Studies   Basser/Fishbane

240083   Ancient Judaism: Debates and Disputes, Third Series   Neusner

240084	Judaic Law from Jesus to the Mishnah	Neusner
240085	Writing with Scripture: Second Printing	Neusner/Green
240086	Foundations of Judaism: Second Printing	Neusner
240087	Judaism and Zoroastrianism at the Dusk of Late Antiquity	Neusner
240088	Judaism States Its Theology	Neusner
240089	The Judaism behind the Texts I.A	Neusner
240090	The Judaism behind the Texts I.B	Neusner
240091	Stranger at Home	Neusner
240092	Pseudo-Rabad: Commentary to Sifre Deuteronomy	Basser
240093	FromText to Historical Context in Rabbinic Judaism	Neusner
240094	Formative Judaism	Neusner
240095	Purity in Rabbinic Judaism	Neusner
240096	Alphonso de Espina and the *Fortalitium Fidei*	McMichael
240097	The Judaism behind the Texts I.C	Neusner
240098	The Judaism behind the Texts II	Neusner
240099	The Judaism behind the Texts III	Neusner
240100	The Judaism behind the Texts IV	Neusner
240101	The Judaism behind the Texts V	Neusner

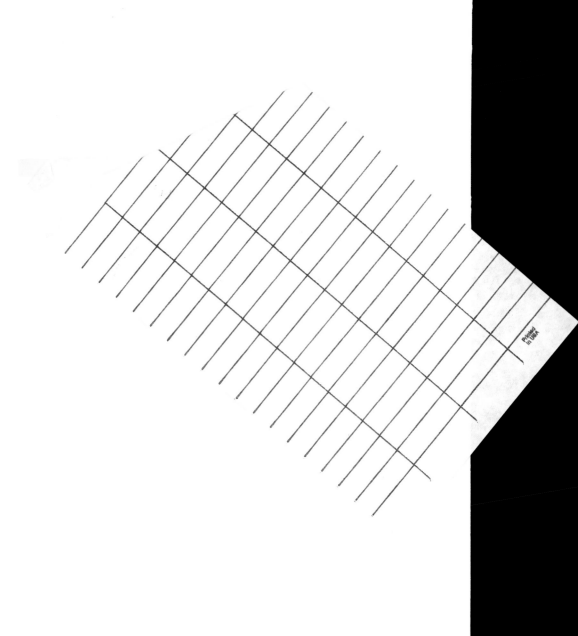

Printed
in USA